DUELING CULTURES,
DAMNABLE LEGACIES

A Nation Divided:
Studies in the Civil War Era

ORVILLE VERNON BURTON AND
ELIZABETH R. VARON, EDITORS

Dueling Cultures, Damnable Legacies

Southern Violence and White Supremacy in the Civil War Era

James Hill Welborn III

University of Virginia Press
Charlottesville and London

University of Virginia Press
© 2023 by the Rector and Visitors of the University of Virginia
All rights reserved
Printed in the United States of America on acid-free paper

First published 2023

1 3 5 7 9 8 6 4 2

Library of Congress Cataloging-in-Publication Data
Names: Welborn, James Hill, III, author.
Title: Dueling cultures, damnable legacies : southern violence and white supremacy in the Civil War era / James Hill Welborn III.
Description: Charlottesville : University of Virginia Press, 2023. | Series: A nation divided : studies in the Civil War era | Includes bibliographical references and index.
Identifiers: LCCN 2023000932 (print) | LCCN 2023000933 (ebook) | ISBN 9780813949314 (hardcover) | ISBN 9780813949321 (paperback) | ISBN 9780813949338 (ebook)
Subjects: LCSH: Honor—Southern States—History—19th century. | Masculinity—Southern States—History—19th century. | Violence—Southern States—History—19th century. | Men, White—Southern States—History—19th century. | White supremacy (Social structure) | Edgefield (S.C.)—History—19th century. | Edgefield (S.C.)—Social life and customs—19th century. | Southern States—Social life and customs—1775–1865. | United States—History—Civil War, 1861–1865.
Classification: LCC F279.E38 W45 2023 (print) | LCC F279.E38 (ebook) | DDC 973.7/1—dc23/eng/20230308
LC record available at https://lccn.loc.gov/2023000932
LC ebook record available at https://lccn.loc.gov/2023000933

Cover art: *Arguments of the Chivalry*, Winslow Homer, 1856. (Library of Congress, Prints and Photographs Division, LC-USZC4-12985 DLC)

For my wife Leslie, son Odin, daughter Myra, and son Tavin
For my parents Jim and Lila Welborn
For my grandmother Margaret Elizabeth Hinson Davis ("Bebbe")
For my great-grandmother Eva Bunch Hinson ("Granny")
Inspirations all

CONTENTS

Acknowledgments — ix

Introduction: Edgefield, South Carolina, as the Birthplace of Southern Righteous Honor — 1

I. Toward a New Southern Ideology

1. Honor: From Colonial Virility to Antebellum Refinement — 21
2. Piety: The Ascent of Evangelical Protestantism — 42
3. Righteous Honor: Merging the Ethics of Honor and Piety in the Early Antebellum Period — 63

II. Righteous Honor in Action

4. Moral Failings: Exorcising Inner Demons during the Sectional Crisis — 91
5. The Conundrum of Slavery: Sanctioning Violence on Moral Grounds — 115
6. 1856: Righteous Honor Triumphant — 139
7. The Civil War and Reconstruction: Violent Conflict as Divine Contest — 165

Epilogue: The Damnable Legacies of Righteous Honor — 185

Notes — 193

Bibliography — 235

Index — 259

ACKNOWLEDGMENTS

I HAVE truly been blessed in my life and work, and doing justice to the many people and places responsible for these blessings is a lesson in humility for which I am eternally grateful. What follows falls far short of what is due, for what I have been given far exceeds what I probably deserve...

My love of history revealed itself at an early age, as ramshackle boat docks, derelict barbecue pits, and lone chimneys standing sentinel over the ruins of long-forgotten homesteads became the subjects of incessant musings about who and what had passed in these places. This novice pursuit of the past in my own backyard and along every roadside to those of family and friends soon expanded to incorporate more noteworthy historical sites, structures, and monuments within my purview, first in my birthplace of Charleston, South Carolina, then in Fernandina Beach, Florida, where I was reared. Historic buildings, cemeteries, and ruins became an obsession, but the craving proved so insatiable that I refused to confine myself to the built environment for sustenance and actively sought out books, films, video games, and any other historically themed productions available as additional fare.

Such intellectual proclivities persisted into my early formal education. I am grateful for all my K–12 teachers in the public school system in Fernandina Beach, Florida, especially Ms. Elizabeth Purvis in first grade at Southside Elementary, who encouraged my enthusiasm for learning and instilled an early and crucial confidence in this shy but eager student. In fifth grade Ms. Helen Edenfield at Emma Love Hardee Elementary empowered me to squeeze every last drop out of each lesson and even enabled me to go beyond the bounds of the lesson plans to further quench my thirst for knowledge. At Fernandina Beach Middle School Ms. Ginny White was an inspiration in every sense of the word, challenging her gifted English classes to engage challenging topics and materials and maximize their potential academically, creatively, and personally. I fondly remember each of our annual encounters with Shakespeare and every "People Fair" project. Mr. Donald Roberts challenged his students to confront history in all its facets and many of those early lessons continue to resonate in my teaching and scholarship. At Fernandina Beach High School two English teachers, Ms. Gail Johnson and Ms. Veronica Williams, both cultivated my love of literature and writing and improved my own writing exponentially, as did Ms. Donna Perry, whose guidance and encouragement in her gifted studies course planted an early seed in my mind that writing might become a professional pursuit. Mr. Steve Rathman's world and European history courses enlightened and enlivened the past in ways that continue to influence my own classroom, while Mr. Ron Sapp's deft combination of wit, humor, and intellectual challenge in his government and economics classes provided an early model for my own teaching perspectives and persona. All did what great teachers do best: encourage, inspire, and empower their students to strive to become the best versions of themselves, and I am humbled and grateful to have benefited from so many truly great teachers along the way.

I entered upon the path to professional historian at Clemson University. There in those hills among the Clemson family I realized my love of the past would be my future. After dabbling in architecture and prelaw I finally settled on an undergraduate history major, and upon graduation, immediately began my graduate studies. Paul Anderson has provided a steady source of inspiration and guidance from these very beginnings. His influence—through candid advice, honest criticism, and encouraging counsel—over the past two decades has been and continues to be a shining example of history—researched, written, and taught—at its finest. Likewise, Rod Andrew also provided a wealth of support and inspiration, and I continue to pattern my perspectives as a teacher and scholar to his exemplary example. The late Tom Oberdan offered me my first employment in academia, first as his graduate teaching assistant and later as a temporary instructor. He provided critical advice and the necessary room to grow as I cultivated my fledgling teaching persona and philosophy, and he will be ever revered and sorely missed.

Having laid this foundation at Clemson, the University of Georgia proved the ideal place to build upon it both personally and professionally. Stephen Berry is a kindred historical spirit, and I was truly fortunate to have him as my dissertation advisor in Athens and remain honored to call him a mentor and a friend whose example as a scholar and writer, teacher and mentor, and overall gracious human I strive to emulate. John Inscoe was the first person I met at UGA and since that summer day in 2008 he has provided kind words, sage advice, and constructive criticism in a manner that personifies the historical profession at its best.

Kathleen Clark's tutelage in gender history sharpened my skills and perspectives in the gender analysis so essential to my scholarship and teaching. And Vernon Burton, of Clemson University, provides the link between Clemson and Athens. I have long looked to Dr. Burton's work as a model and inspiration, and I was elated when he joined the history faculty at my undergraduate alma mater and agreed to serve as an outside reader on my dissertation committee. His unwavering support of the project's transition from dissertation to book has been nothing short of phenomenal, and I am extremely grateful. Dick Holway's editorial patience and guidance of the project has been much appreciated. Nadine Zimmerli assumed the editor's role upon Dick's retirement in 2019, and her steadfast patience, support, and insight since has been incredible. I am also grateful for the feedback from anonymous peer reviewers, for the graciousness of Bob Elder and Tim Williams in taking considerable time and effort to provide substantive feedback that vastly improved this work, and for everyone at the University of Virginia Press whose efforts contributed to the publication of this book.

Research funding provided by grants from UGA Department of History donors Greg and Amanda Gregory and from UGA's Willson Center for the Humanities enabled me to conduct much of the research herein. A research fellowship from the Summersell Center for the Study of the South at the W. S. Hoole Special Collections Library on the campus of the University of Alabama also provided essential research funds toward the completion of this project. Portions of chapter 6 were published previously in *Southern Cultures* (vol. 20, no. 4 [Winter 2014], southerncultures.org) in an article coauthored with Stephen Berry entitled "The Cane of His Existence: Depression, Damage, and the Brooks-Sumner Affair"; portions of the introduction and chapters 4 and 5 were published in the *Journal of Southern Religion* (vol. 23, 2021, jsreligion.org/vol23/welborn) in an article entitled "Like Father, Like Son?: The Emotions of White Southern Manhood, Ministry, and Mastery During the Antebellum Sectional Crisis." They are reprinted here with express permission.

Archives and archivists are the lifeblood of good history, and I have been privileged to work with some amazing people who presided over some outstanding historical collections along the way. The staffs at the following libraries and institutions provided pivotal assistance and guidance toward the completion of this project: the Edgefield County Archives, especially the former head archivist Tricia Price Glenn, who not only opened the doors of the county archives to me but opened my mind to the fascinating history of her adopted home. I am proud to claim her as a fellow historian and a friend; I am also extremely grateful to the Edgefield community, especially Bettis Rainsford and Steve Ferrell, for sharing their love of their home and its history; Jim Farmer graciously allowed me to examine his transcriptions of Whitfield Brooks's personal journal now published under Jim's astute editorial hand and historical mind with Mercer University Press; the Tompkins Genealogical Library in Edgefield, South Carolina, especially Tonya Browder Guy; the Southern Historical Collection at the University of North Carolina; the South Carolina Baptist Collection at Furman University, especially Julia Cowart, Debbielee Landi, and Sarah Masters; the South Caroliniana Library at the University of South Carolina, especially Graham Duncan, who set aside his Gamecock loyalties and overlooked my ubiquitous Clemson orange attire to provide invaluable insights and assistance; the South Carolina Department of Archives and History; the David M. Rubenstein Rare Books and Manuscripts Library at Duke University; the Southern Baptist Historical Library and Archives, especially Taffey Hall; the W. S. Hoole Special Collections Library at the University of Alabama; and the Hargrett Rare Book and Manuscript Library at the University of Georgia.

As Clarence Oddbody wrote in Frank Capra's classic film *It's a Wonderful Life*, "No man is a failure who has friends." If Clarence was right, then any failure on my part has been wholly self-inflicted, because I have been blessed with the best friends anyone could ever hope for. I sincerely appreciate all of my colleagues in the Department of History and Geography at Georgia College and State University, current and former, who have provided a professional home in every sense of the word. I consider myself inestimably lucky to have landed in Milledgeville among such superb scholars, teachers, and friends. I am also grateful for all my fellow UGA #PhDawgs and #DawgMAs who've shared in the triumphs and travails of graduate school within the friendly confines of LeConte Hall. Older friends have been more geographically distant but close in spirit throughout. All of my fellow Tigers—my Clemson family—are never far from my mind. Y'all know who you are (#TheWebOrDie). From "the 'Dina,'" Briton Sparkman will always be "my best friend since third grade," and we wisely brought Jessica Nease White into the fold in middle school and she has put up with our unmerciful sarcasm while keeping us in line ever since. To friends old and new alike, thank you.

Last and most important, I want to thank my family. My mother Lila and father Jim have supported me in everything I have ever done, and in every sense of the phrase I would not be here without them. Their influence was and is indelible, and their example as wife and husband, mother and father, has grounded and inspired me from my earliest memory and will continue to do so until my last breath. My love for them and appreciation for everything they have given me knows no bounds. There truly are no words in any language that come close to conveying all that they mean to me, so I will have to settle for these: thank you and I love you.

My younger brother and sister have both heard me ramble on about historical things for longer than either can probably remember, and both have usually expressed (or at least feigned) interest. My brother Christopher was my first and remains my best friend and I'm immensely proud of the man, husband, and father he has become. My sister Averi has likewise been a constant friend and steadfast source of joy and pride since the day she was born, and I stand in awe of the beautiful, intelligent, and successful, thoughtful, caring, and loving woman she has become. I cherish our siblinghood. And I am so grateful for their respective spouses, Sammie Burman Welborn and Davis Clayton Bean. As my "Granny" Eva Hinson once said, "We don't have in-laws, we're all just family," and y'all have both added immensely to ours.

My Crean family has been a perpetual source of love and support and I cannot thank them all enough: John and Mindy Crean; Kevin, Amanda, Kate, and Jack Crean; Nathan, Mary, Declan, Rowan, Isla, and Callum Schutter; and Jeffrey and Lauren Apeldoorn. My life has truly been enriched with y'all in it, and I appreciate every moment we have shared in the near two decades since I first joined the clan.

And for the most fitting of finales, my love and gratitude for my wife Leslie grows stronger with every passing day, and I am eternally grateful that she said yes to a lifetime together, knowing full well how much time that meant she would have to share me with long-dead historical figures from long-past historical eras, as well as an interminable roster of Clemson sports figures and "Classic Clemson Moments." As a wife and mother, artist and teacher, she inspires me daily and supports me always. The arrival of our son Odin just before the initial submission of this book manuscript changed our lives for the better in almost every way imaginable. Our daughter Myra's arrival amid revisions deepened that joy immeasurably. Our son Tavin's birth just as this book went into production further enhanced our blissful family circle. Watching them grow and learn and prosper, and reveling in every moment, has more than compensated for every minute lost in research and writing as a result. This book and our lives are both better for their presence. I love you all eternally.

S<small>OLI</small> D<small>EO</small> G<small>LORIA</small>

DUELING CULTURES, DAMNABLE LEGACIES

INTRODUCTION

Edgefield, South Carolina, as the Birthplace of Southern Righteous Honor

> Could I even venture to mingle the solemn with the ludicrous, even for the purposes of honourable contrast, I could adduce from this county instances of the most numerous and wonderful transitions, from vice and folly to virtue and holiness, which have ever, perhaps, been witnessed since the days of the apostolic ministry.
>
> —Augustus Baldwin Longstreet, *Georgia Scenes* (1835)

THE WHOLE issue of secession and Civil War in the United States during the mid-nineteenth century—much less postwar racial violence and continued sectional discord, and lesser still the systemic racism that has persisted into modern American society and culture—can hardly be traced solely to the actions of one man or his place of birth. But in many respects, efforts by white southerners in the Civil War era to not only defend but aggressively expand and perpetuate not just racialized slavery but the deeper-seated ideals of white supremacy upon which it had rested must pass through Edgefield, South Carolina, and involve its native son Preston Smith Brooks. By the end of May 1856, Brooks's life had changed beyond recognition. His infamous caning of the Massachusetts senator and ardent abolitionist Charles Sumner on May 22 had thrust him into the national limelight, but the contentious nature of his notoriety on either side of the sectional divide in the aftermath reflected the intensifying divergence between the proslavery South and the free-labor

North during the antebellum period. Brooks and his caning became a lightning rod for an increasingly violent sectional storm that served to harden both sides' enemy images of the other. For antislavery northerners, the proslavery South had become a barbaric region whose inhabitants were bent on foisting a corrupt "slave power" upon the nation and its future. Proslavery southerners, meanwhile, believed the North had been overrun by a fanatical "abolitionist horde" intent on destroying their southern "way of life," by which they clearly and consistently meant the slave system in perpetuity.[1]

For many antebellum Americans on both sides of this divide, the caning embodied the triumph of sectionalism over nationalism, of conflict over compromise in the sectional crisis. And that antebellum crisis had consistently turned on the issue of slavery. Reviled as the caricatured "Bully Brooks" throughout much of the North, especially among abolitionists, Brooks's public image in the South, meanwhile, transformed from that of an obscure moderate among the boisterous South Carolina delegation in Washington, D.C., to *the* symbol of southern sectionalism, especially in the hearts and minds of his fellow South Carolinians and among a broad swath of secessionist "fire-eaters" across the region. Both reactions confirmed for their adherents their enemy images of the opposition. Proslavery southerners rallied around Brooks as their warrior-savior, while abolitionist northerners revered Sumner almost as a living martyr to the cause of freedom. However unlikely a hero to the causes of southern sectionalism, secession, and independence Brooks had appeared to be before his belligerent act, however uncomfortable Brooks seemed with this newfound role in its wake, and however consequential his untimely death just over seven months later proved in vesting him with these sectional glories in cultural memory, Brooks had immediately become more symbol than man. Though he passed away well before the full effect of his violent act would be felt, his spirit lived on in the secession movement, the Confederate rebellion, the postwar white resistance to Reconstruction, and even in the post-Reconstruction rise of the Jim Crow South. Like Sumner, Brooks, too, became a martyr, but his martyrdom revolved around him and the caning as the personification of gendered and racialized political violence marshaled in defense of white supremacy and patriarchal privilege, an image that persists even into the present through prejudicial perspectives and practices that are his deplorable legacy.[2]

Within the antebellum South's racial patriarchy, gender and racial identity and ideology were intimately linked with class, and upper-class white men like Preston Brooks assumed and dispensed supreme authority according to the dictates of both. Better understanding the elite white masculine culture of this "Old South" as it evolved across the Civil War era enables a deeper understanding of the fundamental nature of that society and culture—its limits and excesses—as a whole. The dominant white masculine culture in the region involved two predominant moral and ethical ideals: The first, masculine honor, prioritized the public recognition and defense of white male claims to reputation and authority; it also, to a perhaps lesser degree, emphasized private self-reflective fantasies of worthiness to claim such honor, and self-castigations for consistently falling short. The southern honor code thus sought to maintain order among elite white southern men, that they might then fulfill their duty as self-proclaimed masters to uphold the antebellum South's prevailing racial patriarchy. The second ethic, Christian piety, emphasized moral self-reflection and encouraged believers to curb excessive pride and passion and ready themselves for God's Kingdom, that they might allegedly make good on their paternalistic claims as so-called Christian slave masters. But such self-proclaimed "Christian masters" might also marshal their piety into action for more temporal causes and even—in its most extreme and rarest forms—wield it to sanctify prescribed acts of violence in the name of God.[3]

As *Dueling Cultures, Damnable Legacies* shows, in Edgefield, South Carolina, beginning in the 1830s the lives of a select group of leading white southern families reveal the complexities of their intensely personal and emotional experience of righteous honor as a contentious process of individual identity and public ideology formation and evolution that defined their worldview during the Civil War era. Such experiences became increasingly prominent among a similar class of white southern men in similar contexts across the South as the Civil War loomed, raged, and terminated only to produce a still-combative postwar Reconstruction and a damnable legacy of classism, racism, and sexism reincarnated in the Jim Crow South. And even after Jim Crow's legal death in the mid-twentieth century, the haunting presence of these cultural tensions persisted within prejudicial conceptions of gender and racial identity and ideology that still permeate the contentious cultural, social, and political landscape of the United States in the twenty-first century.

Through its exploration of the emotional experiences or inner lives of this set of leading white southern men and their families, *Dueling Cultures, Damnable Legacies* details the complex ways in which such men attempted to balance these interrelated and composite cultural values of honor and piety during the Civil War era. In so doing these men sought to better define their highly gendered and racialized sectional identity and better secure their associated ideological footing. A conceptual ideal I label "righteous honor" enables a more thorough historical explanation of both the tension and compatibility between these prevailing ideals. Righteous honor illustrates how the ideals of honor and piety interacted with each other in both contradictory and complementary ways in the lived experiences of these men as they conceived of the world and their place within it. In other words, to understand the minds and mores of white southern men holistically—as male, as white, as southern, and as Christian—historians must consider their individual and collective sense of honor through the lens of Christian piety and morality, while also considering their faith, in thought, word, and deed alike, through the lens of the honor code. Only when considered together does the complete worldview of such white southern men come into clearer focus, and only then can the thoughts and actions of such men during the antebellum sectional crisis, the Civil War, and Reconstruction be more fully explained.

The concept of righteous honor provides historians the analytical framework within which to comprehend the minds, motives, and methods of many leading white southern men as they made war in defense of what they deemed their best material interests, social structures, and cultural values, first against Indigenous Americans and Mexicans, then against the American Union itself. But the concept of righteous honor also helps to explain how and why their efforts ultimately failed by revealing the simultaneously constructive *and* destructive potential of both ideology and behavior in deeply personal emotional experiences that nevertheless had profound public consequences. These consequences pervaded the Civil War era, persisted through the Jim Crow era, and left an indelible imprint on prejudicial conceptions of gender and racial identity and ideology even into the twenty-first century, most conspicuously in the form of white Christian nationalism.[4]

Honor and piety could and often did pull a man in different directions. Despite its avowed purpose to promote order and preclude violence among elite white men, the honor code generally assumed an unavoidable role for violence within society and sometimes ended at the dueling grounds. And despite widespread expressions of martial morality as well as pervasive denominational and sectarian divisions, piety ideally ended at the communion table. Piety, to a degree, operated as a check on the more hedonistic and anarchic aspects of honor as perceived by many evangelical

Protestants, just as honor laid claim to a moral and ethical security that purportedly softened its more extreme potentialities. But as *Dueling Cultures, Damnable Legacies* highlights, though honor and piety were often at odds in their proscriptions—especially regarding white masculine vice and violence—in the minds and hands of powerful white men they could also serve as complementary moral ethics that sought to ensure masculine virtue by promoting the proper application of white male prerogative. This conception of righteous honor is essential for historians seeking to better understand how many leading white southern men of the Civil War era could and did lay claim to that prerogative: by emphasizing their "unique" ability to achieve self-mastery while simultaneously empowering themselves to enact righteous violence against anything and anyone that undermined their claims to privilege and authority. Again, a tension both productive and destructive in its potential pervaded their righteous honor ideal and its dual emphasis on self-mastery as the root of white rule and righteous violence as the means of sustaining that supremacy.[5]

Tensions abounded in the public and private lives of the South's leading white men during the Civil War era. Contradictions seemingly plagued their every thought and action. And the weight of these burdens simultaneously gnawed at their individual and collective consciences even as it spurred them toward increasingly deluded expressions of sectional solidarity and ideological conviction. As expressions of confidence, even pride, in southern social systems and cultural values came to dominate white men's public culture during the late antebellum period, privately many struggled more than ever to live up to its dictates. Such men knew well what vices undermined their righteous claims: sensual and sexual desire, alcoholic indulgence, wanton violence, and unrestrained racial exploitation. More than ever, these needed to be conquered: How could the white South hope to do battle with the allegedly heathen North, how could they be prepared for Armageddon, if they could not put their own houses in order? In a heightened sense during the late antebellum period, "*self*-mastery" became key to the public culture of the South.[6] And to unprecedented degree, the struggle (and prevalent inability and/or unwillingness) to achieve or sustain that mastery produced a tension, indeed a fury of "righteous violence," which found its most desperate yet ultimately deficient final release in the Civil War and its aftermath. The resulting dynamic tension constituted righteous honor in thought and action during the era and persisted in myriad forms of archconservatism typically predicated on a volatile combination of patriarchal elitism and white supremacy, often masquerading as populist dissent, from the end of the nineteenth century through the dawn of the twenty-first. And Edgefield, South Carolina, produced early and particularly potent examples of this perpetual pattern.

The historians Bertram Wyatt-Brown, Ed Ayers, Dickson Bruce, Kenneth Greenberg, and John Mayfield and Todd Hagstette have most notably and ably described the "Old South's" honor culture and together have made a persuasive case that a peculiar variant of masculinity prevailed in both its public spaces and private homes. Conceptions of honor played a pivotal role in shaping the complex southern culture and sectional crisis. Honor, as these and other historians have shown, was pervasive in the antebellum South. It privileged white male authority and upheld a strict hierarchical view of society; one that placed white men of wealth at the top and rendered working-class and landless white males, women, and people of color subservient to elite white male authority. Honor, however, was not the sole moral and ethical influence operating upon white southern male minds and mores.[7]

The historians Donald G. Mathews, Anne C. Loveland, John B. Boles, Christine Leigh Heyrman, and Monica Najar, among others, have also long acknowledged the American South as the "Bible Belt" of the nation and have adeptly described the prominence of evangelical Protestant Christians in fastening that moniker upon the region. Expanding upon inroads made during the First Great Awakening of the mid-eighteenth century, evangelical Protestant Methodists, Baptists, and Presbyterians spearheaded the nation's "Second Great Awakening" a half-century later by descending upon the southern interior and igniting a revivalist fervor that waxed and waned for most of the early nineteenth century. In this "Great Revival," as it was often termed in the region, these evangelical Protestant denominations assumed the mantle of defining and expanding religious faith and morality in the South, and their emphasis on the conversion experience lent these revivals an emotional fervor that largely set the tone for a more pervasive religiosity and moral consciousness within the region's cultural values. An evangelical Protestant Christian ethic governed actions, shaped discourse, and defined meaning for many antebellum southerners, regardless of class, race, or gender status. Pious and impious alike employed a spiritual language and engaged in a spiritual outlook that became a pronounced southern cultural trait.[8]

Despite the breadth and depth of each of these historical currents— the honor-bound South and the Bible Belt South—extant works nonetheless exhibit most historians' tendency to dissect what became increasingly undissectable for many leading white men in the Civil War–era South. True, some white southern men eschewed the scriptures and immersed themselves almost exclusively in a secular conception of the honor code, while others chose religion and wholly rejected honor's secular strictures. Yet this dichotomy in the scholarship obscures a more complex and historically compelling reality. By assuming and in some cases overemphasizing the dichotomy, early historians of southern honor and religion oversimplified many leading white southern men's complex and varied experience and deployment of these cultural ideals during the Civil War era and in its legacies in popular cultural memory since that time.[9] As such, a more holistic consideration of the vital roles played by *both* ideals in tension better explains the very nature and evolution of white southern culture and society throughout that era. Moreover, this holistic understanding of the antebellum past that I propose resonates with prevailing historical analyses of archconservatism closer to and encompassing the present, revealing a through-line of often highly emotional and hyperindividualized expressions of identity and ideology rooted in long-standing assumptions of patriarchal elitism and white supremacy that crystalized in the Civil War era.[10]

Dueling Cultures, Damnable Legacies builds upon the work of Ted Ownby and other gender historians such as Joanne Freeman, Amy Greenberg, Craig Friend, and Lorri Glover by engaging the intimate personal and familial lives of several leading white southern men linked to one another in mind and by geography to reveal the often intensely emotional and overtly moral dimensions of their effort to balance sometimes contentious cultural values. In his work on the postwar South, Ownby asserted that "southerners managed to balance the tensions between masculinity and evangelicalism fairly well during the antebellum period," and that in this period, "the nature of Southern life enabled men to take both sides, embracing masculine competitiveness while still respecting evangelical self-control." But Ownby's main focus is the postbellum period, and he takes this passing observation regarding antebellum masculine mores as a given without further explication. *Dueling Cultures, Damnable Legacies* delineates not only how such men managed to strike a balance between honor and piety but also how and why they sought to wield both in mutually reinforcing ways to solidify their standing in southern society and defend it during the sectional crisis, the Civil War, and Reconstruction.[11]

Generational tensions such as those recently explored by historians of southern masculinity in the early republic and antebellum periods guide much of my analytical perspective. As the historians Lorri Glover, Stephen Berry, and Peter Carmichael have most notably shown, nostalgia for the glories that "southern sons" attributed to their fathers in defining "all that makes a man" continually combated present pressures and future specters, lending these two antebellum generations of white southerners a particularly conflicted vision of masculine identity. In *Dueling Cultures, Damnable Legacies* I emphasize the degree to which the elder generation debated the questions over honor and mastery that gave them at least intermittent, though largely still dismissible, moral and ethical pause, while their sons' generation increasingly felt unable and/or unwilling to engage in such debates. Rather, these sons felt compelled to defend themselves and their culture against what they saw as ever more pernicious threats. This conflicted identity and the generational pressures it entailed made both generations eager for glory, personal and communal, regional and national. Personal combat provided one means of achieving such glory, and white southern male honor became pricklier than ever. War provided another outlet—in various "Indian wars," then in the Mexican War, and, once solidly under the direction of the antebellum South's "last generation," even against other Americans in the Civil War. Both personal combat and warfare provided an opportunity for young white southern men to prove their mettle by facing the fire, lending honor and manhood a deadly seriousness that intensified throughout the antebellum period.[12]

As the historian John Mayfield and others have collectively argued, however, honor also proved quite malleable for the white southern men who wielded its power and confronted both real and perceived threats to its sustainability during the era. Internal threats—within themselves and among their race and class—often necessitated that such a stern conception of masculine honor be deflected and deferred, frequently masquerading as literary humor throughout the antebellum period. But the malleability of white masculine honor was not confined to the pages of fiction. Many historians now view such malleability as honor's dominant characteristic within American culture, one that allowed it to pervade the cultural mores of the South and nation by assuming myriad forms applied in various ways across multiple contexts and time periods. *Dueling Cultures, Damnable Legacies* continues in this vein, showing how an implicit ideal of righteous honor enabled some white southern men of power and influence in the Civil War era to exalt their virtues while also confronting the seemingly absurd personal and social contradictions among honor, an expanding market culture, and evangelicalism by emphasizing their self-mastery as the basis of their authority. This concept of righteous honor asked them to prioritize restraint while it simultaneously sanctioned their resort to loosely prescribed forms of righteous violence whenever their sense of righteous honor faced real or perceived peril.[13]

Dueling Cultures, Damnable Legacies makes no assertive claims in answer to the age-old question of whether non-elite southerners wholly adopted the cultural mores of their social superiors. Historians of southern class and gender dynamics have collectively shown that complexities abounded, with myriad factors accounting for both commonalities and differences in expression and behavior across class and gender lines within the region. Certainly, as the historians Stephanie McCurry, Elliot Gorn, Timothy J. Williams, and others have shown, such values promoted by elite men proved widely compelling beyond their relatively select peer group due to the considerable power and influence such men wielded in the antebellum South's racial patriarchy.[14] Other historians such as Jonathan Daniel Wells, Jennifer R. Green, and Amy Plugrad-Jackisch, however, have acknowledged these commonalities while convincingly countering that this very same power and influence could just as easily spawn various forms and degrees of cultural divergence, even among the upper classes.[15]

Obviously, as the presumed privilege and proclaimed purview of elite white southern men, righteous honor consciously excluded enslaved and free Blacks and relegated poor whites and women to a subordinate status. Historians of poor, working-class whites in the South, beginning with Frank Owlsey and continuing to Charles C. Bolton, Scott Culcasure, and Keri Leigh Merritt, have clearly shown the many divergences between these white lower classes and those higher on the social ladder while also fleshing out the ways in which elite ideals functioned, usually in adapted forms, in lower-class lives. The historian Jeff Forrett has notably extended this class analysis across the racial divide to uncover similar dynamics at work among enslaved and free Blacks both within these communities and in their interactions with poor, working-class whites in the region.[16]

Righteous honor never approached monolithic status in the South's cultural value system, even among elite white men most responsible for defining and enforcing its tenets. As Eugene Genovese and Elizabeth Fox-Genovese, as well as Bertram Wyatt-Brown, Dickson D. Bruce, and John Hope Franklin, have most prominently argued, dissension abounded throughout the early republic and early antebellum periods. Many men simply refused to accept or abide by the prevailing religious moral standards, while others, especially landless, dependent, and otherwise poor whites, found themselves beyond the pale of the prevailing honor code's consciously selective jurisdiction. But such dissension drove efforts toward more militant consolidation in the late antebellum period. As *Dueling Cultures, Damnable Legacies* asserts, the larger significance of an implicit ideal of righteous honor, regardless of this dynamic and fluid cultural milieu, rests on powerful men who forcefully asserted such values and concerns during the height of the antebellum sectional crisis, through the Civil War, and in its wake. Whether embraced or rejected by white southern men writ large, the increasingly apparent need to align individual identity and collective ideology in the face of both intra- and extraregional threats during this extended and evolving crisis gave added impetus to the implicit ideal of righteous honor for many, but also tended to heighten their anxieties over its failures. White southern men and their families need not have wholly aligned themselves to this ideal and its mandates to be affected. Righteous honor as an ideal shaped collective identity and regional ideology significantly. In the celebration over its successes, the frustration over its failures, and even the indifference toward both, a sense of righteous honor fueled the animosity of the sectional crisis, the eventual outbreak of war, and the course of the war, as well as reactions to its results.[17]

Dueling Cultures, Damnable Legacies therefore marches in step with a relatively select group of more recent historical studies, by Edward Crowther, A. James Fuller, Charity Carney, David T. Moon, and Robert Elder. All explicitly engage the intersections of white southern honor, religion, and manhood in the Civil War era. All consider honor and piety in relation to each other and reveal many essential aspects of their interrelated role within various white southern communities during the antebellum era. All emphasize, to varying degrees, the compatibility of these moral and ethical ideals, while still acknowledging their obvious points of friction. Crowther in particular argues that "over time, many religious and secular ideals, which were not necessarily dissonant, had fused to produce a hybrid and distinctly southern value, a 'holy honor' that drew on evangelical and martial traditions for its sustenance and animated and, for white southerners, justified southern behavior." The pervasive influence of evangelical morality on their social mores suggests that many powerful white men assumed divine sanction of their privileged place within the southern social order and as such, likely considered their personal and public honor in that same divine light. *Dueling Cultures, Damnable*

Legacies therefore uses the term "righteous" rather than "holy" to describe the dynamic interplay between honor and piety in the lives of elite white southern men during the Civil War era, to better capture this widely held assumption that God, not man, had ordained the prevailing southern social order predicated on white supremacy and patriarchal authority. The mission of white southern men, then, was not one of creation but rather fulfillment of what they considered their divinely sanctioned roles. They strove to render their lives—individual, familial, and social—holy, in order that they might collectively be deemed righteous in the eyes of God. Through the concept of righteous honor, *Dueling Cultures, Damnable Legacies* centers the lived experiences of honor and piety, in tension and compatibility, to better reflect the worldview of the men who most assertively held and upheld them.[18]

Both the tension between and compatibility of these moral and ethical ideals fundamentally shaped elite white men's worldview and guided their thoughts and actions, as private heads of household and as leading public figures. Righteous honor encompasses how such men might have conceived of and applied the ideals of honor and piety in mutually reinforcing ways to secure a social order that rested on the cornerstones of patriarchal authority, white supremacy, Christian morality, and free-market capitalism, especially as the personal and public pressures associated with the sectional crisis over slavery intensified. But this conception of righteous honor also exposes the many ways that such pressures undermined that mutuality and fomented an anxiety among many of these men that portended their potential secular doom and even sacred damnation. Such anxieties and the means pursued to mitigate against them, including especially populist appeals to oppose alleged common enemies, were not confined to the Civil War era but continued to permeate American society and culture from the Jim Crow era to the various "culture wars" of the more recent past. Reflected in and adapted by a litany of archconservative expressions of class, gender, and racial solidarity against perceived threats to white male authority across the twentieth century and into the twenty-first, the hauntingly familiar voices and violent actions displayed on January 6, 2021, were just the latest American political insurgency to invoke the gendered and racial overtones and legacy personified in Preston Brooks and his caning, despite the distance of more than one hundred and sixty years.[19]

No place is better suited to analyze the emergence and evolution of righteous honor, its emphasis on self-mastery, and its inherent sanctioning of righteous violence as the composite bedrock of white supremacy and patriarchal authority than Preston Brooks's hometown of Edgefield, South Carolina, a district widely known in the Civil War era for its pronounced honor culture but one also steeped in evangelical Protestant Christian fervor. Midway up the Savannah River on the state's southern border, the South Carolina state legislature created the Edgefield District in 1785, and by the turn of the nineteenth century it had grown to be the fifth largest in South Carolina. Its population initially consisted mainly of yeomen and middling planters; in 1800 the white population numbered 13,063 while the Black population stood at just 5,067. But thirty years later the Black population (mostly enslaved) had increased threefold, outnumbering the white population 15,522 to 14,957, a trend that continued through 1860, signifying the growing presence and influence of a wealthy white planter class, despite the continued preponderance of yeomen and merchants. The district became increasingly plantation-oriented, with greater reliance upon enslaved labor and cash crop agriculture—namely, cotton—but it never approached the overtly aristocratic stature of many Lowcountry districts.[20]

Whether planter or yeoman, merchant or professional, Edgefield's leading white male population often exhibited belligerently southern mores, boasting a history replete with distinguished soldiers and statesmen who flaunted their bravado and continuously fought and died—against common enemies and one another—in defense of the personal and public honor nearly all held dear. The ideal "Edgefield man" had to be fluent in the language and ritual of southern honor. For him, failure to perform the duties of honor risked dishonor—personal, familial, and communal—that the white Edgefield community would not countenance. This persistent yet evolving Edgefield tradition paraded across the century, pervading the minds of all who bore it witness. Parson Mason Locke Weems reviled early Edgefield as "pandemonium itself, a very district of Devils." A half-century later, the tradition continued, adapted but unabated, warranting the antebellum exclamation, "If you're going to commit a murder, do it in Edgefield, as jurors there understand the idiosyncrasies of a gentleman!" Into the late 1870s, Edgefield's traditional reputation for an acute honor consciousness that often resulted in violence continued to invite ridicule, particularly from Judge Thomas Jefferson Mackey of the state judicial circuit, who once declared, "I am going to hold court in Edgefield, and I expect a somewhat exciting term, as the fall shooting is about to commence."[21]

But alongside the familiar ethic of honor that inflected the obscene number of duels, shootouts, and fisticuffs for which Edgefield men gained infamy, an equally dynamic and pervasive ethic of piety emerged and evolved. Predominantly evangelical Protestant Christian, and overwhelmingly Baptist and Methodist, religious revivals reverberated throughout the Edgefield community during the early nineteenth century. These revivals spawned expansive religious communities with a parallel social ethic. The editor of the Edgefield *Advertiser* captured the "violence" with which this parallel ethic had taken hold in the community when in the summer of 1854 he proclaimed, "There is something primitive in campmeetings that always pleased our fancy as well as satisfied our taste and judgment. . . . Nothing is, or could be, more appropriate than these occasional encampments," he continued, "[for] sinner as we are, we almost fancied ourselves in the camp of war, and preparing mind and body and soul . . . to march into the dreadful conflict." "The camp meetings have a tendency," the editor concluded, "to remind the Christian, Methodist and Baptist, of the great warfare in which they are engaged . . . and to that alone, we attribute all that is great or glorious, or wise beyond other ages, in this generation of men." As Edgefield grew and prospered both honor and piety came to define its communal morality, indelibly linked in the concept of righteous honor that implicitly guided its prevailing conception of ideal white southern manhood within the region's rigid racial patriarchy.[22]

As the renowned Edgefield historian Vernon Burton has argued, Edgefield was extreme: in the preponderance of political leadership at the state and national level who hailed from the district and in the conspicuous role that many of these leaders played in creating and even exalting its traditional reputation for violence. But Burton also argues that Edgefield was "representative in its statistical similarity to South Carolina as a whole and representative of southern values." This perspective on Edgefield finds ready affirmation in the district's cultural duality, which stemmed from its vibrant honor culture and its evangelical Protestant Christian religiosity as they evolved together during the first half of the nineteenth century. In many ways, Edgefield's honor code was more aggressive, assertive, and conspicuous in its most violent applications than elsewhere; the same could be said of the emotional tone and fervency of its religious development. That both developed alongside one another at the same time renders this cultural aspect of this place unique in many respects. But just as historians have long recognized Edgefield's political impact on the South as a whole, so too must historians acknowledge its cultural imprint on the region. Just as Edgefield sons such as George McDuffie, A. P. Butler, James Henry Hammond, Francis W. Pickens, Louis T. Wigfall, Preston S. Brooks, Benjamin R. Tillman, and J. Strom Thurmond wielded immense political power and influence on a regional and national stage, so too did Edgefield sons shape the cultural values of the region and nation from the pulpit and at the polls, in the military ranks and in the pages of the press. Their values reverberated widely across the white South during the Civil War era and beyond.[23]

Each of the families who figure most prominently in the pages that follow exhibited this broad cultural influence and resonance in that, though all had tangible, temporal ties to the Edgefield community either by birthright (the Brooks and Milligan families) or by marriage rites (the Manly and Brookes families), all ventured forth from that community into various others within and even beyond the South. Born in Pittsboro, North Carolina, in 1798, Basil Manly Sr. left North Carolina for South Carolina in the late 1810s to further his fledgling career as a preacher and complete his education at South Carolina College. Upon graduation in 1821 he proceeded to Edgefield as a minister and there started a family while being ordained in his first pastorship, before removing subsequently to Charleston, South Carolina, as pastor of the First Baptist Church (1826–37), then to Tuscaloosa, Alabama, as president of the University of Alabama (1837–55). In the spring of 1855 he returned to Charleston to pastor the Wentworth Street Baptist Church, where he served through the end of 1858. He returned to Alabama in 1859 and there remained through the duration of the Civil War as a pastor and public minister. In 1867 Manly Sr. again returned to South Carolina, where he and his family lived until his death in 1868, close to their two eldest sons, Basil Jr. and Charles.[24]

Basil Manly Jr., born in Edgefield, South Carolina, in 1825, had established himself in Greenville, South Carolina, in the late 1850s after previous stints in Alabama as a young man and minister (1830s), in Massachusetts and New Jersey for seminary studies (1840s), and in Richmond, Virginia, as a church pastor and religious educator (early 1850s). Following the Civil War and his father's death, the younger Manly migrated in 1871 from South Carolina to Covington, Kentucky, to assume the presidency of Georgetown College after struggling since 1865 to sustain the Southern Baptist Theological Seminary (SBTS) he had cofounded in Greenville in 1859. The SBTS relocated to nearby Louisville, Kentucky, in 1877, and by 1879 Basil Jr. had rejoined the faculty there, where he remained until his death in 1892.[25]

His brother Charles, born in Charleston, South Carolina, in 1837, moved with the family that same year to Tuscaloosa, Alabama, where he would spend his childhood before graduating from the University of Alabama in 1854. The next year he accompanied his father and family back to Charleston, where he spent a year itinerating among various Baptist churches in Blackville and the Edgefield district. In 1856 he departed for the Princeton Theological Seminary, graduating in 1858. From that point forward he traveled widely in fulfilling his calling as an ordained Baptist minister and educator, with stints in Alabama as pastor of the First Baptist Church in Tuscaloosa while also serving two terms as co-president of the Alabama Central Female College (1863–64 and 1869–71). He spent periods also in Murfreesboro, Tennessee, as president of Union University (1871–73), and in Staunton, Virginia, where he ministered to several area churches (1873–80). In 1880 Charles Manly and his family moved back to South Carolina, where he assumed the pastorate at First Baptist Church in Greenville (1880–81) before accepting the presidency at Furman University in Greenville (1881–97) and ministering to several rural area churches. Following his resignation from Furman, he returned to full-time ministry with pastorates in Lexington, Missouri (1898–1903), and Lexington, Virginia (1903–14). In 1914 he retired and resided most of the year with his son's family in Chicago, Illinois, but traveled every winter to visit his other children still residing in the South. He died during one of these visits, at his daughter's home in Gaffney, South Carolina, in 1924.[26]

The Reverend Iveson Brookes, another Baptist and North Carolinian, left the Old North State upon graduation from the University of North Carolina in 1819, first for South Carolina as an itinerant preacher, then for Eatonton, Georgia, as an early-career pastor and director of the Eatonton Academy in the mid- to late 1820s. Having married then lost two wives to premature death, by 1831 the widower had married a third time and settled down in the Woodville, South Carolina, community in Edgefield County, where, aside from a brief sojourn as director of the Penfield Female Academy in Penfield, Georgia, from 1842 to 1845, he remained until his death in 1865. Brookes's eldest son Walker would attend Columbian College in Washington, D.C., in the mid-1840s before returning to his native Georgia to manage various plantations in Jasper and Jones counties.[27]

The Brooks family hailed from Edgefield and constituted one of its earliest and longest-tenured clans, and by the antebellum era Whitfield Brooks stood as family patriarch. His eldest son Preston would inherit this mantle upon his father's death in 1851 but resided at least part of the year in Washington, D.C., after his election to the Congressional House of Representatives in 1853 and continuing through his own premature death in 1857.[28]

Dr. Joseph Milligan Jr. also hailed from Edgefield, specifically the town of Hamburg, along the Savannah River in the southernmost part of the county directly opposite Augusta, Georgia. Dr. Milligan practiced medicine in both cities throughout his life. His son Joseph A. S. Milligan attended medical school in Charleston, South Carolina, before returning to the Augusta vicinity to practice medicine and administer a small school in the area.[29]

Edgefield certainly made its mark on all of these men and their families, even as some ventured beyond its immediate environs. Their status and experience as leading white southern men during the Civil War era, perhaps uniquely stamped by their ties to Edgefield, reflected broader cultural patterns and resonated beyond its borders.

It stands to reason, then, that if Edgefield, the assumed microcosm of the familiar antebellum South, can be made unfamiliar to scholars through these families and their intensely emotional experiences of righteous honor, I will have achieved a new look at the Old South as it marched toward civil war, collapsed upon defeat, and resurrected itself in the postwar period. The first three chapters in part 1, "Toward a New Southern Ideology," analyze the most influential cultural characteristics of Edgefield, South Carolina, as they pertained to the dynamic influence of honor and religion in shaping elite white southern male ideals and identities. Chapter 1 establishes Edgefield's nineteenth-century reputation for honor-bound violence. Chapter 2 establishes Edgefield's vibrant spiritual life and fervent religious tenor during the first half of the nineteenth century. Together these chapters establish the context in which a sense of righteous honor emerged and evolved in Edgefield, outlining the ideological precedents informing elite white men's efforts to reconcile perceived cultural contradictions and defend the slave South's racialized patriarchy during the antebellum sectional crisis.

Chapter 3 illustrates how a select group of leading white men in this Edgefield community embraced its dual ethics of honor and religious piety in forming their personal identities and public ideologies as southerners during the early antebellum period. These Edgefield men in many respects personified the earliest antebellum efforts to balance the demands of male honor and religious piety more effectively in a nascent ideal of righteous honor.

Chapters 4, 5, and 6 in part 2, "Righteous Honor in Action," collectively demonstrate how this emerging early antebellum sense of righteous honor evolved through the late antebellum period, amid the sectional crisis and the coming of the Civil War. Chapter 4 describes how individual white southern men relied upon a sense of righteous honor to cope with moral failings and exorcise inner demons. These highly personal travails had a profound impact on their collective public ideals and identities as proslavery southerners. Some men conflated their struggle for self-mastery with the sectional conflict; both were part of the same battle for moral supremacy.

Chapter 5 takes the Reverend Basil Manly Jr., a Baptist pastor, as a case study. Through him, his father, and their Edgefield associates, their evolving perspectives on southern slavery, mastery, and morality during the sectional crisis come into clearer focus. These men's perspectives on the institution of slavery at large and the ideal role of ministers and self-proclaimed masters within it drew upon highly individualized and intensely emotional experiences, which at once prompted them and others like them to redouble efforts to more securely define, attain, and apply their sense of righteous honor as the best means of curbing slavery's apparent and increasingly problematic tendency to promote vice and violence. The tone of both these personal struggles and this public defense places in stark relief a fledgling generational disparity among leading white southern men over how best to view and defend southern slavery.

Chapter 6 takes Preston Smith Brooks as a case study, the personification of righteous honor and violence as conceived and enacted by leading white southern men at the height of the antebellum sectional crisis. The chapter suggests the extent to which many white southern men like Brooks justified loosely prescribed and ritualized forms of violence in defense of their cultural ideals and the society they purportedly upheld. His most famous, and infamous, act would become a lasting symbol of gendered and racialized political violence in defense of white supremacy and patriarchal authority.

The seventh and final chapter carries these themes through the Civil War and its aftermath, again utilizing the Manly family—Basil Sr., his wife Sarah, and their sons Basil Jr. and Charles most conspicuously—to illustrate how their sense of righteous honor—its emphasis on self-mastery and its potential to sanction righteous violence—guided them through the war and survived it, albeit in familiar-yet-adapted form to serve similar-yet-altered postwar purposes stemming from Confederate military defeat and Black emancipation. The Manlys' application of these values to meet new wartime-then-postwar realities suggests that the ideological roots of the "Lost Cause" and the "New South" derived from familiar antebellum ideals to simultaneously serve both reactionary and progressive agendas, lending the mind of the postwar white South much of its divided quality while simultaneously reinforcing the white supremacy and patriarchal authority most clearly embodied in the Jim Crow South.

The epilogue, titled "The Damnable Legacies of Righteous Honor," recounts the evolution of righteous honor as the implicit ideal of elite white southern manhood from the antebellum sectional crisis through the postwar Reconstruction era and projects its legacies into the early twenty-first century. It traces the emotional experiences of these select elite white men and their families as they grappled with slavery, secession, Confederate defeat, and Black freedom from the antebellum era to the end of Reconstruction. Their emotional lives simultaneously illustrate the overarching persistence of these cultural values throughout the period even as they highlight key shifts in identity and ideology that stemmed from both generational contrasts and changing social and cultural contexts. And these tensions over how best to perpetuate the formidable combination of white supremacy and patriarchy permeated the rise of the Jim Crow South and survived its legal demise in the mid-twentieth century to pervade the systemic gendered and racial prejudices still prevalent in the early twenty-first.

Taken whole, *Dueling Cultures, Damnable Legacies: Southern Violence and White Supremacy in the Civil War Era* unmasks the inherently prejudicial personal, emotional, and moral dimensions of ideal white manhood in the South as it lurched toward its self-destructive apotheosis in 1860–61 and cast about for justification, explanation, and direction in the breach (1861–65) and aftermath (1865–80), the benighted legacies of which still resonate in the systemic prejudices of the present day.

PART I

Toward a New Southern Ideology

1

Honor

From Colonial Virility to Antebellum Refinement

> If you're going to commit a murder, do it in Edgefield, as jurors there understand the idiosyncrasies of a gentleman!
>
> —Wade Harrison of Troy, South Carolina

IN (IN)FAMOUSLY codifying the Old South's "code duello" in 1838, the South Carolina governor John Lyde Wilson claimed to be actuated by a fierce sense of morality. Most men, he asserted, went about their lives "in the true spirit of Christian benevolence," and sought only to add "in any way to the sum of human happiness." But when such a man met with "encroachments upon [his] natural rights," "if he be subjected . . . to insult and disgrace," he was duty-bound to "guard [his most sacred] possessions with more watchful zeal than life itself." "When one finds himself avoided in society," Wilson concluded, "and traces all his misfortunes and misery to the slanderous tongue of the calumniator, who . . . has sapped and undermined his reputation, he must be more or less than man to submit in silence."[1]

Wilson denied that in publishing his *Code of Honor*, he "was an advocate of dueling, or that he wished to introduce it as the proper mode of deciding all personal difficulties and misunderstandings." "The indiscriminate and frequent appeal to arms, to settle trivial disputes and misunderstandings, cannot be too severely censured and deprecated," he wrote. Indeed, Wilson saw his published code as a step toward a time when dueling should "cease to exist entirely, in society." Moreover, he hoped to "inculcate in the rising generation" an awareness that "nothing was more derogatory to the honor of a gentleman, than to wound the feelings of any one, however humble." According to Wilson's honor code, the truly moral man would thus endeavor "scrupulously to guard individual honor, by a high personal self-respect, and the practice of every commendable virtue," and in doing so would render such a system of education "universal, [so that] we should seldom hear, if ever, of any more duelling."[2]

In ways historians continue to explicate, religious morality increasingly took hold across the antebellum southern landscape, and even men like Wilson looked for alternatives to the more primal demands of southern honor and manhood. Predictably, however, they were not ready to give up their code entirely, and many felt little compulsion to do so, believing instead that honor and piety might provide complementary means to compatible ends. "If a man be smote on one cheek in public, and he turns the other, which is also smitten, and he offers no resistance, but blesses him that so despitefully used him," Wilson wrote, "I am aware . . . that he is in the exercise of great Christian forbearance, highly recommended and enjoined by many very good men, but utterly repugnant to those feelings which nature and education have implanted in the human character."[3]

Wilson designed his code to reduce the amount of cheek-smiting in the first place; to structure men's language through ritual forms and procedures promised to subdue the passions that so often gave way to wanton personal violence, while also upholding the moral virtues espoused by prevailing religious doctrine. Thus, as Wilson emphasized, his published code did not promote dueling but self-mastery and the primacy of proper conduct toward others. *Controlled* violence was part of good breeding and good manners; in the white mind it was the essence of white rule in the slave South.[4]

Of course, violence did not always play out in the South according to Wilson's code, and many groups across the South questioned the very premise that the type of violence condoned by such a code accomplished anything even remotely resembling "self-control" or "social order." Conspicuous among the latter were evangelical Protestant Christians, who typically decried all personal violence, even that which purported to be honor-bound, and with fervent frequency publicly denounced dueling as immoral. Their rise to social prominence and pronounced cultural influence in Edgefield and the South receives full contextualization and analysis in the next chapter. But their general opposition to dueling did not equate to a complete aversion to southern honor or the white patriarchal prerogatives it purportedly upheld. Honor *could* serve as a deterrent to violence, and within the slave South some violence enacted by white enslavers was widely held to be necessary, however regrettable, by secular-minded and more sacred-minded alike. It was this potential, combined with these prerogatives, that enabled many elite white southern Christian men to exalt both honor and piety as essential elements of both individual and collective moral righteousness. Wilson's *Code* represented one prominent and broadly compelling means of achieving this reconciliatory effort, and the white Edgefield community perhaps most personified its prevalent, though prescribed, cultural embrace.[5]

That the attempt of Wilson and others to circumscribe violence within layers of Christian comportment and internalized self-restraint very nearly failed in Edgefield only intensified the desire to achieve such solidarity, and only exacerbated the fury with which people reacted to failure. That this instability often made violence more rather than less likely only increased the likelihood that so much of that violence would eventually be channeled into sectional rage. The social and cultural development of Edgefield during the early nineteenth century exposed these tensions over honor and violence acutely and provides essential context for the complex process by which such tensions eventually fueled the antebellum emergence of a more conspicuous, though still implicit, conception of righteous honor as part of the white South's increasingly desperate effort to reconcile its internal contradictions and present a united front against burgeoning criticism from abroad.[6]

Edgefield's first white settlers consisted of individuals and families who had ventured as early as 1748 inland from the coast, northward from Augusta, Georgia, and southward from the North Carolina hills and beyond. Conflict between these settlers and local Cherokee Indians culminated in the bloody Cherokee War of 1760–61, when long-standing tensions over land and commercial rights finally erupted into outright warfare. Colonial expeditionary forces and Cherokee war parties engaged in a series of brutal raids involving close, hand-to-hand combat in the sparsely settled backcountry. A 1761 peace treaty quelled tensions by reserving specified lands in the far western portion of the state to the Cherokees and opening the remainder of the backcountry to white settlement. By the end of the decade, rapid in-migration resulted in nearly three-quarters of South Carolina's white population residing in the backcountry.[7]

The social flux that followed then erupted into a series of pitched battles *among* the white settlers. This so-called Regulator movement of the late 1760s brought decades of frustrations—between Lowcountry and backcountry, white settlers and remnant Cherokees, and rival families—to a brutal head. The Anglican itinerant preacher Charles Woodmason traveled extensively in the backcountry during the period, and his observations captured the ambiguous nature of Regulator violence. Woodmason generally excoriated the backcountry populace as men and women of "abandoned morals, and profligate principles—rude, ignorant—void of manners, education or good breeding"; there being "no genteel or polite person among them," they were more or less "continually drunk." In 1767, Woodmason nevertheless empathized with these backcountry people in their exposure to "the depredations of robbers" and their impotence "without laws or government, churches, schools, or Ministers—no police established—and all property quite insecure." In the absence of such authority, Woodmason asserted that they were "neglected and slighted by those in authority" and applauded them as "they rose in arms—pursued the rogues, broke up their gangs . . . and drove the idle, vicious and profligate out of the province."[8]

Even after this wave of violence broke and receded, Woodmason warned that "the Regulators (so the populace call themselves) will not long be passive." And indeed, the Regulators shortly became so violent that Woodmason himself withdrew his support: "Great insolences are now committed by those fellows who call themselves *Regulators*—they are [ever] wanton in wickedness and impudence—and they triumph in their licentiousness." Such tensions persisted until the colonial government finally conceded backcountry demands for greater political representation and a circuit court system in a series of 1769 ordinances. Woodmason's observations and the results of both the Cherokee War and the Regulator movement confirm an early Edgefield familiarity—bordering on comfort—with violence.[9]

Such violence proved relentless, as the American Revolution in the South Carolina backcountry resembled more a blood feud between neighbors than a military engagement between nations. Vicious combat between local Tory and Whig families defined the war in the backcountry and deeply divided the Edgefield populace. These conflicts mingled with intermittent official military actions in the area to make the Revolution in Ninety-Six District (the westernmost of seven colonial judicial districts established in 1769, of which the Edgefield area was a substantial part) one of the bloodiest and most contentious theaters of the war. An editorial in the Augusta *Chronicle* by William and Thomas Butler later recalled the tumult: "We formerly knew William and Robert Melton of Little Saluda

River in Edgefield County," who "during the late war between America and Great Britain . . . were Tories and outliers and plunderers . . . with William Cunningham at the time of those cruel murders, robberies and house burnings in the winter of 1781 and 1782 that were perpetrated by the said William Cunningham and his men."[10]

As part of the fledgling nation created by the Revolution, the South Carolina state legislature created the Edgefield District in 1785 and it quickly emerged as a powerful economic and political force in the state. Its proximity to Augusta, Georgia, on the Savannah River, rendered it an ideal agricultural and commercial center for the burgeoning South Carolina backcountry. Augusta, formally established in 1736, became a pivotal market for the Georgia and South Carolina piedmont. Several trading posts had engaged Native Americans in commerce there as early as the 1740s, and by the first decade of the nineteenth century, Augusta served as the main commercial hub for the piedmont's steadily growing cotton economy. Edgefield's "first families"—the Butlers, Brooks, Jeters, Martins, Ryans, Simkins, and many others—established Edgefield Courthouse as a major way station along the road to Augusta and solidified their prominence, and that of their community, in the Augusta hinterlands.[11]

These families did not solidify their position with "soft" power. Indeed, the early Edgefield populace, high and low alike, presumed a certain level of violence in the exercise of social intercourse. Their exploits littered Edgefield's early court docket, with over four hundred cases of criminal violence recorded in the county. Several cases, most of them involving working class and middling white men, revealed the extent to which brutality colored the early Edgefield scene, as several combatants had an "ear bit off in an affray," or experienced the "gouging out of one eye." Others illuminated the growing "refinement" of Edgefield's violence, especially among its "higher sort," through the formal "sending of a challenge" or honorable "affray." One John Ously's public handbill typified the role of public opinion, and the degree of community sanction, in such affairs of honor: "I do hereby certify that in April last there was a challenge of a duel from me presented to James W. Prather of Lincoln County, Geo. And he has not accepted it. I therefore publish him as a mean, lying rascally coward." All these cases brought down only nominal fines or jail time from the Edgefield Circuit Court.[12]

Parson Mason Locke Weems, the Episcopalian itinerant preacher and book peddler, delighted in haranguing Edgefield for this brutally violent past and present. He published a series of pamphlets designed as religious moral tracts to convert the wayward from sin. Writing in the first two decades of the nineteenth century, Parson Weems penned these stern literary warnings against all manner of ill repute, from drinking, gambling, and adultery to the more life-threatening concerns of domestic abuse, dueling, and murder, and he pawned them off at every rural hamlet and county seat he encountered throughout the South. His frequent travels though Edgefield and the South Carolina backcountry gave him plenty of material from which to draw, and he never shied from dispensing it fully. As Weems's pandemonic "district of devils," Edgefield played host to most of what he despised and inspired much of what he would write. In doing so, Weems unwittingly transformed Edgefield's relatively typical colonial and early republican violence into a sensational popular image, imprinting Edgefield and its inhabitants with an indelible reputation for violence.

That reputation for a violent past—real and imagined—would fundamentally influence Edgefield's future. Subsequent generations would hold themselves to its standard, however hyperbolic it had become relative to its historical origins. And their actions would be judged accordingly from abroad, however sensational such stories became. As Edgefield proceeded through the first decades of the nineteenth century, a fundamental tension developed around this reputation. To be an Edgefield (white) man was to defend all one held dear, violently if necessary. But as Edgefield distanced itself from its frontier origins, its leading men increasingly upheld a more refined sense of honor as a means of maintaining that distance and promoting continued progress. Seeing themselves as men of honor, they reinterpreted Edgefield's past through honor's prism; Edgefield's violent past had prepared them to lead the district and confront the challenges of the future with manly fortitude. But lurking just beneath this emerging belief in the proscriptive potential of honorable violence was a fear of regression into frontier lawlessness, recklessness, and unmanly disorder. This insecurity drove many Edgefield men to exalt the honor code as the best hope of a more promising future, without renouncing the district's more visceral past.[13]

Parson Mason Locke Weems preyed on this insecurity in his writings, which simultaneously served to enshrine this violent reputation and expose the insecurity over it. Weems first aired his disdain for Edgefield in 1808 with his highly popular *God's Revenge against Murder, or The Drown'd Wife*, in which he documented the late eighteenth-century drowning of Mary Findley by her husband Ned Findley, both of Edgefield District, just eight days into their marriage. With classic tongue-in-cheek, Weems proclaimed: "It may excite the surprise of some, that a district now so civilized should ever have given birth to such a monster." In the next sentence he wrote that such "surprise will cease, when it comes to be remembered that Edgefield is a mere *nothing now* to what it was in days *of yore*." He continued: "Even till the last twenty years the citizens of Edgefield, to speak moderately, were a *rapid set*" and "club law of course was mightily in fashion. A tough pull of the snout was *all one* as an indictment—a broken head passed current for a *capital* argument—and a stunning knock to the ground *settled the hash*." In his view, "The people then had no more notion of *restraint*, than the Indians; and if only *touched* by the trammels of law, would jump and kick."[14]

Weems painted a raucous picture of early Edgefield, one in which even its tribunals overflowed with rancor, as he related the story of a defendant whose suit had gone against him "bound[ing] out of the Court house like a shot out of a shovel, and, stripping to the buff, went ripping and tearing about the yard like a mad man!" The enraged defendant then allegedly commenced to "damning both judge and jury for all the pick-pocket sons of bitches he could think of! and daring them to come out, *only to come out*, and he'd shew 'em, '*God damn 'em, what it was to give judgment against a gentleman like him!!*'" Court in those days was likely to reveal, "poor *blackguards* by the dozen, with batter'd jaws and bung'd eyes, poking about like blind dunghill cocks on a *Saft-Tuesday*." And the excitement knew no bounds, for "here you might have heard the bullies hard at it; some laying on each other like mad horses; and others like drunken brutes, bawling out at every blow . . . '*now's your time—Gouge! gouge! damn you, why don't you gouge?*'" Weems then concluded: "This, I am told, was *old Edgefield*, some five and twenty years ago!" all based on "four days which I spent there at a crouded court last month" during which he "had not the pain to see a *single drunkard!* nor a *single fight!*" As some of his later tales would attest, this new Edgefield retained much of its former self in its penchant for violent display.[15]

The "poor Findley" whose story Weems related, "was born in Edgefield when it was a place of but *low degree*; and thence, probably, he took a taint of the old leaven which stuck him to the last." This taint led Findley to murder his wife, and for that murder he hung from the public gallows. Though Weems utilized the story to remind neglectful parents and wayward youths of their religious moral duty, his account of the murder also revealed the role that honor played in Edgefield. Ned Findley had clearly dishonored himself, his family, and the community with his heinous crime, and for that he was duly punished with a suitably shameful death. His violent act did not uphold or adhere to the honor code, and he was summarily sentenced to death for the unmanly affront.[16]

But another Edgefield murder would muddy those waters. Mason Locke Weems's most scathing reproof of the Edgefield District came in his wildly popular pamphlet *The Devil in Petticoats, or God's Revenge against Husband-Killing*, initially published in 1810. In it Weems recounted the life of Mrs. Rebecca "Becky" Cotton of Edgefield in all its grisly detail. In 1794, she had murdered her husband John with an ax "and with arms braced up of hell, drove at his defenceless head a furious blow which . . . bursted the skull and sunk deeply into his brain." Then, "supposing, thence, that he was dead enough, she waked up her brother Davy" and "with his assistance dragged the corpse of her husband into a small meat-house" where "thinking she saw him move an eye, she tied a rope round his neck, and throwing the other end over a rafter, drew him up from the ground" and there left him "half hanging" as she retired to bed. In the darkness of the dawn, she again woke Davy and together they "dragged the corpse into the garden and buried it in the potato vault." But her neighbors soon grew suspicious of her husband's absence and threatened young Davy until he reluctantly revealed the grim truth and its sordid proof. But Becky Cotton avoided immediate capture as she fled westward. Edgefield's concerned citizenry soon formed a posse and in hot pursuit they overcame the murderer within days. All eagerly anticipated her trial and (it was hoped) speedy punishment. "Accordingly, she was tried. But O! strange to tell, and as hard to be believed, she was acquitted! The longing gallows and gibbet were both disappointed . . . the sheriff's branding iron and the constable's cowhide were not permitted to scar, or even to approach her polished skin."[17]

In describing how Becky Cotton thus "came off clear," Parson Weems waxed most eloquently in his derision of her native Edgefield. He laid the fault of her fallen nature at the feet of her father, who had neglected to encourage in her "delights in virtue," and as a result she began "resting her glory and conquest on the immortal charms of mind [that] have confided to all the vain attractions of a little skin-deep beauty." As Weems recounted, Becky Kannady Cotton's father, James Kannady, "the wretched old man! was borne to a bloody grave long before *his eye was dim or his natural strength abated*" because he was "selfish; and his neighbors were not benevolent . . . sordid and selfish as himself, their blood was quickly roused by jarring interest; and their anger as fiercely inflamed by the slightest threat of loss." These "wretched men, with fiery faces and uplifted clubs, met in the fields amidst the mingled roar of worrying dogs and tortured swine" and "a shameful fray ensued, which terminated to the disadvantage of Mr. Kannady who crawled home, barbarously beaten." But James Kannady survived the assault, and successfully argued his case in the Charleston courts, after which he returned to Edgefield and loudly proclaimed that he had "so nicely matched the rascals."[18]

Such a public affront would not long stand in Edgefield. Kannady's antagonists, "burning with tenfold rage ... and seeing no way of escaping the rod of shame and loss which he held over their heads ... bravely struck hands with the Devil to kill him!" They proceeded and "with this infernal view they loaded their guns, and mounting their horses, dashed off in open daylight" whence "they triumphantly exclaimed 'O ho! you old villain! So you are overtaken at last are you? On your knees you damned Rascal, and say your prayers, or you'll be in Hell in three minutes, for you have only that time to live.'" They then placed a "gun to the old man's side and shot him through the heart." Through this tumult, Becky Cotton vainly entreated the mob to spare her father's life, while her husband, John Cotton, "sat petrified with terror during this shocking scene." His inaction sealed his fate, and she later exacted her revenge with one swift ax blow.[19]

Her acquittal by the Edgefield court surprised Parson Weems. The subsequent defense of her character by the Edgefield populace shocked his sensibilities. Her physical beauty bewitched "the admiring throng" who crowded the courthouse while "the stern features of justice were all relaxed, and both lawyers and jury, hanging forward from their seats with fondly rolling eyes were heard to exclaim, 'O Heavens what a charming creature!'" An observing bystander supposedly rejoined, "'Yes, if she had not been such a murderer!'" to which one of the jury indignantly replied, "'A Murderer! A murderer sir! 'tis false. Such an angel could never have been a murderer.'" Her seduction ultimately succeeded not only in acquittal, but betrothal, to a Major Gellis, one of the jury and "a respectable citizen ... of handsome property." Parson Weems concluded that God exacted justice where Edgefield had failed when Becky Cotton was murdered by her brother Stephen on the courthouse steps in 1807, the result of a long-standing tension between them.[20]

Weems meant for his treatment of Becky Cotton's travails to morally instruct, and the immense popularity of this particular tract seemingly confirmed his success. But despite his intent, Weems also gave readers a self-righteous position from which to read an indulgent tale of immorality, and inadvertently confirmed and advertised Edgefield's growing reputation for honor and violence. Honor and shame certainly motivated both James Kannady and his persecutors, whose actions ultimately proved to be the root of Becky Cotton's murder. The Edgefield community assumed that such honor often required a violent defense. This expectation extended even to Becky's murder of her husband, who had repeatedly shown himself bereft of honor, most conspicuously in his failure to defend her or her father in the face of assault. Even her heinous deed could seem justified according to that conception of honor. And as Weems himself lamented, her subsequent acquittal and betrothal to an upstanding Edgefield citizen seemingly affirmed that community response.[21]

The tension between virility and refinement within Edgefield's manhood ideal and its honor code persisted, as did masculine insecurities and community reservations over the proper balance of honor and violence. The U.S. senator George McDuffie personified that balance for many in his Edgefield home. In the summer of 1822, McDuffie engaged his political archrival William Cummings in a formal duel that conspicuously captured these tensions as well as the public eye. McDuffie and Cummings had exchanged insults in the weeks prior to their exchange of shots, with Cummings initiating the public affair of honor by "posting" McDuffie. He asserted that McDuffie had "virtually denied me the satisfaction demanded of him" and pronounced the congressman "an EQUIVOCATING SCOUNDREL AND BASE COWARD!" Cummings then mocked McDuffie's printed response, "a hand-bill in his own best style," by declaring, "He is never afraid of shedding his ink, and generally answers charges of cowardice by words."[22]

McDuffie, in that handbill, returned Cummings's fire with equal fervor: "I gratuitously offered Col. Cumming the satisfaction due to a gentleman when in the estimation of the whole community he was disgraced as unworthy of notice." He continued, "I appointed a day and place and forewarned that I would meet him on no other. He actually refused to meet me; seeking under false pretences, to obtain a day to which he was not entitled." McDuffie then lowered the boom: "I have seen Col. Cumming on the ground of combat embolden his cowardly nerves by artificial stimulants. I know him to be a coward, who has been driven only by desperation to the course he has pursued." He accused Cummings of "the effrontery [of denying] . . . that he stimulated internally by the habitual use of opium in addition to the [spirituous?] liquid in which he washed his face the moment before he took his stand."[23]

Their combat finally took place in the early morning of June 8, 1822, at the Sister's Ferry, just miles below Augusta, Georgia, on the Savannah River. McDuffie fell wounded after the first fire, while Cummings emerged unscathed, and the duel ended. But the affair of honor continued unabated, as both parties (through their seconds) filled the press with declarations, explanations, and justifications aimed at shaping public perception of the affair and claiming victory for their partisan. McDuffie emerged from this war of words the victor, physically wounded but with a heightened reputation, which he carried back to Congress, into a thriving local law practice, and eventually to the South Carolina governorship. McDuffie—and his Edgefield constituents—certainly upheld the Edgefield "tradition" for violent defense of personal, and communal, honor.[24]

However, formal duels in the McDuffie-Cummings mold were few and far between in early Edgefield, at least as publicly rumored, reported, or acknowledged. And bloodless affrays paled in comparison to the heinous bloodlettings that appeared on the county court docket. "Another murder in Edgefield" came to symbolize the district's growing reputation for violence, as newspapers across the state reported Edgefield's "exploits" with derisive ardor. "Another horrid murder was committed in Edgefield District," the Pendleton, South Carolina, *Messenger* proclaimed in 1825, when "Peter Morgan, who resided near the junction of Turkey and Stevens Creek" fell victim to a "horrid deed" by "Alexander Howl, son-in-law to the deceased." In the wake of a "tax gathering" both parties had attended, the Pendleton *South Carolina Republican* related that Morgan and Howl had been engaged in a fierce argument, when Morgan, who "stood high among his neighbors as an honest, upright citizen, . . . one of the survivors of the Revolutionary War [who] was at the siege of Yorktown when Cornwallis was captured," had, after Howl had "pressed harder on the old man," "picked up a board and retreating struck Howl one blow." "Howl then seized him by the throat with his left hand and with the right inflicted a mortal wound in the left groin, with a Spanish knife, which cut the main artery." Morgan "expired in 15 minutes" while Howl "made his escape." This familial brawl became in the hands of Pendleton's editors a symbol of Edgefield's lawlessness, even as they defended the action of one of its honorable citizens, Morgan, who had initiated the violence.[25]

Yet another murder trial made headlines two years later, this one involving a local entrepreneur, Henry Shultz, founder and mayor of the recently incorporated town of Hamburg, South Carolina, located on the Savannah River at the southernmost edge of Edgefield District. Shultz had made his name and a fleeting fortune as a merchant and banker in nearby Augusta, Georgia, during the first two decades of the nineteenth century. But expensive legal battles with rival Augusta banks and merchants increasingly depleted his accounts and weakened his resolve. Sometime around 1820, after several legal setbacks, he desperately thrust a loaded pistol into his own mouth and pulled the trigger. He miraculously survived, and after a brief recuperation seemed little worse for wear. Granted this new lease on life, he fell headlong into his new design—to erect the town of Hamburg, South Carolina, as a commercial rival to Augusta, Georgia, directly across the Savannah River. In this he largely succeeded, and by the mid-1820s Hamburg had siphoned off much of the South Carolina cotton trade that had previously been contracted in Augusta. But success again proved fleeting. In 1824, a theft in one of his Hamburg wagon yards riled Shultz's considerably violent temper, and he ordered the suspected larcenist, a young man named Alexander Boyd, to be severely whipped. When Boyd died from this lashing, the Edgefield District Circuit Court indicted Shultz for murder, though he was convicted on a reduced charge of manslaughter in 1827 and thus avoided the hangman's noose, serving just six months in the Edgefield jail.[26]

Press coverage of this trial echoed that sensationally chronicled by Weems in the Becky Cotton affair and reaffirmed the ambiguous relationship of Edgefield's leading men to violence. Augusta's preeminent newspaper, the *Chronicle*, frequently ridiculed Edgefield, its neighbor across the Savannah, for the prevalence of criminal violence, but in the Shultz case the paper's editors heralded one of Edgefield's most conspicuous perpetrators by declaring, "The character of Mr. Shultz for twenty years past was given by gentlemen of the first respectability from both States, and it was equally gratifying to his friends and those of humanity to find it unequally in acts of charity, humanity, and benevolence," and "on the trial he proved a character for generosity, humanity, and benevolence equaled by few and surpassed by none." They concluded that "even in the unfortunate affair in which he violated the laws, and which has brought on him so much public censure and self-reproach, he was not the voluntary actor," and owing to Shultz's reputation, the jury's verdict of manslaughter "seemed to give general satisfaction." Violence born of a just cause and exacted with proper tact could be tolerated as a necessary defense of honor. Such honor could countenance a wide range of white male transgressions, so long as those men exhibited an honorable character and carried themselves accordingly. The case of Henry Shultz illustrated the lengths to which an honorable reputation could and would permit violent retribution.[27]

A tenuous balance between maintaining honor's virility and curbing its most violent excesses defined the Edgefield tradition. By 1830, many accepted that the formal duel promised to best serve such restraining ends, and its practice became more conspicuous, if only nominally more frequent, in the years that followed. The year 1830 also marked the incorporation of the town of Edgefield Courthouse, signifying for many the supposed advance of the civilizing influences and social order that often accompanied such municipal establishment. While much of the rest of the nation had largely discarded the code duello by 1830, elite white southerners maintained their adherence to this more traditional conception and application of honor, and Edgefield was first among the adherents. Edgefield tradition viewed the honor code as a necessary check on masculine recklessness, and community courts reflected the mores of their constituency by turning a blind eye and a deaf ear to affairs of honor in their midst. Indictments for "sending a challenge" or "affray" disappeared from the judicial record after 1824. Judicial silence, however, did not signal abatement of the practice. And Edgefield's public eye took applauding, if reserved, notice.[28]

This evolving Edgefield tradition for honor-bound violence nevertheless grew stronger, and its adherents more stalwart, with each succeeding duel. On August 9, 1843, the editors of the *Advertiser* reported that James Gardner and "our brother Jones of the *Chronicle and Sentinel*" had recently resorted to "horrida bella" near the town of Hamburg, but "after an exchange of shots, their feelings of resentment seemed to be satiated, and they left the ground." Edgefield's editors congratulated both Georgia men for their "scatheless escape from the field of Mars" but added, "We regret our soil being made the scene of such gladiatorship, and would prefer the gentlemen settling their disputes at home, in Georgia." Another "affair of honor came off" the following year near Hamburg "when Col. John Cunningham and S. McGowan, Esq., both of Abbeville . . . fought with U.S. Yangers, at a distance of thirty paces. Mr. McGowan was severely wounded." According to these accounts, such violence was not necessarily to be shunned, but it should at least include men of Edgefield if the district was to host such bloodshed. These visiting gentlemen obviously knew well Edgefield's reputation for looking the other way when it came to the "idiosyncrasies of a gentleman."[29]

Other affairs of honor involved prominent Edgefield politicians. Senator Andrew Pickens Butler engaged in two such affairs during his congressional tenure. The first began in August of 1848, when Butler challenged the Missouri senator Thomas Hart Benton "to mortal combat, on account of the harsh language used by the latter to him in the course of debate in the Senate on Sunday morning. Col. Benton accepted the challenge, and the time was fixed for the deadly encounter." However, Virginia "police got wind of the matter, and both parties were arrested and bound over to keep the peace. Mutual friends are endeavoring to settle the difficulty." The *Advertiser* then reported on August 17 that "the difficulty between Senators Butler and Benton has been adjusted . . . [and] settled without a meeting. Mr. Butler leaves for home tomorrow morning." The editors concluded, saying, "The conduct of Mr. Benton was that of a bully, while Mr. Butler's was characterized by the cool deliberate courage which neither offers nor submits to insult." By all accounts, the affair was ended. However, the following week's paper brought news of a complication. The editors rescinded their previous report that the affair had been "*honorably adjusted*," citing "statements furnishing the exact version of the matter, which was, that Judge Butler's friend, although urging it for three successive days, could get no reply to his correspondence" from Benton or his second. Benton was thus assumed to have "refused the challenge," to which Edgefield's editors observed, "He did not reply, and thus the affair terminated, at whose expense the public can at once see."[30]

Just three years later, Senator Butler again engaged in an affair of honor with a fellow senator, this time Henry Foote of Mississippi. "It will be seen," the *Advertiser* reported, "that Senator Butler has already encountered Mississippi's Foote, without being upset or in the least degree injured. On the contrary, he has made use of an excellent opportunity of giving the old wrangler a very decent castigation early in the action." For his action, the editors "among many others, return[ed] the Judge . . . sincere thanks, adding the usual cry of 'hit him again' with a hearty good will." Edgefield's tradition served its leaders—of the pen and in politics—well, as long as their collective sense of honor emerged unblemished.[31]

But the line between formal duel and informal rencontre often blurred. Even the perpetrators of Edgefield's most wanton destruction of life—in shootouts, brawls, and various other fisticuffs—evinced a sense of the personal and public honor often at stake. Though eschewing the formal exchange of ink and bullets with pens and pistols that governed the code duello, many of these more frequent violent confrontations partially assumed the mode if not entirely the means of the southern honor code, broadly conceived. The press and the reading public recognized those stakes all too well. Between 1830 and 1860, nearly four hundred such cases came before the Edgefield County Court, and many of these played out conspicuously before the public.

The shooting of Adam Taylor by J. P. Terry found its way onto the pages of the *Advertiser* in the closing weeks of November 1838. Witnesses agreed that Terry went armed with a gun, but did not brandish it "until Taylor advanced with a rock drawn back, threatening to kill Terry—and then it was that the direction of the gun changed." At that point, "Taylor seized the muzzle of the gun with his left hand and 'jerked' it violently" and "the gun fired." On January 4, 1842, the *Advertiser* reported another "melancholy affray" between Samuel Tomkins and Alexander Nixon, the product of "some difference, which resulted in the death of Mr. Tomkins by Nixon shooting him in the left temple, with a ball from a pistol." Nixon initially fled the scene, was later apprehended and tried on the spring court docket, but a jury of his peers found him not guilty.[32]

On September 4, 1844, Joseph W. Glover assaulted Lovett Gomillion on the Edgefield County Courthouse steps. After a public sheriff's sale Glover confronted Gomillion about an alleged insult and exclaimed, "Damn you Gomillion, prepare and defend yourself!" before discharging his pistol. He then advanced steadily toward Gomillion, pistol raised, the latter slowly retreating. At just eight feet apart, Gomillion suddenly turned, pistol ablaze, and shot Glover "in his breast" causing him to "pitch forward into a gully," dead when he hit the ground. Gomillion, who immediately entered into custody, later pled self-defense and was found not guilty of murder.[33] Yet another "fatal rencontre" befell Edgefield the following year, when Charles Price angrily "entered the store of Mr. A.B. Griffin," and upon spotting Benjamin F. Jones in the corner, declared he had "met a rascal he didn't expect to meet and had heard he had said his daughter had sworn a lie." Jones answered this declaration with, "She had sworn a lie!" Price replied by shooting Jones through the heart with a shotgun, killing him instantly. He then "walked out, told witnesses he was done working, and left" the scene. Authorities later apprehended Price, who was convicted for manslaughter, and imprisoned for one year.[34]

While these disputes between relative unknowns over relative trivialities may have stretched the logic of honor in some minds, others condoned such actions as the justifiable result of honor-bound difficulties between white men. Many cases exhibited the extent to which the law, the newspapers, and the reading public conspired to couch seemingly brutal homicides in the language and ritual of the honor code. According to that code, as many interpreted it, otherwise respectable white men in the community sometimes disagreed to the point of physical confrontation. As long as they conducted themselves according to the tenets of honor, their blows—even with deadly results—could be abided as their prerogative. Reared in the Edgefield tradition for honor-bound violence, such men could justify—and could expect community sanction of—such violence if properly pursued.

Several of these occurrences involved local "grog shops" whose "spirituous" offerings "tempt[ed] men to drunkenness and ruin"; yet these cases maintained a ritual formality often lacking in such places. On July 8, 1851, "an argument over money took place near the entrance of Spann's bar room in Edgefield between William Cloud and Phillip Goode," wherein Cloud tried "to back away honorably but Goode would not let him," and despite attempts to calm the two men, who had both been drinking, "Goode pulled out his pistol and shot Cloud in the chest," killing him "almost immediately." Goode eventually stood trial at the fall term of court and was released on the issue of a bench warrant. On the evening of March 2, 1852, "Eldred Glover entered Doby's Bar and demanded that Dr. [Walker] Samuel explain a letter ... Samuel refused an explanation, and challenged Glover to meet him the next Monday at Sand Bar Ferry saying, 'and you shall have satisfaction with the weapons of warfare.'" After Glover ignored this challenge and again inquired about the letter, Samuel vehemently responded that he "wished to have no correspondence with a damned rascal!" and turned away. Glover then punched Samuel, who "dropped his saddlebags and drew his pistol and fired twice at Glover inside the bar." Glover took to the streets, with Samuel in hot pursuit and firing again, this time maiming Glover with "a gunshot wound that entered one side of his abdomen and exited the other." Glover died of his wounds within twenty-four hours. Dr. Samuel offered himself up to authorities and stood trial during the fall term, when he was convicted of manslaughter, fined one thousand dollars and imprisoned for one year.[35]

These inebriated confrontations also spilled out into the public thoroughfares. A shooting on the courthouse square occurred over a game of faro at the local Planters Hotel on the evening of July 21, 1856. George D. Tillman and E. T. Davis were gaming among a crowd of onlookers huddled in their room. A dispute arose over the amount of the bet, and James H. Christian, a local mechanic who was among the spectators, vociferously denied Tillman's claim. After unsuccessfully appealing to the crowd for support, Tillman denounced Christian a "damned rascal and liar!" He then further exclaimed, "You damned scoundrel," to which an incensed Christian replied, "Who do *you* call a damned scoundrel!" The two slowly advanced toward each other when Tillman suddenly fired his pistol, causing Christian to spin around, throw "his arms across his chest," and exclaim, "Tillman, you've killed me!" Tillman evaded the law for two years, absconding with the notorious filibuster and "gray-eyed man of destiny" William Walker to Nicaragua. J. H. Christian's family attempted to "Stop the Murderer!" by offering a reward for Tillman's capture in the *Advertiser*, but to no avail. Upon his return late the following year, Tillman offered himself up to authorities, was tried during the spring of 1858, convicted of manslaughter, fined two thousand dollars, and imprisoned for two years.[36]

Yet another Tillman son found trouble in 1860, when John Tillman (younger brother to George D., both older brothers to Benjamin Ryan Tillman of later infamy) met George C. Mays and his son John along the Plank Road connecting Edgefield Village and the town of Hamburg. Mays shouted at Tillman, calling him a "damned rascal!, pulling his pistol" and refusing to give up the road. Tillman said he was unarmed and declared Mays a "damned liar!," to which the elder Mays replied, "Damn you! I'll kill you anyway!" before hitting Tillman with a pistol shot to the chest. Tillman then told Mays, "'I am a dead man, shoot until you are satisfied,' and Mays fired a second shot hitting him in the arm." John Mays also pulled his pistol and demanded that "Tillman get out of his buggy before he fired 2–3 more balls." Tillman drove off severely wounded and "in great agony" to his family's nearby mill. Dr. Walker B. Samuel there treated Tillman's wounds, but to no avail; he later related how in death Tillman had declared, "It was not worth while to do anything for him ... he was a dead man ... he felt the blood running internally ... he knew he was shot through and ... there was no chance for him." Both George and John Mays were tried in the spring of 1860 and found not guilty.[37]

The town of Hamburg hosted another bloody affray in the final days before South Carolina's secession from the American Union. Three brothers, Joseph, Wade, and Musco Samuel, confronted James Reynolds on December 18, 1860, and accused him of an insult. When Reynolds denied the accusation, Wade Samuel declared that he "told a damn lie!" Joseph Samuel heightened the accusation when he "proceeded to call Reynolds an abolitionist and accuse him of helping free Blacks to the north. He told Reynolds never to speak to him again." Reynolds defiantly "replied he would speak to him or any other man he wished," at which Joseph Samuel "hit Reynolds over the head, apparently killing him instantly." All three Samuel brothers "drew their pistols, but a crowd that had gathered urged them not to shoot." They warned the crowd "that they would shoot any person attempting to aid Reynolds." But despite the warning, Stephen Shaw emerged from the crowd and knelt to assist the dying Reynolds. The three brothers then "fired 10–12 shots at Shaw. Joseph was believed to have fired the fatal shot to Shaw's jaw. Wade also hit Shaw with a very deliberately aimed shot to the side." All were brought to trial in the spring of 1861, when Joseph was convicted of manslaughter, sentenced to two years, six months imprisonment, and fined one thousand dollars. Wade and Musco were found not guilty. All three were released from their recognizance regarding the death of Stephen Shaw.[38]

In all of these cases, from the Taylor-Terry fight in 1838 through the Samuel-Reynolds-Shaw shootout in 1860, the language and ritual of honor governed, however coarsely, the violent action as it unfolded. And Edgefield's juries repeatedly confirmed this in their reduction of murder charges to manslaughter convictions, which carried considerable fines and often nominal jail time but precluded the shame of the hangman's noose at the public gallows. In the evolving Edgefield tradition, one point became increasingly paramount: violence that abided by the code of honor fell under the jurisdiction of white male prerogative, a territory into which the state rarely ventured and public juries typically proved unwilling to invade. That prerogative, according to prevailing ideals, supposedly solidified their society, and the honor alleged to be inherent in these cases and others like them ostensibly preserved that prerogative and the social order.

But honor could not account for all social evils, and it fell far short of justifying all violent acts. Wanton domestic violence against dependents white and Black, as well as impassioned public violence fueled by lust, or greed, or perversion, or alcohol, fell conspicuously beyond the bounds of the honor code. And such violence abounded, despite claims that honor restrained passions and governed the social hierarchy accordingly. Divergence of this sort strained the delicate balance between masculine prerogative and excess and worried the very white men whom honor entitled to heightened social positions, which their tradition for honor-bound violence purportedly sought to ensure.

The case of Martin Posey quite literally brought home the grim reality of what could transpire when honor failed: the household over which supposedly honorable white men presided, and which formed the basis of an orderly slave society, descended into chaos. The entire trial, and the execution of its death sentence, seemed to confirm the chaotic results of such dishonor, as each moment met with considerable excitement. "The Court House was crowded, and the excitement high," the *Advertiser* reported, and "the Jury during the recesses of the Court and at night were put in custody and kept entirely separate from the community." The near-hysteria continued on the day of Posey's public hanging, with the *Advertiser* again reporting it "a day memorable in the annals of our District. The oldest inhabitants do not recollect ever to have seen so many people collected at this Village. The concourse may be estimated from four thousand to five thousand persons." The assembled crowd, "composed of men, women, children and negroes, on streets, stairways and rooftops, on foot, on horseback, in Buggies and Carriages came and went," with the "only events to disturb the calmness and melancholy of the day . . . a few drunken brawls in the afternoon, which ended in several fisticuffs, that produced no more serious results, we believe, than a few scratches and bloody noses." The Edgefield Circuit Court sentenced Martin Posey to "be hanged by the neck until his body be dead" for accessory to the murder of his wife Matilda, and for the murder of his slave Appling, whom he had incited to kill his wife. Posey went to the gallows on February 1, 1850.[39]

This excitement did not cease upon Posey's execution. Nearly ten years later, the *Advertiser* lived up to its name by offering a "record of past days and dark scenes" surrounding "the Trial of MARTIN POSEY for the Murder of his Wife, Matilda H. Posey, and Negro Slave Appling" in "an interesting pamphlet of about 75 pages, giving a true and exact account of a crime committed in Edgefield District in 1849." Edgefield's grisly reputation for violence sold papers, especially when the murder broke the bounds of its honor code. The trial of Martin Posey and cases like it served dual purposes; they were chilling reminders that lost honor meant lost order, as well as scintillating portraits of an often raucous (and cautiously celebrated) community history. The Edgefield tradition bestowed an uneasy comfort with criminal violence. Even that which honor did not condone could still serve honorable ends.[40]

That fine line extended into acts of racial violence. The court dockets and press pages teemed with accounts of white brutality toward enslaved Blacks. The case of Russell Harden epitomized this brutality. Harden appeared before the Edgefield Circuit Court twice within two years for the crime of murdering a slave. The jury revealed the larger community's fears when they found Harden "guilty of killing in a sudden heat of passion." Yet the crime carried only a five-hundred-dollar fine and six months' imprisonment, also revealing the implicit recognition that white racial control sometimes required the corporal punishment of and violent demonstration toward enslaved Blacks. The state only with extreme reticence ventured across the threshold of another white man's household, and even then, decrees came with extreme caution.[41]

Perhaps that implicit acceptance prompted Harden to commit his next brutal act with little fear of legal reprisal. On September 19, 1848, the county coroner investigated the death of another Harden slave, Stephney, eventually ruling that Harden "did feloniously kill the slave Stephney against the peace and dignity of the State." The nature of the crime exacerbated its effects: Harden had severely whipped and paddled Stephney for insubordination twice in the span of two weeks. When Stephney refused Harden's command a third time, Harden became irate. He "tied a chain around the deceased's neck and fastened it to a pole in the . . . hog gallows . . . where they killed and cleaned hogs" in order to "prevent him from running away," but after "two or three hours Stephney died." Harden and his sons Miles and Elbert then loaded Stephney's body into a wagon and "hauled it to the Savannah River about five miles away" where they "fastened a large sledge hammer and a heavy plow hoe to Stephney's body and put him in the river at their landing . . . sometime after midnight and before daylight." They then reported to neighbors "that their slave Stephney had run away." But the body was soon discovered at a nearby plantation and brought under inquest, ultimately resulting in Harden's conviction. Again, reluctance to interfere with white prerogative checked the state's action. Despite a prior record of slave cruelty and even murder, Harden was "admitted to bail in the amount of four thousand dollars with two securities on condition of his appearance in court next term" and that "in the meantime he will be of good behavior and keep the peace toward all the good citizens of this State." After he satisfied these terms, the jury returned a verdict of not guilty during the following session.[42]

The deference that state counsel and jurors paid to white patriarchal prerogative did not apply solely to the household. Such prerogatives could and did play out in very public ways in very public places, and often embroiled state courts despite their reservations.[43] The case of Joseph Williams exemplified the trend. On January 18, 1857, "Williams had been drinking and was antagonistic and yelling for his horse" when he entered S. F. Goode's blacksmith's shop just off the Edgefield Courthouse square. He soon got into an argument with two enslaved men, Hamp and Bill, who worked at the shop. Despite being supported by Bill in the argument, Williams belligerently "told both Bill and Hamp that he was going to shoot them" before "the two men left the shop and Williams fell over. When he got up he pulled out his pistol and said, 'God Dammed you I will shoot you!'" At this point, a third slave named Richmond, who had witnessed the entire exchange, "said to Williams, 'go ahead and shoot,'" to which Williams vehemently "swung his pistol around to Richmond and told him he would shoot him instead." Richmond exclaimed, "'Then shoot me God damn you!'" before "Williams shot him twice in the head and he died instantly." Williams was incarcerated for the murder of a slave following the March court session. His drunkenness had stripped him of his honor to the point of quarreling with enslaved men, a foreboding prospect that struck a sensitive nerve in the white southern psyche. Honor could not abide a drunken lack of control and would not countenance the leveling effect such dishonor could foment between white and Black.[44]

Thus stood the Edgefield tradition on the precipice of the Civil War. Adherents claimed honor acted as a restraint, a controlling moral influence against excessive masculine violence, whether domestic or public in nature, intra- or interracial in execution. Such violence—enacted by certain men toward prescribed ends according to finite rules—was accepted as a necessary part of white patriarchal mastery in a slave society. But a litany of dishonorable violence against dependent Blacks and whites, men and women, exposed just causes for considerable moral concern. The very resort to a greater dependence on honor's proscriptive potential along these lines implicitly revealed such concerns.[45]

Tensions within the white male honor ethic also exposed the reservations these men held about its solidifying influence within their own lives and their slave society. Entering the early antebellum period, as they subtly questioned their ability to control their passions by maintaining honor, they tacitly opened themselves and their society to criticism and ridicule from within and without. These criticisms came in many forms and spawned many responses. A pivotal challenge—and potential ally—arose with the South's other dominant social ethic: evangelical Protestant Christian piety. Edgefield proved equally fertile ground for cultivating that parallel social ethic and reaping the fruits of its moralizing labors.

2

Piety

The Ascent of Evangelical Protestantism

> To give you an idea of the spirit of the [Edgefield] people . . .
> God has indeed in a most signal manner blessed the church . . .
> The work is spreading . . . even where the revival has not yet appeared . . . a sense of eternal things had taken hold of their minds.
>
> —Rev. Basil Manly Sr. (1822)

EDGEFIELD'S RELIGIOUS history before 1820 marked the rise of evangelical Protestant Christianity in the South Carolina interior, and its social ethic predicated on a spiritual "new birth" as the entry point to a more universally accessible path to spiritual salvation formed a cornerstone of the Edgefield community from the outset. The "Great Revival," the spiritual awakening that peaked in intensity between 1800 and 1810 but reverberated in ebbs and flows through the 1830s, brought much of the South Carolina midlands and upstate, including Edgefield, into the evangelical Protestant Christian fold by drawing upon the revival fervor that had enveloped communities across the South. This "Second Great Awakening" wove an emerging evangelical Protestant Christian ethic of piety into the very fabric of the Edgefield community. This communal ethic only increased in its cultural influence and social impact as the century progressed, manifested most conspicuously in the expansion of existing churches and the construction of new ones, with most of this expansion in Edgefield occurring among Baptists and Methodists and initiated by recurrent revivals among those denominations.[1]

But as the Methodist bishop Francis Asbury noted of early Edgefield, "limited preaching meant that when a preacher was available, people of different denominations would attend the same church; hence the values of different denominations were mingled." This mingling of values enabled an awakening of the Edgefield spirit to ameliorate sectarian division and even extend beyond denominational affiliation. Revivals were very public, social affairs, rivaling judicial court days and commercial sale days for the anticipation and attendance of the Edgefield community. Many who remained beyond the evangelical Protestant Christian fold attended revivals as they did these other community events, and thus encountered evangelical Protestant Christian values and teachings. Such encounters led many to join Edgefield churches; it led even more to a familiarity with evangelical Protestant Christian moral and ethical ideals. This ethic of piety broadly embraced spiritual self-reflection and morality, stressing their mutual importance in bringing about religious conversion. While many in the community, especially men, stopped short of conversion and abstained from officially joining a particular denomination or congregation, the esteem of individual spiritual growth and moral concern pervaded, suggesting, as the historian Vernon Burton has surmised, that "at least some of the churches exhibited a degree of tolerance necessary to foster a larger sense of community," one well versed in the morality and language of evangelical Protestantism.[2]

On the brink of the Civil War, Edgefield—like much of the South—exuded a pronounced religiosity, one that promoted a moral consciousness suffused with a decidedly evangelical Protestant Christian tone. The centrality of revival and the ecumenical nature of religious worship in Edgefield meant that even those outside the evangelical Protestant Christian fold often partook of or engaged with its ethic of piety to some degree. This effusive moral concern drove the religious "progress" of the Edgefield community at large. But behind this exuberant Edgefield spirit lurked a gnawing sense of spiritual consternation, especially among white Christian enslavers as sectional divisions over southern slavery and the region's racial patriarchy intensified. For every conversion there remained countless unredeemed; for every revival season there languished years of religious indifference. Despite their celebration of Edgefield's long history of spiritual "progress," the most honest inhabitants could equally lament, "The worst of it with our people seems to be that they won't *stay converted.*" Such tensions over personal and public piety and morality in Edgefield's white community and culture persisted and evolved from the colonial period through the antebellum era, becoming increasingly contentious and conspicuous in the thirty years directly preceding the Civil

War. During this tumultuous period, inconsistencies and incongruities between prevailing ideals (piety prominent among them) and social realities (violence and other forms of sinfulness especially) appeared ever more pernicious and potentially destructive in proslavery white minds amid the intensifying sectional discord over their "peculiar institution."[3]

The steady rise in the stature and influence of those evangelical Protestant Christian denominations most responsible for promoting broader moral concern and greater commitment to piety in Edgefield, and the ebbs and flows of their institutional development and cultural influence within the Edgefield community, provide the context in which their ethic emerged and evolved in that place over that span. New Light Baptists established the first significant inroads in Edgefield as early as 1760, when the Reverend Daniel Marshall began itinerating in the area. A native New Englander then over fifty years of age, Marshall had established himself as an accomplished evangelist by founding vibrant church communities in Virginia and North Carolina. His lifelong pattern of following God's call into new fields of toil brought him to the South Carolina backcountry, where he ultimately settled near Edgefield and began a successful ministry.[4]

Reverend Marshall founded eight churches in and around Edgefield, all of them emanating from the first, Stephen's Creek Baptist, which he founded in 1762. Stephen's Creek, located ten miles north of Augusta, Georgia, provided Marshall a base of operations to evangelize the region. Evidence of his success came with the founding of Horn's Creek Baptist Church, located some six miles south of Edgefield Courthouse, in 1768. The Horn's Creek brethren later praised Marshall as "one of the first ministers of [the Baptist] denomination that ever preached the Gospel in this part of the State, whose faith and zeal in the ministry was very early the means of conviction, and the conversion, of precious souls to God." As the seeds of the American Revolution were being sown, Baptists had staked their claim as Edgefield's spiritual leader.[5]

On the eve of that Revolution, even the stodgy Anglican itinerant Charles Woodmason grudgingly acknowledged the preponderance of these New Light Baptists throughout the South Carolina backcountry. His Anglican affiliation dictated a patronizing, if not wholly dismissive attitude toward the various dissenting sects he encountered. He expressed particular disdain for these Baptists' preference of adult baptism: "They had a numerous progeny for baptism—rather chusing they should grow up to maturity without baptism." He then reluctantly admitted his belief that "some few among [the New Light Baptist clergy] mean well—but they are [un]equal to the task they undertake. They set about effecting in an instant, what requires both labour and time—they apply to the passions, not the understanding of the people." In another encounter, he opined that he "met here with some serious Christians. But the generality very loose, dissolute, idle People—without either religion or goodness—the same may be said of the whole body of the people in these back parts."[6]

Despite his Anglican reluctance to credit New Light Baptist religious advances, Woodmason's backcountry observations clearly revealed an early evangelical Protestant Christian presence. His inability—and those of his denomination—to gain a solid spiritual foothold in the backcountry did not mean religion languished among its residents. The backcountry preference for a more emotional religious experience troubled Anglicans like Woodmason, who decried the tendency to come "to sermon with itching ears only, not with any disposition of heart, or sentiment of mind" and to "assemble out of curiosity, not devotion, and seem so pleased with their native ignorance, as to be offended at any attempts to rouse them out of it." But one man's sinful emotion is another's path to spiritual salvation. Baptist congregations continued to multiply into the post-Revolutionary period and provided a firm spiritual foundation grounded in an emerging evangelical Protestant Christian ethic.[7]

But these Baptists were not alone. Like most Methodist Episcopal Church communities throughout the South, early Edgefield Methodism originated in the work of circuit-riding ministers. According to one local church historian, "The earliest [record of Methodism] discovered so far is a description of the first circuit to cover the Edgefield area—the Cherokee circuit. James Jenkins, an important figure in South Carolina Methodism, notes in his autobiography that the Cherokee circuit was formed in 1789." This sprawling circuit covered nearly three hundred miles and stretched from the Savannah River northward to Saluda and westward to Cherokee Town, enveloping the districts of Edgefield, Abbeville, and Pendleton. In 1791, Butler's Methodist Episcopal Meeting House was established on the property of James Butler. But such permanent houses of worship were rare, as the circuit riders who traversed the Edgefield area more typically preached wherever they could—private homes, public taverns, courthouses, other denominational meeting houses, even outdoors—and as frequently as travel would permit. The Methodist Episcopal bishop Francis Asbury affirmed Edgefield's growing Methodist community with three visits to the area in 1801, 1807, and 1809.[8]

In Edgefield the fervor of the Great Revival spread forth predominantly from these Baptist and Methodist pulpits. In 1809, the Reverends Samuel Marsh and John Landrum of Horn's Creek Baptist Church presided over "a Great and Glorious revival of religion . . . the greatest revival we have known. There were about three hundred members added to this church." During the last of his Edgefield visits, the Methodist Episcopal bishop Francis Asbury credited the extensive Methodist presence in Edgefield for fomenting this spiritual revival in observing, "The Baptists are carrying all before them; they are indebted to Methodist camp meetings for this." Both Methodist camp meetings and Baptist protracted meetings "received by experience" hundreds of members, while also resulting in many a "backslider restored." The nature of the Methodist circuit system certainly contributed to this cross-denominational outpouring of religiosity. Largely without their own permanent houses of worship, Methodist circuit riders frequently borrowed the pulpits of their Baptist brethren. A Methodist revival could thus quickly embrace attending Baptists.[9]

By the 1820s, both the Baptist and Methodist denominations had made annual meetings a regular part of the church calendar, and many of these sparked revivals of several days' duration. Most of these differed from earlier revivals in that they were an established part of the annual clerical calendar rather than spontaneous outpourings of religious fervor. As such, they served as important administrative meetings and outreach expositions, retaining much of the emotion of former revivals but lacking their sense of spontaneity. These revivals came more to resemble reunions, reaffirming rather than pioneering a sense of the spiritual among the church brethren and the community at large. Some proved more emotionally affecting and therefore more protracted than others, but a continuous cycle of revival became a primary means of maintaining the faith within individual churches and promoting a continued religiosity within the broader community.[10]

Local Baptists again took the lead. A young Baptist preacher named Basil Manly Sr. entered Edgefield from Columbia in 1821, where he would soon graduate valedictorian from the South Carolina College. Upon graduation he assumed the pastorate of Little Stephen's Creek Baptist Church, some ten miles north of Edgefield Courthouse, in 1822, and presided over a revival that began during his first full summer there. As he publicly recounted, the revival fervor appeared "suddenly, and like an electric shock, the Divine power seemed to be poured out on the whole congregation . . . it was truly astonishing—I never saw such things before—So universal an effect." This revival gained momentum—and statewide notoriety—throughout the summer and fall of 1822. Manly's name became synonymous with the "Edgefield Revival" he encouraged. This revival success prompted Manly, aided by several prominent families in Edgefield, to found the Edgefield Village Baptist Church in 1823, the first Baptist church in the town of Edgefield proper. As the decade unfolded, both Manly and the Edgefield community thus became driving forces in the advance of South Carolina Baptism.[11]

When the Baptist minister William Bullein Johnson ascended the pulpit at the Edgefield Village Baptist Church for the first time in 1831, he was entering his forty-eighth year, over half of which he had dedicated to Baptist ministerial service. His name stood among those most exalted of South Carolina Baptists—Oliver Hart, Edmund Botsford, and Richard Furman—all of whom he credited with lighting the fire of his own faith, and whom Baptists statewide revered for advancing the faith across the Palmetto State. As an aging veteran of numerous Baptist pulpits in Euhaw and Columbia, South Carolina, as well as Savannah, Georgia, Johnson entered an Edgefield community primed for spiritual expansion. His younger ministerial brother and personal friend Basil Manly Sr. had done much of the priming through the 1820s revivals. Manly's success had led to the founding of the Edgefield Village Baptist Church in 1823, as well as the Edgefield Female Academy, both of which Johnson had been called to direct. Edgefield became a prominent fixture in the annals of South Carolina religious development, and the names of its spiritual leaders, Johnson foremost among them, became familiar across the state and region.[12]

Edgefield Methodists made similar gains during the period. A prominent Methodist society near Sleepy Creek, thirteen miles north of Edgefield Village, had formed McKendree Methodist Church in 1817. The first permanent Methodist church serving the village itself was erected in 1820, just one mile north in Pottersville. And in 1825 the congregation of Harmony Methodist Church established a meeting house some six miles east of the village on the Edgefield and Augusta road. The Quarterly Conference minutes from 1831 lists twenty-five churches within the Saluda Circuit, which encompassed the Edgefield District. Many of these were Baptist meeting houses utilized by Methodist circuit riders at least twice monthly. "The Reverend Stephen Olin, visiting Methodist divine, preached on January 31, 1821," says one report, while another observed that "on September 4th of the same year, Mr. Bray, another Methodist circuit rider, delivered a sermon from Matthew 2:3, giving the Baptists a strong

Wesleyan interpretation of the words, 'How shall we escape if we neglect so great [a] salvation.'" By 1831, this decade of growth culminated in the construction of a Methodist meeting house on Buncombe Street near the home of a local luminary, Hansford Mims, just off the Edgefield Courthouse square.[13]

Revivals were thus a primary means of extending the faith by growing the churches. Edgefield Baptists and Methodists alike relied upon revivals to expand their numbers and influence. Together with the Methodist circuit-riding tradition, these revivals further fomented the community spirit that prevailed in Edgefield. Local church records and the fledgling local press both give credence to the centrality of revivals in this spiritual growth among the Edgefield populace. A series of religious revivals during the next two decades inundated Edgefield in spiritual fervor. The Baptist reverend William B. Johnson guided his own revival shortly after arriving in Edgefield in 1831. From his pulpit at Edgefield Village Baptist Church, the revival fervor commenced on the second Tuesday in August, when "preaching [was] appointed at candlelight," which introduced "some pleasing prospects of a revival" as "Christians began to pray in earnest for the outpouring of the Holy Spirit."[14]

These prospects quickly came to fruition over the next several days as "the Lord began to show himself in a powerful manner. God's people greatly encouraged and sinners began to look about . . . Sinners began to tremble and cry mightily to God what they should do to be saved . . . The spirit of the Lord was evidently seen and felt among the people, and some conversions spoke of." Weekend services affirmed the onset of a fullfledged revival: "Several conversions talked of at this service—all hearts gladdened and much prayer was sent up to God for a continuation of his Holy Spirit upon us . . . The balance of this Holy day [Sunday] was spent in preaching, praying, and exhorting, and it was now most evident, that God intended a mighty display of power among the people." As the progenitor of this revival, Johnson later reflected, "It pleased our Heavenly Father to grant us a spiritual revival, accompanied with the addition of many redeemed souls to the church. I have been present at many such meetings, but none, that I have ever attended, were equal to this."[15]

The interdenominational aspect of this revival captured Johnson's attention most particularly, as he explained that "of those who were, according to their own statements, made recipients of a hope which maketh not ashamed . . . Some of these intend uniting with the Episcopalians, some with the Presbyterians, others have already joined the Methodists" in addition to those claimed by his own Baptists. Johnson credited a Methodist camp meeting the year before as the inspiration for the Edgefield revival.[16]

The impact went beyond even this ecumenical connection, as Johnson's biographer later gleaned from several accounts: "Even persons who professed no religious faith were impressed with the results of the revivals which had spread to other places," with "not fewer than five hundred souls" having ultimately "received deep awakenings."[17] The Horn's Creek Baptist Church confirmed the trend over the next three years, as more than thirty persons experienced conversion and joined the church during protracted meetings, each of several days duration. The Baptist church at Little Stephen's Creek further extended the revival's impact when "several men and women came forward and united themselves to the Church by experience" during protracted meetings in 1833 and 1834. Reverend Johnson himself later observed that the revival "came upon the inhabitants like the mighty shock of an earthquake, overturning the foundations of skepticism and the self-wrought schemes of salvation, and convincing everyone that there was a power and reality in the religion of Jesus Christ ... The impulse given here reached to every part of the District of Edgefield and even beyond its limits in certain directions."[18]

Revival fervor again swept through the Edgefield community between 1838 and 1841, when local Baptist and Methodist churches reported an extensive outpouring of religious spirit among their brethren. Protracted meetings in Johnson's Edgefield Village Baptist Church during the summer of 1838 brought nearly forty new souls into the church and again prompted district-wide revivals among both Baptist and Methodist congregations. The Village Baptist Church felt compelled to record the "public thanks of the church to Almighty God, for this special outpouring of his spirit upon the church and the inhabitants of this place." Little Stephen's Creek Baptist followed suit the next year when their protracted meeting saw thirty-four join the church, thanks in large part to Reverend Johnson, who had accepted an invitation to preach on the occasion.[19]

This latest revival spawned continual protracted meetings throughout the 1840s at both Edgefield Village and Little Stephen's Creek Baptist churches, during which the church secretaries for these congregations recorded "the church was greatly refreshed by the Lord ... The word of God was faithfully preached to the people, many were deeply affected and some were brought to rejoice with salvation of God." "Our Heavenly Father was pleased to pour out his blessing upon us, and revive our drooping spirits." The Edgefield *Advertiser* celebrated the revival in announcing "several very interesting" protracted meetings that "have been and are still going on in various parts of our district," paying particular attention to those at Little Stephen's Creek and the Village Church, as well as others "going on at Antioch and Dry Creek—and we hope they may be blessed in a like manner."[20]

Like the revival a decade before, this one also was ecumenical in tenor, especially among the Edgefield Methodists. The *Advertiser* took note of this when it observed, "A very interesting meeting at Mt. Vernon by the Methodist denomination closed last week, where we understand about forty joined the Church." This meeting occurred at the same time as those among the various Baptist churches the paper had already acknowledged. Methodists continued to witness and experience similar expansion. In August 1844, the *Advertiser* received a letter confirming "that there had been a considerable revival, and that many souls had been happily converted, about forty of which had been already added to the M. E. Church. The meeting was very large, and still in progress, on Monday evening last."[21]

Through 1848, the pages of the *Advertiser* teemed with similar reports of revival meetings among both Methodists and Baptists. This revival fervor culminated over three decades of religious growth and prompted a beaming editorial appraisal of the Edgefield spirit in 1851: "We have in this District, thirty-one Baptist Churches, nearly all of which have large congregations, the general deportment of which, is altogether praiseworthy and such as becomes a Christian people." The author further noted, "We have twenty-three Methodist Churches, and though their congregations are not at all times very large, yet it is exceedingly pleasant to anyone to see the happy greetings and the good feeling that prevail amongst them." The Edgefield spirit was thus firmly grounded in the evangelical Protestant Christian tradition, a tradition that would continue to evolve and shape the religious development of the district for decades to come.[22]

This spiritual growth manifested itself most visibly in the new houses of worship that had pervaded the district by the 1850s. The *Advertiser* took "real satisfaction" in noticing the "great improvement, of late, in our houses of worship throughout the country," citing new buildings at Rocky Creek, Stephen's Creek, Antioch, and Dry Creek churches as in "every way creditable to those congregations of the Baptist denomination." This public praise extended as well to the Methodists, who showed themselves equally "alive to the duty of honoring God with appropriate tabernacles for the observance of His religion, as their improving Chapels throughout the district testify." The paper's editors then admitted, "True, the

Almighty will hear a prayer breathed in a forest as readily as one that goes up from the most magnificent cathedral," before venturing that "He may, nevertheless, be well pleased with that pious solicitude of his people, which seeks to advance the externals of His religion to greater respectability, *that good may come of it.*" They continued: "While men of the world are contributing their thousands to increase the splendor of their Museums and Theatres, should not Christians do something to add attractiveness, in the eyes of non-professors, to the temples where they exhibit the truths of revelation and the wonders of the Trinity! ... We hope to see the day, when men shall think that it does not, at least, interfere with undefiled religion, to increase the beauty of our sanctuaries, within the bounds of propriety and simplicity." In the public eye, these physical refinements matched the spiritual refinement such edifices encouraged.[23]

These houses of worship and the accolades they garnered in the local press bore witness to the continued prosperity of the Edgefield spirit in the communal mind. The dominant Baptist and Methodist denominations appeared especially blessed, as they again experienced several waves of religious revival throughout the 1850s. The first of these originated at Horn's Creek Baptist during a "fourteen days protracted meeting" late in the summer of 1852. According to the *Advertiser* the meeting met "with unusual success. Many have been aroused to a sense of the great importance of renewing their ways, and not a few have gone forward for membership ... The excitement still continues unabated." This excitement quickly spread, as "A religious meeting ... at the Methodist Church ... protracted for several days" and found praise in the public record. A protracted meeting among the congregants at Mt. Tabor Baptist Church, some "six miles North-East of Edgefield C.H.," met with similar excitement the following year. Methodist camp meetings and Baptist protracted meetings abounded throughout the summer of 1854, resulting in a renewed revival fervor that carried over into the following year.[24]

A visiting preacher elicited this outpouring of the spirit in the Edgefield Village Baptist Church. As the *Advertiser* explained, his "powerful reasoning and masterly eloquence" convinced "all of the 'error of their way'" and brought "them to a firm determination to try and serve the Lord. This has been a remarkable season of refreshing to all Christians." All of this the minister accomplished, per the *Advertiser,* with "no unnecessary excitement"; "Nothing has so far occurred to produce any unpleasantness, but everything has been conducted 'decently and in order.'" Again, the fervor spread. On August 29, 1855, the *Advertiser* praised the "religious influence prevailing to an extraordinary extent in this time in many parts of our District," taking particular notice of "a meeting which had been continued for many days at Horn's Creek Baptist Church" that "seemed to indicate no abatement of the religious interest. There was an uncommonly large concourse of people present, and evidently a disposition to linger about the spot with which were associated many pleasing recollections." The Horn's Creek Church was not alone. In editorial reports "from many other sections, we also learn that meetings have been held that have resulted in the accession of large numbers to the Churches, and others are in progress, which promise abundant success. At Little Stephen's Creek we understand over one hundred have recently joined." In reflecting upon this spiritual scene, the *Advertiser* observed, "Our village has not known a period of such intense religious excitement since 1831 as has prevailed in the Baptist congregation" of late. In paying homage to Edgefield's historical legacy of religious revival and the stalwart ministers who had guided it, the editors acknowledged the prominent spirit of Edgefield past and present.[25]

Edgefield's Methodists contributed mightily as well, and they too soon contributed to this latest revival fervor. The *Advertiser* made note of their efforts in early summer of 1855: "A religious revival has been in progress ... for some days under the labors of Rev. Mr. Evans, of the Methodist Church" in the town of Hamburg, some twenty-four miles south of Edgefield Village. This caused the editors much "rejoicing that the 'marble hearts' of [this] community are at length becoming changed into hearts of flesh and blood." Camp meetings at Bethlehem Methodist and Mt. Vernon Campground extended the revival among Edgefield's Methodists. The spirit even spilled the bounds of Edgefield District, enveloping churches in Abbeville, Aiken, and Newberry as well. All of which prompted the editors' approving declaration, "It does indeed seem that the times of 'refreshing from the presence of the Lord' are upon the land."[26]

The latter half of this last antebellum decade witnessed a particularly eventful revival season. Announcements for Methodist camp meetings and Baptist protracted meetings filled the Edgefield press and local church minutes between 1856 and 1860. One meeting in late August 1856 at Dry Creek Baptist Church, about nine miles northeast of Edgefield Village, was reportedly "immense," while later that same month Mt. Lebanon Baptist Church, nine miles north of Hamburg, "experienced a gracious revival" during a protracted meeting. Both churches again experienced revivals in 1858 and 1859. En route to the Dry Creek Baptist meeting, "the

Columbia road was alive with carriages, barouches, buggies, wagons, carts, etc., carrying the old and the young, the good and the bad, male and female, white and black, to the scene of action . . . the rush was immense." An "interesting meeting of sixteen days duration" at Mt. Lebanon Baptist late the following summer added nearly thirty converts. Other area churches followed suit. Red Bank Baptist Church, twenty miles north in Saluda, experienced "accessions [that] were most cheering" while Mt. Tabor Baptist Church, "in this vicinity," likewise witnessed "a very promising meeting." The Edgefield Village Baptist Church too, experienced this ongoing revival. A report in October of 1858 revealed "a series of very interesting meetings" among the Village Baptist brethren, during which "the seed of much good has been sown, which will yet spring up and bring forth fruit in due season."[27]

Edgefield's Methodists rivaled the fervor of their Baptist counterparts during this latter part of the decade. In 1857, the *Advertiser*'s editors declared themselves "highly gratified in announcing that the Methodist Church in our Town is enjoying a refreshing season of Divine favor . . . A goodly number has been added to the Church, and numbers are enquiring after the 'truth as it is in Jesus.'" They then expressed the hope that "the blessings of the Lord still be poured out until there will be none left who are not rejoicing in that 'hope which maketh not ashamed.'" The following year the editors again deemed it "gratifying to learn that numerous additions have been made to the Methodist congregations of the Edgefield circuit during the current year. There has been an unusual degree of religious interest manifested among the churches, and the good work still progresses." This continuous revival fervor convinced these editors that "a strong religious influence appears to have prevailed . . . throughout this District," especially among the Methodist and Baptist denominations. These "first two branches of Christians" "largely preponderate[d] in Edgefield" and could "be said to have swept the District."[28]

The interdenominational aspect of this vibrant Edgefield spirit emerged most fervently during these frequent revival seasons. "Sunday last was a great day in Edgefield," declared the *Advertiser*, with "a Methodist camp-meeting on one side [of the District] and a Baptist association on the other. Large crowds were in attendance at both places," which promoted "a good deal of religious feeling . . . all was harmony and satisfaction." The value of these meetings in fostering a community spirit seemed obvious: "These occasions, besides their religious benefits, serve as pleasant reunions for the people and tend to foster friendlier feelings between different neighborhoods." Religious and nonreligious alike imbibed of the spiritual outpouring such revivals entailed; both individuals and the community derived benefits from these dispensations of faith and morality.[29]

By 1859, these benefits warranted editorial celebration: "It affords us sincere gratification to be permitted to record the fact of considerable religious progress in our quiet community ... This has been especially observable in the Baptist congregation ... But the good work has not been limited to this congregation," as "the Methodist Church, has also been wielding the sword of the spirit with zeal and energy." Even the more typically reserved Trinity Episcopal Church partook of the revival spirit, as its minister "rendered faithful and exemplary service by his earnest and forcible lectures" during "the Baptist meetings, which have been continued nightly for several weeks." The "unselfish devotion to the advancement of the Church Universal" that pervaded this revival certainly confirmed the ecumenical nature of the Edgefield spirit. The editors of the Edgefield's *Advertiser* concluded: "All together, the religious privileges, with which our community is now being blessed, are such as to arrest the respect if not the gratitude of every witness. It is indeed 'a day-spring from on high' which no one surely can mark with indifference."[30]

But as the sectional gulf over slavery widened and deepened, the nagging, gnawing consciousness of inconsistency and even contradiction between proslavery ideals and slavery's lived realities became ever more damning in their destructive potential. Even in Edgefield's most influential church communities, such evidence frequently reared its ugly visage and exposed the concern over these ideological fault lines and the increasingly precarious position of the "southern way of life" amid the growing sectional crisis over slavery. The church records of Edgefield's Baptist and Methodist congregations exposed a pattern of "backsliding" throughout the antebellum period. The pattern exhibits at once the pervasive moral concern that accompanied the growing antebellum Edgefield spirit, as well as the inability of even the most pious men of the Edgefield community to fully realize its evangelical Protestant Christian ideals.[31]

Masculine excesses in drinking, fighting, racial violence, and sexual indiscretion—domestic and public—loomed large in the list of egregious sins for which church members were disciplined. Edgefield's Baptist minister, William B. Johnson, had a long history of censuring such masculine waywardness, and feelings he had expressed as early as 1810 he undoubtedly wielded again twenty years later from his pulpit: "Gross and scandalous sins, the more refined part of mankind, though destitute of true, vital religion, generally censure and avoid." "A Christian," he wrote, "must have departed far already from the line of duty and rectitude, before he can come under very strong temptations . . . to commit such sins which are directly contrary to the law of God and . . . to decency and respect in civil society." Johnson denounced those men, "who have been once decent in their manners, of amiable dispositions, and even virtuous principles," but who "by giving way to a fondness for merry, idle company, have become eventually the wretched slaves of drunkenness, profanity, and debauchery, and of every pernicious, shameful vice, and crime," and were "thus ruined forever!"[32]

In Johnson's view, these wayward souls corrupted not only themselves but also "the souls of their families." He believed that "many wear out their own strength, and life, as well as of their servants and dependents" and are "rigorous, even to cruelty, in exacting the utmost exertions in labor from those under their control." "The result of all is," Johnson concluded, "that the public interests of religion, as well as its spirit, are neglected . . . The pious education of children is neglected," he wrote; they "are permitted to waste their precious time in forming habits for idleness, ignorance, and vice." Moreover, the "religious instruction of servants is entirely neglected, though their labor is exacted in full measure." The excesses of wayward men corrupted the souls of all their acquaintances, domestic and public, personal and professional, man or woman, white or Black.[33]

Such denunciations elicited frequent congregational rebukes of masculine waywardness in Edgefield. Several cases can serve as representative of the whole, beginning with the 1825 "case of Vann Swearingen," whom the Horn's Creek Baptist Church to which he belonged "charged with fighting." Swearingen "plead justification to this charge" for which the church brethren "disciplined and restored [him] to full church fellowship." In acknowledging his transgression and vowing to improve, Swearingen avoided scornful expulsion from the church. Three years later, the "Case of Brother Bettis" did not terminate quite so amiably. Bettis was "charged with rioting" and summarily "expelled from the church." His failure to admit to or repent of the deed suggests that he, unlike his fellow congregant Swearingen, remained defiant and defensive and incurred the harshest of penalties. Penitence was paramount to forgiveness, while recalcitrance provoked stricter censure. In 1834, two members of Little Stephen's Creek Baptist Church, Willis Holstin and Marshall Faulkner, proved this rule. They had reportedly engaged "in personal combat" but received no discipline beyond rebuke and admonishment, due to their confession and repentant expressions. Similarly, when John Quattlebaum, also of Little Stephen's Creek Baptist, "reported Thomas Youngblood had a difficulty at Edgefield Courthouse on sale day," the church "committee found he was 'in no way criminal in what he did.'"[34]

A string of similar cases several years later, again at Horn's Creek Baptist, further demonstrated the anxieties attending such masculine excess. In June 1839, "Brother Edward S. Mays [was] disciplined for fighting." But after an extended biblical rebuke from the church he "confessed his wrong [and was] restored." He was even elected a delegate to the Edgefield Baptist Association annual meeting later that same year. The following winter, "Brother William Doby came forward and informed the church that he had been fighting" frequently with his cousin. After some consideration the "church agreed his that his personal apology to his cousin would be satisfactory." Later that year, the brethren lodged a complaint "against James Whitlock for intoxication and fighting" for which he was "expelled from church membership" outright. In all of these cases, the church seemingly assumed that a repentant sinner could be redeemed but a recalcitrant one could corrupt the whole, and exacted discipline accordingly.[35]

Public drunkenness and frequent intoxication often initiated such violent confrontations, so this particular vice incurred the persistent censure of church brethren. At Little Stephen's Creek Baptist, "Brother Thomas Youngblood came before the church" in 1833 "and professed repentance for having drank too much for which he had resolved for the future to abstain altogether." The following January, his fellow congregant "John Miller professed intoxication, professed repentance [and was] forgiven and restored by the church." Another church member, John Harlin, later "confessed intoxication and trusted he should do so no more, and would try to be a man on his guard for the future."[36]

Many others, including Lewis Bledsoe, John Hill, and John Nicholson, followed suit. Thomas Youngblood, Bledsoe, Harlin, and Miller had "professed repentance" and "resolved . . . to abstain" from such excesses. Others were less repentant. James Youngblood frequently found himself before the church committee for intoxication between 1834 and 1837. In 1840, Charles Parrott, was "expelled due to admittance of drinking too much." Both merely admitted to their transgressions but evinced no signs of repentance or future abstinence, repeatedly falling into liquor's sinful embrace. Parrott declared that he "thought it no harm to keep spirits at home and to get drunk provided he laid down and slept it off." A church committee received his admission of guilt and subsequent lack of remorse "unfavorably" and he was promptly "excluded from church membership." The same sentence earlier befell James Youngblood.[37]

Perhaps these cases prompted the church to more aggressively assert its influence in the lives of its white male members when it took into consideration the "neglect which too many of our Brothers show toward Church by failing to attend our regular church conference days" and resolved that "any member who shall fail to attend for two meetings in succession shall give sufficient excuse—and if failing to attend three meetings in succession shall be under censure of the church." The measure apparently produced little change in result, as over a decade later such disciplinary cases continued to afflict the congregation, prompting another resolution which decreed "that in all cases for the future where a member is guilty of frequency of capital offences, such as intoxication, gambling, dancing, or any other offence that is not in accordance with church discipline and it is known by the church, that we dispose of them—in other words expel them immediately." Dr. Walker Samuel, prominent doctor and active church member, felt the effects of this resolution directly when he was "expelled from the church" in 1853 after a very public altercation with Eldred Glover inside Doby's Bar in the Edgefield district.[38]

This unequivocal harshness betrayed the growing concern and frustration with white masculine transgressions. These excesses jeopardized the sanctity of the church as a congregational body and a social model. That white men invested with both church and social authority should undermine their own cause through these sinful excesses compounded the anxiety. The inability to control themselves made white men's control of their own households seem all the more tenuous. These households included the neglected "servants and dependents," Black and white, male and female, to whom the Reverend Johnson referred when he admonished masculine "indulgence of envy, resentment, malice, and revenge, those fires of hell; and the gratification of sensual, licentious appetites, crimes which are too common in the world."[39]

The disciplinary records of Edgefield's most prominent congregations bear out this persistent apprehension. Domestic discord drew the ire of Edgefield congregations on several occasions. In 1838, the Horn's Creek Baptist Church levied "a charge against Brother Stiron for neglect of his family" for which he was censured by the brethren. In December of 1853, "Brother William H. Mathis reported Brother S. B. Griffin to the church as being in disorder . . . It was concluded that he be expelled from the church." Four years later, Brother E. M. Swearingen reported, "L.B. [illegible] as being in disorder ... the brethren ... thought it best to expel him and acted accordingly. He was therefore expelled." The following year, Dr. Walker Samuel was "reported as being in disorder" and after several months deliberation, the brethren ultimately "thought best to and did expel him." Such familial disorder threatened the sanctity of the home, upon which the stability of society purportedly rested. The persistence of these cases in all of Edgefield's prominent congregations unveils this fundamental anxiety, which shaped all manner of church disciplinary action implicitly designed to secure the social order by maintaining the sanctity of family life.[40]

Cases involving neglect of and brutality toward enslaved persons occurred with relative frequency, threatening to undermine and expose the hypocrisy of white enslavers' professions of Christian paternalism and its claims regarding slavery's virtues. In the spring of 1832, the Horn's Creek Baptist brethren cited "Brother William Walker ... for hiring Negroes to work on the Sabbath" and expelled him from fellowship. During the summer of 1840, "Brother William Colclazuer having accidentally killed one of his own negro boys by striking him in the head with a stick" for which he "disciplined himself" and was issued a stern rebuke from the church, but retained in fellowship. Horn's Creek proves representative of a general trend among Edgefield's churches. If left unchecked, white enslavers' unwarranted violence against—as well as ungoverned leniency or neglect of—those they enslaved could further undermine the sanctity of the home and the purportedly paternalistic order of society. The incessant disciplinary action of the churches along these lines epitomized these concerns and the anxious tension they created between white paternalistic stewardship and patriarchal control.[41]

Perhaps white enslavers' oscillation between negligence and concern regarding their enslaved Black "dependents" prodded the churches to step across the threshold and more actively curb "disobedience" among the enslaved by exacting harsher punishments against enslaved "transgressions." The white members of Horn's Creek Baptist frequently recorded disciplinary measures against their Black church brethren. Alcoholic indulgence accounted for many of these cases, beginning with the citation of "Joe, belonging to M. Mims for intoxication" in late 1828, to which he "came forward" early the next year and "confessed he had drank too much and declared his sorrow and was restored by the church." But later that summer, Joe again crossed the church and was expelled for "living in disorder." These alcoholic excesses on the part of enslaved Blacks never failed to excite white church brethren to disciplinary action. The measures taken by Horn's Creek again prove representative of the Edgefield community of faith on this score. Enslaved congregants frequently came before church tribunals for intoxication and drunkenness, and the discipline they received varied according to the frequency of the crime. One-time offenders typically received leniency if they exhibited a repentant demeanor; but enslaved members who repeatedly fell off the proverbial wagon received little reprieve and were often expelled from the church outright. In this way, the churches' discipline of its imbibing Black members differed little from that administered toward its white ones.[42]

Theft proved a persistent worry, as evidenced by Horn's Creek Baptist's 1831 expulsion of "York, belonging to F. Bettis" who came before the church "for his misconduct" and was expelled during the next month's meeting "for being concerned in hogstealing." At Antioch Baptist, "Brother James Griffin informed against his servants Peter and Peggy for theft," for which the church found them "guilty of said act and therefore declared nonfellowship with them." Again in 1834, the Antioch church levied a charge "against Sister Boyd's Milly for theft," but a lack of proof later proved it untenable and she was "restored to fellowship." Similar cases proliferated among Edgefield's most prominent congregations throughout the antebellum era.[43]

Sexual licentiousness among Black church brethren drew the consistent ire of their white enslavers. Perhaps these sexual transgressions exhibited the slave system's perpetual sensual and sexual temptation too vividly for comfort. "Sally belonging to Thos. Rainsford [was] expelled for adultery" by the Horn's Creek church in the summer of 1833. Antioch Baptist also recorded that year "a charge was laid in against Mr. Land. Williams' Jenny . . . for the sin of adultery" and that a committee "believe[d] her to be guilty of the crime . . . therefore excommunication was declared against her." The Horn's Creek Baptist church meeting in May of the following year had been "rejoiced in since it [was] the finest since the revival of [18]32" before "the feeling of the brethren [was] wounded with the information [that] the black brethren, viz. Spincer, belonging to W. Nobles; Abram, belonging to Col. Buckhalter; and Jeremiah, belonging to Mr. Irving [were] impeached of adultery." In the spring of 1838, "a black sister viz. Rose . . . the property of Francis Bettis" was expelled "for lewd conduct." Later that year, "Jack belonging to Esqr. F. Bettis [was expelled] for the sin of adultery, a repeat offense for which the church deemed him unworthy of fellowship." In May of 1850, "Jim, belonging to John Dobey was cited to the church for a misdemeanor," and the following month, "Jim was expelled for having dismissed [his] lawful wife and tak[en] up with another woman." The discipline administered at Horn's Creek and Antioch for adultery and sexual promiscuity among enslaved Blacks found its equal across the Edgefield evangelical community.[44]

Violence among enslaved Blacks presented the most visceral challenge to racial authority, both secular and sacred, in white minds. In 1833, the Horn's Creek church heard "reports for fighting against Samuel, belonging to Benj. Hatcher," for which he was cited, rebuked, but ultimately restored to church fellowship. Another case against "a negro man of Thomas Rainsford for improper conduct by the name of Namdon" ultimately terminated in his expulsion from fellowship in 1836. Later that year a enslaved man named "Jim, belonging to Simion Dinkins [was found] in disorder," as was another slave, "Jim, belonging to Francis Bettis" who were both "excommunicated from the church." In 1853, "Jim belonging to A.J. Hughes who being expelled from this church a few months ago now complains of being harshly treated" was "disposed of," the church "not thinking him worthy of fellowship," while later that month yet another enslaved man named Jim, "belonging to Br. Bettis was expelled for having a fight with his overseer and for swearing repeatedly." Again, Horn's Creek sets the mold for the broader Edgefield community. Disciplinary cases against overt acts of violence among enslaved Blacks abounded in the records of Edgefield's churches. Like the discipline administered against alcoholic abuse, theft, and sexual transgression among Blacks, that against violence perpetuated the tension between paternalism and patriarchy, between saving a wayward soul and punishing a recalcitrant enslaved congregant.[45]

The persistence of these transgressions exposed the ineffectiveness of church discipline, prompting the Horn's Creek brethren to seek alternative redress. In October of 1841, "Brother H.H. Mayfair . . . suggested the propriety of appointing two of the coloured brethren to overlook the coloured members, which met the cordial approbation of the church." Two particular Black members, "Jack belonging to Mr. Francis Bettis, and Primus the property of Mrs. Ryan, were appointed for that purpose." At a meeting early the following year, the church sought the permission of "Mr. Francis Bettis . . . for Jack to be appointed to overlook and report the conduct of the coloured members," which was granted. This added disciplinary oversight coincided with another proposal to augment the spiritual education of the Black brethren, when "the propriety of an extra sermon to the coloured part of the congregation was laid before the church and they concluded to leave it to the discretion of their minister," who later approved the measure. Such measures on the part of Edgefield's churches maintained their paternalistic posture, but also revealed a persistent anxiety concerning their own self-control and the ever-present temptations afflicting the slave system they inhabited.[46]

The similarity of the discipline imposed on white and Black brethren alike for the same sins of excess revealed not only prevailing racial prejudices but also implied a distrust of white male control—of the self, the home, and the racial hierarchy. Many white men seemed generally indifferent toward any effort to curb their passions, while others proved wholly unwilling to do so. The potential excesses stemming from both attitudes threatened, however nominally given their pronounced privileges and prerogatives within the region's racialized patriarchy, to render their claims to social power suspect and cast a considerable shadow of doubt upon the sanctity of the so-called southern social order. If white men consistently backslid into sin, how could Black community members be expected to meet the same moral obligations, when the southern social hierarchy assumed the absolute supremacy of the former over the latter? This reasoning produced a tension between the necessity of racial control and the primacy of spiritual brotherhood, a tension embodied in the compatible-yet-contentious concepts of patriarchal prerogative and paternalistic duty that in turn produced a palpable moral concern within and over the entire southern social system. Such apprehension manifested itself in the home, the sanctuary, and the very streets of villages like Edgefield that proliferated across the southern landscape.[47]

Drawing on this religious history and heritage, the white Edgefield community in the antebellum period evinced a pervasive evangelical Protestant Christian conception of morality. Those morals had coalesced over more than sixty years of religious development through a markedly evangelical Protestant mode of worship and revival. Led by local Baptist and Methodist congregations, Edgefield's evangelicals had shaped the morals of the community directly and indirectly through both concerted conversion efforts and casual conversations. In expanding their prominence and influence in Edgefield, these evangelical Protestants did much more than convert new souls to fill a growing number of new houses of worship; they grafted a distinct religious moral ethic onto the Edgefield scene, one ecumenical and general in its effects. Members of other denominations— lay and clergy alike—couldn't help but confront its message and methods.

Nonmembers and wayward souls likewise heard its message, experienced its methods, and conversed in its moralized language, even if they refused to formally align with its institutions. By 1830 this evangelical Protestant Christian piety formed the foundation and parameters of morality in Edgefield.

Honor and piety dictated in tandem the moral strictures of the broader Edgefield community. Both moral and ethical ideals privileged white men with authority, but both also exposed and exhibited a fundamental tension between curbing white masculine excess and justifying white masculine prerogative. By 1830 Edgefield's leading white men went well armed with both a prickly sense of honor and a pervasive, even self-righteous, sense of evangelical spiritual morality. These sometimes contentious, sometimes complementary cultures guided these men, their families, and their communities through the antebellum era, and governed their thoughts, words, and actions. The first antebellum generation in Edgefield navigated the tensions within and between both their honor and piety by implicitly combining both moral ethics in a nascent ideal of righteous honor so that they might better secure their personal sanctity, their households', and their communities', and thereby preserve the southern social order predicated on white supremacy and patriarchal power. It was a mandate with both secular and sacred implications, one which this first antebellum generation of leading white men believed paramount to upholding southern mores in the present, so that their sons might inherit them in good standing and apply them in good faith to confront an increasingly ominous sectional discord.[48]

3

Righteous Honor

Merging the Ethics of Honor and Piety in the Early Antebellum Period

> When you have caught the rhythm of Old Edgefield you will discover that here, God and the Devil are often one and the same.
>
> —Tricia Price Glenn, Edgefield County Archivist

When the Episcopal itinerant parson Mason Locke Weems vilified Edgefield as a "very district of devils," he did so in light of the county's well-established tradition for honor-bound violence. His stories had, indeed, amplified Edgefield's reputation on that score. But by recounting its vices in the same breath as he expounded its virtues, Weems exposed an early duality of mind in the Edgefield District. He had turned upon Edgefield repeatedly for its grisly past and present, but in his moralizing he also actively spread the gospel about its more promising future. His accounts of the brutal murders committed by Edgefield's own Ned Findley against his wife, or Becky Cotton against her husband, seemingly confirmed the inherent sinfulness of the devils. By 1830, however, Weems had borne equal witness, however begrudgingly given his Episcopalian credentials, to another prominent Edgefield trait—evangelical Protestant Christian religiosity—even as he continued to disparage the district's lingering demonic tendencies. "Blessed be God for sending such *judges* as Trezevant, Johnson, and Brevard," he said, "and blessed be God for such preachers as Marsh, Lendrum and Marshall: for in no place have the labours of judges and preachers been crown'd with more singular success." He then concluded: "Edgefield, with but *few exceptions*, is now quite a *decent place*, a district of gentlemen and Christians."[1]

Despite Weems's undeniable penchant for hyperbole, his writings regarding Edgefield nevertheless expose a tangible cultural dualism there. It was "Christian gentlemen" such as those Weems chronicled who took up Edgefield's dueling cultures with the greatest alacrity, and whose experience most revealed the incipient ideal of righteous honor during the early antebellum years. By the 1830s, their sense of honor and piety became inextricably linked, though persistently contentious, in this implicit conceptual ideal. Both honor and piety allowed for, even expected, a certain oscillation between rising and falling, momentary passions and forgiveness, backsliding and returning to the fold. The dueling cultural legacy of Edgefield's recent past bore out this fact. It was not the one or the other that made this community work: it was the murder and the return to family, the debauch and the return to Jesus; all displayed the broad range of accepted white male conduct within an overtly patriarchal and white supremacist society and culture, and it played out publicly on the street and in the pews. All underlined at once white male responsibilities *and* illimitable freedoms. There was almost nothing a white man might do for which he would not (eventually) forgive himself, and in turn expect to be forgiven by his family and his community, his congregation (if he had joined one) and ultimately, his maker. But as the sectional crisis between North and South over slavery and its fate within the nation intensified, so too did the perceived need among such leading white southern men to reconcile their cultural contradictions, redeem their transgressions, and unite in defense of southern ideals and institutions. Into this developing firestorm righteous honor emerged in more visible, though still implicit, forms of expression and behavior that drew upon both honor and piety in complementary ways, and within this conflagration it would evolve to simultaneously serve both constructive and destructive ends for the defense of white supremacy, patriarchal authority, and the southern social order predicated on these prejudicial hierarchies.[2]

Three Baptist ministers—Iveson Lewis Brookes, Basil Manly Sr., and William Bullein Johnson—personified in many important respects the ministerial experience of this nascent ideal of righteous honor in early antebellum Edgefield. Several of their nonclerical neighbors—James Bones, Dr. John Hughes, Dr. Joseph Milligan, and Whitfield Brooks—exhibited important facets of the more secular experience of righteous honor and its moral mandates. The private lives of these self-described "Christian gentlemen" reflected Edgefield's cultural duality. Theirs was not a choice between an eye for an eye or turning the other cheek. Both fell within their prerogative, depending on the situation. Their burgeoning sense of righteous honor demanded manly fortitude in upholding the moral tenets they held sacred. Curbing personal vice through self-mastery and channeling personal conflict through righteous violence both loomed especially large in that endeavor and permeated their thoughts, words, and deeds as ministers and laymen, planters and merchants, husbands and fathers. As part of the first generation of white southern men faced with an increasingly dire need to more effectively balance these two predominant ethical traditions into one moral worldview, these leading Edgefield men personified the complex process by which a conception of righteous honor came to govern white masculine mores and define ideal white southern manhood in the decades to come, all in an inherently prejudicial effort to defend white supremacy and patriarchal authority as the basis of social order.[3]

Iveson Lewis Brookes, born in Rockingham County, North Carolina, on November 2, 1793, shared what seemed by all accounts a cordial but distant relationship with his father, Jonathan Brookes. Of the middling planter class, Brookes's filial relationship reflected the expectations typical of his set—to acquire land, slaves, and an honorable reputation that would advance the family name. These expectations, and Brookes's constant efforts to meet them, figured prominently in his correspondence with his father. A veteran of the American Revolution, Jonathan Brookes had acquired considerable status as a planter in North Carolina, and as his eldest son, young Iveson bore the mantle of continuing this familial distinction. His education at the University of North Carolina set him firmly upon a path to prestige, but it also introduced him to his true calling—Iveson Brookes experienced conversion and joined the Baptist church while at university and began his ministerial career during his senior year in 1819. Brookes henceforth remained committed to both his secular father's expectations and his heavenly father's demands and attempted to appease both throughout his life. This tenuous balancing act shaped his beliefs and behaviors henceforth as a son, a father, a spiritual leader, and father figure to his proverbial flock.[4]

Iveson Brookes demonstrated this duality most clearly in his early correspondence with his father. Brookes did not answer the religious call lightly or precipitously. Religion had come to feed his soul, but he continued to bury himself in more secular subjects. "It is to me a dry study," he complained of his curricular demands, "more particularly when so increased as to prevent my attention to other sources of mental improvement and especially when it encroaches on my enjoyment of *religious privileges.*"

Sketch of Rev. Iveson Lewis Brookes, undated, from *History of the Baptist Denomination in Georgia*, Atlanta, GA: J. P. Harrison, 1881. (Special Collections, Ina Dillard Russell Library, Georgia College and State University)

He continued, "I hope the moments spent in reading and meditating on the sacred promises of the Gospel afford me too much real comfort to be exchanged for profession of such knowledge as pertains chiefly to *this world*," before concluding, "I however feel willing to curtail some of my religious engagements for a time and make a sacrifice ... this will certainly tend to my future promotion and usefulness to *this world*. For this reason I am still anxious to continue at college."[5] Brookes very early recognized that in order to be effective in wielding his faith for earthly good, he had to become conversant in the ways of the world, and his collegiate education seemed to promise the best possible foundation of temporal knowledge toward those spiritual ends.

Brookes eventually acted upon these convictions, however fraught, in settling upon his postgraduate professional path. "In regard to my course after leaving college," he told his father, "I have not fully determined the manner in which to proceed. It is probable you have calculated on my attempting to preach the Gospel and could my prospect for usefulness in ministry appear reasonably good it is presumable that you would have no objections to my engaging in that most *exalted and respectable calling*.

Portrait of Rev. Basil Manly Sr., 1840. (University Libraries Special Collections, University of Alabama)

It is my *greatest earthly desire* to preach." By continually balancing sacred and secular in his filial relationship and professional ambition, Brookes was like many if not most aspiring evangelical Protestant Christian ministers of the period. But as a white southern man of the cloth during the advent of sectional tension over slavery in the antebellum era, Brookes's success in applying his faith in this calling would increasingly hinge on his ability to effectively wield the power and privilege ascribed to men of his race and class. That demanded literacy in the language and ritual, if not always the physical manifestations (ostentatious appearance and bearing, and willingness to engage in violence) of southern honor. His experience applying both honor and piety in his life and career at once revealed the predominant nature and perceived necessity of the emerging sense of righteous honor in the early antebellum era, and it was an experience shared by others of a like mind.[6]

Basil Manly Sr.'s life and career proved similar and equally illustrative of that experience. Born in 1798 to Captain John Basil Manly who, like

Jonathan Brookes, had earned his rank and reputation during the American Revolution, Basil Manly Sr.'s father bequeathed this reputation, firmly planted in Pittsboro, just south of Chapel Hill, North Carolina, as a model for his sons to follow. Basil, the second son and namesake of Captain John Basil, bore much of this burden. A singular event altered his course, however, from that of his father or brothers; he experienced conversion to the Baptist faith in 1814 at the age of sixteen. This conversion ushered in a tension between honor and piety that colored the remainder of his days. In an 1819 letter to his father, a young Manly expounded upon his prospects for the coming summer and fall and took special care to enumerate the financial gains attending every option. All involved some form of religious service. Manly closed the letter by saying, "Such are prospects—God knows how they will terminate. I think I desire to throw myself into His Almighty hands to be guided as He sees most fit. I have thought proper to make this explanation to you. I hope you will approve my determinations." He ended with "Believe me as ever your *dutiful* and affectionate son." Here Manly blatantly exhibited his duality of mind, presenting his worldly prospects in answer to his secular father, while throwing himself at the mercy of his heavenly one. He evinced this duality frequently in correspondence with his father, and in so doing revealed his early recognition that he must meet the demands of manhood in order to effectively purvey the promise of his faith in his native South. Those demands included adherence to the honor ideal and its evolving mandates for manly comportment. The ways in which he applied both further reveal the ways in which leading white southern men in the early antebellum era might shape their personal and collective identity according to an emerging sense of righteous honor in the early antebellum era.[7]

In 1819, Iveson Brookes and Basil Manly crossed paths while preaching near Chapel Hill, North Carolina. Both born on the eve of the Second Great Awakening into prosperous southern families, they personified in many respects the first generation of white southern ministers to be faced with the prospect of more effectively balancing secular honor and sacred piety throughout their lives. Given their similar backgrounds and mutual calling to preach the Gospel, the two became instant friends. Both sought to balance earthly distinction and spiritual growth, to make worldly honors serve spiritual ends. That balance could be tenuous. Their calling eventually carried each of them into Edgefield during the early antebellum period, where both easily recognized the tensions between worldly honor and religious piety then presiding among its people. Both men seemed ideally suited to minister such a population. Themselves the product of pressures to adhere to the masculine expectations of more virile and in many ways more primal conceptions of southern honor, they saw in Edgefield, perhaps, a chance to promote an ideal manhood that invoked both religious piety and secular honor. Each left their ministerial mark on Edgefield and fomented the pervasive religious spirit of the early antebellum Edgefield community. In so doing, they provide an intimate glimpse into the often intensely personal and emotional experience of Edgefield's fledgling sense of righteous honor during the early antebellum years.[8]

Basil Manly Sr. took his first pastoral charge at Edgefield's Little Stephen's Creek Baptist Church in 1822, which he quickly parlayed into a resounding religious revival. In the wake of this revival, Manly joined several prominent Edgefield families in founding the Edgefield Village Baptist Church in 1823, and was elected its first minister. These early professional successes met with equal personal happiness; Manly met his wife, Sarah Murray Rudolph, during his first summer in Edgefield and the two married three years later on December 23, 1824. Thus Edgefield secured a permanent and sacred position in Manly's heart and hearth. Even after leaving Edgefield in the spring of 1826 for professional opportunities in Charleston, South Carolina, and later, Tuscaloosa, Alabama, Manly and his family remained intimately tied to the Edgefield community and the state of South Carolina.[9]

In both personal reflections and public projections, Reverend Basil Manly Sr.'s experience bore out the nascent sense of righteous honor increasingly prevalent in Edgefield and prominent in his own life. His sermons frequently touched on the relationship between secular and sacred, with morality the touchstone of a life governed by that conceptual ideal. "Moralists divide law into the law of honour, the Holy Scriptures, [and] the law of the land. But what is this law of honour?," he asked rhetorically before proffering, "It sanctions every enormity. Jabez was honourable on a different law. It was the honour of *usefulness* and *devotion* [to God]." In referencing the Old Testament account of Jabez, whom the Bible described as "more honourable than his brethren" and who had "called on God . . . saying, 'Oh that thou wouldest bless me indeed, and enlarge my coast, and that thine hand might be with me, and that thou wouldest keep *me* from evil, that it may not grieve me!'" Manly renders the common earthly distinction between honor and piety moot. Honor could not be separated into secular and sacred, for any true secular honor inherently contained a sacred sanctification. The two served each other, or honor was absent. Upon this moral foundation of righteous honor Manly seemingly rested his personal manhood and his familial, congregational, communal, regional, and national ideals and identities.[10]

This interconnection between honor, piety, and manhood pervaded his thoughts and actions, both private and public. In an early sermon drawn from the Epistle to the Romans, Manly took up this theme by declaring, "Great as sin and its fruit might be to cast dishonour on God, grace would do him more honour, than if sin had not had existence . . . Sin abounds in the conscience, the sinners own convictions and grace abounds most, usually, where the sense of sin is greatest." He concluded that "if heretofore sin has abounded in our past life, and we have been very zealous in its pursuit, we should now be proportionally zealous that grace may much more abound." This grace would sanction his conclusion that "this only answers to the moral government of God. He devotes moral above natural distinctions. For the purposes of life men are variously endorsed. But for purposes of his moral government all are brought to a level; all stand on the same ground." In another sermon he reiterated the point: "The design of the Gospel is to profit us, it was given to us to reform our manners (morals), to elevate our minds; above all to save our lost and wretched souls . . . Faith in us is necessary to secure this design." Only through faith could men repair "the dishonour heaped on God" by their inherent sinfulness. Here again Manly grappled with the distinction between worldly honor and sacred piety and concluded the two inseparably linked in the overall pursuit of moral righteousness. A moral life invoked both honor and piety in equal measure. In the context of the antebellum slave South, white men of means wielded both power and responsibility as models of this ideal and agents of its application to uphold what they deemed a divinely sanctioned social order.[11]

Much more than mere abstractions designed to appease pious congregants from his Sunday pulpit, Manly evinced this persistent tension between honor and piety throughout his adult life. His entry into the ministry first tested his mettle on this score by bringing him into conflict with Captain Manly's more secular-minded designs for his son, namely planting and politics. That trial foreshadowed many others. While at South Carolina College, Manly gained the renown of his peers as much for his scholarly prowess as his preaching talents. His success in the former confirmed his intention to pursue the latter, but the pursuit was not without its trials and tribulations. His time in college taught him the necessity of projecting a manly comportment in his efforts to touch other men's souls. In his native South, such manliness held honor in utmost esteem, and his peers at South Carolina College ranked among the most fervent adherents. The defense of both in the face of affront sometimes demanded violence—verbal and physical—that often threatened to excite his otherwise composed nature.[12]

Just such an affront brought these personal tensions to a public head on December 3, 1821, when Manly defended his honor against a jealous rival during graduation exercises at South Carolina College. His elder brother Charles later recounted that Manly parried the knife of his rival and "flew upon him like a raging tiger, seizing him by the throat with both hands, bore him to the ground, throwing himself heavily upon his body where the fellow could neither kick nor 'holler.'" The sons of South Carolina's aristocratic gentry who witnessed the scene declared that Manly "had been cowardly attacked without provocation and that he should have his satisfaction." After the assailants were separated and that satisfaction achieved, this genteel audience cheered Manly and "threw up their hats and swore it was the best fight they had ever seen a Baptist preacher make." As their adulation suggests, such physical confrontations were rare among southern evangelical Protestant divines, and Manly's own experience proved the point; this was the only recorded instance in which he resorted to physical assault to answer an affront.[13]

Historians have tended to focus on religious denunciations of dueling and the code duello as corrupting influences that encouraged sinful personal violence, and with good reason; in their public pronouncements and private lives, the overwhelming majority of southern ministers actively avoided physical violence and fervently derided the practice of dueling. Many even went so far as to publicly promote and personally join antidueling societies and associations in order to eradicate the practice. However, opposition to violence generally and dueling specifically fell far short of a complete rejection of southern honor or white patriarchal authority. Many southern ministers exhibited a pronounced familiarity with the language and ritual of southern honor as well the prerogatives of white mastery, wielding both in their personal lives and public positions even as they typically stopped short of actual physical violence and denounced dueling as an effective means of preventing the honor and mastery's potential excesses.[14]

Adherents to the southern honor code nevertheless aspired to propagate its ability to preclude physical confrontation between principals by ritualizing the verbal and written "violence" of these affairs, as John Lyde Wilson's published 1838 code attests. Manly frequently exhibited his embrace of this potential function as he demonstrated his literacy in these ritualized forms. He often found himself embroiled in clerical controversies that played out in the pages of the religious press. Many of these disputes were nothing more than doctrinal or sectarian squabbles, manifested in public press debates. But these public debates often turned into personal disputes. In these "rhetorical duels," the line between spiritual discussion and personal affront blurred.[15]

Manly's sense of righteous honor certainly shaped just such a confrontation with an alleged charlatan named Jesse Denson in the summer of 1827. On June 4 of that year, Manly noted in his church journal a discussion he'd had that morning with a friend named Jacob Axson on the subject of Mr. Denson. Manly recounted, "Denson had been traveling and begging for years in [the] character of a Baptist preacher. Latterly he had not been received by the denomination. On his coming to Charleston in May, I had, in answer to some published inquiries respecting him, caused him to be *published* as no Baptist, and as an *imposter*." He continued, "For this, after a good deal of newspaper writing, he had threatened to prosecute me, unless I gave him *satisfaction*. I could give him none and would not recede from the ground I had taken. Mr. Axson, with the utmost address, obliged him to desist; and obtained from him a written obligation that he would not say or do anything against me." Manly had thus engaged a "second" in Jacob Axson, whose role was to attempt an honorable arbitration of the Denson affair. Clearly, Manly adhered to the form, if only part of the function, of the southern honor code. True to his sense of Christian manliness, he actively averted physical violence. But in achieving this Christian restraint he revealed his intimate knowledge of the language and ritual of the southern honor code.[16]

Manly's personal friend and professional kinsman the Reverend Iveson L. Brookes understood such tensions all too well. Brookes frequently expressed the same tenuous personal balance between secular and sacred, between honor and piety, as his friend Basil Manly. Though Manly ultimately took charge of the Baptist church at Edgefield's Little Stephen's Creek for which both pastors had initially been called, the two friends shared an affinity for Edgefield that persisted even as their callings carried them beyond its borders. Having conceded the Little Stephen's Creek pastorate to Manly, Brookes took his first pastorate that same year some 115 miles west-southwest, in Eatonton, Georgia. Like Manly, he too quickly met and married his first wife during his inaugural year in Eatonton. He and Lucina Sarah Walker were married on September 22,

1822. She bore him his only son Walker in October 1826, but she died just two months later. He married again in 1828, to Prudence Echols Irvin Johnson of Wilkes County, Georgia, but she too passed away, in 1830. He married his third wife, the widow Sarah Julia Oliver Myers, in 1831, and from her received title to plantations near the town of Woodville in the Edgefield District, where he moved shortly after his nuptials and remained the balance of his life. He itinerated between several Edgefield churches from that date forward, leaving for just four years (1842–45) to administer the Penfield Female Academy in Penfield, Georgia. Thus Brookes, like his close friend Manly, developed spiritual, marital, and temporal ties to Edgefield that remained throughout his life.[17]

His permanent residence in Edgefield only honed his earliest inclinations toward the incipient sense of righteous honor that had likely first attracted him to the district. A young Brookes hinted at this inclination when he reflected upon a death in the family of a college acquaintance: "How awful must be the case of a sinner on whom the wrath of God abideth while in life to be forced to enter the gloomy vale of death and launch into an unknown world to appear in the more immediate presence of an angry Judge and experience the realities of eternal despair!" He may have thought of his own failings when he concluded, "What folly is it to spend the days of youth and health in the pleasures of sin or the pursuit of earthly treasures to the neglect of immortality and the concerns of Eternity." In contemplating his future prospects, young Brookes visibly vacillated between secular and sacred desires, and demonstrated the tension between honor and piety that would color his life when he observed, "Men prefer the toys of the world and the pleasures of sense to the treasures of heaven, the salvation of God, the enjoyment of everlasting happiness." These are typical evangelical Protestant reflections for the era, but viewed through the prism of righteous honor, the emotional experience of these ideals as both contentious and compatible by turns becomes clear.[18]

A later letter to his father laid bare these personal tensions: "Whatever station in life may be designed in the purposes of Providence to be filled by me and whatever part of the world may be set apart to be the place of my residence and the theatre of my action are things known with certainty only to God." He then declared, "It is my part to acquiesce in the dispensations of his Providence, to trust implicitly in his Sovereign Mercy and omnipotent Grace and to submit in humility and obedience to the teachings and leadings of His holy spirit . . . yet as creatures of intelligence and foresight we are permitted to consult our reason and deduce such conclusions from present appearances and impressions as justify at least a conditional resolution as to the future course and purposes of our life." Here Brookes showed a common tension present in the lives of evangelical Protestant Christians of the period, but his status as an upper-class white southern man in the slave South fundamentally shaped his experience of this tension; his social station simultaneously provided him the power to wield his faith for good while also revealing the dangerous depths of sinful indulgence such power and prerogative could produce.[19]

Brookes reconciled these competing motives and overcame the fear of these temptations by embracing the opportunity, reasoning that "in drawing inferences from reason and the nature of things to direct us in our pursuits we should be also cautious in our consultations to make the word of God the main of our counsel," as only by "such a method of proceeding we shall be sure to have the glory of God in view as the ultimate end of our purposes and his service set before us as the great end of our existence and the grand source of our action." But he admitted the difficulty in maintaining such spiritual resolve in the face of temporal temptation. He confessed himself "truly fearful" of his belief "that preaching the gospel to sinners is the only employment in which I can engage in a professional character," and cited his "unworthiness and inability" as the reason for his diffidence: "I shrink from the cross and think it impossible for me to fill a station so dignified or perform a task so arduous." Perhaps such reservations rested on his fear of the power his station provided; despite his expressed intention to wield that power for good, he had ample evidence all around him of the myriad ways in which such power could corrupt. His native slave South represented both a bountiful field for reaping the harvests of converted souls and shaping the morals of committed believers as well as a foreboding cesspool of sinfulness that undermined those efforts at every turn.[20]

Brookes came close to explicitly confronting his fear of temptation in a letter to his father: "When the Lord joins with my flesh and conducts me to the point of the mountain (Earthly vanity) I am presented with a very exclusive prospect beautified by all the objects Satan and imagination can exhibit among which the most illustrious and attractive is the Temple of fame." Observing that "in the courts of this temple are to be discovered walking in majesty rulers and officers of state together with a train of professional characters who bear the ensigns of wealth and honor," he ultimately sought to silence his fears by reminding himself that "all its couriers are falling for hasty and inevitable destruction." "It reminds me," he wrote, "of the shortness of time and certain approach of Death bids me behold a world that is lush in inequity and which must shortly appear as the awful tribunal of God." Upon such reflections Iveson Brookes based his ultimate resolution: "That the great object of my life under present circumstances is to attempt to preach the Gospel of Salvation to sinners." He would take up the sword of the spirit to battle the demon of sin in his midst, but in so doing he relied upon the shield of his faith to do so without succumbing to sin's allure.[21]

Another, more senior, Edgefield minister provided further evidence of Edgefield's dueling cultural heritage and its signal role in shaping a sense of righteous honor during the early antebellum period. William Bullein Johnson, born near Beaufort, South Carolina, on June 13, 1782, to Joseph and Mary Bullein Johnson, differed in both age and upbringing from his fellow Edgefield Baptist brethren. In contrast to the filial tensions of their youth, Johnson described his own father as "being of a roving disposition . . . often absent from home" and acknowledged he "was therefore less under his instruction and example than [his] mother's." His mother attempted to fill the paternal void and drew praise from her faithful son as "an intelligent and pious woman." He reminisced, "[She] bestowed great pains on my intellectual and moral culture . . . She sought to imbue my mind, at an early age, with profound reverence for the Holy Scriptures [and] taught me also the great principles of the doctrine of Christ which were so impressed upon my mind that they were of great service to me when I began to preach." Her influence and example drove Johnson's intense religiosity, and though she herself could never supplant his absent father, the love of a higher paternity became his life's calling.[22]

His paternal influence came most fervently from his Baptist mentors— Oliver Hart, Edmund Botsford, and Richard Furman—who shaped his early manhood in their own faithful image. His biographer later described their influence: "The faith of his fathers . . . was his by inheritance and teaching; and it was to become his by regeneration." Like these early mentors, Johnson himself later assumed a paternal role for many within the Baptist faith, a role that carried him into Edgefield to continue to build upon the work of Basil Manly Sr. He came later upon the Edgefield scene, accepting a call to administer the Edgefield Female Academy and to preside over the Edgefield Village Baptist Church in 1830. Both institutions had grown out of the religious revivals of the previous decade, revivals that the younger reverend, Basil Manly Sr., had helped foment, expanding faith communities that Iveson L. Brookes would later minister to as well. Johnson's personal history, like those of these ministerial brothers, reflected a burgeoning sense of righteous honor in the early antebellum Edgefield community. All experienced the constant personal and public tension between secular and sacred, between honor and piety. This cultural duality came to define Edgefield and fundamentally shaped many who fell into the district's embrace, whether by birth, betrothal, or baptism. Reverend Johnson, like Iveson L. Brookes and Basil Manly Sr. before him, personified in many respects the experience of this sense of righteous honor that guided Edgefield's white men through the antebellum era.[23]

In one particularly poignant homily entitled "God is Love," initially composed in 1812 during his early ministerial career but repeatedly revised and redelivered thereafter, Reverend Johnson took up what would continue to be a common evangelical Protestant Christian refrain in assessing and addressing the difficulties confronting such men in a world of iniquity: "Sin has introduced into our world confusion, strife, and every evil work. Hence arise those painful scenes which are presented to our view in the affairs of men. Hurried on to the commission of deeds awfully abandoned, man acts toward his brother man, rather as the enemy of his race, than as a member of the same common family." He concluded that "every man is tempted when he is drawn away of his own lust, and enticed," that men "voluntarily, and in violation of the strongest principles of moral obligation" rebel "against the throne of their Sovereign," the Lord God above. Johnson believed that by embracing the sacred honor of God as paramount, men opened themselves to the moral righteousness that characterized the truest manhood.[24]

This consistent point of emphasis in his sermons in some ways set him apart from the younger Baptist brethren in Edgefield. As a church elder well over ten years their senior, Johnson prioritized sacred matters far more than the younger ministers Manly and Brookes. Such emphasis on otherworldly promise over worldly preoccupations predominated in evangelical Protestant Christian thought generally, but the younger generation more frequently and pointedly applied Christian moral teachings to the most pressing social and cultural concerns of the day. What men of Johnson's generation tended to couch in the more abstract language of spiritual commitment, men like Manly and Brookes had begun to more explicitly confront in the specific context of the antebellum South. In that context, and especially in Johnson's native South Carolina, the degree of abstraction that he preferred became increasingly impossible, and the perceived need to more directly address the specific issues and concerns of the antebellum era became increasingly unavoidable. In the specific context of Edgefield, both honor and piety governed the conception of morality deployed for that purpose, and leading white men drew upon both in defining and defending their purported manly virtues and prerogatives according to the precepts of righteous honor. After a decade in Edgefield, Johnson increasingly aligned himself to these prevailing trends in both his private expressions and public appeals.[25]

The most poignant evidence of this shift in Johnson's thoughts and actions came during the 1840s, when he became embroiled in an ongoing clerical debate between various Baptist ministers and educators—principally James Reynolds, James Mims, and James Furman. The content of this debate—by inference a dispute over the proper relationship between individual churches and denominational conventions—mattered less than the manner in which it unfolded. In a series of newspaper articles between 1846 and 1849, Reynolds, Furman, and Mims jousted in the religious press, generally avoiding the line that often turned such public debates into heated personal disputes. But sometime in late 1846, Reverend Reynolds crossed that line and penned a personal attack against James Mims and James Furman, calling into question their character as Christians and as men.

In a string of letters, Johnson attempted to arbitrate between the various parties and save face for the faith. Assessing Reynolds's character and argument in a letter to James Furman, Johnson observed, "Alas! my brother, how true is it, that 'man at his best estate is altogether vanity.' The defense of [Reynolds] is a sad proof of this truth in himself. The spirit of it is anything but Christian, dignified, or manly." In a later letter to Furman, Johnson again sized up the arguments and the manner of their opponent by asserting, "Reynolds ... I am very sorry to see, descends to an unmanly mode of repelling the thrusts of his antagonist." A letter to James Mims confirmed this opinion of Reynolds, but requested further information regarding the allegations made by him. Clearly, Johnson was toeing a fine line between fulfilling his professional obligations and serving a friend in need, as he made repeated requests for additional information regarding the affair. "I wish to have full information on all points before I write," he said.[26]

All of Johnson's correspondence regarding the matter took this form, as he carefully weighed his duties as Baptist leader against his loyalties as fraternal friend and confidant. In effect he performed the role of second in this rhetorical duel between clerical combatants, arbitrating the conflict through very measured printed responses. In doing so he, like his younger Baptist brothers Basil Manly and Iveson Brookes, revealed an acute literacy in the language and ritual of southern honor and acknowledged its importance in upholding southern Christian manhood during the antebellum era.[27]

These ministers attempted to balance the demands of ideal white southern manhood—embodied in the dueling nature of their personal honor and piety—and thereby reflected the often very personal and emotional experience of these inherent cultural tensions in the early antebellum South. As fostered in Edgefield, honor and piety dominated in these preachers' ministries through their remaining lives; both became inseparably linked in the ministers' nascent sense of righteous honor, and that ideal increasingly defined their identity as white, southern, Christian men through the antebellum era. That they generally abhorred violence and explicitly denounced dueling did not preclude their adherence to the southern honor code; it only shaped their application of it in coordination with the tenets of their faith to actuate their white patriarchal privilege and authority. But one did not have to be a minister to experience such tensions and subscribe to such an ideal to serve similar ends. Many a nonminister navigated the same cultural tensions between secular and sacred, honorable and pious, and arrived at the same conception of righteous honor in all its emotional complexity.[28]

James Bones and Dr. John Hughes both settled their families in Edgefield sometime in the early nineteenth century. Bones had five sons—James Jr., John, Robert, Samuel, and William—who all of came of age in the 1820s and 1830s and became planters and merchants in the Edgefield and Augusta area. He also had a daughter, Martha, who married John H. Hughes, eldest son and namesake of Dr. John Hughes, in 1831. The Hughes and Bones families typified Edgefield's middling planter class by the early antebellum years and maintained an intimate connection with each other and the Edgefield community throughout the antebellum era. Edgefield's tradition for honor-bound violence and its pervasive evangelical Protestant Christian piety permeated both families. Dr. John Hughes's sister Elizabeth married the Baptist preacher Nicholas Ware Hodges of Abbeville and Edgefield in 1820, while one of his cousins, Lucy T. Butler, later married the prominent Edgefield Methodist minister Joseph Moore. Through these personal and community connections, evangelical Protestant morality pervaded the mores of the Hughes and Bones families.

An early note by an unidentified member of the Hughes family (most likely its patriarch Dr. John Hughes) betrays, however, the cultural tensions these families shared with each other and their Edgefield neighbors.

In 1811 reflections on the role of religious clergy in wartime resulted in the declaration that the "clergy is still seeking in a religion which is called the religion of peace for pretenses and the means of discord and of war; it is embroiling families in the hope of dividing the state; so difficult it is for that order of man to be taught to renounce riches and authority . . . There is a great difference betwixt what is incomprehensible by reason and what is contradictory to it." Recognizing such contradictions did not make reconciling them any easier. Copies of two sermons by unidentified preachers that were saved by the family attest to the continued anxieties such tensions spawned. The first, entitled "Those Who Sin against God," proclaimed that such sinners would be "condemned by him as those who live in the open violation of his Law: and although their sins may not be of as aggravated a nature, yet their condemnation will be as sure." It then explained that "sins may be divided into inward and outward, i.e. the sins of the heart and the sins of the life . . . from within, out of the heart of men, proceed *evil* thoughts, adulteries, fornications, murders, thefts, covetousness, wickedness, deceit, lasciviousness, an evil eye, blasphemy, pride, foolishness; All these *evil* things come from within, and defile the man.'" The sermon concluded, "Hence it is very evident that evil or wicked tempers indulged in the heart form the first class of moral *evil*, and is the fountain or source from whence [come] all the evil or bad conversation and conduct that men and women are guilty of" and "from that source proceeds lying, hypocrisy, profane swearing, cheating, defrauding, evil speaking, quarreling, fighting, licentiousness, and in a word, the whole haven of moral *evil* of which men are guilty."[29]

In the view of this unnamed pastor, "When man refuses to obey the will of their maker, sets up his will and pursues it in opposition to the will of God, he often runs into many excesses of moral evil, lives in the practice of sin, both of omission and commission, and brings ruin and destruction upon himself." The only salvation was in "turn[ing] from your evil ways, and seek[ing] the Lord in earnest . . . that you may obtain mercy, and escape all those evils and dreadful consequences of sin, that will overtake the wicked, and the haters of righteousness." The copy of this sermon, expressly requested from its unidentified author and saved for posterity, revealed the self-reflective spiritual doubts so common among evangelical Protestants of the period. But its subject also exposed the pressing temporal concerns that often caused such spiritual consternation. Echoing the moral concerns espoused in the sermons of Edgefield's most prominent Baptist and Methodist leaders, the Hughes family profoundly experienced the same personal and emotional tensions between secular and sacred duty, between temporal honor and religious piety.[30]

A requested copy of another sermon by an unidentified minister nearly ten years later revealed more of the same but offered prescriptive measures to reconcile these cultural tensions. "The Gospel is not merely a negative system . . . It is not enough that we cease to do evil, we must also learn to do well," its anonymous author asserted. "We must not only break off from the practice of every sin and live a blameless life, but we are required to cultivate and have in exercise love, faith, humility, and devotion toward God, purity, chastity, and temperance towards ourselves and righteousness, truth and charity towards our fellow men." The preacher then expressed the worry that "many seem to be regardless of practical piety, and it is to be feared that they accommodate their opinions to their conversation and conduct. They separate the branches of religion and reduce its importance in such a way as that their minds and consciences are easy and quiet although in their lives they are worldly, prayerless, and indifferent to the honor and glory of God." Perhaps counting themselves among the "multitudes [who] deceive themselves by balancing one part of their character against another, and vainly hope to weigh down their sins and irregularities by opposing to them their good qualities," whom this preacher admonished, the Hughes family certainly sought to put into practice the pastor's ideal, which urged, "If men would hearken more to reason and the word of God, and less to the false dictates and prejudices of their own corrupt hearts, we would see holier, better, and more useful Christians."[31]

The first antebellum generation of Bones and Hughes men exhibited this tension between temporal honor and religious piety repeatedly. Personal and familial honor figured prominently in letters from John and Samuel Bones to their father James. In an 1830 missive, John discussed the temporal situation and moral state of his brother Robert. "I must say that Robert being so long from home after the fourth of July was highly improper, and what I did not expect he would have been guilty of. I see no impropriety in his having joined in the festivity of the day with his neighbors, but he ought to have avoided getting into improper company." John then declared, "Without a correct course of conduct he would not expect any aid or assistance from me," but he then admonished his father: "I have observed with great pain that your treatment of Robert has not been such as to make his time agreeable at home. You are much more harsh with him than you are with any of your negroes."[32]

John continued: "[When Robert] left this place to return to you he certainly gave up apparently favorable prospects and is now unfit for any other business than that of a planter, which after all is much the happiest life in this country when people are attentive"; if "a plan by which he might be able to do something for himself" could be devised and "by which he may have an interest in the plantation," John concluded, "I have no doubts [it] will stimulate him to great exertions." In his mind, a planter's status would confer honor upon Robert, the responsibility of which would in turn compel him to moral righteousness and social respectability. Without honor's moral imperatives, Robert might languish under his father's seemingly cruel reproaches and ultimately bring shame upon himself and the family by falling in with "improper company." The attainment of temporal success and manly honor had moral consequences, something both John and his father James understood all too well in their anxious planning on Robert's behalf.[33]

John's younger brother Samuel similarly expressed an intimate understanding of this connection between temporal honor and spiritual morality. James Bones had earlier written his son Samuel to gauge the truth of an allegation made against his character. Samuel responded by declaring himself "a good deal surprised at the contents" of that letter, and assured his father: "As to what the fellow said it only convinces me that the opinion I have formed of him was correct; that he is a damned weak, vain, lying fool. As to our being friends this was false; as to what he said about my drinking too much wine, with my friend at night, he again lies." His honor questioned, Samuel bristled with indignation, not so much at his father's inquiries and implicit remonstrance as at the aspersions made against him by his alleged friend. He parried the affront by wielding the language and rituals of the southern honor code.[34]

He further denied the accusation by explaining, "If it was really the fact, he has never had an opportunity of knowing, for I never have been in his company at night or at any other time except when he came into the store"; he then denounced the accuser: "When I have a friend or associate they must be gentlemen, as such I have never considered him. As to what he said give yourself no anxiousness about it for in the first place it is false and you may rest assured that my friends never will have cause to fear for me on that account." Samuel answered this personal affront by denying his assailant any semblance of the manly honor he himself defended. As a "damned weak, vain, lying fool" his adversary deserved neither the time nor effort that an answer to this affront would require, and Samuel therefore determined, "I will now drop the subject as it is unpleasant to me." His personal honor secured in his father's eyes, an incensed Samuel nonetheless rested on honor's laurels by exhibiting his gentlemanly restraint and deeming his accuser unworthy of further notice.[35]

A third Bones brother, the sickly William, evinced a more overtly religious morality in reflecting upon his own mortality to his older brother John: "God knows that I have had a dreary and lonely time of it ... I have long since given over all idea of ever being partially restored to health, and endeavored to look forward to my fate with as much calmness and resignation as I came possessed of." He then turned to his faith: "May the Almighty give me grace to persevere it and prepare for the awful change. Oh! my dear brother what pleasure and comfort does the reliance on the mercies of a divine Saviour afford a person in my situation. It is a medicine to the soul that is indescribable and will cheer a person at the last moments beyond anything else."[36]

When William later died of his unstated affliction, a family friend named W. G. Stavely offered similarly pious condolences, hinting at the spiritual tenor of the Bones family circle: "It is trying on parents to be disposed of children ... It is their calculation that their children should perform to them the last rites of humanity, but, when it pleases Providence, to invert this order, and when the parent has to perform the duty of the child, Oh, it is most afflictive. To a mind thoroughly imbued with a conviction of an overruling Providence, convinced of immortality, even persuaded that all things are to work good for those who love and serve God, such visitations are divested of everything unseemly and contentment, which the world cannot give, becomes its slave." Stavely added, "It has ever been my hope, as now it is my belief, that such lessons shall not be lost on you ... We should be persuaded that our Redeemer liveth, and that he is able to save for the betterment." In this letter, Stavely implicitly revealed the abounding faith and piety present in the Bones family circle, but he also alluded, however indirectly, to a persistent tendency among the men in that circle to become preoccupied with worldly honors over spiritual matters. The collective portrait gleaned from these brief accounts of the Hughes and Bones men's lives corroborates Stavely's implied assessment and reveal a nascent sense of righteous honor at work among them: they strove for self-mastery, indeed considered their ability to attain it a pillar of white patriarchal prerogative in the slave South. But they also evinced a general sanction of certain forms of violence toward certain social and cultural ends.[37]

Like the Hughes and Bones families, that of Joseph Milligan came to Edgefield around the turn of the nineteenth century. They came bearing a moral stamp of approval from their fellow Presbyterian congregants at nearby Hopewell Long Cane in Abbeville County, South Carolina, who certified that "Joseph Milligan has lived the seven years past in this congregation, been a spirited supporter, lived an honest and useful life both as a citizen and Christian . . . [and] is in full communion in the church and has been for some time past in the station of a lay elder." As such their previous brethren "cordially recommended [them] to any society they may choose to join." The Milligans ultimately settled in the southern part of the Edgefield District near what would later become the town of Hamburg. There they welcomed the birth of their son Joseph Milligan Jr. in 1800. By 1830, Joseph Jr. had established himself as a physician and druggist of some means in Hamburg with a growing family of his own.[38]

Friends and family often wrote to Dr. Milligan upon religious matters, of which he apparently took a sincere interest. In the summer of 1835, John Dickson, a friend from nearby Augusta, wrote the doctor to inform him that "the Baptist Church has received very many accessions. 60 (white and black) were converted last Sunday . . . It is thought the Baptists will have to build another church soon, and I do think it would be good policy for them to do it." He then discussed the effects of this revival on their own mutual Presbyterian denomination by observing, "The attention among the young . . . in the Second Pres[byterian] Ch[urch] has not entirely ceased, but I cannot say I think the work as deep, thorough, or extensive as it was. Pray for us that the Spirit of God may not be withheld." This correspondence reveals Joseph Milligan's persistent interest and concern over religious development and morality in his community, a concern he shared with other members of his family.[39]

Another friend, H. K. Silliman, of Charleston, wrote in the fall of 1847 about a mutual acquaintance who had become a preacher. "I have heard Fleming *preach*, for you must know after all his *rascalities* he turned *minister*, his first church was on James Island," Silliman wrote. "[When] a great many persons thereunto inquired not only from me but others as to his reputation, I merely said time would show and that I did not think they would be pleased long with him. The case came out exactly, for they caught him or suspected him of some dirty tricks and sent him off." He then concluded, "It may be set down as a good rule that unless a man is so constantly and quickly changing the fault is greatly on his side . . . I hate to say it but I believe he is a *damned hypocrite*." As if chastising himself as much as his current subject of derision, Silliman then confessed, "When I told you I was so steady, you must not think I am exactly a Saint yet; I still enjoy myself but in a quieter way than I used to." In sharing the news of Fleming's rise then fall from grace and the pulpit, Silliman further exposes Dr. Milligan's abiding interest in the religious and moral development of friends and acquaintances, however remote. In turning the focus upon his own habits, by implication in answer to Milligan's apparent admonishment regarding Silliman's social habits, this confession of a dear friend implied that Milligan espoused a strict personal piety for himself, his family, and his most intimate friends.[40]

Perhaps this devout sense of piety derived from the influence of his sister, Jane Milligan of Charleston, who frequently expressed her religious feelings in long missives to her brother. In the fall of 1835 she wrote, "My dear Joseph although you have been made to drink deeply of the cup of sorrow at times, yet there has been so much mercy, and grace manifested toward you, and your family, that I cannot but view every event as a link in the chain of Providence, that is to fit you for an inheritance which is incorruptible, undefiled, and that cannot fade away." "Let us then endeavor to view God as a kind and merciful father," she continued, "who never afflicts willingly, but always with the benevolent design of preparing us for usefulness here, and happiness hereafter." Whether he drew his religious strength from his sister, or whether her strong beliefs reflected his own, such fervent expressions of religious faith reveal a mutual moral commitment and concern between brother and sister.[41]

In another letter later that year, Jane revealed the need for such pious remonstrance: "You must excuse me my dear Joseph but I do think that you are wrong in feeling that life has no charms, and inducements for you . . . Our Father knows when, and how to chastise us, and we may rest assured that no other way, than the one he has chosen would be as profitable to us." She further illustrated the point through her own example, saying, "My happiest moments have been those, when I could yield up my own will entirely and feel that I would not have things different from what they are, even if I could," before concluding, "I know that it is much easier to preach, than to practice, but difficult as it may be to attain this frame of mind, still it is attainable, and it is our duty to strive after it." Given their close relationship, his sister certainly influenced much of Dr. Milligan's own religious piety, which undoubtedly shaped the model he set for his growing family.[42]

Though Dr. Milligan repeatedly showed himself to be of a pious mind he also maintained a considerable concern for temporal matters, and was no stranger to the demands of manly honor as exacted in his Edgefield County home. In a letter to his daughter-in-law Octavia during the summer of 1848, Dr. Milligan made a casual observation about a mutual acquaintance: "Fred Selleck made a speech the other day, Friday, at a barbeque given to the returned Abbeville Volunteers. They say that Fred is about to get into a duel. I don't know the name of the other party." He then revealed the close nature of his acquaintance in announcing, "Fred will be invited to a barbeque to be given on the 10th August... I hope he may come over, for I would be pleased to see him." His friend Selleck had obviously given offense with his speech, and from the reaction of Dr. Milligan we understand he had to face the consequences in an affair of honor. Never party to an affair of honor himself and presumably opposed to such an affair on religious moral grounds, Dr. Milligan nonetheless countenanced just such an affair involving a close personal friend, never hinting even the slightest reservation or venturing even the faintest recrimination. For a man who seemingly admonished friends and family alike for their moral transgressions (and according to his sister Jane, bemoaned his own moral failings at every turn), this eagerness to consort with a potential duelist unveils the extent to which the honor code might permeate the worldview of southern men like Dr. Milligan; violence in defense of honor sometimes became unavoidable if not necessary. Men like Dr. Milligan were common in the antebellum South. Relatively few engaged in affairs of honor, while fewer still fought duels. Many espoused basic tenets of religious morality and did so in a decidedly evangelical Protestant Christian tone even if they remained outside the fold of those denominations that heralded such a moral ethic most fervently.[43]

Whitfield Brooks further epitomized the type. The Brooks family ranked among the oldest and most venerated in the history of Edgefield, where Whitfield himself was born in 1790 to Zachariah and Elizabeth Butler Brooks. Zachariah Brooks had gained renown as a captain during the Revolutionary War and had served under Colonel William Butler, Whitfield's maternal grandfather. Whitfield Brooks's own family perpetuated the privileged status of the Brooks name into the early antebellum years as a member of Edgefield's planter elite. He personified Edgefield's dueling cultural heritage of honor and piety. Though himself a founding member of the socially elite Trinity Episcopal Church in Edgefield, he and his wife, Mary Parsons Carroll Brooks, had been among a group of several Edgefield paragons to sponsor the founding of the

Portrait of Whitfield Brooks, 1844, by William Harrison Scarborough. (Edgefield County Historical Society; Edgefield Discovery Center)

Edgefield Village Baptist Church, and he occasionally attended Baptist and Methodist worship services and protracted meetings. Through such ecumenical interaction the evangelical Protestant ethic entered his home and mind and contributed to a nascent sense of righteous honor within his growing family. As an implicit moral standard that held both honor and piety in high esteem and deemed both paramount to the maintenance of southern manhood, this sense of righteous honor pervaded both the public and private affairs of Whitfield Brooks.

Though Brooks regularly attended worship services at the Episcopal church to which he formally belonged, he also listened to local Baptist and Methodist preaching with some frequency, and as a pious and emotionally reserved Episcopalian Brooks rarely failed to express his distaste for some of their more audacious practices: "My great objection to these public exhibitions by children [among the Baptists] is that it places them in an unnatural position, which they soon feel to be both false and embarrassing and which too generally ends in open apostasy or in hypocrisy, either of which has a pernicious effect upon the young mind," as well as their lack of education: "The [Baptist] ministers are good men but without education or intelligence." Such assessments obviously expose the considerable limits governing his tacit embrace of evangelical Protestant mores and practices.[44]

Despite these doctrinal and liturgical reservations, however, Brooks still frequented their services and generally commended their moral tenets. One passage in his journal revealed his reflective piety and its intimate connection to the more temporal concerns he had for himself and his family. In it, Brooks asserted his belief that "a reasonable mind should be content and should be especially thankful to the great Giver of every good gift, that our lot has been cast in a land of plenty and of social, religious and political liberty." He added, "If we will perform our part and faithfully employ our time in the attainment of moral and intellectual excellence there can be no doubt, that we shall enjoy our due share of the happiness, prosperity and success, that crown the labors of the deserving and meritorious in this life." Temporal honors rewarded spiritual morality, and when properly attained and deployed, the former could and should enlarge the latter. Brooks often committed such statements of his beliefs and other pious thoughts to his journal, revealing an inner piety that shaped his outward morality, one steeped in a sense of righteous honor.[45]

These nonclerical "Christian gentlemen" mirrored their ministerial counterparts in both their honor-consciousness and their spiritual commitment and moral concern; they all held common communion under the strictures of the righteous honor ideal. Collectively, theirs was a male world of love and ritual; the love of and for family, friends, and in a severely circumscribed and inherently prejudicial sense, even the enslaved, were all governed by the rituals of this nascent sense of righteous honor. But mothers and sisters, wives and daughters all played an especially prominent role in fostering the religiosity of these men: in bringing religious moral tenets into their intimate spaces; in softening the rough edges of their masculine interactions; in helping these men to master themselves so that they might more effectively master those dependent upon them; and in rendering their exercise of authority more righteous in white minds.[46]

Or so these men claimed and consciously sought to affirm in the conduct of their personal lives and public affairs. William Johnson explicitly credited his mother for the strength of his faith and its attendant moral fortitude; Whitfield Brooks pointed to his wife's pivotal role in shaping his moral outlook and helping him toe the proper moral line as an enslaver and patriarch; Joseph Milligan leaned on his sister's fervent faith in good times and bad and sought her moral counsel at frequent intervals. Though their public interactions with one another largely determined their status—sacred and secular—in one another's eyes, white southern men's ideals and identities never strayed far—in mind, body, or spirit—from the women in their lives. Though the concept of righteous honor was decidedly patriarchal in its assumptions and influence—the very foundation of their southern manhood—southern women served as ever-present sources of spiritual strength and symbolic reminders of what it was all for.[47]

Whether clerics or politicians, doctors or lawyers, merchants or planters, Edgefield's leading men in the early antebellum era carved out a tenuous balance between personal honor and piety, manifesting a nascent masculine ideal of righteous honor that they hoped would guide them, their families, community, state, and region into the increasingly foreboding years ahead. Much of their success would depend on their sons, to whom they passed this masculine standard of morality, and over whom they anxiously fretted when it (and they collectively) faltered. As one of the sermons saved by the family of John H. Hughes expressed it, "One design for which the family relation was instituted was that there a holy end might be trained up for the service of God, and he has promised his blessing to all who will seek to train their offspring for him." That their sons would indeed falter was expected; the balance, after all, was recognizably tenuous, as their own lives could attest. The masculine angst afflicting honor and piety within the South's strict hierarchies of race and gender persisted. But the implicit standard of righteous honor embodied for many proslavery whites the best hope of a more promising future, and the sons of Edgefield's—and the South's—first antebellum generation would be the ultimate arbiters of that supposed promise as they confronted the raging sectional crisis of the late antebellum years.[48]

PART II

Righteous Honor in Action

4

Moral Failings

Exorcising Inner Demons during the Sectional Crisis

> All things are delivered unto me of my Father: and no man knoweth the Son, but the Father; neither knoweth any man the Father, save the Son, and he to whomsoever the Son will reveal him.
>
> —Matthew 11:27

WALKER BROOKES was frantic as the summer of 1846 came to a close. During a recent break in his studies at Columbian College in Washington, D.C., he returned home to South Carolina and there confessed to his father, Iveson Lewis Brookes, a Southern Baptist preacher, his regrettable propensity toward "[an] illicit gratification of lust [and] excess of self-abuse [in the] stolen pleasures [of the] solitary vice." He later professed his extreme anxiety that such indulgences would render him physically and morally deficient for marriage. This anxiety prompted him to seek medical advice when he returned to school, which only amplified his worst fears. Medical professionals and health reformers at the time widely cited blindness, impotence, muscular atrophy, and even insanity as the most probable results of masturbatory indulgence. Burdened with this knowledge of the potential dire straits into which he had so wantonly waded, Walker wrote his father seeking counsel shortly thereafter, in utter despair and drowning in his own self-debasement. Over a decade later in 1859 Reverend Brookes fielded a similarly anxious admission of masturbatory mania from his nephew John M. Carter, who like his older cousin before him was away at college and in the prime of his early manhood.[1]

All three men clearly deemed the issue a spiritual failing with deep spiritual consequences, but each also recognized the secular dishonor implicit in such failings. They understood such dishonor undermined any claims they, as white men, might make to authority in the South's rigid racial patriarchy, predicated as it was on the "legitimacy" of those claims and the "proper" application of that authority. This sense of personal crisis only intensified in the crucible of the sectional crisis between North and South, free-state and slave-state. Others shared the Brookes family's concerns regarding southern cultural values, their place in southern society, and the emotional struggles entailed therein. Brookes's personal friend, professional associate, and sometime Edgefield resident Reverend Basil Manly Sr. drew similar connections between personal and public morality in the South. These ministers considered it their duty to administer sound moral principles to their families, their flocks, and southern society at large. Their place at the head of their households, their congregations, and—as white men—the southern racial patriarchy mandated that they themselves exhibit the self-mastery widely considered the basis of their authority according to the implied strictures of righteous honor.[2]

But one need not have been a preacher to experience the moral tensions of righteous honor and its emphasis on self-mastery as the basis of white supremacy and patriarchal power. Other Edgefield patriarchs outside the clerical profession exhibited similar and related concerns for the morality of their families and communities in this respect. The families of Whitfield Brooks and Dr. Joseph Milligan expressed equally fervent moral concern, and similarly sought to instill such a concern in their sons. Such tensions pervaded the masculine culture of the Civil War–era South and, though manifested in myriad ways, touched the lives of most white men to some degree, especially those in the upper strata of the social hierarchy. For these fathers, inculcating their sons in their inherent moral and ethical duties assumed primacy in their exercise of authority. For these sons, learning and applying these lessons to satisfy both secular and sacred filial duties while also preparing to fulfill paternal, political, and racial expectations in the future, seemed paramount.

The series of emotional biographies that follow illustrate how the distance separating such personal pitfalls and being forced to choose, between the downfall of the entire southern social order or the dissolution of the American Union and civil war, might well have seemed small for these men during the height of the antebellum sectional crisis. These southern fathers' crusade to prevent the former and either stave off or better prepare for the latter began at home, as they attempted to purge themselves, their households, and especially their sons of vice. And their sons bore the weight of this burden more acutely as they came of age during the height of the sectional crisis. All believed that only in fulfilling their duty to one another as fathers and sons could they confidently assert their white masculine claims to privilege and authority and enact the prerogatives that their privileged and powerful place in the southern social order purportedly demanded of them. All understood that the future of white supremacy and patriarchal authority as the basis of that social order rested in their hands.[3]

In their frank discussion of transgression and its consequences in the late antebellum period, the Reverend Iveson Brookes, his son Walker, and nephew John revealed a conviction shared by many white southern men of a similar station: that self-mastery was the linchpin of individual and collective destiny. All manner of vices—particularly alcohol, gambling, covetousness, and illicit sensual and sexual practices—tempted white southern men for whom the path to sin was always right in front of them. Stills, grog shops, and gambling dens were rife in the South, all of which white men considered immoral temptations, an appellation they also callously applied to enslaved women. (An unidentified southern merchant interviewed by Frederick Law Olmsted reluctantly admitted that there were but two lads in his small town in Alabama who were not paying the "penalty of licentiousness" [venereal disease] for their conduct with enslaved women. We "might as well have [our sons] educated in a brothel at once, as in the way they [are] growing up," he admitted.) But if the temptations were many, the consequences were grave. If white southern men could not control their own physical and emotional urges, how could they answer to themselves much less the North, to say nothing of the Father Almighty? How could they justify the social and political power that secured their peculiar prerogatives in the slave South, prerogatives most believed to be divinely sanctioned?[4]

Reverend Brookes certainly recognized the slippery slope of southern vices and made the connection explicit time and again in his letters of advice to his son and nephew. When first apprised of his son's depravity, Reverend Brookes tried to be reassuring, and referenced the professional opinion of a Doctor Chapman who had said "that your case has nothing alarming about it and moral treatment is all that is necessary; that you had become unnecessarily alarmed by the misrepresentations of a quack. As to the opinion of the authors you have read differing from that of Doctor

Chapman," Brookes continued, "you will find in those fatal cases that the subjects had long indulged most exceptionally and unnaturally and were perhaps so given over of God to work their destruction with greediness that they could not cease from their wicked acts, some repeating the act not only daily but from 10 to 20 times per day." He also reminded his son that such had been his own opinion upon their most recent farewell: "I told you that in so young a person who had discovered the wickedness and numerous consequences of such practices, and had abandoned the actual indulgence, restoration would be effected in due time by carefully abstaining from all causes of excitement to these organs. I am still of just the same opinion." Concerning the prospect of marriage, the elder Brookes gave his son this advice: "Simply let yourself alone and attend to your lawful and proper pursuits... In due time you will be relieved and be in a fit condition for marriage... as soon as you will have fixed upon the course you may determine to pursue and be sufficiently matured in judgment and experience to make a wise choice in selecting a partner for life."[5]

In offering solace for his son's fears, however, the elder Brookes revealed his own, as well as the tensions that shaped his moral purview. His God wielded both condemnation and compassion with a heavy providential hand; both Old and New Testaments shaped his view of God's role in human affairs. Judgment was unbending; forgiveness hard to come by. As befitting a man of the cloth, his paternal advice concerning his son's sinful self-pollution invoked these religious principles. "I tell you, my son, you must look to God as your great Physician," Reverend Brookes advised; "His grace is the sovereign remedy for the effects of sins and that alone can restrain the corruptions of poor fallen human nature and enable the reformed sensualist to keep his body under. I hope you have learned a practical lesson of experience in reference to lust and you may rest assured that all carnal indulgences turn to excess and are ruinous in their results." He then warned, "The Devil puts the unwary youth to work in onerous ways, promising him the reward of happiness, but his wages are misery here and eternal death hereafter. But God's order is to mortify the members while upon the earth, deny yourself of all ungodliness to worldly lusts, and live soberly, righteously, and Godly in this present life." "Let not the demon of hell any longer deceive you with his flattering tales," he said, before concluding: "You know those who follow his dictates in the illicit indulgences of the unclean passion must reap a copious crop of misery."[6]

Indeed, this belief in God's wrath seemed to set Brookes off, for after assuaging his son's fears he began admonishing his faults, launching into a general harangue against the vices plaguing all mankind. He warned young Walker that submission to one vice very often resulted in enslavement to all. "No chain is more galling and despotic than that with which the devil binds the unfortunate immoderate," Brookes asserted, and the "indulgence of an appetite for stimulating drinks is no less deceptive [than carnal lust] and in its results equally ruinous to body, mind, and soul." "My dear boy," he continued, "resolve deliberately and voluntary to sign the temperance pledge and be a freeman." Brookes clearly believed that self-pollution of any kind led easily into self-pollution of every kind. All constituted forms of self-enslavement.[7]

Brookes considered gambling equally sinful, deeming it as "demoralizing and fatally ruinous perhaps as any branch of the devil's services." "Like all Satan's plans of destruction," Brookes cautioned, "the initiatory step is called innocent but the grades are few to the top of this vice." Singling out chess, dice, cards, and faro as particular pitfalls, Reverend Brookes observed that the gambler, like his archetype the devil, would, once fallen, "only thenceforth goeth up and down and to and fro seeking whom he may devour." "My son," Brookes concluded, "if you have been tempted to engage at any of these usually called innocent games, remember that they are [the] beginning of the worst of vices."[8]

Walker Brookes earnestly sought to apply his father's moral teachings but frequently exhibited the anxieties attending the effort. And while his struggle consumed him, it also enveloped his family. Just three years after these exchanges with his father, his sister Virginia expressed a constant concern over her brother's tendency toward an unspecified sinfulness. "My darling, my only Brother," she wrote, "I pass many, many, sad reflections on you. I fear you are too careless about your immortal soul. I beg you, I implore you, to turn from your wicked ways and devote the remainder of your life to the service of God." She then urged, "Let not Satan tempt you to die in your sins. Oh! How long will you be wedded to this world; how long will you find pleasure in its follies." In another letter she reiterated the theme by declaring, "I hope those admonitions you have so often received will yet profit you and you may not die as one who knows no God, as those who pass through life in prosperity and forget they have a maker."[9]

Four years later in 1853, Walker, by then married and striving to settle into family life, continued to bemoan his personal failings and echoed his sister's earlier assessment of him by admitting to his father, "I have been rather extravagant in my habits [and] am anxious ... I am still floundering in [spiritual] darkness." But he declared himself "fully resolved with the help of God never to give up prayer again and to read more attentively the Scriptures." His wife Harriet, however, harbored doubts, which she shared with her father-in-law: "I am more than ever exercised and greatly troubled about my beloved husband's choosing the God of Abraham and Israel and Jesus as his God. Oh! I see clearly that he has everything to urge and encourage more than ever a Christian course." She then prayed, "God grant that the solemn warnings of his Providence may melt his heart. God has blessed him in every way all his life." Harriet's anxiety over Walker's continued "floundering" prompted her to implore Reverend Brookes to join her in daily, earnest prayers for her husband's salvation. "My dear husband appears to be in a troubled state of mind and I notice his constant searching of the sacred scriptures," she shared before exclaiming, "Oh! I cannot give up his precious soul . . . Oh! May God set him in the right way and make him a blessing to the church and his family and servants."[10]

Walker Brookes put himself on the spiritual rack in an attempt to master his bodily urges and emotional desires, but his personal travails became family trials, as his father, sister, and wife fervently tried to hold him accountable. That collective effort to purge the hearth and home of vice and render these domestic spaces the progenitor of virtue might well have been reenacted many times over across the antebellum South, as middling and elite white southern families strove to purify themselves in order to better defend their society against attack. Such efforts sometimes even extended beyond the nuclear family. On the precipice of secession and national disunion, thirteen years after his son Walker's travails, Iveson Brookes responded to his nephew John Carter's very similar confession of masturbatory mania and exposed an intersectional commonality within his moral vision. He urged upon his nephew many of the same religious principles with much the same tone of reassurance he had earlier proffered to his son. But he also similarly admonished his nephew for potentially provoking God's wrath and its dishonorable consequences by asserting that the white man can either master himself or find himself the slave of his desires. "Let your habits be in accordance to health and pure morality and they will prove a great blessing. But if corrupt and unchaste they will prove to be tyrants and will inflict curse upon soul and body," he declared. Such an emphasis was not unique to the South during the late antebellum period, however, a point that Brookes himself revealed when he advised his nephew to read the *Lecture to Young Men on Chastity*, first published in 1834 by the Connecticut-born Presbyterian minister Reverend Sylvester Graham.[11]

Reverend Graham had gained national renown during the antebellum period as a moral and dietary reformer and published many of his lectures, none more prominent or provocative than the *Lecture to Young Men on Chastity*, which outlined the physical and moral causes of youthful lust while proffering various means of abating it. Graham conveyed the import of his undertaking when he declared, "There is no point of morality of more importance ... Through a fear of contaminating the minds of youth, it has long been considered the wisest measure to keep them in ignorance ... so that while parents have been resting securely in the idea of the ignorance and purity of their children, these have been drinking in the most corrupt and depraving knowledge."[12]

Graham thus laid the onus of social corruption at the feet of neglectful (or naive) parents, and sought to inform both parent and child about the sins of the flesh and to instruct them on how to drive out the evil. "In the first place," Graham continued in the same *Lecture to Young Men*, "self-pollution is actually a very great and rapidly increasingly evil in our country," as is "illicit commerce between the sexes ... [and] sexual excess within the pale of wedlock," while "efforts to encourage illicit and promiscuous commerce between the sexes are already very extensive, and are daily becoming more extensive, bold, and efficient." "Are they who know the truth to hold their peace ... and see this destroying flood of error and pollution roll over the earth?" asked Graham, before responding, "Humanity, Virtue, Religion answer—'No!'"[13]

Reverend Brookes's belief in self-mastery thus exhibited his alignment to an important part of an emerging middle-class conception of masculine morality that crossed the sectional divide. As a slave-owning southern divine, Brookes could invoke the northern-born Reverend Graham's instructions even in the midst of sectional turmoil because they both believed that irreverent self-pollution begot rampant social corruption and eroded national righteousness. The disparate ends to which Brookes and Graham pursued that end, however, constituted the primary distinction between northern middle-class emphases on masculine self-control and southern masculine mores emphasizing self-mastery. Graham counted many of the most prominent antebellum abolitionists among his closest associates, including William Lloyd Garrison, Theodore Weld, Sarah and Angelina Grimke, Horace Greeley, Arthur and Lewis Tappan, William Goodell, and Joshua Lewis, all of whom became devoted adherents of the "Graham system" of moral reform through dietary restriction. Graham conversed and corresponded frequently with these and other ardent abolitionists; the "Graham boardinghouses and hotels" that emerged as the institutional manifestation of the "Grahamite system" became widely noted as dens of abolitionism; and Graham even contemplated authoring his own political history of American slavery. Though his social reform efforts concentrated most fervently on the alleged sins stemming from unrestrained sexuality and an unrestricted diet, his intimate and long-standing associations with abolitionist advocates suggests that he believed slavery, too, constituted an indulgence and a sin. Brookes on the other hand believed that slave mastery underlined and demonstrated the white right to rule. Indeed, so this inherently prejudicial logic went, enslaved blacks were enslaved in part because they were incapable of mastering themselves.[14]

Whatever reservations Brookes might have harbored for himself, his son, and his nephew concerning their moral righteousness, however, his public defense of southern slavery deliberately refused to dwell on such vices in order to exalt the alleged virtues of the southern social order as compared to the North. In Brookes's mind the North had proven itself incapable of self-mastery because its free-labor ideals tended to throw society into flux by promoting competition and upward social mobility as the hallmarks of civilization and progress. This stood in stark contrast to his conception of southern slavery, with its social hierarchy predicated on white supremacy, as the most effective means of ensuring social stability. From Brookes's vantage point northerners so often succumbed to the temptations of lust, avarice, prostitution, and free love that the region seemed a second Sodom and Gomorrah well worthy of southern derision.[15]

The North's singular hypocrisy in casting aspersions upon southern slavery most galled Brookes as he contemplated the growing sectional divide. New Englanders too, so Brookes argued, had "what they modestly call their helps," people Brookes genuinely believed had been marked out for "a state of slavery, under other names it is true, but for the most part far worse than our state of negro slavery. These [New England servants] all through life are engaged in hard and drudgery service," he continued, "for which the pittance they get barely affords food and clothes, and often through the freak of the employer, or for their own faults they are turned off, homeless and penniless, finding it difficult without a recommendation to get their heads into a shelter on any terms." He urged anyone to "go look into the back streets and crowded cellars of London, and New York, the metropolitan cities of the old and new world, not to refer you to Boston, and you will see a condition of squalidness, hunger and sickness without medical aid." Brookes thought it unfathomable that this debased northern society, as he saw it, dared to cast moral judgment on *his* native South; that northerners posited their social structure as the high road to moral righteousness, as opposed to the low (southern) road to hellfire and damnation.[16]

Brookes most resented the tendency among even northern ministers to join in the fray, with stones in one hand and the Bible in the other, ready to pillory the South for its peculiar institution: "What the clergy of the North will do with the Bible," Brookes observed, "as the text book from which the rule of human duty and obligation should be primarily drawn I cannot conceive." All of it appeared, ironically given his own delusions regarding the "proper" racial and gendered social order, a self-righteous delusion to Brookes, and one that threatened to undermine the southern social order where he believed self-mastery stood the best chance of success. The "bright galaxy of talents for which the south has long been, and is now distinguished, give the negative to the defamatory rantings of northern [radicals]," Brookes declared before concluding, "We think that instead of such barbarism [as is alleged by northerners], truth and impartial history must concede to the slaveholding states, the traits of noble-mindedness, kind-heartedness, benevolence, generosity, hospitality, politeness and polish of manners, as characteristic of citizens of the South."[17]

But such self-righteous delusion cut both ways, and despite such public proclamations of southern superiority, the specter of the North as they imagined it sometimes hit disturbingly close to home for men like Brookes. In discussing his son Walker in correspondence with an old college friend on the eve of southern secession in 1859, Iveson Brookes admitted, "I have long hoped God intends to make a preacher of him but he says he has not received a call to preach ... He derived from his grandfather a pretty property and married a Baptist girl of equal estate and is perhaps too much immersed in the world like his father to preach much." Brookes recognized that any lecture he might give his son, he had already given ineffectually to himself long ago: "On settling and engaging in planting, the devil too readily persuaded me to give up study and recover health by an active life. The result was I became too much engrossed in the finances of the world and my usefulness in the ministry has been greatly cut short."[18]

The elder Brookes had utilized this confession as a warning for his son to guard against avarice as early as 1848. At that time he had deemed the present state of commerce "truly discouraging" and called "for retrenchment and economy" before admitting that for several years he had "foolishly caught the wild mania for getting rich which so universally prevailed ... and [had gone] largely in debt on the credit system." The father then effectively asked his son to "do as I say and not as I do": he reminded him that he had "frequently cautioned [Walker] against extravagance," and was repeating that advice now: "Retrench from your course of several years passed or you will inevitably find yourself involved in pecuniary matters." "My advice to you," he finished, "is to set down to your proper course studies making decency rather than show your model of life." Brookes took solace, over a decade later, in Walker's attention to his church: "[Walker] is an active church member ... a deacon, conducts the Sunday school, leads prayer meetings and in absence of their preacher lectures the congregation." But the paths of both men to such respectable moral standing proved arduous. By the end of the 1850s they recognized more clearly than ever the very same moral failings in themselves that they so vehemently despised when they looked disparagingly at the North. The very same capitalistic greed that they believed had overrun the North threatened now more than ever to penetrate the South, corrupt its soul, and undermine its claims to mastery.[19]

In his sermons Reverend Basil Manly Sr. frequently expounded upon similar themes of youthful passion and heedless ambition and the threat they posed to allegedly sanctified southern traits, no doubt thinking of his eldest son and namesake, Basil Manly Jr., as he proffered moral advice from his Sunday pulpits. In one sermon, Reverend Manly declared, "*Character* depends on purity. Whatever reputation may be gained without it is either the *bubble of accidental circumstances*, the *whitewash of hypocrisy*, or the *dreadful distinction of devils*." In his view, "Remorse of conscience follows the sins of youth on every remembrance," but purity "stamps character with solid worth." After quoting the ninth verse of Psalm 119, which asks, "Wherewithal shall a young man cleanse his way?" Manly commented: "By the *way* of a young man is meant whatever in him is likely to be affected by purity or impurity, to his principles as well as to his conduct, his character as well as habits ... To change his way is to commit and avoid whatever may be considered *low* and *impure*."[20]

A proper religious frame of mind, then, constituted "the foundation of all true happiness and success," and Manly argued in several sermons that this foundation was best laid early in life. "Youth affords advantages for obtaining religion beyond any other period of life. The heart is then tender, the habits unformed, the attention capable of concentration," he argued, and as such, "those who come to religion late labor under many disadvantages and are wanting in the tender[ness] and beauty of religion, as well as the joy." But if instilled with an "early piety," Manly believed the mind "undergoes timely discipline, takes a holy, lovely direction, whence easy and perpetual improvements are made." Upon that rock, so he thought, innocent youth should build their faith and practice their piety, and the southern social order could rest assured of its place in the right.[21]

In most cases, Manly did not direct such messages at the youth in his flock. He, like Sylvester Graham, had sense enough to know that parents were more likely to listen and act, and Manly Sr. often wove parenting advice into his sermons. "Parents," he hectored one Sunday, this concern for the proper moral instruction and deportment of youth "is not without its interest to you. For though you may be gathered to your grave before the evil come on them ... does not the apprehension fill you with the deepest anxiety?"[22] "The character," Manly Sr. asserted, when cultivated through a religious frame of mind, "acquires all the solidarity of confirmed habit, and the young Christian is saved despair of those perpetual backslidings to which some good men are exposed."[23]

Carnality, obviously, was the besetting sin of youth, but Basil Manly Sr., like his Baptist brother Iveson Brookes, saw in himself and his son countless other failures in the face of temptations that embroiled both individual and public morality in precariousness. Ambition and greed, particularly as they looked north, had become so widely and deeply indulged that Manly Sr. feared for the soul of the nation. "'Seekest thou great things for thyself?" he asked his congregation. "Seek them not." "[We must offer] *a check to inordinate ambition* so common to young minds," he urged. "That ambition of *elevated station* is to be distinguished from a desire for true *excellence of character*. The latter is a most commendable ambition." "It is a very common temptation," as "all young minds are sanguine, romantic," to "expect and desire something considerable." But by "seeking great things" in this way, youthful minds pursue "a worse ambition, an ambition of ease and indolence at the expense of God's cause." "This should be corrected," he concluded, so as to "throw into shade all desires after wealth, fame, etc." for their own sake, and rather promote their achievement according to the designs of Providence.[24]

But in his private reflections Basil Manly Sr. revealed much about his own moral misgivings behind this public mask of self-righteous conviction. Like many preachers, Manly Sr. frequently noted his unworthiness for his calling. He wrote, in his journal: "A cold and dull frame has seized me, and long absence from duty has destroyed my facilities of connection and expression." He later complained, "Thoughts incessantly wandering. I impute the wandering state of my thoughts, which has now become a *habitual moral disease*, to the hurried and *superficial* manner in which all my reading and reflection have for some months been conducted ... and [to] occupation in worldly things." "My experience for some months has been very peculiar," Manly Sr. admitted; "my frames [of mind] have exhibited almost constant barrenness and destitution, and if a gleam of tenderness has at any time visited me it has been but seldom and momentary." He worried over this frequently depressed spiritual state precisely because of the awesome responsibility he felt as the head of a burgeoning family, the pastor of a burgeoning church, and a white man in a burgeoning slave society. If he, as a minister of the sacred gospels, constantly struggled to uphold the moral tenets of his faith and station, how could less pious men be expected to resist the temptations surrounding them within the slave South and bearing down on them from the allegedly hedonistic North?[25]

In a fashion altogether typical of religious clerics, Manly Sr. attempted to salve his fears and answer his own critique by attributing this personal spiritual discomfort to divine workings. "I think I have been made willing to walk on in darkness if this should be God's chosen method of bringing souls to the knowledge of the truth," he suggested, before confessing, "I think indeed that my proneness to pride is such that I could not *bear* both blessings at once, i.e. usefulness and personal comfort." Similar bouts with a melancholy spiritual state plagued Manly Sr. throughout his life, as he frequently expressed feelings of depression and languidness concerning his spiritual frame of mind. He attributed most of this to his own moral failings and an excessive worldly pride and consciousness.[26]

His heavy responsibility as both a biological and spiritual father only heightened the burden of what he felt to be damning evidence of his personal depravity. He well understood the familial and even sectional consequences of these personal travails. As a moral example for his family and his congregations, he personified the moral standard with which they could and should collectively combat the North. In this light, his personal failings became southern failings, and these southern failings portended the dissolution of the very authority to which he laid claim and upon which southern society itself rested.

Basil Manly Jr. eventually rivaled his father's renown as a Baptist minister and spiritual leader in the South. Their strikingly similar career paths confirmed their personal similarities, chief among them continual self-reflection and cycles of lamentation and recommitment to spiritual betterment. As a young man, Manly Jr. declared his resolve to cultivate his own sense of self-mastery: "The habits I now form, the character I now assume, and the reputation and standing among men I now acquire will be very liable to be permanent. If I can now preserve a manly, mild, honorable, and in a word Christian deportment, if I conduct myself with decency and order and prudence, I shall not only acquire a reputation for being so but will necessarily become of that temper and frame of mind." And on that foundation Manly Jr. would build his church. To achieve all his spiritual and secular goals, he took his father as his model and prioritized self-mastery in his daily walk and social worldview.[27]

Early in life, however, Manly Jr. recognized the difficulties of upholding the ideals of the moral manhood that he, like his father, professed. "*Heavenly minded men* are indeed rare," the younger Manly noted. "[Even] my [own] thoughts . . . when running in pious channels . . . on usefulness in the world [frequently stray and] piety becomes like the indistinct flashes and sudden but inconstant gleams of the Aurora Borealis." "There is nothing that grieves me more than these alternate religious and sinful frames [of mind]," he observed. "Not that I dislike the first, but the last, they give me more doubts and fears and anxieties than anything else and drive me sometimes to the very brink of despair." Manly Jr. most fervently prayed that his religion would bring an end to such self-wrangling; he wanted to surrender himself to control himself; if God would just take the helm, he could rely on faith to guide him: "[It] shall at *all times* [rule] *my affections* as well as my reason." But such capitulation contradicted his acknowledged station and duties on earth, as a son, a fledgling minister, and a white man in a slave society. Only with God's guidance could he master himself and exhibit the righteous honor required of him as a master of others dependent on his authority in this world.[28]

The vice-ridden temptations threatening to undermine this effort appear frequently in Manly Jr.'s diary—the place that captured, and sponsored, his spiritual struggles. His father had long kept a diary to give voice to certain thoughts and emotions too honest and self-disparaging for public consumption in the South. He confided to his diary as a secret receptacle for those most private of feelings. Basil Manly Jr. followed his father's example very early in life, and quickly surpassed his father in his devotion to this emotional release. His diary became for him a sort of sacramental ritual in which he confessed and confronted his deepest personal fears and most threatening moral failings. "If now when my mind is, as it were, being molded for life," he observed while in college, "I throw . . .

dirt chips and trash into the mold, so as to fill it up with anything but the right thing, when it comes into use these sticks and trash will be forever in the way. And what is more, I will know that they have taken the place of more important matters." He wrote, "[I] yielded up myself an easy prey to all kinds of temptations and have lost almost all my self-control." His diary became the primary place to express his need for self-mastery as well as his persistent failures in achieving it. It chronicled his attempt to be good while also serving as the place to confess consistent shortfalls; it provided him with a certain solace that accompanied such a record of accountability, of learning to fall and to pick himself up again in an endless cycle of despair, regret, and recommitment.[29]

In the sequestered safety of this diary Manly Jr. further confessed, "I have been sadly deficient in private duty . . . Secret sins have crept in and have met with unrestrained indulgence . . . I am indeed low down . . . The older I get and the longer I live the more evidences do I see of the perverseness of my own heart." "Passions wild and ungovernable course through my mind with a powerful yet unperceived effect," he later wrote. "Imagination calls up fanciful scenes of danger, of insult, of temptation, and then all the strong passions . . . whirl like a tempest within my bosom." That tempest proved unrelenting. He expressed his belief, "I feel a strong desire to do something in winning souls to Christ" as a minister of the gospel, and also his strong remorse: "I have *backslidden!* I have *backslidden!*"[30]

Such backsliding, as his father had long warned and he himself had consistently worried, imperiled his temporal happiness and spiritual progress. Self-mastery was rooted in unstable ground, and the slightest indulgence of vice and concession to temptation could result in irreparable moral erosion that could destroy his life and condemn his soul. Erosion of this kind—in someone aspiring to save souls and in so doing, to redeem the South in all its peculiarity—would not do and could not be permitted. Knowing that habits formed in youth could prove hard to shake, the burden of this responsibility weighed heavily upon young Manly Jr. as he confronted his own moral misgivings and prepared himself to meet the dual challenges of ministering to the slave South and defending it against aspersions—and alleged corruptions—from the North.

Basil Manly Jr. understood the inherent difficulties of bearing these burdens and meeting these challenges. "How soon, how easily, how imperceptibly does the careless Christian fall!" he commented. "With what silent, gradual enticements is he lured away from his love! Without alarming him, without shocking him, but with soothing devices and flattering suggestions, the Devil leads him on and causes him to fall." Like his father, Basil Manly Jr. struggled throughout his life to reconcile his desire for secular success with the demands of his spiritual calling. Both demanded he master himself by curbing his desires and channeling his ambitions toward morally sanctified ends. This effort to effectively exhibit and apply manly honor and piety in his daily walk, to become the man his secular standing and spiritual station decreed, personifies the ideal of righteous honor at work during the period. Only then could he speak confidently of the divine sanction attending southern institutions and ward off perceived northern threats. If he failed, southern society might fail with him and follow the North down the benighted path of excessive capitalistic aggrandizement, unchecked greed, and unrestrained passion. Abhorrent as it seemed, such a fate beckoned each time his vices overtook him, each time his morality succumbed to temptation, each time he failed to master his bodily lusts or emotional urges. Such weakness undermined his claims to authority, which endangered the southern social order that very authority purportedly upheld.[31]

As religious divines the Brookes and Manly men collectively understood and confronted, perhaps more directly than most, the complexities of a self-evident truth: that the southern virtue ensconced in their implicit ideal of righteous honor demanded white masculine self-mastery as a prerequisite for effective white supremacy and proper social order. But these ministers were not alone in their moral struggles or recognition of the stakes such struggles entailed. Some of their Edgefield neighbors and acquaintances confronted the same vices and worried over the same backsliding tendencies and their effects in the pages of the Edgefield *Advertiser*. Its editors frequently voiced their moral concerns, especially concerning alcohol abuse and the degradations it inflicted on men, their households, and the community at large. In the early spring of 1845, these editors decried "the sad events to which [they had] alluded so frequently, from wanton gambling and promiscuous sexuality to reckless violence and loss of life, [which] undoubtedly are in great measure to be ascribed to the unfortunate use of strong drink, and we hope the day is not distant when such a course of riot and confusion will no longer be felt." They resolved that "when all who are now engaged in selling, and all who drink, shall be *persuaded* to abandon their practices—then we shall be freed from occurrences" such as these.[32]

Their call for temperance seemingly fell on deaf ears, however, for fifteen years later, they again lamented "the many sad and deplorable occurrences that are brought about directly through the agency of the licensed rum shops that are scattered here and there over this otherwise great and glorious land—shops that are kept without any regard to law or order, where midnight revelry and all manner of wickedness is carried on, and where, even in the sunlight of Heaven our blessed Sabbath day is desecrated by men drunk and maddened with the poisonous drinks of the present age." "Such dens, although few and far between in this District, should be exterminated forthwith and forever," they urged, and it was "the duty of all good citizens to arise in their majesty and expugn from their community these loathsome places of resort, or see that the laws are rigidly and strictly enforced against those who may fearlessly and wantonly violate them." In their view, passions ran amuck when alcohol flowed freely, and control—of the self and society—was predicated on white men's ability to harness their passions and hold their liquor.[33]

These vices—so publicly reviled—stemmed from the same moral failings that bedeviled the families of the Reverends Brookes and Manly and seemed equally poised to rend the hearts and hearths of their nonclerical neighbors and acquaintances, the Milligan and Brooks families. Joseph Milligan Jr. achieved success as a physician in Hamburg, South Carolina, and gained considerable prestige across the Edgefield District. This success enabled him to send his son, Joseph A. S. Milligan., to medical school in Charleston. As a family of middle-class professionals and devout Presbyterians, father and son revealed in their frequent correspondence the primacy of self-mastery in their calculations of both temporal and spiritual success. "Our Lord tells us that 'a man's life consisteth not in the abundances of things which he possesseth.' It is a blunder to think that money brings happiness. Contentment only does it," Dr. Milligan wrote to his son. "If you deport yourself with dignity (*not haughtiness*, for a great mistake is often made here) and exhibit and feel in your intercourse with others a sincere desire to make them happy, and crush within yourself the tidings of a selfish spirit, you will be beloved and success will follow you." He continued, "Trust in God, and everything will come out right. If you do not trust in Him, He will thwart all your plans." In a later letter, Dr. Milligan expressed his most earnest desire: "May He guide you in the way of all truth and enable you to lead a useful life, a life of self-denial and devotion to your duties both to God and man." The doctor expected his son to deny indulgence of more secular urges, especially those of avarice for wealth and station, and to seek instead a personal piety and moral righteousness, through which all other secular success would come in time. Honor in this world—personal and professional—demanded honor to God through a pious moral bearing. Such righteous honor was best achieved through mastery of the self. Such self-mastery was the bedrock of the southern slave system and the best means of securing its purported moral sanctity as a defense against northern affronts.[34]

Joseph A. S. Milligan, however, also evinced a propensity to indulge the very desires that most threatened both his professional prospects and spiritual state. "We think his most prominent fault is that of spending money foolishly," his aunt Jane Milligan Bruns once confided to her brother, Joseph's father. "We often tell him of it, and as both you and Henry Bruns [her husband] have been very faithful in pointing out this to him, I hope he will be brought to see his error in time." Joseph's uncle, the same Henry Bruns, affirmed this tendency to prioritize secular over sacred concerns when he wrote Dr. Milligan urging him to "examine Joe's knees medically. I am afraid he is weak about those parts, as he has been in the habit of always sitting in church in time of prayer. The fashion in church with us is to stand on this occasion. If you can do any for him in this respect, pray don't neglect it."[35]

Confronted with his son's moral shortcomings, Dr. Milligan prayed, "May God bless you, and give you the inclination to persevere in the habits of industry which your friends so highly commend in you," and beseeched young Joseph to "ask the assistance of the Almighty to strengthen those habits, to correct whatever is wrong in the *motives* which actuate you, and to enable you to devote the learning and wisdom you are now acquiring to the glory of His name and the benefit of mankind." The doctor here confirmed a long-standing desire for his son: "I wish that you could be impressed with the truth that your soul is of more value to you than everything else." He later warned young Joseph against excessive pride and the avarice that so often accompanied it by observing, "There are some persons who are spoiled by commendations of the kind you are receiving. They think that under such circumstances they may safely intermit, or altogether suspend, future exertions and become inflated with vanity and self-esteem." "I trust," he concluded, "that you have too much good sense to be affected in this way, and that expressions of approbation of your moral and intellectual habits will only spur you on to higher developments of those sentiments and faculties which raise man to the position which it was originally intended he should occupy by his benevolent creator." This sense of righteous honor guided both father and son in what would become their shared professions as medical physicians and Presbyterians. As such, they comprehended both their secular professions and spiritual affinity as forms of moral stewardship and knew that such stewardship was essential to combating assaults against their society from abroad.[36]

Others outside the cloth in the Edgefield community took up the call for improved morality and stressed the tenets of righteous honor to achieve those ends. Whitfield Brooks, the antebellum patriarch of a prosperous Edgefield family dynasty, emphasized self-mastery as the cornerstone of an implied sense of righteous honor. He demanded both of himself and especially of his eldest son, Preston. "We should not neglect to employ every means that it is calculated to improve the heart and to purify it from the low passions and desires, which a love of this world and its treasures is sure to inspire," he once professed to his journal. He believed resolutely that the "one distinguishing difference between a good and bad man is, that the good man mortifies and controls his passions while the bad yields to and is governed by them." Wanton drinking, gambling, and other nefarious "pleasures" could easily enslave men to vice and immorality. The elder Brooks later assessed his eldest son accordingly, deeming him "deficient in moral energy and decision, in mental activity" and "too indulgent in more physical gratifications," before asserting, "The spiritual man must overcome the more corporeal." Whitfield Brooks thus echoed precisely the tenor of his ministerial neighbors' admonitions to their sons and mirrored the same personal tensions between honor and piety that plagued those religious divines.[37]

Though not of the same evangelical Protestant fold as the Brookes, Manly, or Milligan men, Whitfield Brooks stood as a founding member of Edgefield's more socially prestigious and emotionally reserved Trinity Episcopal Church. He nonetheless imbibed much of the pervasive evangelical Protestant ethic of his Baptist, Methodist, and Presbyterian neighbors, chiefly because he and his wife, the former Mary Parsons Carroll, had cosponsored the establishment of a Baptist church in Edgefield proper during the 1830s, contributing to that denomination's expansion in their community and bringing much of its message into their lives. Furthermore, in the absence of an Episcopal priest, or during revivals in the Edgefield evangelical churches, Whitfield frequently heard sermons by Baptist and Methodist ministers, and presumably conversed even more frequently with members of these particularly well-represented denominations in his daily affairs. A similar moral concern therefore bound the Edgefield community of faith together, and pervaded their thoughts, words, and deeds as they presided over their farms and families, all the while pondering their futures. Even the unchurched and irreligious encountered this pervasive moral concern frequently and felt its influence in myriad ways that ranged from subconscious incorporation to contentious opposition. But even in resistance, the conspicuous moral concerns of the faithful made their mark on the wider community.

Like his evangelical Protestant neighbors, Whitfield wanted his own life to serve as a fitting example for his sons to follow, and he strove to uphold the tenets befitting the "good man" he so often reiterated for himself and his progeny. The elder Brooks frequently decried the prevailing tendency toward drunkenness and debauchery in his native district, and through his diatribes he sought to deter his sons from similar transgressions. "This is sale day and so very clear and inviting that I anticipate a large gathering at the Village," he wrote in 1841, and he fully expected the day to be attended by "cases of drunkenness in the afternoon." Another sale day several months later evoked the same commentary on "several cases of drunkenness" enacted by "a number of persons collected from all quarters of the district." A particularly disdainful note in his journal recounted "a disgusting exhibition of drunkenness at the sale among the crowd generally and many instances among the self-righteous Baptists" at Stephen's Creek. Such sentiments were again aroused in the early spring of 1843 when he ruefully noted a recent pottery sale where he "learned that almost every one of the company got shamefully drunk, among whom, were some young gentleman, of whom better things and higher hopes were anticipated." Brooks rarely missed an opportunity to point out the pitfalls of drunkenness and its attending immoralities.[38]

But the father struggled to maintain the standard for himself and example to his son. In describing a party he attended in the spring of 1842, the elder Brooks noted, "There was neither wine nor other strong drink and neither seemed to be necessary to the comfort of the company. It is a good example and I am *tempted* to follow it. There would be more honor in the observance than in the break of it." In saying this, he revealed his continued preference for temperance and moderation, but implied a gnawing inability to abide by his own precepts. During the summer of 1842, Brooks recorded his attendance at "a meeting of the temperance society last evening in the Courthouse," at which the "society was dissolved and a union formed with the new mechanic's Washingtonian abstinence Society." Here Whitfield witnessed a local shift from temperance to teetotal abstention but he did not count himself among the converts.[39]

He further exhibited his weakening resolve in commenting on a Washingtonian Society meeting the following year. "A gentleman from Baltimore by the name of Carey has been lecturing in the Village on the subject of temperance to large audiences," he recorded. "I heard him on Monday night & was rather pleased with the tenor and scope of his remarks and particularly with his explanation of the principles, on which the Washingtonian temperance society was organized." He further noted, "It is regarded in the light of a social reform, to be affected by social and voluntary associations, disconnected & independent of both church and State," but expressed reservations that "he [Mr. Carey] is not however the plain, unpretending and simple-hearted man, that he has been represented, who tells his story of sorrow and suffering in modest subdued & heart touching language but his vanity induces him to play the actor and occasionally to aspire to the honors of the orator." Brooks then concluded, "I fear that he is converting what was at first a disinterested experiment in the cause of benevolence, into a trade for making money. The moment he loses sight of his original purpose and prostitutes his powers to selfish ends, he becomes a contemptible mountebank."[40]

Brooks's reservations apparently found public voice later that month when he noted, "No news except in regard to a little dissatisfaction between the Temperance and non-temperance portions of the Villagers in regard to some proceeding of the former in relation to the observance, not celebration, of the 4th of July" upcoming. By September, Brooks despaired that "a more riotous, drunken, and fighting company have not been seen in the public square in five years." This prevailing spirit of intemperance literally came close to home the following spring when Brooks reported "evidence of a good deal of drunkenness through the sense of hearing as many noisy and drunken men passed my house," while the following Fourth of July celebrations witnessed "a large quantity of ardent spirits drank." At a temperance convention held in Edgefield that August, Brooks professed, "[I was] much entertained and gratified with the proceedings ... and here record my approbation of their principles and purposes." "I was an attentive observer and listener and really at last was very much in the condition of Agrippa before Paul—'I was almost persuaded to give my signature to the pledge.'"[41]

But pledge he did not, for after a party given by Colonel Andrew Pickens the following November, Brooks noted, "His dinner was excellent and his wines various and choice," but its consequence painful: "a paroxism of headache from which I suffered through the entire day." He observed,

"It is a great drawback upon my happiness that I cannot participate in the social pleasures of the festive board without paying a heavy penalty in suffering the succeeding day, be my indulgence ever so temperate and cautious." Despite continued interest in and support of the local temperance movement, Whitfield Brooks stopped short of taking the abstinence pledge, and failed to curb his indulgence at the "festive board."[42]

Perhaps his own alcoholic indulgence heightened his sensitivity to such abuses in his midst, for Brooks continued to decry the local prevalence of an intemperate spirit. "I returned home in the afternoon," he noted in the winter of 1845, "witnessing on the road several exhibitions of drunkenness and immorality, [schocking?] to the feelings of every friend of good order and social reform and improvement." In the spring he again deplored this local propensity for alcoholic excess when he observed "an exhibition of beastly drunkenness, discreditable to the District and offensive to the eye of decency. The temperance societies," he continued, "have reformed a portion of the drinking community but the other portion now drink to greater excess, than formerly and in their drunken debaucheries have less regard for decency and public opinion than they ever had." Temperance and moderation promised temporal success and spiritual salvation, but such restraint proved difficult to enact and even harder to sustain. His own lapses only heightened his anxieties over the moral failings of others, none more so than those of his eldest son. All seemed to threaten the moral foundation of southern society at large, a threat only aggravated by ever-more frequent reports of northern derision of the slave South. If Brooks and his sons couldn't control themselves, if their neighbors continued in their debauches, how could they justify their gender and racial prerogatives against criticism from abroad? How could they win the sectional conflict over the nation's moral destiny?[43]

For men like Whitfield Brooks, success in that conflict and the promise of the future rested with their sons, and as the eldest son in the Brooks family, Preston Brooks bore the lion's share of this burden. Preston sorely felt the weight of these expectations throughout his life, and frequently expressed his admiration for his father's honorable and pious example. Despite his father's personal bouts with intemperance and immoderation, Preston still declared to his diary, "He is a model character for purity and justice," and "a better husband and father never lived." Upon his father's death in 1851, Preston expressed thirty-two years of pent-up feelings for one he had so long revered and from whom he had inherited his own sense of righteous honor and the burden of expectations it entailed. "May

God bless the best of Fathers and truest of men with all the rewards permissive to the 'just man,'" he prayed at Christmas in 1851. "God bless him. Even in his suffering and near approach to death, he takes interest in all family matters like a well man." Just three days later, Whitfield passed away, prompting Preston to declare, "It pleased God to release my beloved father from the suffering he had been enduring for years past. I was with him during the last day & a half & he died in my arms. A kinder parent never lived nor a juster man than Whitfield Brooks."[44]

In reflecting on his father's model of the righteous honor ideal, Preston turned his thoughts inward, fervently praying in his journal, "God grant that the blessing which my father bestowed on me, with his hand on my head, may stimulate me to be in his language 'an upright, virtuous man' and that I may emulate his example and meet [him] in Heaven! . . . Oh! May my life be as honorable and useful and my end be as composed and confident as his was." In his lifelong attempt to live up to their mutual ideal of manhood, Preston evinced a fervent commitment to, if faltering attainment of, the same righteous honor he attributed to his "noble father."[45]

The moral demands of that implicit ideal, and his perceived inability to meet them, plagued Preston throughout his life. He often grappled with his father's earlier assessment of his character, as evidenced by an 1849 confession to his diary: "I have not been well for nearly a year. I am a great sinner but trust in the all atoning blood of an immaculate Savior to blot out my past transgressions and fervently pray that He will enable me to lead a new life, to discharge my duty with honesty and propriety, and to become one whose walk may be viewed even as a holy man." He admitted, "This looks strange from me but I feel what I write and 'His blood can redeem, though our sins be like scarlet and made white as snow.'" He then declared, "I rose this morning with strong feelings of gratitude to my Heavenly Father for the innumerable blessings He has given me in almost everything I could desire, but especially for His continued forbearance towards my multitudinous and oft-repeated sins, and His permitting me to live in comfort when justice might long since have cast me off." "[I] hope yet to be known to the wicked of the world as an avowed consistent and humble Christian and that my own heart and my daily acts may be my most steadfast approvers." Strengthened by this resolve, he proclaimed, "Now I feel right!" In the same journal entry, however, he confided the utter lack of faith he felt in being able to hold fast to this newfound spiritual resolve: "What a commentary it is upon the sinfulness of my nature and the villainy of humanity, when my understanding tells me that should temptation assail me, I will sin grievously before night. Oh! Deliver me from temptation and make me, my Father, such as I know happiness, respectability, earthly and heavenly good but reasonably require."[46]

Preston knew as well as his father had that there was more than just individual happiness and salvation at stake; the sanctity of southern families, the stability of southern society, and the moral fate of the nation hung in the balance. His personal struggle to overcome temptation personified to considerable degree the white South's struggles to overcome its faults and present a united, morally justifiable front against northern aspersion, and to defend itself against the threat of perceived northern corruptions. For Brooks, his infamous caning of Massachusetts's famed abolitionist Senator Charles Sumner several years after these diary entries would release a lifetime of frustrations on that score into one violent moment, and for many southerners it would stand as *the* symbolic defense of those contentious southern claims to higher moral virtue at the height of the sectional crisis.

Collectively, these fathers and sons exhibited the tensions that pervaded conceptions of ideal white southern manhood in the Civil War era and personified the struggle to uphold the sense of righteous honor such manhood commanded. By emphasizing their ability to achieve self-mastery as the basis of their patriarchal authority, the Brookes and Manly men vividly illustrated the emotional convergence of personal and public honor and piety, as well as the central role these ethics played in dictating the moral tenets of masculine virtue in the slave South. Threatened at every turn by vice, these men strove to attain the manly virtues inherent in their sense of righteous honor and did so as part of their larger effort to sustain their privileged place in the southern social order. Their particular experience as ministers captured the most explicit merging of these white southern values but pointed toward a broader white masculine experience of moral tension that enveloped minister and master, planter and professional alike during the antebellum era. The Milligan and Brooks men experienced this more secular tension between honor and piety. All called Edgefield home for formative periods, if not all, of their lives, and reflected its particular history of honor and religiosity in their intensely emotional pursuit of personal and public moral righteousness. Their own consciences, their Edgefield ties, and their southern sectional identity all led them to embrace a sense of righteous honor in defining manhood and claiming self-mastery as justification for the patriarchal privileges and racial power embedded in that ideal.[47]

Their sense of righteous honor deluded them, however, with regard to the sanctity of their cause and the wickedness of the North. In their eyes, the North embodied the debased results of unrestrained lust and greed; the corruption of true religious faith and piety; the complete loss of honor. Despite reading the same Bible and praying to the same God, despite battling the same vices and coveting the same virtues, white men north and south increasingly drew upon these common moral teachings to serve fundamentally different ends that reinforced their sectional identity in opposition to the enemy images they simultaneously developed of one another. Those identities and those images both revolved around the contentious subject of slavery—as an economic and social system as well as a political and moral issue—and its place in the nation's increasingly sectionalized present, as well as its fate in the increasingly divergent sectional visions for that nation's future.

5

The Conundrum of Slavery

Sanctioning Violence on Moral Grounds

> They are surrounded by their bondsmen and dependents; and the customary intercourse of society familiarizes their minds to the relation of high and low degree.
> —John Pendleton Kennedy, *Swallow Barn* (1832)

In 1821 Basil Manly Sr., while still at college, revealed nascent antislavery sentiments in a text he composed on southern slavery: "Slavery is an evil under which this country has long groaned. Introduced at first from motives of avarice, it had been perpetuated in this country partly as a convenience, partly through necessity, without exciting, till within a few years past, any general apprehension. But now, its prevalence and continual increase are such as compels us to ask, whether there be not danger in its further continuance, while the injuries inflicted on its wretched victims make the long-neglected appeal to the feelings of humanity to devise, if possible, a plan for its removal." He recognized particularly the regional lines beginning to harden on the question, claiming, "If contending parties are not reconciled, the fair fabric of our Union (I shudder to think of it) must totter to its basis."[1]

Basil Manly Sr. was born into a family of enslavers, and eventually became an enslaving patriarch in his own right. In many respects he embodied a generation of leading white southern men who had been the first to marry prevailing forms of masculine honor to emerging modes of evangelical Protestant morality amid an increasingly prevalent sectionalism; the first, too, to bend honor's more primal virility in compliance with religious moral mandates; and the first to conceive of religious piety in the context of a ritualized honor code. His generation implicitly modeled the antebellum South's nascent sense of righteous honor. As such, Manly Sr. and his peers had been woefully aware of their cultural contradictions. They were enslavers who persisted in proclaiming that all men were created equal in their right to life, liberty, and the pursuit of happiness; they were men of honor prone to excessive pride and passion, who denounced violence but often made recourse to it in defense of honor; and they were men who could see slavery as an evil, though they continued to believe it a necessary one.[2]

Once antislavery sentiments and abolitionist harangues began to issue forth from northern pulpits, presses, and parlors with greater frequency and urgency beginning in the 1830s, however, such self-criticism among white southerners smacked of treason. Men like Basil Manly Sr. strove to inculcate their sons with a sense of righteous honor, but as sectional tensions heightened, this carefully balanced moral ethic—perpetually strained—threatened to break under the pressure. All northern critiques of the slave South became part of the abolitionist menace in the white southern mind, an affront to southern honor and a potential perversion of southern morality. This menace was, for many leading white southern men, unbecoming, threatening, and insulting, and it warranted a response, one that should and would be in accordance with their implicit righteous honor ideal.[3]

Reverend Manly Sr.'s son, Basil Manly Jr., personified this tumultuous shift away from self-criticism toward self-justification and self-defense. Whereas his father's generation had been allowed to look inward in their attempts to reconcile contradictions and correct moral wrongs, Basil Manly Jr.'s generation considered such self-doubt perilous. The persistent evidence of personal failings and social deficiencies only heightened their anxiety as they desperately attempted to thwart the northern threat. This generation gap became a pivotal factor in shaping how Basil Manly Jr. and many of his peers ultimately decided that withdrawal from the American Union was their best, though perhaps most desperate, chance of successfully reconciling their ideals and their institutions. But even as the sons began to mistrust their fathers' tendency to express these doubts, they nonetheless hungered for paternal advice and craved paternal models that might provide some, any, means of resolving their personal misgivings over slavery's internal contradictions. And despite the apparent divergence in their conception of slavery and the most expedient means of characterizing it, many if not most of these southern fathers resembled Manly Sr.

Photograph of Rev. Basil Manly Jr., undated. (Boyce Digital Library, Southern Baptist Theological Seminary, Louisville, KY)

in eventually guiding then following their sons' course by jettisoning previous ambivalence centered on slavery as a "necessary evil" and embracing a more overt and aggressive proslavery defense predicated on slavery as a "positive good."[4]

For Manly Sr., slavery had at one time in his youth seemed, as he phrased it in his college oration, "utterly repugnant to the spirit of our republican institutions." Like Thomas Jefferson before him, Manly Sr. took some solace in the notion that slavery had been thrust upon the South, particularly by the British, leaving his society with a moral conundrum. Slavery, so he had claimed to believe, was obviously bad for the enslaved. But, again like Jefferson, he also saw its degrading potential for white society. "Who can say," he said, "that some such and powerful combination will not trample on the liberties and privileges of the common people, whom many are even now learning to consider little superior to their slaves."[5]

Added to this anxiety was the readily observable fact, as he saw it at that time, that "the slave population, increasing so much faster than that of the white, will almost certainly be dangerous to the lives and liberties of the people of this country." He admitted that "in their present uninformed state, little danger need be apprehended from an insurrection of the slaves.

But they are becoming gradually more and more informed," especially as "their daily intercourse with their masters and observations of manners and customs, their necessary employments, their privileges, nay their very opinions will become the means of improvement to them." Armed with the very revolutionary rhetoric generally held sacred in American hearts throughout the early republic and into the early antebellum era, Manly Sr. had little trouble imagining their "ardor and enthusiasm naturally arising out of such considerations," and supposing them "able to number a population equal to that of the white," assuming they would be thus "prepared for any act of violence to which a long oppression can prompt a revengeful mind." Overburdened by this fear of racial vengeance, and referring specifically to the Santo Domingo slave revolt, Manly Sr. argued that, "if the emancipation and transportation of slaves be necessary to the permanent safety and interest of our country, we should be justifiable in sending them," and "emancipation can at least be defended on this principle."[6]

But alongside this animating fear was a nettlesome sense of moral responsibility. He stated that "justice demands it at our hands for that ill-fated people, and their injuries and long servitude call upon us loudly . . . not only to restore to them the enjoyment of their ancient rights and privileges, but along with these, to endeavor according to our ability to bestow on them the blessings of civil and religious society." He stated, as a given, that "the fault of our ancestors, or of the universe, cannot disannul the law of Heaven which brings all men into this world equally free," and, from this, argued that "however the laws of inheritance sanctioned by the Constitution . . . and the improbability of effecting their emancipation at once, may palliate the charge of tyranny and injustice to which we are exposed, they can never wholly vindicate us from it." "Nor," he continued, "can they for a moment free us from the obligation of attempting to serve the cause of freedom in every practicable method."[7]

But this question of "what is a practicable method—one which promises to serve the double purpose of our safety and their freedom," remained unanswered, even unanswerable, in his mind. As he said at the time, "To invest [enslaved people] with the privileges of freedom in promiscuous distribution amongst us, or to assign them a territory even in the remotest of our western wilds, would be fatal either to them or ourselves. So that the question of emancipation at length resolves itself into that of colonization at a distance from us."[8] "I cannot avoid indulging the pleasing anticipation," he concluded, "that in the progress of civilization, of liberty and religion, which are all engaged to support this cause, the time may yet arrive when the government may with propriety declare herself the friend of universal emancipation."[9]

Reverend Manly Sr.'s friends and Edgefield associates had at various times expressed similar misgivings regarding the evil tendencies of the southern slave system. Manly Sr.'s professional associate, sometime Edgefield neighbor, and personal friend, the Baptist minister Iveson L. Brookes once declared "when at Chapel Hill I was a sort of abolitionist." Their Edgefield associate Whitfield Brooks revealed a similar uncertainty concerning the morality of slavery when he described its inherent travails. "It is a difficult task to perform our duties towards [the slaves] of our household with reference to their proper and necessary government and to our sense of humanity," he noted; "Without the enforcement of perfect subordination the slave becomes unruly and troublesome and the rigid enforcement of discipline is painful and distasteful to the owner so that upon the whole it is often a conflict between duty and feeling." All three men expressed genuine reservations regarding southern slavery, but as patriarchal enslavers all, each would also resort to paternalistic expressions regarding fulfillment of the mutual responsibilities assigned to self-proclaimed masters and those they enslaved as the best means of resolving the dilemma.[10]

All three southern elders increasingly felt compelled to lay these reservations aside as northern abolitionist critiques of southern slavery emerged in the late 1820s and 1830s and intensified the more general antislavery sentiment already present there. Each of these elder white southern men eventually developed staunch proslavery positions that applied a sense of righteous honor to the moral dilemma presented by southern slavery amidst the burgeoning sectional divide. Each sought to instill this perspective in the rising generation. But the result, for both fathers and sons, never approached the moral certainty they so often projected and so earnestly sought. Their sense of moral righteousness and grievance, allegedly affirmed by their patriarchal prerogatives, failed to fully silence the inherent moral tensions of their ideals, which fundamentally informed their identities as white southern men embroiled in the sectional struggle for the future of slavery and the nation.[11]

That struggle began not with abstract political principles but with deeply personal moral philosophies. As Whitfield Brooks privately expressed to his journal in the fall of 1840: "The happiness or misery of man depends more on his physical organization and temper of mind, than upon the accidental circumstances of State or conditions in which he is placed." "Self-possession and acquiescence amidst and to the changes and conditions of life, which lie beyond our power of prevention or control," he continued, "is the best possible philosophy for the contentment or happiness of the subject." In other words, a man must content himself with his station in life and strive to maximize his potential within that sphere of influence. Only then would he find the peace and tranquility attending success and happiness. It is ironic, even telling, that Brooks's advice to himself to surrender to circumstance undoubtedly echoed his advice to those he enslaved. Both he and they, so the paternalistic argument went, had had little to say in defining their respective roles, but such was the lot ordained for them, and the duty of man—master and servant alike—was to fulfill his role without question. "The world is thus" has ever been a powerful argument for those who effectively order the world in their collective, daily decisions, and Brooks personified the type in the antebellum South.[12]

The only thing that remained for white southern enslavers, then, was to accept the station to which they had risen and to dutifully exercise its paternalistic responsibilities and, conveniently, its patriarchal prerogatives. The hardest thing to master, of course, was the household of the self from whence all else purportedly sprang. Whitfield Brooks made the connection explicit when he noted, "Political consistency is the rarest of all virtues in the life of a public man" and life's temptations, especially in "the game of politics" tended to "gradually undermine and sap the moral principle." In observing various public figures in his native Edgefield, he saw that time and again a man would "become the antipode of himself in his political opinions, principles and conduct and yet can look at the change without a blush or a feeling of shame." This, in his view, would not do. For to "preserve the Soul's whiteness is one of the first dictates of Sound wisdom, if we wish a peaceful conscience." Only certain men were capable of achieving the level of self-awareness and self-mastery that fully justified, in their own minds, their considerable social control as patriarchal enslavers.[13]

Believing that divine wisdom emanated from these philosophies, men such as Whitfield Brooks, Iveson Brookes, and Basil Manly Sr. had searched most of their lives for confirmation of their own moral righteousness. In ministering to his flocks, Reverend Manly Sr. had often encountered what he perceived as signs of the Lord's work among the Black members of his church. Early in his career, he took special notice of two such cases. The first involved an enslaved preacher named Sambo Deas, whose story Manly Sr. declared himself "very much impressed in hearing." "He was licensed in writing by Dr. [Richard] Furman to preach to coloured persons," Manly Sr. remembered, "and while in the exercise of this duty he was seized by a patrol, and very severely whipped, and his license taken from him. He said before the church afterward, that the Lord so strengthened him, he severely felt the lashes as they laid open his flesh, that he could bear ten times as much for Christ." After praising several other sacrificial acts on the part of this Sambo Deas, Reverend Manly happily reported that "the old man died in the enjoyment of that peace" which comes from a life well-lived according to divine teachings.[14]

Just months later Manly Sr. recorded another case involving an enslaved member of his church named Langford, who had served the church for years, according to Manly Sr., as sexton. "This day came to see me in some distress of mind one of the oldest coloured members of our church," Manly recounted before detailing Langford's personal history as it was known to him. Native to Africa, he had been orphaned at an early age, and sold into slavery at just eight or ten years old. "On the passage," Manly narrated, "a dreadful storm arose which prevented any from standing on deck. While the slaves were in the hold the Captain and sailors went into the cabin, and [Langford] heard them saying, 'Oh! Lord, Oh! Lord!' He knew not then the language, or what it meant, yet he remembered the words." Manly Sr. then moved the narrative several years forward, when a young Langford was confronted by an elderly Black member of the Baptist Church about his relationship to Christ. "'Do you know Jesus Christ?' He said 'no.' He was tempted to say 'yes' as he thought he might by that means get rid of the old woman's exhortation, but conscience triumphed, and he answered promptly 'no.' The old woman then spoke further to him, and from that moment conviction fastened on his mind. He felt his sin, and his lost estate." Manly Sr. gleaned personal and religious meaning from the old man's tale, giving a full account of it: "Now it came to his mind that this very person who was teaching him his need, was the one that the Captain and Sailors had called Lord ... Not long after Jesus revealed himself to him. He joined the church." Manly then expressed with awe his belief that "the old man has been a great blessing to his colour ... [and] It is truly affecting to hear the old man tell all his travail, and all the goodness of God to him, and see him weep for his want of love." Manly concluded, "He seems to bless God for bringing him to this country, slave as he has been; and I believe he has ever maintained a truly pious course."[15]

In both cases, Manly Sr. interpreted the stories of these enslaved people through the prism of his own sense of righteous honor and assumptions of white supremacy. From his deeply prejudiced perspective, their benighted state of enslavement, and the admittedly horrific trials inflicted upon them thereof, were but God's way of bringing them into the light of Christ. It was their cross to bear. In this perverse logic, the very existence of the slave system proved the salvation of these enslaved souls. Without bondage, so Manly Sr. surmised, these enslaved people would have remained lost in the spiritual darkness of a heathen land. And what's more, as he garnered from the personal history of Langford, these enslaved people themselves counted their enslavement and subsequent introduction to Christ among God's blessings. To his mind, his sense of righteous honor sanctioned *both* his patriarchal power to enslave, as well as his paternalistic responsibility to morally instruct those he enslaved.

Reverend Manly Sr.'s interpretations and perspectives resonated with many of his Edgefield associates and white southern brethren. A fellow Baptist itinerant, Reverend William P. Hill, frequently took note of the religious exercises of the enslaved in traversing the Edgefield District. Many of these observations reflected on the relationship between patriarchal control of the enslaved and the perceived parallel duty to instruct them in the sacred mysteries. In one note on a local planter named "Brother L. Ayer," Hill recorded that "his servants had a house in which they met 3 nights in each week for worship. [Three] of his men read the Scriptures and exhort and pray with their fellow servants. I agreed to preach for them." He then recounted, "After tea, a servant (the leader) met me at the door with a candle and conducted me to their house of worship, where I found all the servants collected, singing. I preached during the service [and] they were remarkably attentive." Reverend Hill then remembered with satisfaction, "After leaving the pulpit several came to me and expressed their thankfulness for the service rendered," and declared, "On this plantation, the servants are contented, well fed, and moderately worked, which is the general character of the neighborhood." So long as enslavers fulfilled their paternalistic responsibilities, so the prevailing logic went, slavery represented not a blight upon humanity but a benefit to mankind.[16]

Whitfield Brooks included a similarly self-righteous account in his journal in 1844. "Mrs. B[rooks] directed all our little negroes to be dressed this morning and to attend at Sunday school. It was no unpleasant sight to a benevolent mind," he reflected, "to see them with clean dresses and newly combed heads marching towards the Church, to meet the Pastor and his assistants, their faces beaming with smiles and gratification." From such paternalistic gratification he then turned to assess his patriarchal position by asserting, "We and our household are in health and enjoying a reasonable share of success and prosperity in whatever appertains to this life. I humbly pray unto God that he would keep us in such a subdued and thankful frame of mind, so that we may never be unmindful or insensible to his great blessings and of our utter and total dependence upon his munificent hand."[17]

He returned to the theme two years later when he reflected upon the day's survey of his plantation and crops. Accompanied by several local planters and friends, Brooks had observed with glee the progress and overall success of his domain. "I cannot close my remarks, without noting the fact, that this excursion was one of the most instructive and agreeable in which I have participated for many a day. The weather was clear and mild and the company intelligent and entertaining," he reflected before concluding: "They ought to occur more frequently as a means of social improvement and as a stimulus to our agents and negroes, who are made to take pride in the exhibition of a good crop and well-ordered plantation." Despite confessing that he felt "warranted in pronouncing [his own crop] the most inferior one that [he had] ever had at this period of the year," he nevertheless seemed buoyed by his friends' favorable appraisals. His gratification on this score seemingly paled only in comparison to the personal satisfaction he gained from the proper mode by which it had been accomplished. In his view, he presided over a well-ordered household, peopled by industrious servants and contented dependents who all looked up to him with pride in their hearts. This, so he thought, was the embodiment of domestic peace and racial harmony, such as only could come from a well-managed slave system.[18]

Only an anxious concern for his sons Preston and Whitfield Jr. as they served with General Winfield Scott's army in its Mexican War campaign could dim his otherwise heady outlook on life in 1847. And yet even amid this anxiousness he sought and found solace in the perceived affirmation of his paternalistic vision. In what would prove to be the last letter he received from his son while the young man yet lived, a still apparently healthy Whitfield Jr. wrote his father with encouraging words about his most faithful slave in May of 1847. "Our son Whitfield . . . wrote in fine spirits, informing us his health was never better. He also makes a favorable report . . . of my old Servant Joseph, whom I have owned for thirty years. He states that he has been faithful and attentive and contented to remain with his young Master Whitfield with great cheerfulness because he thought that I would be better satisfied, than for him to return." Whitfield Sr. then declared of Joseph, "He has been a faithful servant to me and carries out his fidelity to my children, which is very gratifying to my feelings and for which he shall receive a due reward." Such loyalty, he believed, could not be bought or compelled, but had to be earned through intimate relation and cultivated through genuine exchange of feeling.[19]

In such soothing examples of moral sanctity and sanctimoniousness, these Edgefield fathers had taken their solace. But they had also been constantly confronted with the ominous reality that could tear it all apart. In the winter of 1833, Basil Manly Sr. had, for instance, finally closed the book on a case that had troubled him for several years. He made special note that he had recently purchased a woman named Lydia Frierson from a Mr. Asa Russ, "one of the heirs of Mr. Frierson," the woman's previous enslaver. Reverend Manly Sr. noted with pleasure that the woman now served as "our worthy and respected old nurse," a role she would fill until her death six years later. Earlier in the summer of 1829, he had first mentioned this woman in his church journal, "who in the honesty of her heart confesses to me that her master *compels* her to live in constant adultery with him." He observed that she was a member of the church and seemed "broken-hearted on account of [her master's repeated rapes]. Although this was a secret known only to God and herself . . . she has abstained from communion for years on account of it." Manly Sr. then recounted his incredibly naive response wherein he had "advised her to remonstrate kindly with her master, and firmly and decidedly to tell him that she could not consent to sin if he would not hear her mild remonstrance." Predictably, Manly later reported that she had "been to me today to say that she has used every means in her power, and that he threatens her most dreadfully if she resisted him. I assured her that it is better for her to die, than to sin, [and] that she surely can prevent the evil if she be resolute and firm," before saying, "God will not hold her guiltless while any possible means of preventing it, even to the risk of life itself, remains untried." Obviously Manly Sr. was obtuse enough not to see that he was blaming a woman for her own repeated rape; nor did such events quite coalesce in his mind to an indictment of the whole slave system. But such examples gradually did eat at the corners of his conscience and threatened to erode the foundations of his sense of righteous honor and the virtues it purportedly ensured. His purchase of Lydia Frierson fits squarely within his conception of paternalistic duty, but likely also served to salve his troubled conscience.[20]

Nearly two full decades later, the pastor confronted a similarly uncomfortable reality that exposed the tensions between his paternalistic claims and his patriarchal prerogatives when he declared, "My mind is made up on several points, with relation to the . . . nearly 40 negroes of all sorts, some of which I must keep, whom I cannot separate, and I would not know what to do with the money if I were to sell them." He resolved to settle them on a farm somewhere in the Alabama countryside, as he saw "no alternative . . . but to keep them, dispose of them safely to myself, beneficently to them, and make the best of a necessity that I can no longer wade or defer." In explanation of this decision, he expressed his "wish to settle them in . . . such a region as would be desirable for health and religious institutions." "I do not wish to place them in a region . . . of interminable negro quarters, without the neighborhood of churches, the practicability of religious instructions, and the meliorating influences, except the lash of the overseer." "I will not place people in such a situation if I can help it," he said, "for they have no defense but the protection of the master; and this would look like delivering over the sheep to the wolves for safe keeping." "It would not be an insufferable difficulty," he concluded, "provided the place were in itself desirable, and surrounded with adequate religious advantages for *that class of people*." The nature of southern slavery dictated that even the most conscientious of enslavers, as Manly at least appeared to be in this case, found themselves engaged in constant combat with what was possible (and often most profitable) according to their patriarchal prerogatives, and what was morally right (or at least tenable) according to their paternalistic ideals, inherently prejudiced though they were.[21]

By emphasizing their concerted, self-sacrificing efforts to wield their patriarchal prerogatives toward paternalistic ends, men like Manly Sr. sought to somehow quarantine the slave system from itself, and they from it. Believing they constituted a model for others to emulate, they felt justified in defending the morally righteous potential of the slave system even as they felt compelled to criticize its most egregious moral transgressions. The next generation could not afford to toe this tenuous line or play these treacherous mental games. The issue had become too pressing, too personal, too pivotal for white southern sons like Basil Manly Jr. to prevaricate any longer. For every good reason, the North and the enslaved themselves saw past temporizing for precisely what it was, and they now sought to precipitate a crisis at once as psychological as material. That privileged white southern men experienced these very personal and highly emotional travails in a time of immense public turmoil drove many in their efforts to place their proclaimed southern virtues on firmer ideological ground. They did so by simultaneously emphasizing their own self-mastery as justification for their enactment of righteous violence, a complementary moral and ethical perspective at the center of their more assertive sense of righteous honor.

By 1844 Basil Manly Jr. observed the perceived abolitionist threat at the heart of national discussions over slavery's future as a student at the Newton Theological Institute in Massachusetts. "I see that the Christian Reflector, published in Boston, announced a prize of 25 dollars for the best essay on, 'The Motives Which Should Induce Christians at the South to Make Efforts for the Abolition of Slavery,'" he noted before saying, "I suppose [the author] intends to circulate it far and wide among us poor benighted Southerners, and thereby rouse us to action." Manly Jr. then declared, ambivalently, "I wish heartily he could. I wish light will spread among us to rouse us to our duty and to cause us, not perhaps to liberate [the slaves] but to send them the word of God and to give them better instruction in the principles of the doctrines of Christ. I should like to say something about this. I may some of these days."[22]

That day finally came in Richmond, Virginia, ten years later when Manly Jr., by then a leading Baptist minister and educator in that bustling city, publicly acknowledged how closely his subject of "The South in the Nation" would "come home to every man's life and daily thoughts." "It cannot be disguised either from ourselves or others that the citizens of the Southern states of this Confederacy stand, in a moral position, not only peculiar but isolated and alone." He then explained what must have been glaringly apparent to his audience after thirty years of political turmoil and the more recent controversy in Kansas. "Amid much that we have in common with other nations and with other parts of our own nation," Manly Jr. explained, "there are some facts in our case, so prominent in their distinctiveness and so influential in their bearing as to mark us for a peculiar destiny. Whatever that destiny may be, it is the part of manliness not to shrink from it."[23]

In playing that "part of manliness," Basil Manly Jr. and his generation perceived a growing crisis, one that they feared would rock them and their society to its core. Reared in a tradition that exalted past achievements and human progress with equal fervor, Basil Manly Jr. felt the burden of that tradition bearing down upon him with each and every rhetorical salvo fired across the sectional divide. In giving voice to this burden he tried desperately to salve his troubled mind and soul by declaring, "We are apt to feel too little our connection with the past, and with one another, and to look on ourselves as solitary individuals living in an isolated present," but, he continued, "the connections between us and our fellow men are almost infinitely numerous. No man liveth to himself. Each influences and is influenced by all the remainder ... Nor does this influence die with the death of individuals." "We stand upon the building of former ages," and "they have not lived in vain," for "other generations shall come after us whose feet shall rest upon that which our hands have built." Here then Manly recognized and verbalized an eternal truth: the past is created *in the present* with a thousand choices made and *un*made.[24]

Indeed, the trouble for Basil Manly Jr. stemmed from his father's generation and their grossly indecisive views on southern slavery. They had lamented and wrung their hands and declared slavery "an evil they knew not well how to deal with." How then was Manly Jr. to convince himself that his traditions, handed down by his father, were sound; that southern slavery as an institution *was* just, though the southern founders had said that it wasn't; that he (and other) so-called Christian masters *were* divinely ordained to shore up what was once understood to be an evil, not by debating its merits (as their fathers had done) but by defending them?[25]

"We are not what or where our fathers were. We have the experience of the ages that are passed," Manly Jr. tried to explain in Richmond in 1854, as much to himself as to his assembled audience. "We stand on the shoulders of the giants that were on the earth, and have an advantage over them, even though intellectually their inferiors." But with all those alleged advantages, Manly Jr.'s generation was, except for the more desperate sectional situation, little different from his father's—flawed, struggling, self-justifying, half-denying, half-acknowledging, always-temporizing, always delaying, always shrugging and throwing up their hands at all that has been "thrust" upon them by God and circumstance, never allowing all that *was* in their power—all because tomorrow was another day, with bills to pay and children to send to school. "It is a cheering thought if we have faith to believe," he asserted, "that there is a law of progress in human nature according to which God is bringing to pass all things and it is a glorious thing to look at history thus in the light of its relations to God's principles." Thus, as helplessly as his father before him, did Manly Jr. lay the entire dilemma at the feet of the Almighty.[26]

Basil Manly Jr. earnestly sought to see himself and his native region in a morally righteous light. He yearned for the moral and ethical fortitude and forbearance he ascribed to self-proclaimed white Christian masters, that he and they might render southern slavery not as a blight upon human history but as the progression of the exalted principles inherited from past generations. Such paternalistic aspirations, he hoped and prayed, might soften the roughest edges of his native South's peculiar institution and patriarchal order, and in so doing redeem it in the eyes of both his God and his fellow men. By 1854 he could not deny, however, that the South stood increasingly alone on the planet in this endeavor. In that same Richmond, Virginia, address he explicitly acknowledged this fundamental point of sectional demarcation from national and international trends: "Leaving untouched now all influences which grow out of the general spirit of the age, and all which affect us in common with other portions of our country, I propose to consider *the Peculiar Agencies operating on Southern Character*," the foremost among them emanating from "our social constitution . . . an institution of slavery" by which "we are separated from almost all the civilized world."[27]

Basil Manly Jr. could never quite admit that maybe the South found itself isolated precisely because it actually stood on the wrong side of history. He sought his solace, the way his father did, in the notion that "the world is thus," never admitting "thus have I made the world." And so, many of his generation lost their grasp on rational logic in ways their fathers had largely avoided. Forced by the sectional tumult that enveloped their generation to more directly confront and more effectively minimize their inconsistencies, they consistently proved unable to reconcile the ideological and cultural contradictions embedded in their "way of life," so they increasingly lashed out at any who pointed out the contradictions. But such defensiveness hardly precluded more private confessions admitting these persistent inconsistencies. Their inability to wholly ignore these contradictions, despite their best efforts to either explain or reform them out of existence by implicitly casting themselves, their society and culture in the light of righteous honor, only further exposed their faults and failures and intensified their frustrations.[28]

Basil Manly Jr. was deeply ambivalent about the ways in which living in a slave society had stamped his own peculiar character. In 1844, when a school friend was called out in front of his peers for failing to return a library book, Manly Jr. had concluded, "I am happy that it was not I who was thus roughly treated, for I should have been apt to make some harsh reply, which I should regret having done . . . *but such things will not do.*" Manly Jr. had then explained this righteous indignation over the affair: "Taken in connection with the *tone and manner,* the *public time and place* at which it was uttered, seems to me an outrage on Newhall's feelings. Because one of us, for the convenience of the rest undertakes a duty of this kind, he is not thereby *degraded to the level of a slave*, and liable to be publicly taunted and called to account in that way." Despite his claims to superior self-mastery, he evinced an equally fervent belief in the efficacy and even legitimacy of righteous violence if and when affronted.[29]

Later that year Manly Jr. similarly exposed the complexities involved in trying to live out his sense of righteous honor in the slave South when he reflected, in his diary, on a trip he had taken with his father the previous spring. As he remembered it, during the trip he and his father "had some conversation about Grandfather Manly. He spoke of his being, particularly in his later years, a man of such vehemence when he was roused that no one dared meddle with him or could pretend to do anything with him." "Father said that *he* perceived the same violent terrible spirit encroaching on himself more and more in his later years, [that] when he was younger all this was more restrained but now he could hardly contain himself when anything exciting entered his mind." Basil Jr. then admitted, "I perceive, I think, the symptoms of the same hereditary malady in myself." This hot temper "if indulged may lead to an utter ruin of my usefulness and not impossibly to derangement." "While at home, I was compelled to restrain myself and was rather remarkable for staidness and collectedness and quietness in my way of doing things. Yet internally and to myself there were symptoms of the same violence when roused." "'This same tendency of mind to run into a terrible and unreasonable pitch of excitement when roused, may be indicated by the thoughts I have recorded in many places ... of this journal. If this growing habit be not repressed it will take full possession of me and I shall become 'such a son of Belial that a man cannot speak unto me.'" Manly Jr. did not and could not go so far as to blame his upbringing in a slave society for encouraging his hot-headedness. Indeed, he managed to draw the opposite conclusion: "I think that having slaves under me, or at least obedient to my orders tended in great measure to reduce this instability, for I find it has risen much since I have been [in the North]." He explained, "Their incapability of resistance and utter subjection made it constantly necessary for me to restrain myself. Here no such necessity for watching and restraint has been impressed on me."[30]

For Manly Jr., then, slave mastery and self-mastery were intimately related. He did not question the right of slaveholding but was preoccupied by questions of how to do it right. "The right of slavery I hold to be undeniable. Whatever noisy demagogues and turbulent agitators may [say] about human rights, freedom, and equality," he once declared, "it cannot be denied that the Bible sanctions slavery under a form as to all important circumstances similar to America's, and enjoined upon the slave the duty of obedience." But the institution enjoined whites also. "By the Golden Rule we are bound to do unto others as we would that others should do unto us. Applying this rule to the case of the slave are we not found to teach them the way to God, the manner in which a sinner may be justified and his soul saved? By the general duty of benevolence we would be bound to give them this instruction. They are men as we; they have minds as we; they have souls as we, immortal souls capable of an infinity of weal or woe. As men, as Christians, we are bound to care for them."[31]

This paternalistic conviction motivated him to act. As early as 1843, he had privately decried the prevailing position of the Baptist Church toward missionary work among the enslaved and claimed that "none but the Methodist Church pretends to pay any attention to the blacks. Even the members of our church, and the very preachers . . . know almost nothing about doctrine" as it related to slavery. This Manly Jr. based on his observation that "the sermons which were preached last year were far, far above [the slaves'] comprehension and did them not the smallest particle of good . . . [and] no other means of instructing them was adopted." He considered the enslaved thus instructed "left as sheep without a shepherd" and reiterated, "It is the duty it seems to me of the whites, since they deprive [slaves] of the privilege of reading the word of God, to instruct them themselves." He advocated for a Black Sunday School, which he privately expressed his willingness to lead. "Without any extravagant opinion of my own acquirement," Manly Jr. ventured, "I suppose it pretty certain that I know more of the doctrine and meaning of the Bible than most of our colored people." Vaguely conscious that in making such a proposal he was overstepping his bounds, Manly Jr. nevertheless asserted, "As to shame I don't think I shall be or at any rate ought to be ashamed of doing good."[32]

In a letter to a Baptist colleague two years later, Manly Jr. expressed the same concern for the religious instruction of the enslaved: "I want to urge upon you what I know is near your heart, the situation of our colored population," a subject that he believed "presents serious and important questions applying to the conscience and the feelings of every other Southerner," most prominent among them: "Are we doing our duty to our slaves in point of religious instruction? What more *can* we do? What more *might* we, in conscience and morality, and in a view of our relations to them and to *our* Master, to do? How are we to do it, so as to secure their best interests, and ours? These questions appeal to us all for an answer, and who can answer them with satisfaction?!"[33]

Later in the same letter to his colleague, Manly Jr. wrote that the "character and amount of religious instruction to [slaves] are both lamentably deficient" and observed that "few indeed receive any instruction except as to their work ... And when the instruction that is pretended to be given is examined," one finds that "they are taught that in shouting and noise, in unseemly indecencies and long 'experiences,' consists the essence of true religion." In this manner, he believed, "they are taught to put their trust in bodily exercise which profiteth little, in meetings and songs [and] outward observances, neglecting altogether the weightier matters of faith and love to God." Manly Jr. expressed his "grief and horror" at the tendency of such instruction "to encourage and produce lustful passions and the worst sort of vices" among the enslaved, with the ultimate result being that "the negroes regard a great shouting and noise on Sunday as a full and complete atonement for all the negligence of the week." He then asked, "Is this the Christian religion? Is this the religion we owe to our servants?" His inherently prejudiced paternalistic convictions determined his response. He believed that proper Christian slave mastery, so called, meant the proper moral instruction of enslaved blacks by their white enslavers. Only then could the southern slave system make claims to divine sanctification. Only then could self-proclaimed Christian masters exalt their virtues in an allegedly benevolent slave regime.[34]

But even as Basil Manly Jr. reiterated his concern for the moral and spiritual state of enslaved Blacks, he recognized the social obstacles confronting its resolution, and many if not most of them stemmed from the wide berth granted to white enslavers by their patriarchal prerogatives. "In whatever we do with regard to ameliorating their religious condition," he said, "the *greatest* caution and circumspection must be used. The laws of this state" curtailing the rights of enslavers to instruct those they enslaved "are unusually severe, but we must take care always to be within the law so that no one can accuse us of transgressing them in the slightest particular." Though he acknowledged the general reticence of both the state and courts to cross the threshold of white male households by observing that, "in practice ... and in reality these laws are not *usually* observed," he still decreed, "Our rule must be nevertheless to 'give no one occasion of offense to any one,' to give no one an opportunity to interrupt or molest us, on any reasonable plea or pretext whatsoever." The fate of the souls of those they enslaved as well as their own demanded that they "provide against the possibility of any such interruption by introducing ... persons of such weight and respectability into the work as to frown down malcontents and evil doers." The growing sectional hostility no doubt prompted Manly Jr. to then state, "I regard the present time, the exact present, as a most favorable juncture for commencing . . . now is the time," and "in the arrangements regard must be had not only to their influence on the blacks but also to the way in which the owners will relish them. Everything must not only be but *seem* fair and open and inviting examination." In short, cultivating the support of prominent enslavers in pursuing this mission to the enslaved was paramount to its success in his fundamentally prejudiced worldview.[35]

Manly's overarching desire to secure the ideological footing of the slave South in order to better defend it shone through continually, for even as he actively sought to reform slavery from within he fervently railed against the social reformers of the North who assailed it from without. He announced himself actively opposed to "interference with our institutions from any foreign quarter," and decreed that "slavery, whether a curse or a blessing, whether a wise or an unwise institution, belongs to the Southern people and none but they can interfere with it or with any of its consequences and any interference will be liable to suspicion and opposition." He well knew "our Northern neighbors think otherwise," but conceded that "if they were content with holding their opinions and leaving others to the enjoyments of their rights and privileges all would be well." In Manly's view, unsolicited and unnecessary meddling by such reformers wholly ignorant regarding the southern "way of life" would only complicate and frustrate the paternalistic pursuits of enslavers like him who claimed to be bound by an implicit ideal of righteous honor.[36]

This tendency among northern abolitionists to engage in and foment "outside agitation" most incensed Manly Jr. To his mind, such northern transgressions made the slave system worse by pursuing its destruction while the white Christian South generally and Manly Jr. specifically sought to make it better. "The practical effect" of abolitionist agitation on the enslaved, Manly Jr. said, "has been to change a comparatively easy lot into a much more severe one and to deprive our slaves of many privileges and gratifications which could once be granted to them." He even blamed northerners for the illiteracy of the enslaved population, or as he put it, "the peculiar situation in which our laws place [the slaves]." Though "we, the authors and sustainers of those laws," he explained, "are bound to give them religious instruction," the encroachment of the North had rendered it "necessary to prohibit teaching them to read. Hence they are [not] enabled to read their Bibles and one great source of information open to every white man however poor, provided he be anxious to learn, is closed to them." Because of this state of affairs, foisted, as Manly Jr. saw it, upon the South from abroad, "we are therefore bound, so long as this law exists (and it is an obviously necessary one) to compensate them for the loss ... of knowledge." According to Manly Jr., because of abolitionist propaganda emanating from northern pulpits and presses, white southerner enslavers had been forced into a more rigid application of the worst patriarchal prerogatives at the expense of the most promising prospects of their paternalistic intentions.[37]

Such was the tangled and tortured logic of men like Basil Manly Jr. They would reform the system if they could, and they could vaguely acknowledge it had gone from bad to worse, but it wasn't their fault, and if only they could be left alone to reform it themselves, all would be well and good. "The fact that of all these melancholy results take place," he said, "we, the South, Southern men, Southern students, ministers, churches, are not to blame for it. We excluded nobody. We shut out nobody. We only demanded that we should be admitted to the common society on terms of perfect equality, and this was denied to us. *We have been excluded*, and the foundation of that Chinese wall has been laid by other hands than ours." He later repeated the denunciation by charging that the abolitionists "all think slavery a great sin, and pray loudly that oppression may cease in the earth. I like to see conscientiousness, but not for other people's sins. I like to see confession of one's own offenses, not of another person's ... Yet such it seems to me is much of the strictness of New England Christianity." Manly Jr. proved increasingly unable and even unwilling to separate the sectional crisis over slavery from his efforts to fulfill his personal role and responsibilities as a self-proclaimed slave master beholden to the implicit ideal of righteous honor in the slave South.[38]

The spiritual bind in which Manly Jr. found himself—the crisis of faith and confidence, the plaintive lashing out at the North for problems that originated in a southern system all once knew as evil—was of course entirely what the abolitionists had hoped to promote. By the time Manly Jr. had entered his profession, he had for the whole of his life felt besieged, self-righteous yet also self-despised. But he had made his choice when he had left the Newton Theological Institute in 1845 because of its growing abolitionist sympathies for the Princeton Theological Seminary, where white southern enslavers met with less opposition. The formal sectional split of the national American Baptist Association that same year had prompted this departure, and though he eventually decided to stay and complete his studies at Princeton by 1847, he remained on the defensive against what he perceived to be a growing abolitionist sentiment around him throughout the ordeal. "If the South should absolutely have to withdraw" from national Baptist institutions, he wrote at the time, it "may make it unpleasant for me to remain [in the North]." He thought perhaps his own edification and the moral future of his native South best served by returning South. Only there could he actively uphold his sense of righteous honor and wield its prerogatives toward the morally righteous ends he proclaimed possible in his home region, ends which promised the type of well-ordered slave society that, in his view, appeared increasingly preferable to that being propounded in the North.[39]

He justified this conclusion by admitting that if he stayed, he would "be looked down on here as low spirited and sneered at in the South as a sneak." "[I would] be taking an equivocal position before my Southern Brethren," he wrote. "All my feelings are with them. I am one of the South. I believe as they do. I feel as they do." With his southern brethren thus "cast out . . . to remain contentedly and quietly under the very shade of the body from which they are expelled, would be to say the least a very ambiguous position. It would be saying," he continued, "you indeed are insulted but I am not, and therefore I am not one of you. I join in justifying the act which shuts you out." "But such is not my feeling," he continued, and such ambiguity "might hinder my future usefulness in the South." "The South is my home," he declared, and "there I expect to live and labor and there I expect to die. There if anywhere is my call, among the poor and destitute. I am bound to do nothing *unnecessarily* which shall impair their confidence in me as a whole-souled Southerner." As such he resolved that he had to do his duty: "a duty which I am afraid we have been neglecting to Southern Institutions. If all who *can* go away, it will be long before any good Institutions are raised at the South." He owed his allegiance to the South, and felt he had a responsibility to render its institutions, both social and religious, closer to his ideal conception, and he resolved to return South in order to fight the sectional fight alongside his brethren.[40]

As vociferously as he had proclaimed his allegiance to the South and his intention to depart from the North forthwith, Manly Jr. also expressed reservations about the efficacy of that decision. He admitted that the controversy over slavery would only follow him south, and that his removal or the removal of any and all southerners from northern institutions would not abate the sectional fervor but, rather more likely, exacerbate it. He wrote, "The intercourse with persons so different from myself and our Southern people [is] no contemptible advantage. They differ in opinions, in feelings, in habits," and in frequently interacting with them he could compare himself with them, "and neither yielding to a stiffened prejudice, nor to a hasty adoption of any and everything new, may learn much from such associations." With these justifications for staying, Basil Manly Jr. effectively paralyzed himself as he vacillated between extremes. In one moment he believed he had "made up [his] mind pretty fully to stay," while in the next contrary evidence would throw him "all aback" into "an unsettled state of mind, excited, roused, unable to do anything else" but contemplate anew "all [his] doubts and fears and waverings as to the subject." Crippled with indecision, Manly Jr. practiced what he would later preach; he looked to his father for answers.[41]

Just before he left Newton he wrote his parents in an effort to clarify the workings of his own mind. "In the first place it seems to me there is an obligation . . . on Southern young men to sustain Southern Institutions. If those who are able run off to the North to get their education," he reasoned, "it sanctions the vainglorious boast that we can do nothing without the North, and are dependent on it" while "at the same time it depresses the character of our own institutions by draining off the cream of the South to a Northern soil and it depressed the reputation of them too." "Northern men," he had observed, "interpret the coming of each man as adding his testimony to the fact that a good education cannot be obtained at the South [and] that there are not men enough of intelligence and liberal training to build up literary institutions." This "seem[ed] to point the Southerner" home. In their series of missives during the spring of 1845, the son expressed to his father the hope that he would "not consider [his] views the rash judgments of a heated mind." "I am roused I confess," he wrote. "The spirit of my father is in me and I feel like wrapping myself in my own dignity and retiring." But he asserted, "I have been calm, cool, patient. I have come, I have seen, I am satisfied . . . we could not in honor act otherwise."[42]

Manly Jr.'s incessant dithering exposed the growing discomfiture of his generation in the face of seemingly deficient ideals, a debased slave system, and a northern threat to expose both. But he could not so fully turn against his father's generation, against his filial duty, against his native region. "My prejudices," he confessed, "are all on the side of my forefathers and countrymen and while I have at various times . . . entertained doubts as to the morality of slavery, my prevailing opinion has always been that it was not in itself a sin to be the owner of a slave. In that conviction I am deeply and firmly settled." The problem, of course, was the system's "great liability to abuse," a liability which rendered slavery "an *evil*" in his mind, one which he would "be glad when, by proper peaceful and Christian-like means, it shall be everywhere abolished." But when and by what means that abolition would occur, if not now and by abolitionists? These were the places Manly Jr.'s mind could not and would not go; these were places he and his generation (ultimately) would rather kill or die than go.⁴³

In looking haplessly to his father's generation for consolation and guidance, Basil Manly Jr. exemplified the reaction of many leading white southern sons across the South as the crisis grew direr. The sectional struggle for the soul of the nation played out in extremely personal terms that were woven into the social, political, and religious fabric of the country. White southern patriarchs—aging fathers and maturing sons alike—understood the stakes all too well and remained conscious of the connection between past and present, between personal and public, throughout the ordeal. As Basil Manly Jr. himself confessed, "This whole matter has caused a severe mental struggle in me, which has made me look forward and backward into my past history and my future prospects, which has brought still nearer to me the 'stern realities of life,' . . . and which has revealed to me secrets in my own nature which I never knew so fully before." That soul-searching quest for answers—to the slavery question and the nagging self-doubt over its morality—drew many white southern men together across generational gaps and myriad social divisions.⁴⁴

Basil Manly Jr.'s personal journey along this path mirrored that of many others of his class in his native region as the 1840s came to a close and the 1850s unfolded. "To me indeed self-study has seemed for the last several years *the most important study* and accordingly my private thoughts, my nightly meditations, have been many of them turned inward upon myself, to see and know for myself who and what that 'myself' might be," he wrote before admitting his simultaneous preoccupation with public perception: "I was comparing myself with myself or with others and I know not but this was often carried to an excess, leading to morbid sensibility, vanity, and selfishness. Everything I did everything I saw or heard was made to contribute by comparison to forming an estimate of myself." Ultimately the result of all this introspection was to find a place where a combination of denial, transference, projection, and contradictory consciousness allowed Manly Jr. to come to some kind of peace in the choices he had made. The months he had spent at Princeton, he wrote, had "placed on surer foundations" his estimate of myself. "I feel now certain of things which formerly I did but dimly conjecture, and suppose, and hope, with regard to myself. And I now reconcile self-judgments which formerly seemed contradictory."[45]

Having achieved this personal reconciliation, Manly Jr. turned his attention to the sectional divide slavery had created. The young pastor now seemed affirmed in his ideological beliefs and resolved to act upon the sense of righteous honor that his father had exalted and which he himself sought to enact. "I suppose the separation [of North and South] to be inevitable and have just made up my mind to it as one of those things disagreeable indeed and unhoped for but which must come to pass," Manly Jr. reasoned before declaring, "The truth is abolition or not, slavery or not, there are many other important reasons for a division." Resigned to the dissolution of the American Union that had been so long in coming, Manly Jr. simultaneously looked back to this turbulent past as he contemplated the potential of an even more turbulent future, seeking justification in the former so as to better prepare for the latter.[46]

Even as he came to this tortured resolution, he sought his father's blessing, and explained both the difficulty in reaching this decision ("You can conceive of the difficulty of it, by remembering how hard it probably was during Nullification times to keep from being suspected of undue leaning to one or the other party"), as well as the moral necessity of seeing it through ("Is this the atmosphere for piety to blossom in? Yet Oh! [that] it is not [one] which will cause a declension in piety. It is inward corruption and absence from God, and these will blind the *soul* at any time.") He confessed a fear: "I am not watchful as I should be. May God help me. I don't want to *talk* about this matter, but to *feel* and to *act*, to come and implore [the] grace of him that is mighty to save." If white southern men held true to their sense of righteous honor, Manly Jr. fervently believed that God would sanction southern separation from an increasingly aggressive abolitionist North. In that he absolutely *had* to have faith.[47]

This very personal mission played out many times over in varying ways in the hearts and minds of leading white southern men across the South during the decade and a half that followed, bringing them face to face with a sobering reality: the dissolution of their slave society, the American Union, or both. At the height of the sectional crisis, southern slavery presented them with the ultimate moral dilemma; either confess their sinfulness, admit their dishonor, and relent to the abolitionist onslaught, or marshal both their religious beliefs and their sense of honor to defend themselves and their way of life. Their aggrieved sense of righteous honor and their power of denial preordained their decision, even as it potentially imperiled the very social order they held sacred to an unprecedented degree.

This implicit righteous honor ideal would require constant defense against such corruption and vice, a defense that promoted a peaceable maintenance of personal and public virtue when possible but sanctioned prescribed forms of "righteous violence" enacted by the "proper" white male authorities when such virtue came under attack. Adherents to this implied sense of righteous honor understood self-mastery and its corollary, righteous violence, as the key to sustaining proper slave mastery, and to meeting domestic and foreign aspersions against southern institutions grounded in white supremacy and patriarchy with professed moral certainty. Alleged northern vices would oppress purported southern virtues if righteous honor was not upheld and defended—peaceably if possible, violently if necessary—by the very southern men it invested with authority.

6

1856

Righteous Honor Triumphant

> On the table, and on each side of him, lay—strangely associated—
> his bible and his pistols. He had been about to refer, with an ev-
> eryday philosophy, to one or the other of them for consolation.
>   —William Gilmore Simms, *Martin Faber* (1833)

Preston Brooks of Edgefield, South Carolina, exhibited a propensity for violence very early on, long before he battered the famed abolitionist of Massachusetts, the U.S. senator Charles Sumner, with his gutta-percha cane. Violent retributions against fellow students, local law enforcement, and political rivals during his youth presaged later impressions of him as a "southern Hotspur," *the* symbol of white southern male recklessness shaped by the barbaric slave regime. His 1856 attack on Senator Sumner and divergent reactions to it north and south only fortified the image. But acceptance of this caricatured "Bully Brooks" oversimplifies the complex moral purview of Preston Smith Brooks, in particular, and many leading antebellum southern white men, in general. Though undeniably protective of his own honor, and sensitive to the point of bloodshed when faced with an affront, Brooks resembled other southern men in the genuineness of his spiritual struggles. Precisely because of their ardent adherence to prejudicial assumptions of white supremacy and patriarchal authority as the basis of a well-ordered society, many white southerners came to view Brooks and his caning of Sumner as auspicious symbols of righteous honor wielded in defense of that inherently prejudiced social order.[1]

For Brooks and many white southern men of the era, violence was a necessary and even salutary aspect of society. The southern code of honor,

Portrait of Congressman Preston Smith Brooks, U.S. House of Representatives, 1856. (Library of Congress)

as they saw it, did not promote but contained violence to its proper forms and ends. The point was not to kill men but to *be* men. "Death before dishonor" was every man's creed—and ritualized forms of facing death underlined white self-mastery. In the white southern mind, the fact that Africans had allowed themselves to be enslaved was evidence enough of their worthiness to be such; the fact that American Indians seemed to prefer racial extermination was one of the more admirable things about them.[2]

In such an environment, religion acted less as a check on the honor code than as a complementary influence. While obviously reared in a religious tradition that centered on Christ's redeeming love, white southerners had internalized an Old Testament outlook toward social relations and the role of violence in their version of Christianity. God, in short, was less leveling love than hierarchical authority, and white men were his self-proclaimed agents on earth, smiting vice and corruption to maintain the proper social order predicated on assumptions of white supremacy and patriarchal authority. Such righteous violence, then, served sacred and honorable ends by ensuring that all did their duty to themselves, their society, and their

God. Men like Preston Brooks, then, became as conscious of their awesome responsibility as they were of their awesome power.[3]

Brooks had stood above his peers at South Carolina College during the late 1830s for his exploits in honor-bound belligerence, no insignificant feat in a place noted for its turbulent student-faculty relations and frequent fisticuffs among the student body. In Brooks's four years alone, numerous violent confrontations involving concealed weapons, drunkenness, and riot littered the school's disciplinary record. The faculty expelled two students in 1837 for homicide. The following year the student body incited open rebellion against the faculty after the expulsion of a member of the junior class, prompting a series of subsequent outbursts. South Carolina College was, in short, a rough-and-tumble place, despite drawing its student body from the finest aristocratic families in the state. In spite or perhaps because of these sons' pretensions to honor, recklessness and violence pervaded their collegiate years, and Preston Brooks often led the charge.[4]

In 1838, Brooks's exploits provoked a special meeting of the Board of Trustees, when the college president learned that Brooks and a fellow student named Lewis Simons had recently been "involved in some difficulty," wherein "a challenge had been sent by one of the parties" resulting in a "quarrel between them." Simons had confessed to sending Brooks a challenge and had argued that he "could not avoid this course; the insult being of such a nature that he felt compelled to notice it in this way." Brooks provided the trustees with a more detailed explanation, claiming that both he and Simons were distinguished members of the school's "Clariosophic Society" and both had come up for the same elected position. Initially, according to Brooks, Simons had deferred, promising "he would not electioneer against him." But after his opponent reneged on this agreement, Brooks admitted that "he said to some of his friends that Simons had falsified his word, which coming to the notice of the latter he sent . . . a challenge to fight a duel." Brooks accepted the challenge, and both "repaired to Mr. Simon's room," where Brooks told his antagonist, "they were both boys and under College laws, that he would give him a boy's satisfaction, but would not fight while in college."[5]

After considerable speculation by both parties the following day as to whether the other was scouting the campus with pistols and malicious intent, the two finally squared off when Simons confronted Brooks in the schoolyard and handed him a formal challenge. Brooks accepted it, at which Simons "drew a horse whip and gave him a cut," prompting Brooks to draw his pistols and bid his adversary to "stand off and defend himself."

Simons then backed up several paces and "exclaimed, 'I am not armed!'" "On hearing this," the trustees' report said, Brooks by his own account "threw away the pistol" and said "'I will now give you a boy's satisfaction if that is what you wish,'" and "they engaged in a personal encounter again, and here the matter ended." The board summarily expelled Simons and suspended Brooks for carrying a deadly weapon and threatening the life of a fellow student. Though readmitted the following semester, Brooks did little to settle down.[6]

Indeed Brooks's prickly sense of honor again embroiled him in controversy during his senior year of 1839, when he assailed the local Columbia jail after hearing a report that his younger brother James Carroll Brooks "had been carried by the town marshal in an ignominious manner to the guard house." Brandishing two pistols given him by a friend, Brooks procured some ammunition from a local shop, "loaded his pistols and proceeded to the Guard House with the design of rescuing his brother from his supposed ignominious treatment." Upon arriving to find his brother no longer in confinement, he admitted at the college faculty's internal enquiry that "he continued to display his pistols in a threatening manner and proclaimed his intention of shooting the aggressors." Citing the defense of his family's name and honor, "he urged in extenuation of his conduct that he had not considered himself subject to the discipline of the college, because his examinations were completed." He further explained "that his offense against the laws of morality and the land, which he did not wish to justify, was one which the natural excitement of the circumstances [and] the fervor of youth should render venial." Brooks was expelled and thus never officially graduated, but this mattered little in a time when a college degree was unnecessary for pursuing a career in law and politics. Besides, unlike the college faculty, Brooks's Edgefield peers only admired his conduct. Brooks had shown himself well versed in the form and ritual of the southern honor code and exhibited the lengths to which he was willing to go to defend that honor against all comers. He thus entered manhood well armed, with personal honor, a penchant for violently defending it, and community sanction of both.[7]

Preston Brooks quickly parlayed his honorable reputation into professional success, studying law under the tutelage of Senator George McDuffie of Edgefield. Brooks's star seemed on the rise, as McDuffie also introduced him to the Edgefield political scene that determined much of the state's political course. One of his earliest forays into this political world would have a lasting impact on his prospects and perspective, both personal and political. Tensions ran high during the 1840 South Carolina gubernatorial election between John P. Richardson and Edgefield's own James Henry Hammond, and both Brooks and his fellow Edgefield rival Louis T. Wigfall fanned the flames that engulfed the campaign. Perceived insults from both camps led to several violent rencontres, one resulting in the death of Brooks's nephew, Thomas Bird, at the hands of Wigfall. Upon hearing of his nephew's death, Brooks reportedly vowed, "I'll kill Wigfall!" As his father later recounted, "My son Preston challenged Wigfall, which was accepted," at the conclusion of a "hostile meeting" between Wigfall and a relative of Brooks, Colonel James P. Carroll, on November 4, 1840. With his cousin (the former governor of South Carolina, later colonel of the Palmetto Regiment in Mexico) Pierce Mason Butler acting as second, young Preston proceeded with the affair a week later on a "small, sterile, and bleak island in the [Savannah] River, called goat island ... having no accommodations but its insulated situation which protected the party from interruption."[8]

Preston's father, Whitfield Brooks, exhibited his own sense of righteous honor most poignantly in this very public affair, as he considered the entire ordeal one "of trial, suffering, and solicitude of a painful nature, beyond anything that [he had] encountered in all [his] past life."[9] He solemnly declared, "One man [Louis T. Wigfall], has caused me more grief, vexation and suffering than I have had to bear from all the other crosses, losses, or misfortunes of a life of fifty years. May God take mercy on him for the mischief he has done and correct the error of his ways, and may he have mercy upon me and forgive whatever faults and sins I may have committed in the unpleasant warfare with this rash and misguided young man, which has been forced upon me and upon my family." "I hereby attest," he continued, "in the presence of Heaven, that a quarrel with that young man was not sought by me, nor was it acceptable to my wishes and purposes. I was willing to do everything consistent with truth and honor to avoid any hostility with him" but "in an unguarded hour ... he suffered himself to be seduced into the support of a cause, which finally absorbed all his thoughts and engrossed all his wishes and hopes and in defence of which, he was prepared to sacrifice all the social relations of life, with the feelings of kindness and sympathy to which they usually give birth." Brooks then vividly displayed his sense of impending moral judgment: "I leave this record to vindicate myself, when the passing of the hour shall have passed away and when truth may claim her empire, with some hopes of being heard and respected." Here the elder Brooks chastised not only Wigfall but his eldest son Preston as well, considering both young men's actions to be reckless. To his mind, both Preston and Louis Wigfall lacked self-mastery, and their impending rencontre on the field of honor seemed to him void of any claim to righteous violence. And yet still he played his part as witness to the exchange of shots. It was not the duel itself that Whitfield objected to, but the unnecessary resort to it in this case as he saw it.[10]

Such fatherly remonstrance surely stung. But Preston, despite having what his father described as "hurried into the fight without the necessary preparation," had doggedly refused to back down, and the battle with Wigfall nevertheless came to fruition. As his father later narrated, "The first shot was ineffectual . . . at the second fire both were wounded and both fell. *I saw my son fall.* My feelings at that occurrence, may be more easily conceived than described." Upon examining Preston's wound it was discovered that "the ball had entered near the spine, passing through the fleshy part of the left hip and touching the bone, and then passing through the left arm, shattering one of the bones," while Wigfall had been "shot through both thighs." Due to the isolated location of this duel, the two men "were forced to remain on the island during the night, on the very spots, where they fell." Preston was attended to by a surgeon, but his prospects worsened: it was a long night, he was wet on account of the rain, and was running a fever. He spent the remainder of the month on the mend, but bouts with fever bedeviled his recovery at every turn.[11]

Over a year later, Whitfield Brooks reflected on the incident: "On this day twelve months past my son Preston and Wigfall had a hostile meeting in the Savannah River . . . So far the day resembles the one on which they met. My situation and feelings are however widely different. I and my family are now in the enjoyment of health and contentment." By implication, his son's heedless passion had imperiled not only his personal safety but the security of the entire family. The family's honor thus secured, however regrettably, Whitfield shifted his thoughts into more pleasant channels: "I thank God that my worldly condition is easy and my worldly prospects as cheering and as prosperous as I have reason to expect or as falls to the lot of most men. I desire in the spirit of humility to return thanks and adoration to God for his many mercies and privileges." The temporal and spiritual sanctity of the family mingled in the personal honor and piety of the father and projected onto the son. When Preston was finally out of danger of dying, his physical injuries were less of a burden than the psychological damage inflicted by these paternal rebukes, as his later thoughts and actions would bear out.[12]

Whitfield Brooks struggled, nevertheless, to maintain a consistent example to his son and conveyed mixed messages regarding the more violent passions. Temperance and moderation purportedly guided his actions at the "festive board" as well on the "field of honor," and he frequently decried Edgefield's prevailing tendency toward both excessive inebriation and violence. In these tirades against excessive violence in the Edgefield District especially, he pursued a resolute purpose: to deter Preston from indulging his more indiscreet inclinations. The admonitions Whitfield heaped upon Preston after the Wigfall duel followed a familiar pattern, which the elder Brooks often exhibited in referencing such cases in their native Edgefield District. "Within the last four years more deaths by violence and casualty have occurred in this District than in any of the old states in the Union," he noted in early 1843, before listing the more violent outrages, none more personally mournful than when "Wigfall shot my poor nephew Thomas Bird in a street rencounter." "In fact the violence and bloodshed," he continued, "have almost rivaled the new states of Mississippi or Arkansas." His own familial loss mirrored countless others felt throughout the Edgefield District, and Brooks lamented the affliction even if he still resented Wigfall's attack and the family turmoil it engendered.[13]

Brooks frequently exhibited such tensions in his personal philosophy toward violence, as he often seemed to oppose the public nature of these affairs more than the violence they entailed. As he conceived of it, the powerful social station of public men often demanded such violence, but they and the press should have the sense to keep such occurrences from disturbing the public peace. In addressing another local affair of honor in the wake of his nephew's quarrel with Wigfall, Whitfield Brooks declared, "It is always a matter of regret for private quarrels to be blazoned before the public in the columns of a newspaper. It is a sort of prostitution of the public press." He reiterated the theme that same summer when he observed another "quarrel and the publications in the papers [that] were the topics of conversation in every coterie. This personal affair has assumed a very vituperative character and has already involved the families of high respectability." "These personal altercations," he continued, "should be excluded from the public prints, and not thrust upon the eye in disregard of all propriety and in some instances even of decency." In short, the duel—when properly applied—enabled this requisite masculine violence to proceed without embroiling the entire community in physical carnage and emotional chaos. When allowed to spill over into the press, the duel lost its efficacy and its actors forfeited their claims to honor, rendering themselves no better than those who succumbed to their violent passions and shot it out on the public square.[14]

He poignantly revealed this perspective in detailing yet another violent rencontre in the district on sale day the following September, when "Joseph Glover came up and calling upon Lovett Gomillion to defend himself drew a pistol and fired" as both parties descended the Edgefield Courthouse steps. "The ball passed through the coat of Gomillion in 2 or 3 places but did not touch his body," Brooks noted, and "Gomillion also fired his pistol charged with buckshot," injuring an innocent bystander. "He also discharged another pistol at Glover, which entered Glover's side" and "killed him instantly. Several other persons were in eminent danger" as well. Brooks then observed, "I have seen no one who condemns Gomillion, as he was forced in self-defense to shoot Glover or be run out of the Village. Glover had sworn to kill him and the attack was deliberate and premeditated." "This spot of ground has been the theatre of two bloody encounters with firearms in each of which life was taken," he continued before asking, "Is there no method by legislative enactment to punish offenders, who carry about them deadly weapons in such manner as to prevent a pernicious and savage practice, now too much in vogue among riotous and quarrelsome men? It is much to be desired that some remedy be devised to put this practice down." Though acknowledging—along with the wider Edgefield community—that Gomillion was honor-bound to retaliate, Brooks nevertheless implied that such scenes of public violence constituted an egregious misapplication of the southern honor code in that the actors exhibited a gross lack of self-mastery, resulting in wanton violence devoid of any righteousness that threatened the very moral sanctity of the men and community they enveloped in bloodshed.[15]

Brooks's desire to see such scenes eradicated from the Edgefield landscape went unfulfilled, for in the spring of 1845 he complained, "There is also prevailing in the District a sanguinary spirit of revenge, that has made violence and bloodshed common occurrences in our Village on public occasions." "Whenever a dispute arises and proceeds to violence," he continued, "the use of deadly weapons is constantly resorted to and the spilling of human blood or taking human life is regarded with very little more repugnance or abhorrence than killing a wild beast. In fact there is no portion of the United States, where life is regarded at so cheap a rate and I regret to say that public opinion in this District is greatly at fault in this matter." He concluded, "Death by violence has become so common, that it has ceased to shock public sentiment, [and] the consequence is, that the law is disregarded and the offender escapes punishment." Seeing it increasingly inured to the conspicuous and wanton violence among even its leading citizens, Brooks worried over the fate and future stability of his community if such heedlessness continued to undermine the social order.[16]

But Whitfield Brooks proved equally fervent in his support of and participation in the rituals of the honor code; indeed he considered them an essential white masculine prerogative, the very foundation of that social order. One particular personal affair of honor prompted Whitfield Brooks to convene with "Judge [Andrew Pickens] Butler, Col. [Pierce Mason] Butler, [Dr. Maximilian] Laborde, [John or Abner?] Blocker, and James Carroll" in June of 1841 to take "a question under consultation." The question mainly concerned his son Preston, and as Brooks recorded, "There finally was little or no difference among us. Our decision was to fight." This family council and its decision stemmed from an extensive correspondence between Louis Wigfall, Preston Brooks, and their respective supporters that succeeded their near deadly duel of 1840. Perhaps Whitfield's lingering resentment of Wigfall for the distress he caused the Brooks family urged this response. All parties were presumably happy, however, when the affair was honorably adjusted without a second recourse to pistols at dawn. Despite this sober termination of the affair, Whitfield Brooks had nonetheless evinced his own propensity toward violent retribution when personal and familial honor faced affront. Religious scruples aside, sometimes the preservation of a life dedicated to what Brooks would later exalt as "the attainment of moral and intellectual excellence... deserving and meritorious" of divine favor demanded violent defense, and any man worthy of the name would not fail to meet the challenge with a stout resolution grounded in the fervent belief that his cause was indeed morally righteous. With so much and so many dependent on his manly bearing, a man like Whitfield Brooks saw clearly that both honor and religious piety should govern his words and deeds and guide the family whose moral instruction and bodily protection was his solemn vow. This sense of righteous honor inflected much of his, his family's, and his society's moral standards and manly identity.[17]

Whitfield Brooks's sense of righteous honor, then, produced a wavering attitude toward honor-bound violence, which resurfaced with yet another Edgefield affair of honor in 1841. He took special notice of two visiting men from Charleston and declared: "Their object in coming to this place at this time was to interpose their kind offices, in terminating a private quarrel, which has continued to agitate the society of this place for the last twelve months. I am sure that they did no good, and I fear they may have made matters worse." Maybe their shortcomings urged him to more resolutely pursue a similar function in an honorable rencontre the following summer. "I left home with Mr. Lipscomb for Greenwood in Abbeville to offer our friendly mediation to effect a reconciliation between the two adverse parties at that place," he later recounted to his journal. "We arrived . . . and sought an interview first with one party and then the other and found each in a proper temper of mind, to admit of reconciliation." "After hearing the statement of each party," he continued, "we drew up the terms of reconciliation, to which in the end by patience and perseverance, we got them to accede, which happily terminated the dispute and adjusted all their difficulties." Thus Brooks succeeded in this dispute where the Charleston delegates had failed the previous summer. He maintained the primacy of honor while avoiding the violent scenes he deplored but did so by invoking the very same honor of the men he had been called upon to serve as second. In his experience, defense of honor did not inevitably result in violence, but could in fact curb such violence in favor of more reasoned and dispassionate consultation. But Brooks also recognized the tenuous nature of this balance and knew as well as his honor-conscious peers that such a defense sometimes rendered violence unavoidable.[18]

"Heard this morning of several affairs of honor, which are expected to terminate in a fight unless compromised by friends," Brooks observed in the summer of 1843. During that same year he reported another affair of honor in which "Mr. Yancy had cursed Mr. Wilson of Abbeville in the public square in front of Goodman's hotel," but made a hopeful note "that Wilson did not resent it." Such affairs persisted, however, for in March 1844 Brooks noted to his journal, "It is reported that the difficulty between Yancy and Alexander has been compromised." He then denounced these affairs in a familiar tone: "They raised a storm and waged a bitter war of words to the great excitement and annoyance of the public." But Brooks again wavered in his professed abhorrence at such honor-bound difficulties when he concluded that the affair had given "their friends an opportunity of displaying their diplomatic ingenuity and talents of restoring sweet peace between the belligerents. It is better to waste ink than to spill blood." But as he also noted, "The repeated recurrence of these personal quarrels and affairs of honor is brutalizing the feelings of our people and inculcating false tastes and principles into our children. They ought and must be discountenanced."[19]

This concern for the district's youth hit home the following year, when his son Preston again found himself in honor-bound difficulty, and Whitfield expressed his frustration over the affair and its handling. "Mr. Cross made a demand on our son Preston to retract certain unspecified but alleged injurious remarks in disparagement of his character through his special and confidential friend Col. Eldred Simkins, who," Brooks noted, "seems in the way of my family whenever mischief and strife are threatened. We certainly have great reason to entertain good will and kindness toward this peacemaking gentleman for lending himself to any adventurer, who happens to take offense with a member of my family." He then concluded, "I had arranged to go to my plantation but was induced to postpone my departure in the hope of seeing a settlement of the difficulty between my son Preston and Mr. Cross." This he presumably did before the affair came to shots fired. Later that month, Brooks continued his harangue against Colonel Simkins and his family: "I was considerably indisposed a part of the day but the very reality that Col. S[imkins], with his meddling, pragmatical wife, had taken their permanent departure from our neighborhood was a sort of compensation for present suffering. This gentleman and his lady have suffered no occasion to pass where an opportunity was afforded, of exhibiting unfriendly and even hostile feeling toward me and my family. I cannot account for it for I never designed to give them cause. I am gratified at their departure." However, after making these comments, he asserted: "I follow them with no resentful feeling, at least I wish them no harm, but rather as full proportion of Heaven's blessings, as they may hereafter merit." Personal and family honor mingled with personal piety at every turn and enveloped every relationship—with his family, his neighbors, and his maker.[20]

Brooks continued to vacillate in his response to Edgefield's honor-bound violence. In March of 1844, he was overtaken by the same passions he had supposedly suppressed under the strictures of the honor code. "I went over to Augusta, purchased a few articles and returned to Hamburg," where that night "a fracas commenced between my father's Servant Phill and a forward son of Hubbards, which resulted in violence to the servant by the son and a good deal of insolence on the part of the father to me who" he deemed "a drunken, cowardly beast and who has no knowledge of the conduct, due to a gentleman. He was so offensive to me that I left his house and took quarters at Hunters.'" His dander up, Brooks later that very same month commented on an honorable affair between two "Abbeville Belligerents, Messrs. Cunningham and McGowan," who, "with a portion of their friends are in our Village, waging a war of words and shedding of ink, which must end in a hostile meeting if the parties have the requisite pluck." He then asserted, "It is a woman's privilege to scold and quarrel but men should either fight at once or keep the peace." Fight they did, as Brooks observed several days later: "It is understood that the hostile party from Abbeville have left this place for Augusta under an arrangement to fight on Saturday next with rifles." His passions apparently cooled, for he expressed his "fear that one of the combatants may be killed for the quarrel is bitter and the weapons deadly." He later "learned that McGowan and Cunningham had met, fought with rifles, and that McCowan was shot in the head, but it was supposed not to be mortal. It is to be hoped that this quarrel will end here and further bloodshed be spared." Thus in a span of only a few days, Brooks exhibited his impassioned excitement when affronted and his willingness to abide violent response in at least some such cases, as well as his regret over the dangerous and sometimes deadly results such violence promoted.[21]

Perhaps these trials of personal and communal honor increased his resolve to avoid such violence if at all possible. In the summer of 1845 he was back in a conciliatory role, having "made an effort ... to settle an angry dispute between Mr. Spann and the Reverend Mr. McCorkadale, which has already and is likely to involve several families." "Spann exhibited a good temper and willingness to compromise the dispute," he noted, whereas "Mr. McCorkadale was not very lamblike, although he professed a wish to settle the matter. I hope that I may succeed." In this conciliatory role, Whitfield Brooks most resembled his clerical Edgefield neighbors. All expected much from themselves and their progeny, but their masculine standard offered a mixed message for their eldest sons to follow. Restraint jockeyed with obduracy in the righteous honor of the fathers and, perhaps predictably, did the same in the sons."[22]

Significantly, not everyone in antebellum white southern society experienced such pronounced internal conflict over the practice of dueling. Many, in fact, abhorred the practice, at least in their public pronouncements and extant private reflections. One of Edgefield's own, the Episcopal minister Reverend Arthur Wigfall (older brother to Louis T. Wigfall of the 1840 Brooks-Wigfall duel), perhaps due to the frequent example of dueling's shortcomings that his brother had provided, repeatedly sermonized against the practice. One of these sermons found its way into print in 1856. In it, Wigfall publicly expressed what many leading southern men, clerics and nonclerics alike, claimed to privately profess: that dueling was morally suspect if not wholly wrong. But outside the cloth, most of these private professions stopped well short of public denouncements or outright refusals to engage in affairs of honor. And opposition to dueling was by no means equivalent to a rejection of southern honor at large. Southern men of honor could and did frequently express misgivings about dueling and still fulfill their expected role in affairs of honor, including those resulting in a duel. The debate (and derision by those opposed to dueling) centered on whether or not dueling tended to prevent or promote violence. Ardent advocates exalted the practice as a means of abating personal violence; stringent opponents denied this assertion as a complete fallacy. Most leading white southern men fell somewhere between.[23]

Always the focus of Whitfield's wary gaze, Preston Brooks felt it more intensely and critically than ever in the wake of his duel with Louis Wigfall. As his collegiate record and early political career indicated, Preston rarely backed away from an affront. But he strove just as ardently to become the "upright, virtuous man" his father so often invoked. The burden of a father's expectations for his first son carried additional weight after the Wigfall duel that Preston would continue to bear—with a limp and a cane—into all future endeavors.

The added weights of expectation and physical debility converged during the Mexican War, in which Preston Brooks sought desperately to fulfill the former and overcome the latter in a cloak of martial glory. As this war with Mexico grew imminent, Whitfield Brooks expressed pride and satisfaction at his son's efforts: "My Son Preston is endeavoring to form a company" drawn from "the young men of the District," and had aligned himself to the "great unanimity and enthusiasm prevail[ing] in every quarter" at this "most gratifying evidence of the patriotism and spirit of our people." He then declared, "This is the time to test the mettle of men." That spirit and mettle received affirmation when Colonel Pierce Mason Butler granted his Edgefield cousin Preston Brooks a captain's commission in the Palmetto Regiment of the South Carolina Volunteers and showered praise upon his cousin, the district, and its men: "I am *much* gratified at the spirit and patriotism evinced by yourself and other officers. From Old Edgefield, nothing less was expected." Whitfield Brooks also heralded his son who, he recorded, "was elected Captain without opposition." He then praised Preston's "warm and patriotic appeal to [the men of Edgefield's] gallantry and State pride, to rally under the Palmetto banner, to march to the theatre, where glory and honor invite them." He even lauded the "pretty flag, which Miss Susan Pickens was working for the Volunteer company, called [the] 'Old 96 Boys.'" "Commanded by my son Preston," he added, who, "upon receiving the colours . . . responded in a manly speech, in which the thoughts were happily conceived and eloquently delivered." "[It was] one of the most imposing and interesting ceremonies that I have ever witnessed. It was a beautiful pageant or in the language of a spectator it was a 'perfect picture.'"[24]

Whitfield's jubilation added to the chorus of Edgefield inhabitants who gathered to send these gallant sons off to war: "To me the occasion was deeply exciting as two of my sons were among the Volunteers and taking an active part in making up the company." He commented, "If high spirit, ardent patriotism, and manly bearing are qualities of which a father should be proud in his offspring, I feel that I have reason to be satisfied with my sons." "They carry with them my blessing and my earnest prayers," he continued, "that the God of the Universe may protect and guard them from danger and injury in the perils, which lie before them and after they shall have discharged their duty to their Country to restore them safe and unhurt to their homes." "The entire audience seemed inspired with patriotic ardour and the day passed off finely and very much to the gratification of every citizen, who felt an interest in the honor and character of the District." He singled out Preston by noting that "the Captain of the Volunteers is exceedingly popular with his men at this time" for having contributed to what "was a glorious occasion for Old Edgefield and long to be remembered as a proud day in her annals."[25]

When these sons of Edgefield finally embarked for Mexico, Whitfield could scarcely contain his paternal and communal pride: "The occasion was solemn and interesting to all and especially to those who had children and relatives—The hoary father and the gentle maiden dropped a tear by the side of the agonized mother at parting with those gallant spirits." Through it all he fervently prayed, "May the God of battles shield them in the hour of peril, cover them with his aegis in the day of trial and bring them, after they shall have faithfully served their Country, back to their homes and their families." At that, he and his family "parted with our sons and with heavy hearts and moist eyes directed our course homewards," concluding a scene that "was impressive and affecting and will long be remembered by the Palmetto regiment and the people of this District."[26]

The necessity of community and religious sanction did not escape the military leaders tasked with leading these sons off to battle. Colonel Pierce Mason Butler, commander of the Palmetto Regiment—relative to some and neighbor to most in its Company D "The Old 96 Boys"—understood this ideal of righteous honor all too well. He praised the South Carolina Methodist bishop Whitefoord Smith for his parting address to the troops as they assembled in Charleston, bound for Mexico. In a personal letter to Reverend Smith, Colonel Butler commended the address and observed, "The peculiar appropriateness of your discourse today before the Volunteers was regarded as happy to all. The effect was apparent." The colonel then requested a printed copy, as "no idle complement" but rather for the purpose of printing "as many as one thousand copies, in the best form for the use of the Volunteers and a few friends." He considered the bishop's words "most solemn and impressive"; they would, he wrote "render service to me and the Regiment and I sincerely hope be the means of disseminating the Holy Christian faith of our land."[27]

No wonder an Edgefield son like Preston Brooks placed such importance on achieving glory in Mexico. His Edgefield community expected much of its sons as they paraded off to war, and Preston occupied a prominent place in the procession. This communal pressure only heightened more personal ones. After disappointing his "noble father" during the Wigfall affair, he avidly sought a chance to redeem himself in his father's eyes. The war with Mexico seemed the perfect chance to fulfill both. But fate did not comply, and Preston's past transgressions would continue to afflict his future prospects. After landing in Mexico, Preston's injured hip inflamed. He limped down interminable Mexican roads with what the regimental surgeon described as a "singular movement in his gait" and a "curious drag of the left leg." A sweltering tropical heat compounded his agony as piercing leg pangs crippled his every stride. Yet he strove on, refusing rest and recuperation in a desperate effort to keep apace. His relentless exertions brought on "a severe attack" of "roasting typhoid fever," rendering him "too unwell to resume the duties of his office *for months to come.*" Just weeks after landing with his Old 96 Boys in Vera Cruz, Mexico, Captain Brooks found himself laid up behind the lines—far removed from his place at the head of the column.

Granted official sick leave and consigned to recruiting duties back home in Edgefield, Captain Preston Brooks fought to meet enlistment quotas rather than Mexican soldiers. As the war raged without him, he felt the tinge of doubt being cast upon his character by the homefolk; having failed to achieve glory in the field, he met with equally dismal success behind the lines, reporting "the spirit of volunteering in this state ... quite destroyed."[28]

Shackled to a desk and denied his main chance, Captain Brooks surely brooded over the cause of this late misfortune—the moment when he defended with near-deadly determination the very honor now so imperiled—his duel with Wigfall. This brooding fueled his desperate desire to return to grace in his father's eyes via military distinction in Mexico. To rejoin the fight appeared his only means to regain some degree of his former status: "before the people of my district the confidence and respect of which I value more than life itself" and to overcome "the extreme regret and mortification ... that I feel on account of [my absence] being denied [my part] the privilege of playing my part in the great battles" of the war. (In the original text, Brooks had written and then struck out the phrases shown here in brackets.) He refused to accept any suggestion that a peace treaty was imminent and the war concluded and remained determined to realize such "stirring and glorious events ... and opportunity for distinctions for which he had volunteered and for which his soul panted." This "first wish of his heart" consumed him to the point that he sought "every chance for a fight" and did "not feel fear." He hounded his superiors to get back into the fray and citing "a peculiar obligation to return to my men" he "respectfully ask[ed] to be ordered to [his] regiment." His persistence—and his family's influence—ultimately prevailed, as he received orders to "proceed without delay to join [his] company now serving with the main army under Major General Scott, in or near the City of Mexico." His "undisguised rapture" at this news, however, proved short-lived. Captain Preston Smith Brooks landed in Mexico to find the fighting nearly finished and the war all but over.[29]

General Winfield Scott's army, South Carolina's Palmetto Regiment, and Edgefield's own Old 96 Boys had succeeded in capturing Mexico City just weeks earlier. Preston's prospects for glory fell with the Mexican capital and the many relatives and neighbors slain in its conquest. Colonel Pierce Mason Butler, Preston's cousin and commander, fell at the battle of Churubusco, his horse and legs shot out from under him. But Butler had refused to relinquish command for more than a moment, returning to the field "dragging his wounded limbs along as he went from company to company instructing the commander of each." His gallant return was rewarded with a shot to the head, which killed him instantly. Another cousin, Sergeant William Butler Blocker "was cut in two by a cannon ball, while leading [his] company in their intrepid charge upon the [Ciudadela]," while still another cousin, "Dick Watson, belonged to the storming party and was wounded in three places." He ultimately perished of his wounds. The most crushing blow, however, came when Preston's younger brother Whitfield Jr. succumbed to wounds received at the battle of Churubusco. Their father was inconsolable: he had lost two cousins, one nephew, and one son—his namesake and favorite. "It would be difficult to find a man," the elder Brooks grieved, "the blood of whose family has been poured out more copiously or freely on the soil of Mexico," where "at the Battle of Churubusco, I lost . . . the noblest son that *father* ever raised."[30]

His less noble eldest son took the loss especially hard, in no small part because his father praised the younger Whitfield with such zeal and lamented his demise with such heartache. The boy had been "so young, so buoyant, so full of hope and bright anticipation" that it was difficult to part with him. In his intense mourning of Whitfield Jr.'s heroic death Preston ironically garnered his father's admiration: "Poor fellow . . . the death of his brother [has] crushed him to the very earth . . . He now pants for an opportunity of doing something to repair, what he conceives he has lost." They both agreed that Whitfield Jr. had been the best of them and found mutual solace in the knowledge that the boy had died "like a chevalier knight in the cause of his country and defense of her standard while his heart was yet pure and untouched by selfishness and unsullied by vice." But such a noble death had eluded Preston despite his reckless "panting" for an opportunity, and he felt responsible for not having been there to sacrifice his own life that the hero may have lived, to protect the "noble boy" whom he loved and admired and his father unconditionally adored. Despite his father's sympathy and consolation, Preston sorely felt the pain of yet another failure, and the losses—of his brother, of his father's confidence, and of his honor—were devastating. Added to these family losses was the loss of over thirty of his own Company D, Edgefield's Old 96 Boys. Captain Preston Brooks had missed it. *All* of it.[31]

Mexico cast a long, cold shadow over the remainder of Preston Brooks's life, and his depression proved as protracted as it was deep. Two years after the war, he still went regularly to his brother's tomb. "My grief for the dear boy is yet green," he admitted to his diary, "and I doubt I will ever be able to speak of him with composure." And death seemed to have followed him home, for it plagued his family at every turn. In April of 1849, the near-loss of his pregnant wife in a carriage accident seemed benign compared to the chain of death that followed on its heels. His young daughter—born while he was in Mexico—took sick and died unexpectedly that year, and his father died in his arms just two years later, after a prolonged illness. A severely depressed Preston Brooks confessed in 1851 that his heart felt the "most painful forebodings. It is my fate to lose almost all I dearly love . . . It seems as if I am destined to lose everything associated with the Mexican campaign."³²

These grim feelings shadowed even the brightest moments of Preston Brooks' remaining years. When he entered the United States House of Representatives on March 4, 1853, his first thoughts were of his deceased father: "How my beloved Father would have rejoiced in my victory. God bless his memory." After finally realizing a modicum of the success for which he had yearned and which his father had always expected, even this "victory" felt hollow. From the grave, his father's expectations—and his consistent disappointment of them—continued to haunt Representative Brooks. His most infamous act—the caning of the Massachusetts senator Charles Sumner, during his second term in Congress—presented one final chance at distinction, at making his mark in the heat of battle. It had been long in ferment.³³

On May 19 and 20, 1856, all of Washington had been captivated by Senator Charles Sumner's strident castigation of the "Slave Power" in a speech entitled "The Crime against Kansas." In his remarks, Sumner personally insulted the South Carolina senator Andrew Pickens Butler, Brooks's second cousin. "The senator from South Carolina," Sumner noted, "has read many books of chivalry, and believes himself a chivalrous knight . . . honor[able] and courage[ous]. Of course he has chosen a mistress to whom he has made his vows, and who, though ugly to others, is always lovely to him; though polluted in the sight of the world, is chaste in his sight—I mean the harlot, slavery." This implication that Butler slept with those he enslaved was just the beginning, however. A recent stroke victim, Butler occasionally wore a small spittoon around his neck to catch the saliva he could no longer control. Sumner had no qualms in folding this handicap into his attack. Butler, he said, "overflowed with rage" and "with incoherent phrases, discharged the loose expectoration of his speech, now upon her [Kansas's] representative, and then upon her people." "The senator touches nothing which he does not disfigure," Sumner concluded. "He cannot open his mouth, but out there flies a blunder."³⁴

The "Slave Power" Butler so shamelessly represented and defended, Sumner claimed, was motivated by an uncommon lust, a fiendish desire to "rape a virgin Territory." Chaste, lily-white Kansas had been overpowered, pressed into the "hateful embrace of slavery," and now she would bear a "heinous offspring," the ultimate object of the South's depraved longing, a dusky new slave state. "Here in our Republic," Sumner noted, "*force*—aye, sir, FORCE—has been openly employed in compelling Kansas to this pollution." In casting the South as the black rapist of white civilization, Sumner had pressed *the* button; he knew it ("I shall pronounce the most thorough Philippic ever uttered in a legislative body," he said), and his audience knew it ("That damn fool is going to get himself shot by some other damned fool!" exclaimed Stephen A. Douglas, pacing the back of the chamber). It wasn't merely that Sumner had insulted Andrew Butler, or run down South Carolina's revolutionary heritage, or even implied that southerners slept with those they enslaved. He had leveled the ultimate insult; he had rendered even the South's noblest impulses—its claims to benevolent Christian mastery and an enlightened social order—wholly monstrous. That insult demanded a response, and Preston Brooks was primed to oblige.[35]

For Brooks, the caning distilled a lifetime of frustrations into one potent batch of emotional release. With his fellow South Carolina representative Laurence M. Keitt always at his elbow and by his ear, Brooks vented these frustrations with "thirty first-rate stripes . . . every lick . . . where it was intended," shattering his gutta-percha cane and causing Sumner to "bellow like a calf." The ubiquitous cane—symbol of Preston's youthful intemperance, filial failings, and fall from grace at his brother's death in Mexico—brought this lifelong burden down on Sumner's head. In the process he vindicated himself according to his father's lessons in righteous honor. Steeped in the southern code of honor, the violent outburst smacked of Old Testament moral righteousness, where God's earthly instrument wielded the divine sword to smite out perceived injustice. It embodied the masculine moral standard of righteous honor implicitly upheld by many antebellum southern men. Brooks captured the connection best when he noted, "The fragments of the stick are begged for as *sacred relicts*. Every southern man is delighted."[36]

Brooks certainly had ample evidence readily at his disposal affirming such general acclaim, especially in his home state of South Carolina. In the immediate wake of the caning, numerous newspaper editorials heaped praise upon Brooks and his belligerent act. On May 28, Brooks's hometown newspaper, the Edgefield *Advertiser*, began its editorial response with the now infamous refrain "Hit him again," which would be repeated often in the press and in public commemoration ceremonies held in Brooks's honor from Virginia to South Carolina in the several months that followed the "affair." These ceremonies frequently entailed the presentation of replacement canes carrying this inscription or some similar iteration of its overarching sentiment. The *Advertiser* described the caning as "an admirable occasion" and "handsome drubbing ... The beating is said by all the reporters to have been a thorough one. Some say he [Sumner] received fifty stripes; yet we very much doubt if the Captain cared to exceed the legal number of thirty-nine, usually applied to scamps ... For our own part," the editors continued, "we feel that our Representative did exactly right; and we are sure his people will commend him highly for it. We have often heard of a word in good season, but his is *an act* in good season ... We have borne insult long enough, and now let the conflict come if it must."[37]

The Charleston *Mercury* evinced a similar tone and sentiment two days later in direct response to a critical editorial published in the Pittsburgh, Pennsylvania, *Gazette*: "It seems that if aggression is to be the policy of the North, it is necessary to have the armed band, as well as the venomed tongue and malignant vote. We are surprised that the North has not opened its eyes to this fact long since. To suppose that war in Congress, and war in Kansas, could be successfully conducted to its issue by such champions as Sumner ... was a dream in which fanaticism alone could indulge, and which is like to be dispelled by the recent developments."[38] The editors then proclaimed that "the South certainly has become generally convinced that it is by hard blows, and not by loud blustering and insulting denunciation, that the sectional quarrel is to be settled. We need not say that this has been our opinion for the last twenty years." The editors of the Laurensville, South Carolina, *Herald* heartily agreed: "We can only give our most hearty endorsement of the conduct of Mr. Brooks ... Our Representatives have been heretofore quietly submitting to the vile calumnies and slanders that have of late years, at every opportunity, been heaped upon the South by our enemies, and we have often wondered at the calmness and discretion of Southern members under such circumstances; but there is a point when forbearance ceases to be a virtue, and Sumner's speech, which brought upon him the merited chastisement, it must be evident the fanatical fool had passed that boundary and it was not in the nature of such a man as Preston S. Brooks to submit to it. Argument, reason, courtesy, and conciliation had long since proved ineffectual to silence the wild calumniators." They then concluded, "We sincerely hope it will prove a salutary lesson to others who may have the temerity to provoke a like act."[39]

The Richmond, Virginia, *Enquirer* weighed in on June 3 by denouncing Sumner and his "Northern Abolitionists" who, they claimed, "do not let a day pass without showing to the world that they are as little fitted to be trusted with liberty as thieves with keys or children with firearms. Their daily abuse of liberty of speech and of the press, and of freedom of religion, are but the means which they habitually employ for greater mischief and crime ... A community of Abolitionists could only be governed by a penitentiary system. They are as unfit for liberty as maniacs, criminals, or wild beasts." The editors then said, "If the noxious heresy of abolition and its kindred isms are not arrested; if a salutary reaction does not take place, ere long, even good men, religious men and patriots, would prefer the quiet of despotism to the discord, licentiousness, the anarchy and crime, which those men practice and invoke. Yet we neither fear nor tremble for the future," they continued, before concluding, "The edifice of American liberty, the most glorious structure of freedom the world has ever seen, is not destined to be sapped and undermined by pismires, nor carried by the assaults of crazy lilliputians. These creatures will be soon driven from their places, and lashed into obscurity by an indignant people, whose confidence they have betrayed and abused."[40]

Even those who denounced the caning as an illegitimate and unjustifiable response shared the expressed convictions of these other proslavery southerners regarding Sumner, northern abolitionism, and southern sectional priorities. The Louisville, Kentucky, *Journal* said that "the assault is deeply to be regretted" as "a great outrage in itself," and that "it will ... greatly strengthen the anti-slavery and anti-Southern feeling in the Northern States and thus help the Black Republican party." Though they deemed Sumner's speech "violent and incendiary and disgraceful" and asserted that they "have no sympathy for Sumner. He has deported himself as a pestilent enemy of the peace and harmony of the country and no doubt deserved more punishment than he has received," they nevertheless believed that "every consideration of propriety and of the public good demands that Mr. Brooks shall be expelled from the House of Representatives." In other words, they objected to the manner of the punishment, not to the punishment itself or the legitimacy of its cause. That such a violent act would be enacted by a South Carolinian and celebrated by nearly all South Carolinians they viewed with no surprise, deriding the residents of that state as "a violent people ... We don't think they ever fail to approve an act of violence against what they hate ... The absurd and wicked resolutions which the South Carolina people are adopting will serve only to exasperate to a still greater degree the public sentiment of the North. But this is what South Carolinians want. They rejoiced in whatever seems likely to promote the dissolution of the Union."[41] The

Wilmington, North Carolina, *Herald* largely agreed: "We think Sumner deserved what he got, but we do not approve the conduct of Brooks" and, though "granting that the provocation was sufficient, he [Brooks] has yet given a good handle for the Northern people to seize, in denunciation of his course, and deprived the South of the opportunity of justification."[42]

Public commemorative rallies greeted Brooks wherever he went in South Carolina and elicited a further outpouring of public support in speeches delivered and widely reprinted in the state's newspapers. The largest of these public celebrations predictably took place near his home Edgefield District in Ninety Six, South Carolina, in early October 1856. Though unable to attend in person, the occasion drew a letter from Brooks's fellow South Carolina congressman John McQueen that fervently expressed proslavery southerners' sectional sentiment, which by that fall clearly rested upon Brooks's laureled brow in commemoration of the beating he had administered to Sumner. "When his State, and his venerable and distinguished relative, than whom no nobler spirit, or truer heart, ever adored the counsels of our once happy confederacy; were ruthlessly assailed with an assassin-like slander; the hands of a crazy and libelous fanatic," McQueen said, "your Representative at the right time, in the right place, and in the right manner, administered to him my argument, the only kind in my judgment, that will now avail against impudent, arrogant and mad fanaticism, that regards no truth, no right, no justice, no honour, no law or compact. And when the fires of black fanatical fury and revenge were kindled against him at the hands of an unscrupulous majority, and the shaft of personal insult was feebly attempted to be hurled at him, he met it with a firmness and repelled it with a promptness that would do honour to a Roman, as they well entitle him to the admiration of every one who is at all endowed with true feelings of manliness."[43]

After further lambasting the radicalism of Sumner and the abolitionists and warning against their growing strength in the national government as a precursor to their ultimate desire "to subdue the South below the condition of province, to destroy her honour and rights, and ultimately, to reduce us to equality, with our slaves, and authorize them to claim (as now by Law in Massachusetts) to associate in our families and marry our children," McQueen declared: "If they succeed in this election, I trust all will agree with me that the Union is dissolved and *ought to be dissolved*, for there can no longer be union of interest, or right, of property, of sentiment, of honour or equality." He then added a prophetic coda: "In my judgment the year 1860, in any event, will settle the matter," and "If forced by the North into a Southern Confederacy, I have no gloomy apprehensions either for our honour, our happiness, or the institution of slavery ... I am doubting more and more, that a Republic can exist without the institution of slavery." His conclusion then invoked the manly honor and sacred morality he and his audience mutually professed: "A very large proportion of the North constitutes now but a mad fanatical rabble, with all the wicked isms of which man can conceive—repudiating God, the Bible, the law, marital rights or the constitution, and if it were not for ... the conservatism of the South, they would ere this, have been consumed by the infernal fires of their own abominations. The South, the beloved South," he proclaimed, "she will never be reduced to the condition of Massachusetts as long as the example of Col. Brooks is in the memory of her sons."[44]

Personal correspondence addressed directly to Preston Brooks further affirmed the pronounced acclaim his act typically garnered among South Carolinians and proslavery sectionalists. W. F. Holmes of Newberry, South Carolina, in a letter dated May 27, wrote: "I am so delighted with your cool, classical caning of Mr. Sumner that I cannot refrain [from writing]. You have immortalized yourself in the opinions of your immediate constituency. With one tremendous bound you have cleared all the intermediate rounds, and alighted on the summit of Fame's ladder." Holmes then reported, "I heard one of your whilom strenuous defamers say today that he would vote for your to fill the distinguished post of President to a Southern Confederacy." He counseled, "That's right, address your arguments to the skin, to the physical sensibilities. The moral perceptions and the mental faculties of the freesoilers have been preached to long enough. Give it to them over the shoulders."[45] Seaborn Jones, another South Carolinian, wrote to Brooks on June 1 proclaiming, "I have just seen the glorious news ... of the severe castigation you have given Charles Sumner ... It is what the Rascal has wanted a long time, and he has only received a small portion of what he deserves if you had given him ten times as much not a lick would have been amiss, upon his damn hide." He continued: "Let them abolitionists crack their whips while there is a dollar in South Carolina ... You have the good wishes of everyone I have heard speak on the subject and everyone is full of it."[46]

But perhaps the most telling evidence of the strongly supportive nature of South Carolinians' and proslavery sectionalists' reactions comes from letters they addressed to Senator Sumner himself. One especially, from an anonymous "Friend Indeed" of Columbia, South Carolina, exposes the sectional feeling inspired by the act, the fundamentally white supremacist and patriarchal assumptions undergirding that sectional feeling, and the willing resort to violence as the "proper" recourse in defense against alleged transgressions to the southern social order predicated on these prejudicial hierarchies and their perpetuity. The "Friend" informed Sumner, "I am very well pleased at the castigation you [received] recently at the hands of an honorable member from the Palmetto State. You have learned from painful experience that the forbearance of the South has limits which even *you* dare not impinge without impunity. Sir the insults you have heaped on the South are so many and so aggravated in kind, that if I had not a little charity in my heart, I could have wished Mr. Brooks had used other and more deadly weapons against you than a mere horsewhip or cowhide." He then declared, "We will not tolerate your insolence longer. If you infernal abolitionists don't mind your own business at home, and let ours alone, the People at the South, will take the matter in hand themselves, and go in mass to the Capital—tar and feather—horsewhip and expel every rascal of yours."[47]

Collectively these responses to Brooks's caning reveal that many proslavery whites in South Carolina, the Deep South, and in perhaps more qualified terms, even the South at large approved both the man and the act according to their sense of righteous honor. And in so doing they clearly exposed that ideal's fundamentally prejudiced assumptions of white supremacy and patriarchy as the bedrock of good social order, a social order embodied, in their minds, in the southern slave system, in defense of which they espoused an increasingly aggressive tenor and violent posture to denounce and combat any opposition to their convictions.

These Edgefield men—Whitfield Brooks, his son Preston, their family and friends, neighbors and constituents—personified the ideal of righteous honor that implicitly guided many antebellum white southern men into their embattled futures. Their Edgefield home, with its cultural duality, convinced them that cultivating this ideal promoted the very self-mastery with which those futures would be secured. Violence had long pervaded the Edgefield scene, and frequently forced men to confront its often heinous results. Fathers and sons drew upon their sense of righteous honor to mitigate, as well as consecrate, such violence as they deemed appropriate. The effort added personal and emotional depth to a more concerted sense of distinct southern regional identity in the late antebellum years. This sense of righteous honor demanded white male self-mastery but sanctioned white men's resort to righteous violence whenever the white supremacy upon which the southern social order rested came under fire.

Whitfield and Preston Brooks in many ways personified the intensely emotional lived experience of this ideal. But neither would live to see if the ends justified such means. Whitfield had died in 1851, while Preston fell prey to complications from the croup just seven months after the caning, at just thirty-seven years old. Neither would bear arms in defense of their ideals against perceived threats from abroad; neither had to endure the mental anguish and bodily trials unleashed by the war they had wrought. But in their deaths they became martyrs to an ideal as yet untested; symbols of righteous honor undefiled and unassailed. Their experience personified the perpetuation of this sense of southern righteous honor beyond the Brooks family and the Edgefield community: in Whitfield Sr. as an example and inspiration to his son, and in Preston as symbol for much of the proslavery South as a whole. From the white, proslavery perspective, Preston had successfully defended that righteous honor by the fervent administration of righteous violence before a premature death claimed him. And so, like his brother Whitfield Jr. before him, whose untimely death had preserved him in perfection, Preston's early demise suspended him in a symbolic perfection he had yearned for—and failed to attain—all his life.

Senator Sumner's rhetorical assault had indeed been personal, but it had been so much more. It struck at the very core of many elite white southern men reared in a slave society. It had defamed that whole society, and had disgraced an entire region by allusion, implication, and outright brazenness, saying what abolitionists had persistently alleged and what many white southern men themselves had long feared (or willfully ignored): that southern slavery corrupted all it touched by condoning and encouraging the very urges that their sense of righteous honor purportedly regulated. In death, even one as inglorious as that which befell Preston Brooks, he accomplished what his caning alone could not; he provided the symbolic sword to complement the shield of southern righteous honor. Through him, the weapon and the Bible symbolically merged in the thoughts, words, and deeds of countless white southern sons as the sectional crisis reached fever pitch with secession, the outbreak of war, and its aftermath, rendering the personal and local regionally and nationally significant and constructing the altar upon which the rapidly growing nation would determine its moral destiny by bloody sacrifice.

The assertive effort by powerful white southern men to reconcile their internal contradictions and project unity of thought and purpose—represented in the implicit ideal of righteous honor, its emphasis on self-mastery and its prescribed sanction of righteous violence—gave them the language and ideology to secede and make war and, indeed, seemingly served to accelerate the onset of that outcome. But by bringing on that long anticipated crisis, they also unwittingly sowed the seeds of their own destruction, as it exposed to unprecedented degree how desperate they had become in their futile efforts to align reality with their fictive ideal. By 1861 the free-labor, abolitionist North had become the nagging, infuriating conscience that had to be demonized into the sin itself, and then destroyed. Such views transformed antebellum sectional difference into irreconcilable sectional discord, producing an apocalyptic vision that ultimately demanded the trial by fire that was the Civil War.[48]

7

The Civil War and Reconstruction

Violent Conflict as Divine Contest

> But know this, that in the last days perilous times will come: For men will be lovers of themselves, lovers of money, boasters, proud, blasphemers, disobedient to parents, unthankful, unholy, unloving, unforgiving, slanderers, without self-control, brutal despisers of good, traitors, headstrong, haughty, lovers of pleasure rather than lovers of God, having a form of godliness but denying its power.
>
> —Timothy 3:1–5

THE WAR did, indeed, come. It raged for four years and took the lives of more than 700,000 American men, dismembered and disfigured tens of thousands of others, and left the entire nation searching its soul. Some issues that had long confounded the nation this civil war had resolved: the bloodletting forcefully determined that racial slavery would cease to exist in the United States, and further mandated that the power of the federal government in its relation to the individual states would be expanded—these United States became *the* United States.[1]

But these answers begot even more confounding questions still plagued by the persistent prevalence of white supremacist and patriarchal assumptions: what effect would the unprecedented death, dismemberment, and destruction have on the nation's future? Could North and South reconcile? Was a peaceful reunification and reunion possible and what would it look like? What would emancipation mean for freed people's rights and privileges—full equality? Second-class citizenship? Race war? Their ultimate demise? In what directions would federal power extend? Would it expand unilaterally to conspicuously enter the lives of individuals, or selectively in response to particular issues in particular places at particular times? How far and to what ends would the federal government go to shape the fate of Black southerners, formerly free and formerly enslaved alike?[2]

These questions, which confronted the entire nation in some form from the time the shooting commenced until well after it finally ceased, would be answered by many leading white southern men according to their implicit righteous honor ideal. Their experience of war—as soldiers and civilians—would alter that ideal, as would the economic and social changes that followed in the war's wake. When the shooting subsided, many of these white southern men looked forward and backward simultaneously, haunted by specters of their past and future. Some, like the South Carolinian James Chesnut, husband of the famous diarist Mary Chesnut, would retreat to their porches and drink themselves into a gray haze. Others, like the Virginian Edmund Ruffin, made quicker work of it, putting a bullet through his brain rather than live with defeat and emancipation. But most elite white southern men, gradually, determined to pick up the pieces. Their altered sense of righteous honor would help them to rationalize defeat and to remake themselves, their households, and their society in the face of new realities.[3]

What emerged—the "Lost Cause" and the "New South"—would *both* be profoundly shaped by a persistent sense of righteous honor, its emphasis on self-mastery and its continued sanction of righteous violence. As they entered the war many Confederates, despite their projected convictions of moral certainty, showed signs of being constantly in the throes of deep moral crisis, subject to bouts of recrimination and castigation whose force fell alternately inward and out, on one's self, one's sons, and one's enemy. And even the ordeal of combat and privation failed to quiet the demon of self-doubt, but rather intensified its rage through the eventual military defeat and emancipation that followed in its wake. For many elite white southern men who survived the war to inherit the fundamentally altered future it wrought, their sense of righteous honor would not perish but would become more wrathful, increasingly shifting their ire from the conquering "Yankees" to the newly freed people.[4]

The Reverends Manly—the aging Basil Sr. and his two eldest sons, Basil Jr. and Charles—personified this trend. All three oscillated between self-condemning despair and self-righteous indignation as secession unfolded and the Civil War drew near. Such oscillation continued through the conflict, as they desperately cast about for signs that God's favor rested with the South, while simultaneously interpreting every Confederate setback as evidence of God's chastisement. As Southern Baptists, it was a cycle they knew well, however novel its current political shape and consequences. Basil Manly Jr. felt in the fall of 1860 that "the prospects in politics are dark. We are drifting we know not whither," but resolved that "God knows, and God rules, that is all, and that is enough." But he had little faith in the leadership of men, especially those rising to the fore throughout the South on the eve of secession. "Between fanatics on the one hand, and silly braggadocios, whose best excuse is their lack of the power of serious thought [on the other]," Manly Jr. bitterly concluded, "we are likely to have our public affairs nicely managed."[5]

Despite his son's expressed reservations, in the wake of Abraham Lincoln's November 1860 election Basil Manly Sr. asserted: "Whenever, and however, [the statesmen and people of my country] throw themselves on their independency to maintain Southern rights, I expect to be with them." In January 1861, when asked to participate in Alabama's secession convention, Manly Sr. evinced mixed feelings, however. On the one hand, he admitted, "I am afraid there is some snare of the Devil laid under this seeming honor," while on the other he declared his long-standing doubts as to whether "the South can safely remain in this Union." But he ultimately reiterated, "For the last 32 years [I have been] in favor of the formation of a Southern Confederacy, peaceably, if we might, but was willing to *fight it out*, if we must. I am of the same mind still."[6]

Amid the first wave of southern secession in the seven Deep South states from December 1860 to February 1861, Basil Manly Sr. and his family cautiously celebrated the measure. Reverend Manly Sr. dubbed northerners "ignorant infatuated tyrants" and declared "*the Union is dissolved, and can never be re-constructed. All the world in arms cannot force us back into it. No concessions or promises they can make, with tears in their eyes and ropes on their necks, can win our confidence. 200,000!!! Let them come!*" "I will not believe, till it occurs, that men can be such fools." Such incredulity did not prevent him, however, from declaring, "The bridges are cut down, and the ships are burnt behind us. The sword is drawn, and the scabbard is thrown away. We never intend to be in any sort of dependence upon those men again. If they make war upon us," he concluded, "then all friendly intercourse, for generations and ages, will cease. We can get along without them, and not withstanding them. But I am getting wrathy, again . . . I hope that the work of secession will go steadily on."[7]

Throughout early 1861 Manly Sr. repeatedly expressed his resolve regarding the necessity and irreversibility of southern secession as well as the perceived folly of the northern threat of arms. "[The North] will wake up one day to find that the Union is dissolved, and can never be reconstructed; that the South is resolved, and can never be conquered. They do not know that we can fight on for a century, if need be," he asserted. "The cotton we make, when spun into threads, binds the heart of the world to us. The Yankees will find out that we occupy no subaltern or precarious position in the great world ... If I were sure we should have war for a century, as the consequence of our position, I would not recede an inch from it." He continued, "Since they know of no bond of Union but force, it is well we have found it out, and taken our affairs into our own hands. Were there no other ground for the utter and final disruption of the Union, *this is enough*." He remained doubtful that northerners would actually take up arms, even as late as early April 1861, when he assured his eldest son, "You need not be afraid of any drill or mustering at the North. There will be no war." By then, however, his dander was up: "If there could be a war, it would be a mighty help and make reconstruction impossible."[8]

Clearly riled by recent events, Manly Sr. nonetheless believed the entire impending trial would be a test from God. Wary though he was of "power accumulated in bad hands" within the fledgling Confederate nation, he took solace in reflecting that even that power "is permitted in the Government of God; *always* for *their own overthrow* at last, but sometimes a temporary purpose is served in chastising guilty nations, even God's own people, and then, having used the rod for its destined purpose, He *breaks it up*, and *throws it into the fire*." "If we are fulfilling the will of God in what are doing," he wrote to his son, "our deeds are to give luster to the days on which they were done. Let our acts stand by themselves, bad or good. If God blesses them, our posterity will have national holidays all their own, made illustrious by what we are now doing." Even as Reverend Manly Sr. touted the righteousness of the Confederate cause, he also left room for its failing. Believing even the best of men to be inherently sinful, even the best of causes, which he believed the Confederate experiment to be, could prove but the folly of man.[9]

In spite of such qualifiers, however, Basil Manly Sr. continued to set a predominantly defiant tone for his entire family to follow as the weather and military action heated up in the summer of 1861, declaring, "A day of retribution is at hand ... God defend the Right!" "It seems to me, that a thousand adverse battles would not shake my resolution to go on while any head can be made against the foe." Acting on this paternal example, the Manly sons all served the Confederate cause, the two youngest—Fuller and James—in the Confederate army, and the two eldest—Basil Jr. and Charles—from their pulpits on the home front. That same summer of 1861, Charles ruminated in a letter to his mother, "I feel just this way about this war: that life, property (shall I say?) religion itself will be worthless, unless we are successful in it." In the spring of 1862, his father was still contending, in a letter to Basil Jr., that he was "too sternly set, to give voice to joy, even when peace returns." "[I] shall retain," he wrote, "the same grave sternness, to stand on the defensive, forever, against every form of approach. If I ever get to Heaven, and see any good Yankees there, I hope I shall rejoice then. There will be no need of stern reserve and vigilance then."[10]

The course of the war would, however, challenge these convictions and test this faith in both the Confederate cause and divine sanction of it. Such challenges exposed nagging doubts lurking just beneath their confident expressions of resolve, doubts seemingly affirmed with every Union advance and Confederate setback during the war's first two years. Manly Sr. had even admitted in the summer of 1861, "It grieves me to hear of [Yankee] feet polluting and cursing a foot of our soil. God, I trust, will overrule it for good." "If God intends to chastise us, we shall be chastised. That will be for our good. If it be the will of God, I do not wish to survive the subjugation of my country. But this is a result, I by no means apprehend." His son Basil Jr. expressed his own ambivalence: "For us, not to be beaten is to conquer. But I rejoice with trembling. It is a terrible girdle of fire with which they have striven to encircle us, and their malice, and command of the means of offense are unfortunately both unlimited, while we have to fight with our *hands tied*. But I trust we should be enabled to maintain our ground." "I suppose the real crisis of the war has yet to come," Charles Manly wrote in February 1862, "and many more of our men will be needed on the battlefield ... things are coming rapidly to a serious issue and must be seriously met." In August 1862, he wrote, in the wake of the Shiloh defeat, "Surely, a righteous God will avenge such things. What a horrid war they are forcing upon us. 'No quarter,' it is as the sound of a knell." All evinced the same fearful hope expressed by their patriarch, Basil Sr., back in February of that year, when he prayed, "The Lord deliver us out of the hand of our enemies!, that we may lead a quiet and peaceable life, in holiness and righteousness, all our days."[11]

This emotional burden grew with every defeat, intensifying the earnestness of their prayers. It also quickened their pulse and roused the family into more concerted action. Basil Sr. in a letter, wrote, "The effect of disasters on my boys is to make them anxious to enter the war. Charles, James, and Fuller have all written about it. So far from discouraging them, I have an idea that when they get located, I will go and join them." "All our faith, courage, fortitude, endurance, and martial resources will now be required," he continued, "or we shall be overrun ... Life is not too precious to be offered in such a cause." He concluded the letter with a prayer: "The Lord direct and preserve us all!, and bring our country out of trouble!"[12]

What could Manly sons do except echo such sentiments? His son Charles asked, "How can I bear it that an insolent enemy pollutes our soil, [and] seriously threatens the structure of all we hold dear?" "If the pinch comes," he resolved, "let all [of us] meet the enemy, *if it be but to die* defending our homes. Life is nothing if our liberty be gone." He nevertheless held to his belief that "the stress on our country greater now than ever before." "In Him is all our hope. If He be for us, we must succeed, finally." Basil Jr. concurred, even after the Confederate losses at Forts Henry and Donelson in early 1862. "This mighty war, how it is stretching out to proportions and protraction far beyond the imagination of the puny mortals who thought they controlled it!" he lamented; "Who knows what revelations it may still make, of humble character or of divine purpose? We have learned some lessons, but the impression is not yet deep enough, or broad enough. The burning iron must be still deeper stamped into the scorched flesh."[13]

As wife to Basil Manly Sr. and mother to their four sons, Sarah Murray Rudolph Manly exemplified how the patriarchal ideals embedded within their southern society and culture prescribed women's roles while also revealing women's often complex emotional experience of that era's prevailing patriarchal order. In her relationships with her husband and sons, Sarah Manly evinced much the same sectional identity and ideologies as these men in whom their native South invested ultimate power and authority, not only as men, but as elite white enslavers. As such, her worldview often mirrored theirs in its assumptions about the "proper" social order, one predicated on white supremacy and patriarchal control. Though Sarah Manly decidedly "stood by her men" as social convention demanded, in fulfilling this feminine duty she also exhibited a keen intellect, perceptive political savvy, and piercing social awareness upon which all in her family clearly relied and demonstrably revered.[14]

Sarah Manly often reinforced their sense of manly duty, especially as the advent of southern secession unfolded and the prospect of civil war loomed: "I have always desired my children to do their duty as Christians and faithful, honorable citizens," she wrote to her son Richard in April 1861. In the wake of Fort Sumter's bombardment that month she supported her sons' desire to serve the Confederacy in whatever capacity they chose: "I believe our cause is just," she declared, "and that God can deliver us from all our enemies, but it is not to be expected that we shall have another *bloodless victory*' and God only knows whether my sons may not fall a sacrifice to their country's cause . . . God prepare us for all that is before us," she concluded.[15]

But she and they also recognized the many ways in which a seemingly just war could come undone through moral corruption dispensed under the leadership of false prophets misguided by false doctrines. All therefore sought to ensure that their cause continued to be worthy of their ardent support and yet feared all too frequently that it was not. But the fate of the Confederate cause mingled with more tangible concerns much closer to their hearts and hearths. Sarah Manly expressed concerns like those of her husband and sons regarding the absence of white men mustered into service and its effects on the home front, especially regarding the management of the enslaved. She especially worried for her family members from whom the war often separated her to unprecedented and troubling degree. Despite her frequent expressions of hopeful optimism and steadfastness, Sarah Manly worried for her husband, sons, and son-in-law enlisted in various capacities of Confederate service, as well as for her own and her daughters' isolation and vulnerability in their absence. These expressions of optimism and resolute faith seemingly served to salve her own fears and counsel her own mind as much as it sought to comfort and inspire those to whom she expressed them, and she remained consistently fearful throughout the conflict.

From such persistent anxieties Sarah Manly came to view the war as the cross that God now called her family to bear. "Most true it is that the religion of Jesus is the religion of the cross, and that there never was a true Christian without a cross," she had written in 1861. Her family had enjoyed such abundance and good fortune in the antebellum period; her boys were strapping and fine. This made the ominous clouds of war gathering around them in the spring and summer of 1861 seem even darker, and in a letter to her children she admitted her "painful misgiving arising from the exemption [they had enjoyed] from the crosses which others bear." She continued, "The heart-searching and prayer, the earnestness and anxiety which this conviction produces may be just the self-discipline which those peculiar trials, from the absence of which you auger ill against yourself, are designed to effect. God can as richly teach and as deeply sanctify us, by the *absence* as by the presence of trial! I have not *coveted* afflictions, but I have often thought that as a family we have been *remarkably* exempt from deep searching afflictions." Her greatest hope was that in their present and impending trial God would protect them: "God knows the condition of each loved one, and can minister to the individual relief of each, and I believe will do for all, that which is most for their spiritual as well as temporal benefit. I desire to lie quiet in His hands and trust in Him at all times."[16]

Though the Confederate forces held their own through the war's first several months, their failure to bring about the quick and decisive end of hostilities that many had expected cast doubt into the minds of the Manlys. By the late summer and fall of 1861 Sarah Manly certainly evinced such misgivings. For her the war now seemed to portend afflictions in abundance and cast a shadow over even the most joyous of occasions. When her niece Virginia Rudolph gave birth to a son that July, she cautiously celebrated the occasion while also lamenting its wartime context: "I think people had better neither marry nor have children while these troublous times continue. I should be thankful if we as a family could get nearer together, but do not see how it can be accomplished. We are more separated than we have ever been." Just two months later she expressed her fears for her son Fuller in the army by admitting, "I hope you will not be required to display your military training, although just now, the prospect seems very gloomy for us." Such family burdens weighed heavily upon her mind, shaped her outlook on the war, and tested her faith. "My trust is alone in God, who is able to defend us against our invaders," she wrote to Fuller before rather ominously citing a string of biblical verses: "'Where heroes were deified, the land ceased to produce heroes; where God was honored, as the source of all success and blessing, heroes sprang up in abundance.' 'He that abaseth himself shall be exalted.' 'Before honor is humility.' 'Them that honor me, I will honor; and he that despiseth me shall be lightly esteemed.'"[17]

In February of 1862, Sarah Manly wrote her daughter, "Our boys are all anxious to volunteer and we have consented to their doing so . . . We received accounts of a terrible battle going on at Fort Donaldson and trust our people had sunk the enemy's gunboats and were pursuing the Yankees. Also a *rumor* that a fight was going on at Bowling Green. We do not know whether to credit these reports." Just three days later in a letter to her son Charles these uncertainties had become full-fledged doubts, most of them stemming not from the fragility of the "cause" but rather the vulnerability of her family: "My mind is bewildered, and I cannot express what I want to say. But this much I do say, let me entreat you not to allow yourself to be entangled in the wishes of military despotism. Whatever you do, let it be freely." She then lamented, "I feel wounded at the unfairness of those men who allowed James to accept of transportation where they knew that it would bind him [to the army] as much as if he had been 'mustered in.' Where was the use of pretending to allow him to come and consult with his parents?" She continued: "I am fearful that Fuller, too, will fall a victim to the mismanagement of his care after his spell lately. His symptoms cause me much apprehension and there is no chance for me to get to him. The R.R. is engrossed by the Government. We all feel very sad and anxious . . . God only knows how long we will need to be troubled about each other."[18]

In early March 1862, she professed, "I fear Charles too must fall into the hands of the enemy . . . God is able to give us the victory, but I fear our sins are so great and numerous that we will have to be more severely chastised before we are prepared for a blessing." Thus confronted with what she deemed the dismal prospects for her sons, Sarah Manly confessed to them her hopes and her fears: "My heart was with you all yesterday. I tried to pray that God would bless you. I feel sad, very sad, at the prospect of all my sons going away to be under the control of those, who have not the fear of God before them . . . I feel a sort of apprehension that some calamity is impending, which will render your presence needful to us. God only knows. I have striven to resist the feeling and so to occupy my mind with useful labor, as to banish the feelings, but it comes back." She then concluded, "This is indeed a time of perplexity and gloom. The Yankees have taken Newbern [North Carolina] and Confederates run!'"[19]

Intensely personal travails and anxieties thus jockeyed with official military setbacks and perceived political blunders for primacy in the Manlys' minds. Between early May and late August of 1862, Sarah Manly repeatedly expressed her worries, fears, and doubts about her family's prospects and those of the Confederate cause to her husband, sons, and daughters by turns. In tangible ways, the already close association between personal privations and public failures intensified in her mind. In May she worried over the proximity of "Yankee" prisoners held captive near her in Alabama, but also over the impending presence of Confederate troops dispatched for "guard duty" over these prisoners. In her view both boded equally ill for the family's access to already slim provisions. She reluctantly resolved, to her husband and herself, "I feel that I must school myself to endure such things patiently," yet nonetheless lamented, "I feel anxious about you and my boys ... I fear we will never all meet together again in this world." In June she wrote her husband seemingly resigned to accepting God's will in light of her powerlessness to aid her son Fuller during an extended bout with sickness in the ranks: "God bless, guide, and preserve our dear child, and cause him to acknowledge God in all his ways that he may direct his steps, and if we never meet again in this world, I pray that we *may all* be permitted to surround the throne of God, accepted throne of our Lord Jesus Christ." She persisted in this tone at the end of July in a letter to her son Charles: "When I hear in various ways of the sufferings of the soldiers from sickness and tyranny of those who are in power, I feel as though I shall lose my senses. If it is God's will to prepare us for it, I shall be thankful if we can be released from the scene of sin and trouble. Pray for me that I may not be rebellious, but that our trials may be sanctified and tend to purify our hearts."[20]

Sarah Manly's misgivings echoed those of her husband and sons, as did her conflation of personal travails with mounting military defeats, perceived political weaknesses, and alleged cultural corruptions. Throughout February and March of 1862, Reverend Manly Sr. laid blame on the Confederate command: "Drunken officers, incompetent, and inattentive to the necessary wants of the men are the bane of our army. If we are beaten, the fault lies there." He repeated this point in a later letter to his son Basil Jr.: "I fear incompetency or unfaithfulness in the governing powers, and I fear that drunkenness is to ruin us all ... The worst things that I see are not the enemy, or their armaments, but the universal drunkenness that everywhere sweeps over high and low." Such degradation worried him, for in his view, it threatened to provoke God's wrath against the Confederacy. "It looks like the sluice of ruin is rolling over us fast." "Have we been mistaken in our men?" he continued. "Are we to be betrayed, insulted, and ruined by the persons we have chosen to conduct this revolution? It really seems so. And we may have before us the alternative of *another* revolution, or *subjugation* [for] when people have lost their public virtue, and public agents are not brought to stern responsibility, the few pious and good fall with the rest. Their only safe resort is the grave."[21]

His eldest son Basil Jr. was similarly despondent and defiant by turns. "I feel chagrined, disappointed, disheartened," he admitted in November 1862. "These alternating extremes of protracted lethargy and sudden convulsive alarms, these late discoveries of amazing and irreparable neglects, these calls on private liberality, enterprise, and patriotism to remedy official stupidity, indolence, and negligence, these loud boastings beforehand and shameful confessions afterward are enough to drive a wise man mad." He echoed his father's pessimism, declaring, "I have begun to think that we may look out for subjugation, that we are doomed, that our earthly all is fated to ruin, that we are to be conquered, not by the energy or valor of our outnumbering enemies, but by our own supineness and neglect." He concluded that if such corruption continued, the Confederacy would find itself "not fit to be free," its men "not fit to be masters of our own soil, or rulers of ourselves."[22]

By the fall of 1863, especially in light of the momentous Confederate defeats at Gettysburg and Vicksburg, Sarah Manly seemed to affirm her husband and sons' dire prediction, and resigned herself to this verdict and its consequences, expressing only a selfish yet still self-righteous hope to her daughter: "If my sons were only *free* [from their military service and/or obligations as chaplains], and this wretched war was over, how happily we could live with God's blessing."[23]

Predictably, the prospect of emancipation figured as the most egregious potential result of possible military and political defeat in the Manlys' minds. Even in the first months of the war, Basil Sr. had seen clearly that the war would fundamentally alter race relations in the South and the nation. He observed that "many negroes in all our towns, male and female, can read, and they see the papers regularly ... and hear our conversations. They seem not to attend, but they form their own conclusions *in silence*." He saw in such conclusions a potential catastrophe, a conclusion confirmed by repeated newspaper reports, as he recounted in a letter to his son Basil: "Many negroes have turned against their houses, have joined the enemy, and have even helped them to plans for capturing their owners, as well as for obtaining supplies. The Yankees, now talk of freedom for them." He considered all the proposed plans for such an end merely "golden visions and delusions, which the negro has not sagacity to dispel. Unless the hand of God interpose, they will be allured and entangled, and the result of any extended outbreak will be the destruction (annihilation) of their race, perhaps of the other [white] race, too."[24]

But Reverend Manly Sr.'s derision of U.S. emancipation proposals and his decidedly white supremacist prejudices against enslaved Blacks did not preclude him from assessing his own relationship to the enslaved in his midst. He expressed particular concern over the spiritual state of those he himself enslaved, as well as the enslaved members of his congregation and his community. How to reach them and make good on paternalistic claims to their proper moral instruction was a persistent source of consternation for the aging minister. "It is the most difficult problem of the Southern Pastor, to know what to do with [the enslaved population] and do it." The issue, which had plagued his conscience since youth, engrossed his every thought in the midst of war and in the face of possible Confederate defeat and emancipation.[25]

Confronted with the prospect of Black emancipation, Basil Jr. shared his father's paternalistic concern for the moral state of Black southerners, as well as the white supremacist and patriarchal assumptions from which such concerns sprang. "Slavery I consider drawing near its end, let the conflict terminate however it may," he reasoned in early 1865. "Nor is it a source of profound regret in my mind. It has elevated the slave. It has sundered but not elevated the master. Perhaps some new system, serfdom or peonage, or some semi-feudal arrangement may grow up out of the confusion and chaos which the war is breeding," he speculated, before predicting that such prospects might "serve to elevate both master and slave, or in some way fulfill providential designs." Citing recent southern proposals to arm enslaved Blacks in Confederate military service as proof, he reckoned that even if the Confederate States achieved independence, its system of slavery would be no more. "Already the indications are very obvious of a striking change of sentiment in reference to this subject among the thoughtful men of the army," he noted. "Events move rapidly in Revolutions when melted in the crucible of war, people become much more fluid and capable of abandoning long cherished views and deep-rooted sentiments."[26]

In coming to terms with this increasingly probable outcome of the war, he speculated on the possible means by which it would be enacted. From his home near Greenville, South Carolina, in May of 1865, he recorded the results of a recent meeting with his own enslaved laborers regarding their emancipation. "Perhaps it was premature," he wrote to his parents, "but we know they had heard and would hear a good deal on the subject, and perhaps much that was incorrect, and we might do good by a plain talk. I told them that there were movements going on which could not well be understood yet, but there was a probability that they might after a while become free and have to shift for themselves, and . . . I had no intention to resist it, nor fall out with them about it." He recalled that he had told them he "should probably give them a part of the crop . . . so they ought to do their best, without watching or urging," and that "as long as they stayed on the place we must have order and obedience, as their master [Manly Jr. himself] expected to make no difference in [his] treatment of them and should stand no airs nor assumptions on their part." He concluded the letter, "Of course they all wanted to stay." As a pastor with a decidedly prejudiced paternalistic worldview, Basil Manly Jr.'s attitude toward the prospective freed people and his proposals regarding the proper white response to their possible emancipation followed predictably pious, albeit pervasively biased, channels.[27]

Along these lines, he shared with his father a resolution his church had recently made regarding its Black congregants, one which sought to answer the question "What arrangements under existing circumstances are best for the discipline and instruction of our colored members?" He told his father that his mind had been "unsettled as to the course that ought to be pursued" but that the final resolution reflected his "convictions that our serenity as citizens and our happiness as Christians depends on our attempting faithfully to discharge the duty of instructing them." He justified these convictions by proclaiming, "It can't be wrong to teach sinful men God's word, and to strive with Christian zeal to win their confidence that we may lead them to Heaven."[28]

One of the resolution's animating concerns was that "in many of the churches [the freed people] are more numerous than the whites," and the members worried that "the novel circumstances of their condition" had "alienated them from their former owners . . . [and] shaken a large portion of them from their adherence to Jesus." To avoid such alienation, the congregation had resolved, "We should not withhold from our colored members kind, earnest, scriptural instruction and faithful discipline. So long as they dwell among us, self-interest as well as benevolence and regard for the honor of Christians requires such care, however laborious it may be."[29]

Despite this expressed concern for the moral state of former enslavers and the formerly enslaved alike, the realities of Confederate defeat soon forced Basil Jr. to shift his focus to the more temporal concerns attending emancipation. "Everything here seems settling down solidly and stolidly into the conclusion that the war is over, that we must just take the best we can get, and comport ourselves by the assurance that 'what is to be, will be,'" he remarked in May 1865. "We hear that the negroes in this state are declared free," he noted later that month, "but are advised to stay with their so-called owners, making contracts to work out the present crop and be paid in a part of the proceeds."[30]

Manly Jr. proceeded to outline the stipulations of the Union policy toward freed people as he understood it, citing specifically the mandate that any labor contracts with the formerly enslaved had to be in writing and had to meet the approval of the local military commander. He further explained the clause requiring planters to reserve half their crops for "fair" distribution to the laborers, and to provide "all necessary subsistence tools." Failure to secure such contracts, he then explained, would result in the planter's forfeiture of the entire crop. If a planter tried to avoid these mandates by refusing to cultivate his land, it would be seized by the government to be distributed among colonies of freed people. He predicted the policy would result in "most of the valuable plantations ... becom[ing] government property and ... [being] disposed of to benefit these colonies of blacks from the interior." Manly then speculated that "the region lining the coast appears to be set apart for the Paradise of Darkeydom, whither the 'freedmen from the interior' are to be transported and have lots assigned them. That may have the effect of depleting the upper country at least to some extent, and delivering us in part of the lazy and fickle who look for freedom as meaning a life without work, and who long for some change of locality if of nothing else."[31]

And so Basil Manly Jr's cautiously optimistic paternalism proved fleeting in the face of his increasingly cynical conception of the Union policy toward freed people and its consequences. Such cynicism eventually engendered a palpable pessimism regarding the future of both races in the postwar South. Basil Jr. vented this growing bitterness toward Confederate defeat, subsequent postwar Reconstruction policies, and freed people, in a letter to his parents: "Much has been said of the violations of the marriage relation by masters who break it up by removals. But there will be more families broken up and more negro women and children left worse than widows and orphans in one year after freedom than has been the case in 20 years altogether" under slavery. "For all these events, however, *we* are not responsible. Still the effects of it we shall have to bear as well as witness. Our eyes will be pained by the sight of misery which we shall lack means to relieve, our ears will be assailed with applications perhaps from our own former slaves ... while the scanty remains of former affluence will be insufficient to provide for our own wants, and bestow upon them too." He predicted that rampant "stealing will provoke killing, and that will be revenged by midnight burnings and aggressive action," before concluding, "Nice country this will be to live in."[32]

It was with such low expectations that he set about reordering his own economic affairs. "I have just returned from an ineffectual effort to make a 'contract' with my plantation hands," he wrote to his father in August 1865. "They refuse to *sign any paper*. I suppose this arises from a report which it is likely the negro troops set afloat, that signing a contract signs away their liberty, and brings them again into bondage." He then explained that "they do not object to the terms I offer" but were nevertheless "going ahead in rather a slipshod way." He observed that most "*profess* to be at work, and are quite civil and respectful, [and] have no notion of leaving," but that after the new year he would be forced to "see to my own children and their support and have the darkies to see to theirs." He then expressed his despair in the face of what he deemed "dark times, proceedings, humiliations, doubts, [and] but little sunshine or joy or hope except Heavenwards," before praying, "Let the days past be gone, swiftly, silently, irrevocably ... may God forgive what was amiss, and bless any feeble attempts to do good."[33]

Like his son Basil Jr., Basil Manly Sr., who had long advised his fellow "Christian masters" to fulfill their paternalistic duties to those they enslaved, continued in that vein after emancipation by urging these former enslavers to look to the welfare of those they formerly enslaved as they navigated the tumultuous road of newfound freedom. But he too eventually threw up his hands in dejection as Reconstruction proceeded into its "Radical Republican" phase. In early 1868 he wrote to his children, "We are destined to get better servants and cheaper, by slow degrees. The negroes will die out and disappear, except the few that early learn to be industrious and managing. And they will be glad to keep a place, when they get it." As for the rest, he wrote, "We scarcely need to commiserate any of the poor negroes now. They will run their course rapidly to extinction." By that summer he reiterated, "I expect gradual impoverishment and the utter waste of all that we possess.... I think the most of [the freed people] will die out before they learn to make the necessary change"; in the meantime, he deemed it imperative that they "be watched and held to a rigid account." Clearly straitened circumstances, armed Blacks, and widespread uncertainty had soured the Manlys' more paternalistic notions and replaced them with distrust, disgust, and despair.[34]

Such hopeful conciliation-turned-bitter despondency did not wholly stifle the Manly spirit, however. In the summer following the war's end, Manly Sr. had seriously contemplated expatriating to Brazil or some other South American country: "Here are many more that would gladly leave if they could save enough out of the wreck of their fortunes to take them away." But he checked himself: "I am too old, and too much of an invalid, to lead in an enterprise of emigration. Else I think I should prefer some other country to that which now remains, encumbered as it is." He then admitted, "For some time I thought there would be no need of my taking any oath to the Yankee Government," but "as time has passed I become informed that not only will no right be regarded or recognized or protected without it, but I may be proceeded against as worth more than $20,000. I have therefore taken the customary oath and have applied for *pardon*." But such concessions did not preclude, and perhaps even fueled, his defiant conclusion three years later: "I am becoming less and less inclined to any intercourse with the northern people. Their very framework of mind and principles is different from ours. Their civilization is different. They seem to have a religion that pushes them on with zeal and a certain liberality in the use of money," he noted, "but I have failed to discern anything love-some in their character. When we get into another world, we may understand each other better."[35]

Sarah Manly's emotional struggles both inflected and reflected those of her husband and sons during the postwar Reconstruction period. By the latter half of 1868, her emotions had run much the same gamut as theirs. In writing to her eldest son Basil Jr. that September, Sarah Manly praised her son's "moderation" toward federal officers stationed in his vicinity as likely the best course of action, but then asserted, "It must have been singularly difficult to keep hands off there impudent officials. Can there ever be a feeling of common respect for the Yankee as such? *Some* good Yankees there *may* be." Just two months later, however, her rancor had subsided substantially as her thoughts turned inward to her heart and hearthstone. She related and reiterated her husband's recent assertion: "As a family we have within ourselves, with God's blessing, the ability to make a comfortable support for ourselves, and those dependent on us." In this tone she then counted her blessings rather than compiling her grievances: "We feel humbly grateful that God has blessed our dear children with spiritual mercies and permitted our sons to labor in His cause as ministers and now our youngest is called to serve His church as a Deacon." Though now in response to confirmed military defeat and Black emancipation, Sarah Manly's perspective carried over into the postwar years largely unabated, revealing the degree to which her and her family remained convinced in their faith and their culture's values despite these new realities and possibly even in steadfast resistance to them.[36]

Basil Manly Sr. died in December 1868—just over a month short of his seventy-first birthday—leaving it to his sons and daughters and their widowed mother to reconcile themselves to defeat and emancipation. Basil Manly Jr. personified their continued emotional struggle in reflecting on a recent trip to Arlington, Virginia, in 1870. He admitted that the sight of Robert E. Lee's former plantation awakened "some bitter feelings, born of the war and its results," but quickly asserted that these eventually gave way "to more overwhelming, and I trust more profitable thoughts." He proceeded to laud the character and career of General Lee as a model of southern righteous honor and white southern manhood, and in so doing anticipated a pillar of what would become the postwar South's civil religion—the "Lost Cause." "The same spirit of unassuming simplicity and self-sacrifice, which moved him through the war," Manly Jr. argued, "controlled his course at its close, and decided the direction of his subsequent labors. It is easier to rise gracefully than to descend, but to bear losses and humiliation and overwhelming disaster is the severest test of true magnanimity... It is not difficult to be grand in victory. It requires greatness to be grand in defeat." Despite the great odds stacked against him during his command of the Confederate Army of Northern Virginia, Lee had, Manly Jr. claimed, indeed remained "grand in defeat," in life and even in death.[37]

Manly Jr. singled out Lee's Christian restraint as the source of his virtue and the strength of his manhood. Lee, in short, exemplified the implicit ideal of white southern righteous honor, both in the self-mastery he had so frequently exhibited and in the righteous violence he had enacted as the commander of Confederate armies. Even after defeat, Manly Jr. insisted, "he spoke only to calm the raging passions, or cheer the despairing energies of the people for whom he would gladly have died, to counsel trust in God, quiet industry, honest endeavors to build up the mind fragments, and retrieve in peace what we had lost in fatal war." This Lee did, according to Manly Jr., "with scarcely an external indication of the volcanic emotions which he restrained and controlled." Lee thus embodied the best of the southern Confederacy and especially the men who had fought for it, those "thoughtful men, who threw themselves into that war... not actuated by blind passion," not "influenced by regard to their present and immediate interests, by the value of their slave property," but rather "actuated by a noble motive, sincere and honorable, even if misguided."[38]

In giving this tribute to Lee, Basil Manly Jr. presaged countless reassertions of this southern righteous honor and ideal white manhood that would follow in the coming decades. As federal Reconstruction ended and white southern men "redeemed" their state governments, they whitewashed the public memory of the Civil War and Reconstruction and eventually reasserted white supremacy through legal disfranchisement in tandem with the segregation of—and extralegal violence toward—Black southerners. The implicit white southern moral and ethical ideal of righteous honor and attendant conceptions of "true manliness" reflected and promoted the change.[39]

But try as they might to both remember their turbulent past and project their vision of the future in the most virtuous light, leading white southern men in the postwar South could never quite escape the contradictions inherent in their righteous honor ideal. Self-mastery had proven deficient, righteous violence ineffective, in defending their inherently prejudicial claims to power and virtue. That failure—embodied in military defeat and emancipation—fundamentally foundered their worldview. And yet they clung to its vestiges like the shards of a shattered legendary sword, exalting elements of its cultural values and social structures like sacred relics, a sense of masculine righteous honor grounded in an overt belief in white supremacy and patriarchal authority foremost among them. Despite this failure, these mores and mandates proved compelling for many white southerners simultaneously seeking to redeem their questionable past and ensure a prosperous future for their race and their region.

In the tumult of postwar Reconstruction, this sense of righteous honor could and did serve various means toward these ends, especially in the more conspicuous and often violent assertion of white supremacy necessitated (in the minds of many white southerners) by the emancipation of the formerly enslaved and the eradication of the racial patriarchy that had structured race relations within the antebellum southern slave system. Racial prejudice and hierarchy did not fade away much less disappear with slavery's demise. Instead, white assertions of supremacy intensified and were reinforced at every turn by equally fervent assertions of patriarchal authority within this overarching postwar agenda. Righteous honor implicitly provided the ideological constructs to guide individual and collective white southern identity through these self-described travails. An emphasis on whites' superior ability to achieve self-mastery became more important than ever, as did the ability to resort to righteous violence whenever this sense of righteous honor and its white supremacist claims were threatened.[40]

In 1876, amidst a hotly contested and, in the South especially, pervasively corrupt and violent national presidential election that saw white Democrats forcibly regain political control at the local and state level, a white Democrat from Edgefield, South Carolina, named Abner W. Atkinson clearly evinced the overarching persistence of righteous honor and its subtle evolution in response to altered postwar circumstances. Just weeks before the infamous Hamburg Massacre (July 1876) and Ellenton Riot (September 1876) in which white Democrats deployed racialized violence to ensure a Democratic victory in the forthcoming November election, Atkinson fervently pressed a formerly enslaved local Black man named Jerry Thornton Moore to join the local Democratic club and vote Democratic in the coming election. He even went so far as to pronounce: "Well I can tell you if you don't do it you will be put out of doors. You can't stay on my land, and you can't come on nobody's land. You will have to leave. The land is all owned by the white people, and we are going to have the election in spite of everything. We will have it if we have to wade in blood knee deep." When Moore responded, "You tried that once, and what's the use to start that thing again?" Atkinson retorted, "But, I tell you, our sons won't stand it. We can't keep them down."[41]

Atkinson's insistence that the rising generation of white southern men would be less accommodating than his own had purportedly been, that they especially would not relent in their efforts to reassert white supremacy and patriarchal authority in the region, underlined much of the shift in rhetoric and action so vividly personified in the Manlys' experience during the Civil War and its aftermath, as well as in subsequent efforts by white southern Democrats to end "Radical Reconstruction" in 1876–77 and usher in the rise of the Jim Crow South in the 1880s and 1890s. The gendered and racially prejudiced assumptions and legacies of an altered-yet-persistent sense of righteous honor and its applications would set the dominant tone for the white South's collective—and selective—memory (and willful amnesia) regarding the Civil War era for generations to come.[42]

Epilogue

The Damnable Legacies of Righteous Honor

> Unconquered still in soul, tho' now o'er-run,
> In peace, in war, the battle's just begun!
> Once this Thyestean banquet o'er,
> Grown strong the few who bide their hour,
> Shall rise and hurl its drunken guests from power,
> In the land where we were dreaming!
> —Daniel Bedinger Lucas, "In the Land Where
>   We Were Dreaming"

> Forth from its scabbard all in vain
> Bright flashed the sword of Lee;
> 'Tis shrouded now in its sheath again,
> It sleeps the sleep of our noble slain,
> Defeated, yet without stain,
> Proudly and peacefully!
> —Father Abram Joseph Ryan,
>   "The Sword of Robert Lee"

A COMMENCEMENT SPEECH delivered at the University of Georgia in 1879 poignantly illustrated the extent to which altered though familiar conceptions of righteous honor and southern manhood still permeated white society and culture in the wake of Reconstruction. Elijah Alexander Brown delivered his speech nearly a decade after Basil Manly Jr. penned his tribute to Robert E. Lee and just three years after

Abner W. Atkinson expressed the demeanor of many white southerners who had refused to concede power and authority in the face of defeat, emancipation, and federal Reconstruction. Brown epitomized the rising generation of elite white southern men. The son of Georgia's famed wartime governor Joseph Emerson Brown and just eight years old when the Civil War ended, Elijah Brown came of age during Reconstruction, like others of his generation, their mission in life to secure the "Redemption" that formally ended it and fomented the rise of Jim Crow. As such, Brown and his speech revealed the degree to which white southerners had successfully begun to reassert their dominance in the southern social and political order following the Compromise of 1877 and the formal end of federal Reconstruction it enacted. Feeling burdened with the fallout from their fathers' exploits, they inherited and revised the Lost Cause faith and authored the New South creed that together would, they claimed, guide the South into its future, a future in which they would secure white supremacy, ensure black dependency, and thereby assure an inherently gendered and racially prejudiced definition of progress and prosperity for the region at large. To justify their claims to authority, they adapted their fathers' sense of righteous honor—its emphasis on self-mastery as well as its sanction of righteous violence—to new social and economic circumstances while simultaneously commemorating the region's past by memorializing its Confederate martyrs and revering its Confederate veterans as idols. Using this white-washed historical vision they would pave the path toward a New South at least nominally reconciled to the North so long as white northerners agreed with (or at least turned a blind eye to) their reassertion of white supremacy in the South, all at the conscious and conspicuous expense of Black southerners' rights.[1]

Brown's 1879 commencement speech portrayed such themes in their best light, ignoring their more nefarious desired ends: "One of the noblest and most pleasing, as well as the most admirable and highly appreciated traits in the human character is that of *true manliness*," he declared in his opening statement. "It is 'a pearl of great price' for the attainment of which each and *every one of us* should assiduously labor, and in which we should strive to perfect ourselves. One of our greatest aims," he continued, "should be to thoroughly know ourselves, without which we cannot attain to the highest rank of true manhood, which will prepare us to live for *our country*, and make every necessary sacrifice in her behalf, and to devote ourselves to the cause of that 'religion which is pure and undefiled.'"[2]

Having reasserted the primacy of white self-mastery as the bedrock of righteous honor, and this sense of righteous honor as the cornerstone of true (white) southern manhood, Brown then proceeded to specify "the lofty traits of true manliness" in the postwar South: "Fidelity to our country and to our God, [firmness (of purpose, steadiness of deportment, courtesy),] stability of character, promptness in meeting every engagement, [(nobleness of mind),] courage in the discharge of every duty, justice to all, unwavering integrity, and strict conformity to the path of virtue and rectitude." (In the original text, Brown had written and then struck out the phrases shown here in brackets.) "A true man," he continued, "is one whose virtues cannot justly be impeached by even the bitterest of his enemies: whose *reputation* is not stained by the least degree of intolerance or enmity: whose kindness of heart is such as to restrain his lips from utterance tending to wound even his conquered foes."[3]

Brown had placed a finger on the pulse of elite white society and culture in the wake of federal Reconstruction and amid the ascent of the "Solid South" that would reign for generations to come in the impending Jim Crow era. But the "true manliness" that Brown emphasized drew upon long-standing moral and ethical ideals rooted in the racial patriarchy of a mythologized Old South even as it anticipated the emergence and expansion of the New South. His melding of secular ethics and sacred morals to fashion an ideal white manhood predicated on the precepts of righteous honor repurposed the antebellum proslavery defense for the postwar, post-emancipation world, and did so in ways at once familiar and novel. A commitment to upholding white supremacy constituted the common denominator across the eras, as did an equally fervent commitment to patriarchal order. Even after military defeat and the destruction of the slave system, elite white men of Brown's generation still posited themselves as uniquely qualified, even divinely ordained, to oversee the "progress" of the New South, just as their fathers and grandfathers had done in the old.[4] Jim Crow was their progeny and legacy, and though declared legally dead during the civil rights movement of the 1960s, his ghost continues to haunt the nation through persistent though adaptive adherence to and application of white supremacist ideals manifested in myriad forms of racial inequality and discrimination clearly visible to anyone willing to look through the veil of colorblind platitudes deliberately deployed to obscure them.[5]

The first antebellum generation of elite white southern men, represented most conspicuously in the lives of Basil Manly Sr., Iveson Lewis Brookes,

Whitfield Brooks, and Joseph Milligan Jr., began to conceive of their personal and public honor and piety in increasingly distinct ways from their forebears. Neither value system originated in the antebellum period, but both prevailed alongside each other during this era in unprecedented ways. And their simultaneous cultural prevalence both inflected and reflected the emerging sectional divide in the antebellum United States, a divide that hinged on increasingly contentious sectional visions for the nation's future and the role of slavery within it. As sectional identity became more and more pronounced, so too did the perceived need to present a united ideological front in the region's public culture. Many within this first antebellum generation transformed their views on southern slavery, honor, and piety amid this growing tension, and these transformations manifested in both their private and public lives in interrelated ways.

Many had harbored doubts about the moral and ethical sanctity of the South's slave system in their youth. But as they became self-proclaimed masters of their own private households in the early antebellum period, they came to conceive of both their personal honor and piety as the basis of their patriarchal power and paternalistic responsibility within the southern slave system. This conception of their personal lives shaped their thoughts and actions in public affairs, whether as ministers or statesmen, planters or professionals. Slavery began to transform in their minds from a "necessary evil" to a "positive good," though the transformation remained fraught with doubt and vulnerable to insecurity. Honor and piety, patriarchal power and paternalistic responsibility became two sides of the same moral and ethical coin, often in tension to be sure, but compatible, even complementary in ways they increasingly emphasized as they confronted both personal misgivings and cultural contradictions. As elite white southern men privileged with ultimate authority in the South's slave regime, they came to assert their self-mastery as the basis of that authority and invoked prescribed forms of righteous violence as their particular prerogative in executing it. Together these points of emphasis, readily observed in their personal lives and public affairs, constituted their sense of righteous honor, by which they sought to sanctify themselves, their families, and their society.

Their sons, Basil Manly Jr. and Charles Manly, Walker Brookes, Preston Brooks, and Joseph A. S. Milligan inherited this sense of righteous honor. But the late antebellum world in which they came of age precluded the same degree of doubt and vulnerability afforded their fathers' generation. Whereas their fathers had once lamented slavery as a necessary evil, these sons had only ever considered it as a positive good; whereas their fathers had at least nominally admitted the fault lines in their moral and ethnical code, even sometimes in public, these sons publicly denied such faults, however much they privately shared the persistent doubts and felt the persistent vulnerabilities. The heightened sectional controversies that necessitated the shift in their fathers' thinking embedded the same values and worldview in these sons from the very beginning. The proslavery defense that their fathers had not fully developed or articulated consumed these sons and their sectional identities and ideologies from the outset, and it rested upon the fundamentally white supremacist and patriarchal assumptions of hierarchical social order. These sons, like their fathers before them, knew that they sat atop these hierarchies, knew the power provided them, but also felt the strain of expectations to effectively wield that power, felt the burden of responsibility attending that duty in all its private and public manifestations. Even more than their fathers, these sons felt compelled to justify that power, fulfill those responsibilities, and defend that social order by invoking both secular ethics and sacred morals beginning in the late antebellum period and continuing through the Civil War and into Reconstruction.

The heightened sectional animosity of the late antebellum period eventually prompted them to support secession, the Confederacy, and the reassertion of white supremacy in the wake of Confederate defeat and emancipation. Publicly they spoke with conviction in support of these causes, but privately they periodically gave voice to continued doubt and insecurity. The often intensely emotional ebb and flow attending this effort to meet perceived public demands for faith and confidence, all while privately struggling to quiet disbelief, infused their collective identities and ideals rooted in a sense of righteous honor. Each generation came to this understanding of the world and their place within it by different paths, and responded to the challenges of sectional division, civil war, and postwar power struggles in their own ways. But the emotional experience of the persistent tensions attending their efforts to fulfill their alleged purpose in both their private lives and public positions found common ground in their sense of righteous honor. Its dual emphasis on, first, self-mastery as the foundation of white supremacy and patriarchal order and, second, righteous violence as the necessary prerogative of those invested with supreme authority within that social order continued to predominate.

Both generations of the Manly, Brookes, Brooks, and Milligan families experienced some semblance of these tensions throughout their lives, and such tensions yet remained in Elijah Brown's post-Reconstruction oration. They, like Brown's generation, had struggled to reconcile cultural contradictions and overcome the tensions pervading their social system. They, like Brown's generation, had fought to defend these values, however fraught, against both internal dissent and external assault. They, like Brown's generation, publicly professed the righteousness of their cause even as they privately confessed its flaws; believed themselves uniquely endowed and especially empowered to ensure the former and extenuate the latter. But with the exception of Basil Manly Jr. and his brother Charles, who lived through the Reconstruction period into the Jim Crow era, they, unlike Brown's generation, had failed to effectively wield their authority to preserve their social system. Worse, they had precipitated its dissolution through secession, defeat in the Civil War, and the emancipation that followed.

Rather than dissuade Brown's postwar generation from adopting similar values as virtues, however, these postwar realities prompted men of Brown's generation to redouble their old allegiance. They succeeded where their forebears had faltered; they secured the perpetuation of white supremacy in southern politics and society and justified the means by which they did so by invoking the very same claims to self-mastery as the basis of white power and by wielding the very same righteous violence such power provided them. Only now they lorded these methods and mores over freed people and their white allies to inaugurate, then perpetuate, Jim Crow disfranchisement, segregation, and violence for generations to come. Brown spoke with supreme conviction because his generation had begun to turn the final corner in completing the arduous process of securing national sanction (or at least tacit complicity enabling the assertion) of white supremacy and patriarchal rule as the "proper" social order in the postwar South that had eluded previous generations of elite white southerners. And they did so not by discarding the memories and lessons of past generations, but by revering them as the bedrock of their Lost Cause faith and the cornerstone of their New South creed.[6]

Perhaps the conviction with which Elijah Brown and his generation spoke and acted enabled Basil Manly Jr. and his sons to return to more familiar ground with a similar confidence a decade later in 1889. During that year Manly Jr. published an article in *Seminary Magazine* entitled "Our Brother in Black," in which his optimistic and conciliatory tone at least superficially sounds a progressively hopeful note for race relations in the New South. In the article he seemed determined to confront the issue of Black freedom and Black rights directly, to salve his personal fears and resolve a regional (and national) dilemma: what was to become of the freed people and their progeny? The issue, as he explained it, was one of paramount concern: "The history of the black man in America is one of the most striking chapters in the providential designs of God with this country. He is a factor that enters, sometimes most perplexingly, into every problem—social, financial, religious, or political—that agitates the public mind." Despite white fears, reservations, and prejudices, the Black man, he wrote, "is here, and he is going to stay ... It is a part of [our] business to see what becomes of him. I am not ascribing exaggerated importance to the negro, when I say that he cannot be ignored or neglected without harm to the gravest interest of our country: for I am but uttering what is the glory of our land, that no class in it, however humble, can be ignored or despised without affecting the welfare of all."[7]

Having laid out the import of his subject, he then struck a nominally progressive, if still prejudiced and paternalistic, tone: "The only way then to deal with the black man whom we find in America—is to give him his rights, cordially, frankly, fully," he declared before asserting a decidedly paternalistic perspective: "The freedman is a man, neither more nor less ... His past condition of servitude is not unimportant, as affecting his present state and our present responsibilities." In Manly Jr.'s mind, "The momentous question is not what he was, but what he is, and especially what he is going to be ... he is not a babe, to be fondled and pitied. He is not a brute, to be trampled and despised. He is not a fiend or a savage to be shunned and dreaded, nor an angel to be admired and flattered. He is simply a man." He then exclaimed, "Oh! how hard it is to know, and how harder still to do just what is right!" before asserting, "The question is—not how much can be got out of the colored man as a worker, nor how much use can be made of him as a voter—but how much can be put into him as a man, how much can be done for him as an immortal?"[8]

But the trend in the region's race relations during the interim between Elijah Brown's commencement speech and Basil Manly Jr.'s article undermined the authenticity of such sentiments and exposed the persistence of deep-seated racial prejudices continuing to parade under the guise of elite white Christian paternalism. This guise shrouded the more sinister reality in which elite white southerners had enthroned the Jim Crow regime through black disfranchisement, racial segregation, and racial violence in the 1880s and 1890s, and invoked a familiar sense of righteous honor to defend the means by which they had done so. Following the landmark

Plessy v. Ferguson case in 1896, when the U.S. Supreme Court endorsed the "separate but equal" racial status quo in the region, the paths of many elite white southerners of both Basil Manly Jr.'s and Elijah Brown's respective generations largely converged. No longer threatened by external derision or internal dissension from most whites and having reinstituted white patriarchal control in southern society, they retained a sense of righteous honor, but one no longer grounded in the tenuous moral and ethical balance of the besieged but in the confidence of the powerful.[9] As historians examining the intersection of Civil War memory and racial politics and culture, alongside other scholars of racial, gendered, religious, and political dynamics have collectively shown, the nefarious results of that shift were far reaching and remain ingrained in the American psyche, ensconced in American society, and embedded in American culture: the lasting, lamentable legacy of the nation's long-standing embrace of white supremacy that spans the colonial era to the contentious present.[10]

NOTES

Abbreviations

BMSr	Basil Manly Sr. Papers, Furman
EBC	Edgefield Baptist Church Records, TGL
ECA	Edgefield County Archives
Furman	James Buchanan Duke Special Collections Library, Furman University
HCB	Horn's Creek Baptist Church Minutes, 1824–1860, TGL
HFP	Hughes Family papers, UNC
ILB-UNC	Iveson Lewis Brookes Papers, UNC
ILB-USC	Iveson Lewis Brooks Papers, 1793–1865, USC
LSCB	Little Stephen's Creek Baptist Church Records, TGL
MaFP-Furman	Manly Family Papers, Furman
MaFP-SBHL	Manly Family Papers, Southern Baptist Historical Library and Archives
MiFP	Milligan Family Papers, UNC
PSB	Preston S. Brooks papers, USC
TGL	Tompkins Genealogical Library
UNC	Southern Historical Collection, UNC
USC	South Caroliniana Library, University of South Carolina
WBJ	William Bullein Johnson Papers, Furman

Introduction

1. Williamjames Hull Hoffer, *The Caning of Charles Sumner*, 1–65; Manisha Sinha, "The Caning of Charles Sumner," 233–62; T. Lloyd Benson, *The Caning of Senator Sumner*, 1–156.
2. Robert Neil Mathis, "Preston Brooks: The Man and His Image," 296–310; Hoffer, *The Caning of Charles Sumner*, 66–133; Sinha, "The Caning of Charles Sumner," 233–62; Benson, *The Caning of Senator Sumner*, 157–222; Stephen Berry and James Hill Welborn III, "The Cane of His Existence," 5–21. This conception of Brooks, the caning, and their legacy in myriad forms and expressions of patriarchal white supremacy and violence since echoes the recent reassessment of Brooks's even more notorious fellow South Carolina politician, John C. Calhoun, by Robert Elder in *Calhoun*, xii–xiv, 525–46.

3. The theoretical approach and historical perspective applied here in relation to honor within southern culture during the Civil War era extends the analyses of religion and violence within American culture embodied in the following selected works: John D. Carlson and Jonathan H. Ebel, eds., *From Jeremiad to Jihad*, 1–28, 91–110, 128–42; Jon Pahl, *Empire of Sacrifice*, 1–34, 63–84; Carroll Smith-Rosenberg, *This Violent Empire*; Jeffrey Williams, *Religion and Violence in Early Methodism*, 93–130, 161–78; Andrew Preston, *Sword of the Spirit, Shield of the Faith*, 3–232.
4. Michael Woods, *Emotional and Sectional Conflict in the Antebellum United States*; James J. Broomall, *Private Confederacies*. The application of "emotions history" to the antebellum U.S. and Civil War South as deployed by Woods and Broomall most directly inform the "inner lives" approach outlined here. The foundation of emotions history lies in the following germinal works: Peter N. Stearns and Carol Z. Stearns, *Anger* and *Emotion and Social Change*; Peter N. Stearns and Jan Lewis, eds., *An Emotional History of the United States*.
5. The most pertinent studies informing this conception of the role of white violence in southern society during the Civil War era include Clement Eaton, *The Growth of Southern Civilization*, 271–78; Richard E. Nisbett and David Cohen, *Culture of Honor*; Jack Kenny Williams, *Vogues in Villainy*; Richard Maxwell Brown, *Strain of Violence*.
6. For related analyses of self-mastery in southern masculine culture, see especially Christine Leigh Heyrman, *Southern Cross*, 246–50, and Timothy J. Williams, *Intellectual Manhood*, 19–22, 93–95, 141–68. The most pertinent works to acknowledge the importance of self-control or self-discipline within southern masculine ethics are Edward L. Ayers, *Vengeance and Justice*, 27–33; Dickson D. Bruce Jr., *Violence and Culture in the Antebellum South*, 8–12, 233–40; Steven M. Stowe, *Intimacy and Power in the Old South*, x–xviii, 1–49.
7. Bertram Wyatt-Brown, *Southern Honor* and *The Shaping of Southern Culture*; Edward L. Ayers, *Vengeance and Justice*; Kenneth Greenberg, *Honor and Slavery*; John Mayfield and Todd Hagstette, eds., *The Field of Honor*.
8. Donald G. Mathews, *Religion in the Old South*; Anne C. Loveland, *Southern Evangelicals and the Social Order*; Rhys Isaac, *The Transformation of Virginia*; Robert M. Calhoon, *Evangelicals and Conservatives in the Early South*; John B. Boles, *The Great Revival*; Heyrman, *Southern Cross*; Cynthia Lynn Lyerly, *Methodism and the Southern Mind*; Philip N. Mulder, *A Controversial Spirit*; Monica Najar, *Evangelizing the South*.
9. Ayers, *Vengeance and Justice*, 27–31; Bruce, *Violence and Culture*, 233–40; Wyatt-Brown, *Southern Honor*, 88–116, and *The Shaping of Southern Culture*, 83–135; William H. Swatos, *Mediating Capitalism and Slavery*. Clement Eaton also explored the intersection of these ideals within white southern

society and culture in *The Mind of the Old South*, 23, 200–223, 245–312. Both Ayers and Bruce acknowledge the mutually reinforcing *potential* inherent in the cultural values associated with the dominant ideals of honor and piety in the antebellum South, but both conclude that distinct groups tended to align to one or the other ideal in exclusionary ways that precluded effective or extended combination in either individual or collective identity and ideology. Wyatt-Brown investigates the mutuality of these ideals more thoroughly and concludes that the concepts of "gentility" and "grace" provided the common ground for honor and religion, respectively, to both exercise considerable power and influence within antebellum southern culture. Swatos arrives at a similar conclusion to explain how white Christians conceived of their racialized slave system in relation to prevailing ethical and moral codes. These conceptions of religion tempering honor fails to fully account, however, for the often violent ways in which both could be marshalled into the service of proslavery sectionalism during the antebellum sectional crisis, the secession crisis, the Civil War, and even extended to reassert white supremacy and resist federal intervention during the postwar battles to define and dictate the terms of peace and prosperity in the Reconstruction Era and into the "New South" and Jim Crow era.

10. Heather Cox Richardson, *How the South Won the Civil War*, xiii–xxix, 179–205; Adam Domby, *The False Cause*, 145–70; Karen L. Cox, *No Common Ground*, 106–74; David Blight, "The Civil War Lies on Us Like a Sleeping Dragon," *Guardian* (August 20, 2017), reprinted in Catherin Clinton, ed., *Confederate Statues and Memorialization*, 93–102; Ty Seidule, *Robert E. Lee and Me*, 1–9, 248–56.
11. Ted Ownby, *Subduing Satan*, 167; Joanne Freeman, *Affairs of Honor*; Amy Greenberg, *Manifest Manhood and the Antebellum*; Craig Friend and Lorri Glover, eds., *Southern Manhood*; and Friend, ed., *Southern Masculinity*. For more on this tension within prevailing conceptions of manhood and masculinity in the broader context of the Victorian Era, see especially Norman Vance, *The Sinews of the Spirit*, 1–28, 166–206; Charles H. Lippy, *Do Real Men Pray?*
12. Lorri Glover, *Southern Sons*; Stephen W. Berry, *All That Makes a Man*; Peter S. Carmichael, *The Last Generation*.
13. John Mayfield, "'The Soul of a Man!'" 477–500, and *Counterfeit Gentlemen*; Mayfield and Hagstette, *The Field of Honor*.
14. Tom Downey, *Planting a Capitalist South*; Elliot J. Gorn, "'Gouge and Bite, Pull Hair and Scratch,'" 18–43; Stephanie McCurry, *Masters of Small Worlds*; Timothy J. Williams, *Intellectual Manhood*; Evelyn D. Causey, "The Character of a Gentleman."
15. Ami Pflugrad-Jackisch, *Brothers of a Vow*; Jennifer R. Green, *Military Education and the Emerging Middle Class in the Old South*; Jonathan Daniel

Wells, *The Origins of the Southern Middle Class*; Jonathan Daniel Wells and Jennifer R. Green, eds., *The Southern Middle Class in the Long Nineteenth Century*.

16. Frank L. Owsley, *Plain Folk of the Old South*; Charles C. Bolton, *Poor Whites of the Antebellum South*, and Edward Isham, *The Confessions of Edward Isham*, ed. Charles C. Bolton and Scott P. Culcasure; Keri Leigh Merritt, *Masterless Men*; Jeff Forret, *Race Relations at the Margins*, and *Slave against Slave*.

17. Eugene D. Genovese, *The Slaveholders' Dilemma*; Elizabeth Fox-Genovese and Eugene D. Genovese, *The Mind of the Master Class*; Bertram Wyatt-Brown, *Yankee Saints and Southern Sinners*, 131–213, and *The Shaping of Southern Culture*, 136–202; Bruce, *Violence and Culture*, 161–77; John Hope Franklin, *The Militant South*.

18. Edward R. Crowther, "Holy Honor," 619–20: A. James Fuller, *Chaplain to the Confederacy*; Charity R. Carney, *Ministers and Masters*; David T. Moon, "Southern Baptists and Southern Men," 563–606; Robert Elder, *The Sacred Mirror*.

19. On the role of this prejudicial legacy in the rise of Jim Crow, see especially Carol Emberton, *Beyond Redemption*; Grace Elizabeth Hale, *Making Whiteness*; Kristina DuRocher, *Raising Racists*; Stephanie Cole and Natalie J. Ring, eds., *The Folly of Jim Crow*; Sarah Haley, *No Mercy Here*; Bruce E. Baker, *What Reconstruction Meant*, 1–68; Domby, *The False Cause*, 1–75; Richardson, *How the South Won the Civil War*, xiii–123; Hoffer, *Plessy v. Ferguson*; Henry Louis Gates, *Stony the Road*; Glenda E. Gilmore, *Gender and Jim Crow*. On the intersection of Civil War memory and prejudicial gender and racial politics in American history and culture since 1896, see especially Baker, *What Reconstruction Meant*, 1–12, 21–170; Domby, *The False Cause*, 76–170; Richardson, *How the South Won the Civil War*, 124–205; Cox, *No Common Ground*, 1–174; Blight, "The Civil War Lies on Us," reprinted in Clinton, ed., *Confederate Statues and Memorialization*, 93–102; Levin, *Searching for Black Confederates*, 68–184; Seidule, *Robert E. Lee and Me*, 1–256; Victoria E. Bynum, *The Long Shadow of the Civil War*, 101–48; Nina Silber, *This War Ain't Over*, 1–187; Kevin M. Levin, *Searching for Black Confederates*, 123–84. On the broader history and contemporary cultural legacies of such prejudicial dynamics within American society, culture, and politics see especially Mark Kann, *A Republic of Men*, 155–78; Carol Faulkner and Alison M. Parker, eds., *Interconnections*; Manisha Sinha and Penny Von Eschen, eds., *Contested Democracy*; David A. Bateman, Ira Katznelson, and John S. Lapinski, *Southern Nation*. On the religious dimensions and manifestations of this legacy, see especially Elizabeth L. Jemison, *Christian Citizens*; Michael O. Emerson and Christian Smith, *Divided by Faith*; Robert P. Jones, *White Too Long*; Anthea Butler, *White Evangelical Racism*;

Jemar Tisby, *The Color of Compromise*; Eric Weed, *The Religion of White Supremacy in the United States*; Khyati Y. Joshi, *White Christian Privilege*; Damon T. Berry, *Blood and Faith*; J. Russell Hawkins, *The Bible Told Them So*, and Hawkins and Phillip Luke Sinitiere, eds., *Christians and the Color Line*; Jesse Curtis, *The Myth of Colorblind Christians*; Kevin M. Kruse, *One Nation under God*; Darren E. Grem, *The Blessings of Business*; Kristin Kobes Du Mez, *Jesus and John Wayne*; Daniel K. Williams, *God's Own Party*; Talia Lavin, *Culture Warlords*.

20. Orville Vernon Burton, *In My Father's House Are Many Mansions*, 5, 19–20.
21. Mason Lock Weems, *The Devil in Petticoats*, 1; The quote concerning the "idiosyncrasies of a gentleman" attributed to Wade Harrison of Troy, South Carolina, sometime in the antebellum period, is representative of the reputation Edgefield "enjoyed" across South Carolina. Though no printed record of the quote exists, the oral history of the Edgefield community confirms that during his seventy-five years, Mr. Harrison's father and grandfather told him this fact many times over, and that the elder Harrison gentlemen were fond of repeating it. The prominence of this adage within the community's oral history is affirmed by Bettis Rainsford (local Edgefield historian), Tricia Price Glenn (Edgefield County archivist), and the offices of the Edgefield County Historical Society, the Edgefield County Archives, and the Tompkins Genealogical Library; Ulysses R. Brooks, *South Carolina Bench and Bar*, vol. 1, 199. The most thorough historical analyses of this Edgefield "tradition" for honor and violence are Burton, *In My Father's House*, xviii–21, 47–147; Richard Maxwell Brown, *Strain of Violence*, 37–103; John A. Chapman, *History of Edgefield County*, 5–90; Lacy K. Ford Jr., "Origins of the Edgefield Tradition," 328–48; John B. Edmunds Jr., *Francis W. Pickens and the Politics of Destruction*.
22. Arthur Simkins, "The Mount Vernon Camp-Meeting, August 17, 1854," Edgefield *Advertiser*. Edgefield's nineteenth-century religious development has typically garnered less popular attention than its tradition of honor-bound violence, but the following works most thoroughly analyze the major epochs in this history: Burton, *In My Father's House*, 21–28; Chapman, *History of Edgefield County*, 72–74, 91–92, 290–98, 306–28; Lacy K. Ford Jr., *Origins of Southern Radicalism*, 26–28; Rachel N. Klein, *Unification of a Slave State*, 42–45; 269–302; Lewis Leary, *The Book-Peddling Parson*, 117–40; James L. Underwood and William Lewis Burke, eds., *The Dawn of Religious Freedom in South Carolina*, 146–64.
23. Orville Vernon Burton, "In My Father's House Are Many Leaders," 23–32.
24. Louise Manly, *The Manly Family*, 71–132; Fuller, *Chaplain to the Confederacy*, 11–317; Daniel Lee Cloyd, "Basil Manly Sr.," in *Encyclopedia of Religion in the South*, 2nd ed., ed. Samuel S. Hill, Charles H. Lippy, and Charles Reagan Wilson, 488; Amber Wilson, "Biographical Sketch, The

Manly Family Papers," Southern Baptist Historical Library and Archives, Nashville, TN; April Burnett, "Biographical/Historical Overview," Manly Family Papers, William S. Hoole Special Collections Library, University of Alabama; "Collection Overview, Basil Manly Papers, 1849–1869," Southern Historical Collection, University of North Carolina.

25. Manly, *The Manly Family*, 197–230; Fuller, *Chaplain to the Confederacy*, 228–40; Daniel Lee Cloyd, "Basil Manly Jr.," 487; David Hoard, Jason Fowler, and Stephen Jones, "Biographical Note, Basil Manly Jr. Papers, 1842–1889," Southern Baptist Theological Seminary Archives, Louisville, KY; Wilson, "Biographical Sketch"; Burnett, "Biographical/Historical Note"; "Collection Overview, Basil Manly Papers, 1842–1893," Southern Historical Collection, University of North Carolina.

26. Manly, *The Manly Family*, 253–74; Fuller, *Chaplain to the Confederacy*, 228–40.

27. "Collection Overview, Iveson L. Brookes Papers, 1785–1868," Southern Historical Collection, University of North Carolina; Kevin Ray, "Biographical/Historical Note, Iveson L. Brookes Papers," William S. Hoole Special Collections Library, University of Alabama.

28. James O. Farmer Jr., in Whitfield Brooks, *An Edgefield Planter and His World*, xix–lxii.

29. "Collection Overview, Milligan Family Papers, 1771–1885," Southern Historical Collection, University of North Carolina.

1. Honor

1. John Lyde Wilson, *The Code of Honor*, 1.
2. Wilson, *The Code of Honor*, 2; J. Grahame Long, *Dueling in Charleston*, 45–54. Long discusses Wilson's published code of honor as an attempt to check the wanton violence provoked by the political tensions surrounding the Nullification Controversy. This chapter extends this perspective by explicitly connecting the published code to religious developments. Few scholarly works have analyzed Wilson's published honor code in this or any other context. The most extensive analysis of the southern honor code's emphasis on masculine self-control can be found in Steven M. Stowe, *Intimacy and Power in the Old South*, 6–49, and Jack Kenny Williams, "The Code of Honor in Antebellum South Carolina," 113–28, and *Dueling in the Old South*; Warren F. Schwartz, Keith Baxter and David Ryan, "The Duel," 321–55; Matthew Byron, "Crime and Punishment?"
3. Wilson, *The Code of Honor*, 1–2.
4. For works that explore the mutuality between honor and religion in the Civil War–era South, see especially Edward R. Crowther, "Holy Honor," 619–36; Eugene Genovese, "The Chivalric Tradition in the Old South,"

188–205; Charity R. Carney, *Ministers and Masters*; Robert Elder, *The Sacred Mirror*; A. James Fuller, *Chaplain to the Confederacy*; David T. Moon, "Southern Baptists and Southern Men." These works extend insights by Bertram Wyatt-Brown, first in *Southern Honor*, vii–xix, 14–15, 60–61, 99–114, 129–47, 298–99, 493, and later expanded in *The Shaping of Southern Culture*, xi–xix, 83–105.

5. For works that generally emphasize the oppositional nature of honor and religion in the Civil War–era South, see especially Edward Ayers, *Vengeance and Justice*, 9–33, 118–25; Dickson D. Bruce Jr., *Violence and Culture in the Antebellum South*, 12–14, 112–13, 233–40; Ted Ownby, *Subduing Satan*, ix–xii, 1–18, 19–99, 101–64. On the manifestation of such opposition in antidueling activism, see especially Thomas J. Carmody, "The Anti-Dueling Movement," 41–366; William S. Cossen, "Blood, Honor, Reform, and God," 23–45.

6. For more on antebellum southern honor in its most virulently violent forms, see especially Richard Maxwell Brown, *Strain of Violence*, 3–103; John Hope Franklin, *The Militant South*, 2–13, 33–79; Clement Eaton, *The Growth of Southern Civilization*, 271–78, and *The Mind of the Old South*, 23, 396–97; Richard E. Nisbett and David Cohen, *Culture of Honor*; Jack Kenny Williams, *Vogues in Villainy*; Elliot J. Gorn, "Gouge and Bite, Pull Hair and Scratch," 18–43; Sally E. Hadden, *Slave Patrols*, 41–104, 130. For broader Victorian-era associations of manhood and violence, see especially Pieter C. Spierenburg, *Men and Violence*.

7. For more on the Cherokee War, see Robert M. Weir, *Colonial South Carolina*, 265–75. For more on relations between Native Americans and British authorities and white settlers in South Carolina during the colonial and revolutionary era, see especially Tom Hatley, *The Dividing Paths*.

8. Charles Woodmason, *The Carolina Backcountry on the Eve of the Revolution*, 27–28, 54.

9. Woodmason, *The Carolina Backcountry*, 27–28, 54. For more on the Regulator movement in South Carolina, see Weir, *Colonial South Carolina*, 275–89; Walter Edgar, *South Carolina*, 211–16; Rachel N. Klein, *Unification of a Slave State*, 36–77; Woodmason, *The Carolina Backcountry*, 165–296. For more on these tensions in Edgefield, see John A. Chapman, *History of Edgefield County*, 5–71; Orville Vernon Burton, *In My Father's House Are Many Mansions*, 18–21.

10. "South Carolina, Edgefield County," March 14, 1794, Augusta *Chronicle*. For more on the American Revolution in South Carolina, see Edgar, *South Carolina*, 226–46, and *Partisans and Redcoats*; Weir, *Colonial South Carolina*, 321–29; Klein, *Unification of a Slave State*, 78–148.

11. John Rigdon, *First Families of Edgefield*; Chapman, *History of Edgefield*, 5–71.

12. Between 1785 and 1830 (the year that the Village of Edgefield was officially incorporated as the county seat) there are on record 424 cases of violence, with twenty-seven of these cases being for murder. The following cases are the most representative of this broader trend toward violence, and refer only to white crime, predominantly between white men, and include the charges of assault, assault and battery, riot, manslaughter, murder, sending a challenge, affray, assault with intent to murder: "On motion of Samuel Evans by Charles Goodwyn his attorney; it being proved by the oath of John Harris that his (Evans) ear was bit off in an affray. Ordered that this proof be admitted to the records of this court," Spring Term, 1786; "Ordered on the motion of Henry Bolton who had his ear bit off in an affray, proved by John Perryman, be admitted to the records of this court," Winter Term, 1789; "The State v. Harry Martin, Assault and gouging out one of the eyes of Richard Mirchum," Fall Term, 1804; "On motion of the Solicitor—ordered that a bench warrant be issued against Henry Martin, a bill of indictment being found against him for assaulting and gouging out one of the eyes of Richard Michum," Fall Term, 1805; Edgefield District Judge of Probate: Minutes of the General Sessions Court, ECA; "Davis Parkins affidavit. Personally appeared and made oath that he was present and did see A. Boddy in a skirmish with Young P. Salter and did see him bite a piece out of the said Salter's right ear," October 4, 1824; "Edgefield District—Personally appeared Lot Etheridge and John Jennings and sayeth on their oath that they were personally present and did see Allen Corley bite off a part of Solomon Richardson's left ear on the 28th day of August, 1815. Also, the said Allen Corley sayeth on his oath that he did bite the said Richardson's ear off as above mentioned, sworn before me this 16th day of November 1815, Spear Price J.P.," November 16, 1815—Solomon Richardson from Lot Etheridge, Edgefield District Deed Book 46, p. 406, ECA; "Ordered that a bench warrant be issued against Nathan Barker and Sampson Butler Esq. for sending and carrying a challenge to Phillip Burt," Spring Term, 1804; "The State v. Dr. Nathan Barker—For sending a challenge. Guilty. To stand committed until a fine of fifty dollars if paid," Fall Term, 1804; "The State v. Nathan Barker, sending a challenge," Spring Term, 1805; "The State v. Nathan Barker, sending a challenge," Fall Term, 1805; "The State v. William (or Walter) Taylor, sending a challenge," Spring Term, 1813; "The State v. David Barrontine and Nathan Joiner, Affray," Fall Term, 1824, Edgefield District, Minutes of the General Sessions Court, ECA; "Notification to the Public," October 1, 1808, Augusta *Chronicle*.
13. Mason Locke Weems, *The Devil in Petticoats*, 1. This post–Civil War edition was just one in a long line of reprinted Weems works. As was his custom throughout his career as an author, peddler, and religious cleric, Weems himself published multiple editions of this story, the last of which appeared

in 1823 under the revised title, *The Bad Wife's Looking Glass, or God's Revenge against Cruelty to Husbands*. This 1823 edition was consulted for the account of the Cotton murder that follows. For more on Weems and his tales, see Catherine Clinton, "Wallowing in a Swamp of Sin: Parson Weems, Sex, and Murder in Early South Carolina," in Catherine Clinton and Michele Gillespie, eds., *The Devil's Lane*, 24–36. For more on Edgefield's violent history in both reality and reputation, see especially Brown, *Strain of Violence*, 6, 39–40, 58–59, 67–90; Burton, *In My Father's House*, xviii, 6, 73–75, 90–95; Lacy K. Ford, "Origins of the Edgefield Tradition," 328–48.

14. Mason Locke Weems, *God's Revenge against Murder, or The Drown'd Wife*, 3–4.
15. Weems, *God's Revenge against Murder*, 4–5.
16. Weems, *God's Revenge against Murder*, 5, 6–40.
17. Weems, *The Bad Wife's Looking Glass*, 19–26.
18. Weems, *The Bad Wife's Looking Glass*, 4–8, 26.
19. Weems, *The Bad Wife's Looking Glass*, 8–11.
20. Weems, *The Bad Wife's Looking Glass*, 26–41.
21. Clinton, "Wallowing in a Swamp of Sin," 31–36. Clinton does not engage in an analysis of the masculine honor culture latent in Weems's accounts, but she does argue that Weems was pivotal in perpetuating a particular reputation for Edgefield, in particular, and South Carolina and even the South more broadly, one of an early and violent infamy that was slowly curbed in the wake of religious awakenings in the early nineteenth century. Despite his typically Episcopalian reservations regarding those evangelical Protestant denominations most responsible for it, Weems undoubtedly saw himself, as an itinerate preacher and moralizing author, at the vanguard of this religious moralizing crusade to save the southern backcountry from itself and its formerly sinful ways.
22. "Copy: Greenville, 5th September, 1822," September 19, 1822, Augusta *Chronicle*.
23. "Copy: Mr. McDuffie's Handbill Posted up at Greenville Courthouse," September 24, 1822, Augusta *Chronicle*.
24. "The Duel," June 19, 1822; "Duel," June 26, 1822; "Reply," July 24, 1822; "Captain Elmore's statement," July 24, 1822; Pendleton *Messenger*. "Copy-Mr. McDuffie's Handbill posted up at Greenville Courthouse," September 24, 1822; "Explanatory Statement-published in Handbills in Augusta," September 24, 1822; "For the Chronicle," September 28, 1822; "For the Chronicle," October 12, 1822; Augusta *Chronicle*.
25. "Another horrid murder;" April 20, 1825, Pendleton *Messenger*; "Another horrid murder," April 20, 1825, Pendleton *South Carolina Republican*. A similar incident five years later also drew derision from the Augusta press, as one "Jonathan Williams inflicted a mortal wound, with a rifle, upon John W.

Yates, whereof he died on the 12th. The Jury of Inquest rendered a verdict of Murder. Williams has escaped from justice," as reported in "From the Edgefield (S.C.) Carolinian," October 27, 1830; "We were misinformed," November 11, 1830, Augusta *Chronicle*. Another, similar murder appeared that same year, wherein Joseph M. Knapp murdered his alleged in-law, a Mr. White, for what appeared to the editors to be the killing of "an aged old man, whose only crime was the accumulation, by honesty and industry, of large estate for ungrateful heirs": "Murder of Mr. White," June 25, 1830, Edgefield *Hive*.

26. Edwin J. Scott, *Random Recollections of a Long Life*, 25–28; Charles G. Cordle, *Henry Shultz and the Founding of Hamburg, South Carolina*, 79–93.

27. "The Trial of Henry Shultz and Alexander Boyd," October 13, 1827; "Extract of a letter dated 'Edgefield Court House, 5th Oct. 1827,'" October 27, 1827. In the same article, another murder trial receives cursory mention ("Absalom Roe was tried for the killing of his brother, Wm. Roe, and found guilty of murder"), further displaying the extent of violence, in reputation and in deed, "enjoyed" by Edgefield's citizens among their neighboring communities; Augusta *Chronicle*.

28. Between 1830 and 1860, 386 cases of violence were brought to trial, including thirty-two cases of murder. These figures refer only to cases involving white crime, predominantly between white men, and include charges of assault, assault and battery, riot, affray, and murder as indicated in the court minutes. In this sense they follow the pattern revealed earlier in the cases referenced between 1785 and 1830, with two notable exceptions: only one of these cases involved an "affray" and none carried the charge of "dueling" or the "sending of a challenge," Edgefield County, General Sessions Court Minutes, ECA.

29. "A Duel," August 9, 1843, Edgefield *Advertiser*. This duel involved one of the newspaper editors from nearby Augusta, Georgia. At that time, the paper was owned and edited by two brothers, William S. Jones and James W. Jones. It is unclear which of the Jones brothers engaged in this particular duel, but in any case the action confirms several prevailing antebellum assumptions about Edgefield (for violence, and a lenient attitude toward affairs of honor) and newspaper men (for their rather frequent engagement in affairs of this kind); "Duel," March 20, 1844, Edgefield *Advertiser*.

30. "Duel in Prospect—Messrs. Butler and Benton," August 9, 1848; "Difficulty between Judge A. P. Butler and Hon. Thomas Benton," August 22, 1848; "In our last number," August 30, 1848; Edgefield *Advertiser*. The editors of the *Advertiser* also took notice of other duels on the national stage, even when Edgefield men were not involved: "The difficulty existing between Messrs. [Thomas H.] Baly [of VA] and [Garret] Davis [of KY] of the House of Representatives has been settled"; "The Duel," January 13, 1847, Edgefield *Advertiser*.

31. "Butler vs. Foote," December 18, 1851, Edgefield *Advertiser*.
32. "On the 3rd inst.," November 15, 1838; "Mr. Editor," November 22, 1838; and "We cheerfully give place," November 22, 1838; Edgefield *Advertiser*. Another affray involving assault with a rock occurred just two years later, between Ansley J. Colvin and Philip Falkner: "Colvin came to his death, by a wound inflicted on the left side of the head, with a rock, by one Philip Falkner," in "An Inquest was held," August 19, 1841; "Melancholy Affray," January 4, 1842; Edgefield *Advertiser*.
33. "Inquisition into the death of Joseph W. Glover," September 2, 1844, Edgefield County, Coroner's Book of Inquisitions, 1844–1868; "Fatal Rencontre," September 4, 1844, Edgefield *Advertiser*.
34. "An Inquisition into the death of Benjamin F. Jones," March 24, 1845, Coroner's Book of Inquisitions, ECA; "Fatal Rencontre," March 25, 1845, Edgefield *Advertiser*; "The State v. Charles Price," Fall Term, 1845, Minutes of the General Sessions Court, ECA.
35. "For the Advertiser," July 17, 1851, Edgefield *Advertiser*; "Inquisition into the death of William Cloud," Coroner's Book of Inquisitions, ECA; "A Startling Tragedy," July 10, 1851, Edgefield *Advertiser*; "The State v. Phillip P. Goode," Fall Term, 1852, Minutes of the General Sessions Court, ECA; "Inquisition into the death of Eldred Glover," March 2, 1852, Coroner's Book of Inquisition, ECA; "Melancholy Affray," March 4, 1852, Edgefield *Advertiser*; "The State v. Walker B. Samuel," Fall Term, 1852, Minutes of the General Sessions Court, ECA.
36. "The death of J. H. Christian by George D. Tillman," July 21, 1856, Coroner's Book of Inquisition, ECA. "Most Melancholy Occurrence," July 23, 1856; "Stop the Murderer!," October 15, 1856; "Mr. George D. Tillman," November 25, 1857; "G. D. Tillman, Esq.," February 10, 1858; "Second Week of Court," March 10, 1858, all in Edgefield *Advertiser*; "The State v. George Tillman," Spring Term, 1858, Minutes of the General Sessions Court, ECA. Reference to William Walker, the gray-eyed man of destiny, and his filibustering exploits in Nicaragua, are taken from Amy S. Greenberg, *Manifest Manhood and the Antebellum American Empire*, 135–69. For more on antebellum filibustering, see especially Robert E. May, *Manifest Destiny's Underworld*.
37. "Inquisition into the death of John M. Tillman," May 6, 1860, Coroner's Book of Inquisitions, ECA. "Death of Mr. John M. Tillman," May 9, 1860; "Court Week," October 1860, both in Edgefield *Advertiser*.
38. "Inquisition into the death of James Reynolds" and "Inquisition into the death of Stephen Shaw," December 18, 1860, Coroner's Book of Inquisitions, ECA; "The State v. Jos. G. Samuel, Wade Samuel, and Musco Samuel Jr.," Spring Term, 1861, Minutes of the General Sessions Court, ECA.
39. "Inquisition into the death of Matilda Posey," February 26, 1849; "Inquisition into the death of a slave named Appling, the property of Martin Posey,"

April 5, 1849, Coroner's Book of Inquisitions, ECA. "Trial of Martin Posey," October 10, 1849; "State Trials," October 17, 1849; "The Trial of Martin Posey," December 26, 1849; "It will be seen by reference," December 26, 1849; "The Great Attraction," February 6, 1850; Edgefield *Advertiser*.

40. "Trial of Martin Posey!," March 17, 1858, Edgefield *Advertiser*; "The State v. Martin Posey; Murder of Matilda H. Posey;" "The State v. Martin Posey, Murder of his slave named Appling," Minutes of the General Sessions Court, ECA; Several other cases involving domestic violence against household dependents similarly stretched the bounds of honor and its ability to maintain familial and social control: The early cases of Rebecca Cotton (1794) and Ned Findley (1804), popularized in the writings of Mason Locke Weems, captured the family and social crises that befell a man bereft of honor. The Cotton case found the pages of the *Advertiser* again in 1857, when an advertisement entitled "Edgefield Fifty Years Ago! Life and Death of Becky Cotton, The Devil in Petticoats, or God's Revenge Against Husband Killing!" ran with the declaring, "This work is replete with interest, especially so to the citizens of Edgefield District, as it contains quite a fair "showing up" of the dark days and murderous deeds of old Edgefield a half century since," October 7, 1857, Edgefield *Advertiser*; "The State v. Edward Findley," Spring Term, 1804, Minutes of the General Sessions Court, ECA.

41. "The State v. Russell Harden, Murder of a slave," Spring Term, 1846; Fall Term, 1846, Minutes of the General Sessions Court, ECA. For more on the tenuous balance of power between southern courts, law enforcement, and social mores, especially notions of patriarchy and the white masculine honor culture, see Peter W. Bardaglio, *Reconstructing the Household*, 3–36; Ariela J. Gross, *Double Character*, 47–71, 98–121; Sally E. Hadden, *Slave Patrols*, 68–152; Jack Kenny Williams, "The Criminal Lawyer in Antebellum South Carolina," 138–50, and "White Lawbreakers in Antebellum South Carolina," 360–73; Laura F. Edwards, "Law, Domestic Violence, and the Limits of Patriarchal Authority in the Antebellum South," *Journal of Southern History*, 733–70.

42. "The State v. Russell, Miles, Elbert, Isiah Harden, unlawfully beating a slave," Fall Term, 1848; "The State v. Russell Harden, Murder of a slave," Fall Term, 1848; Spring Term, 1848; Minutes of the General Sessions Court, ECA; "Inquisition into the death of Stephney, a slave belonging to Russell Harden," September 19, 1848, Coroner's Book of Inquisitions, ECA.

43. A string of cases involving white violence toward enslaved Blacks fill the Edgefield record: Murder of a negro, 1 count; Murdering a slave, 24 counts; Killing a negro, 4 counts; Assault with intent to murder a slave, 2 counts; Cruel treatment of a slave, 1 count; Unlawfully beating and whipping a slave, 33 counts; Minutes of the General Sessions Court, ECA; "An inquisition held on the body of a negro man slave named Pleasant," March 23, 1836;

"The dead body of Peter, property of Joel Abney," June 15, 1838; "An inquisition into the death of the slave Randall, property of Francis Bettis," May 9, 1844; "Inquisition into the death of Rose, the slave of Michael Long," March 9, 1846; "Inquisition into the death of Robert a slave, property of Edward Hampton," April 6, 1847; "Inquisition into the death of Ann, the slave of B. F. Landrum," November 23, 1848; "Inquisition into the death of William, the slave of Chesley Wells," February 8, 1849; "Inquisition into the death of Dina, the slave of Michael Long," May 21, 1849; "Inquisition into the death of a slave named Henry, the property of William H. Moss," June 2, 1849; "Inquisition into the death of Green, a slave belonging to John Cheatham," July 21, 1850; "Inquest into the death of a slave named Minda, the property of George Robinson," August 18, 1851; "Inquisition into the death of a slave named Aaron, the property of Larkin Swearingen," December 3, 1851; "The dead body of Henry, a slave of Arthur Glover," April 30, 1857; "Inquisition into the slave of David M. Glover," September 13, 1860; Coroner's Book of Inquisitions, ECA; "Another Homicide," September 19, 1849; "Another Homicide," November 7, 1849, Edgefield *Advertiser*.

44. Alcohol fueled this purportedly dishonorable violence to an alarming degree in Edgefield: "Inquisition into the death of a slave Richmond, the property of Col. A. Simkins," January 18, 1857; "Inquisition into the death of William Bailey," July 18, 1846; Coroner's Book of Inquisitions/ECA; "Melancholy Affray," July 22, 1846; "Trial of Thomas Prince," October 14, 1846, Edgefield *Advertiser*; "Inquisition into the death of Edmund Brown of Greenville District," February 25, 1853; "Inquisition into the death of Simon C. Wood," December 25, 1857; "Inquest into the dead body of Eldridge Padget," February 9, 1859; "Inquest into the dead body of A.G. Leek," February 23, 1859, Coroner's Book of Inquisitions, ECA; "Sale day and court," October 3, 1855; "Effect of No License," October 31, 1855; "Found dead," November 21, 1855, Edgefield *Advertiser*. For more on the complications posed to southern ethics, ideologies, and institutions by various forms of interracial social intercourse, see especially Jeff Forret, *Race Relations at the Margins*, 1–19, 157–83.

45. For more on honor and mastery in the evolving conceptions of antebellum southern manhood emphasized herein, see especially Craig Thompson Friend and Lorri Glover, eds., *Southern Manhood*, vii–xvii, 1–16, 22–42, 92–107, 113–31, 174–88; Lorri Glover, *Southern Sons*, 1–5, 9–34, 83–111; Ted Ownby, *Subduing Satan*, ix–xii, 1–18.

2. Piety

1. Orville Vernon Burton, *In My Father's House Are Many Mansions*, 21–28.
2. Francis Asbury, quoted in Burton, *In My Father's House*, 22–23; Burton, *In My Father's House*, 23.

3. "Revivals, November 2nd, 1854," Edgefield *Advertiser*.
4. Thomas Ray, *Daniel and Abraham Marshall*.
5. William Robertson, "Early History of the [Horn's Creek Baptist] Church, May 11, 1824," in HCB, TGL; Thomas Ray, *Daniel and Abraham Marshall*.
6. Charles Woodmason, *The Carolina Backcountry on the Eve of the Revolution*, ed. Richard J. Hooker, 6–14, 117.
7. Woodmason, *The Carolina Backcountry*, 13. For more on this emerging evangelical Protestant Christian ethic as it developed and evolved in late eighteenth- and early nineteenth-century South Carolina, see especially Lacy K. Ford, *Origins of Southern Radicalism*, 19–43; Rachel N. Klein, *Unification of a Slave State*, 269–302; Stephanie McCurry, *Masters of Small Worlds*, 130–207; Alan Gallay, *The Formation of a Planter Elite*, 30–54.
8. Kevin Cooley, "Clues of Early Methodism in Edgefield County"; "A Brief History of Edgefield United Methodist Church," Edgefield United Methodist Church Records, TGL.
9. Robertson, "Early History."
10. For a more detailed analysis of the early growth of the evangelical Protestant Christian ethic in Edgefield, see especially Burton, *In My Father's House*, 21–69; Hortense C. Woodson, *Giant in the Land*, 55–90; A. James Fuller, *Chaplain to the Confederacy*, 39–55; John A. Chapman, *History of Edgefield County*, 73–74, 91–92.
11. Basil Manly Sr., "Letter to the Editor," *Southern Intelligencer* 1 (August 10, 1822), 127, as quoted in Fuller, *Chaplain to the Confederacy*, 44–49. These religious developments in Edgefield mirrored those across the South from the end of the eighteenth century through the first few decades of the nineteenth, especially amid the religious revival movements collectively known as the Second Great Awakening. The organizational process apparent in Edgefield as delineated here was typical of the Awakening's religious developments more broadly, as most clearly explicated in Donald G. Mathews, "The Second Great Awakening as an Organizing Process," 23–43.
12. Woodson, *Giant in the Land*, 1–79; Fuller, *Chaplain to the Confederacy*, 41–55.
13. Cooley, "Clues of Early Methodism"; M. N. Rainsford, "Edgefield Methodism," undated, Edgefield United Methodist Church Records, TGL.
14. August 1831, EBC, TGL. Edgefield largely mirrored regional trends in Methodist and Baptist growth in particular and religious growth in general during the period, especially with regard to the prominence of revivals in the expansion of the evangelical Protestant ethic. For more on these broad regional trends in religious growth, see especially Clement Eaton, *The Mind of the Old South*, 200–223, and *A History of the Old South*, 82–83, 111, 451–53; John B. Boles, *The Great Revival*, 1–24, 70–142; Donald G. Mathews, *Religion in the Old South*, 1–97; Nathan O. Hatch, *The Democratization of*

American Christianity, 3–161, 220–26; Rhys Isaac, *The Transformation of Virginia*, 144–77, 241–322; Philip N. Mulder, *A Controversial Spirit*, 3–88, 110–48; Mark A. Noll, *America's God*, 3–18, 73–92, 159–224, 330–64; John Wigger, *American Saint*, 1–13, 47–85, 313–28, 401–18; Monica Najar, *Evangelizing the South*; Beth Barton Schweiger and Donald G. Mathews, eds., *Religion in the American South*, 31–66; Roger Robins, "Vernacular American Landscape," *Religion and American Culture*, 165–91.

15. August 1831, EBC, TGL; William B. Johnson, quoted in Woodson, *Giant in the Land*, 73–74.
16. William B. Johnson, quoted in Woodson, *Giant in the Land*, 74, 76.
17. Woodson, *Giant in the Land*, 74, 79.
18. August 1831, 1832, 1834, HCB, TGL; August 1833, 1834, LSCB, TGL; William B. Johnson, quoted in Woodson, *Giant in the Land*, 77–78.
19. August and September 1838, EBC, TGL; July and August 1839, LSCB, TGL.
20. September 1842, August 1843, EBC, TGL; August 1843, LSCB, TGL; "Protracted Meetings, August 26th, 1841," Edgefield *Advertiser*.
21. "Revival, August 1844," Edgefield *Advertiser*.
22. "For the Advertiser, April 3rd, 1851," Edgefield *Advertiser*.
23. "Our Country Churches, June 19th, 1851," Edgefield *Advertiser*.
24. September 1852, HCB, TGL; "Revival of Religion, September 29th, 1852," "Camp Meeting, July 6th, 1854," "Religious Items, August 10th, 1854," "Religious Items, September 10th, 1854," "Revivals, November 2nd, 1854," "Revivals, April 18th, 1855"; Edgefield *Advertiser*.
25. "Religious Revival, April 18th, 1855," "Revivals, August 29th, 1855"; Edgefield *Advertiser*.
26. "More Revivals, May 2nd, 1855," Edgefield *Advertiser*.
27. "Camp Meeting, July 16th, 1856," "Religious Notice, August 20th, 1856," "Camp Meeting, August 20th, 1856," "Camp Meeting, August 5th, 1857," "Edgefield Baptist Association, September 2nd, 1857," "Protracted Meeting, October 7th, 1857," "Camp Meeting at Mt. Vernon, August 4th, 1858," "Large Religious Meeting, August 25th, 1858," "Camp Meeting, September 15th, 1858," "Religious Meetings, August 10th, 1859," "Religious Meetings, August 31st, 1859," "Religious, September 7th, 1859," "Big Meetings, August 27th, 1856," "Large Religious Meeting, August 25th, 1858," "Religious News, September 21st, 1859," "Religious, October 6th, 1858"; Edgefield *Advertiser*.
28. "Revival in the Methodist Church, September 9th, 1857," "Methodist Revival, October 27th, 1858," "State of the Churches, September 19th, 1855"; Edgefield *Advertiser*.
29. "Camp Meeting and Association, September 17th, 1856," Edgefield *Advertiser*. For more on the national scope of revivalism in 1857–58 and its divergence from earlier periods of intense revivalism see especially Kathryn Long, "The Power of Interpretation," 77–105.

30. "Religious Progress, June 22nd, 1859," Edgefield *Advertiser*.
31. For the most relevant historical analyses of these persistent anxieties within and between southern culture and southern religion—over the institution of slavery most particularly—as emphasized herein, see especially John B. Boles, ed., *Masters and Slaves in the House of the Lord*, 1–126; Eugene D. Genovese, *The Slaveholder's Dilemma*, 1–73; Christine Leigh Heyrman, *Southern Cross*, 28–76, 117–60, 193–252; Charles F. Irons, *The Origins of Proslavery Christianity*, 1–21, 52–62, 96–104, 133–209; Anne C. Loveland, *Southern Evangelicals and the Social Order*, 91–256; Cynthia Lynn Lyerly, *Methodism and the Southern Mind*, 3–10, 146–86; Ted Ownby, ed., *Black and White*, ix–xix, 55–88; Beth Barton Schweiger, *The Gospel Working Up*, 3–89.
32. William B. Johnson, "An Admonition against Worldly Conformity: The Circular Letter of the Charleston Baptist Association (1810)," in Woodson, *Giant in the Land*, app. B, 175–79. For more on disciplinary oversight in Southern Baptist communities, see especially Gregory A. Wills, *Democratic Religion*, 3–115; Janet Moore Lindman, *Bodies of Belief*.
33. Johnson, "An Admonition against Worldly Conformity," in Woodson, *Giant in the Land*, 175–79.
34. Case of Vann Swearingen, February 1825, and Case of Mr. Bettis, July 1828, HCB, TGL; January 1837, LSCB, TGL.
35. June 1839; February 1840; November 1840; HCB, TGL.
36. September 6, 1833, Thomas Youngblood; Charles Parrott; January 11, 1834; March and April 1834, James Youngblood; John Hill; September 1834; October 1835, John Harlin; LSCB, TGL.
37. December 13, 1835; March 1836, Lewis Bledsoe; December 1836, John Nicholson; March 1837, James Youngblood; LSCB, TGL.
38. June 1840; June 1853, HCB, TGL.
39. Johnson, "An Admonition against Worldly Conformity," in Woodson, *Giant in the Land*, 178.
40. May 1838; March 1857; July, August, October, November 1838, March, April, May, June 1839; HCB, TGL. The church minutes from other prominent Edgefield evangelical churches all evince a record of disciplinary measures between 1830 and 1860 similar to those explicitly referenced from Horn's Creek and Antioch Baptist in the pages that follow. These archived church minutes include Big Stephen's Creek Baptist, Dry Creek Baptist, Philippi Baptist, Red Oak Grove Baptist, Republican Baptist, and Mt. Lebanon (now Sweetwater) Baptist, all Furman; and Edgefield Baptist and Little Steven's Creek Baptist, both TGL.
41. May 1832; June, July 1840; HCB, TGL.
42. December 1828; February, August 1829; HCB, TGL.
43. November, December 1831; HCB, TGL; August 1832; March, June 1834; Antioch Baptist Church, Furman.

44. "August 1833," HCB; "July 1833," Antioch Baptist Church, Furman; May, June 1834; May 1838; May, June 1850; HCB, TGL.
45. December 1833, February 1834; September 1835, November 1839; February 1836; June 1853; HCB, TGL.
46. October 1841, January 1842; HCB, TGL.
47. For more on the masculine anxieties within southern religion as emphasized herein, see especially Charity R. Carney, *Ministers and Masters*, 1–37; Heyrman, *Southern Cross*, 117–252; Fuller, *Chaplain to the Confederacy*, 1–25, Janet Moore Lindman, "Acting the Manly Christian," 393–416; Loveland, *Southern Evangelicals and the Social Order*, 30–64, 91–129; Lyerly, *Methodism and the Southern Mind*, 73–186; Mathews, *Religion in the Old South*, 20–38, 120–24; John Mayfield, *Counterfeit Gentlemen*, xiii–xxvii, 25–47; McCurry, *Masters of Small Worlds*, 171–207; Steven M. Stowe, *Intimacy and Power in the Old South*, xiii–xviii, 1–49. For more on the tenuous balance of power between southern courts, law enforcement, and social mores, especially notions of patriarchy and the paternalistic ideals of white southern religion, see Peter W. Bardaglio, *Reconstructing the Household*, 3–36; Ariela J. Gross, *Double Character*, 47–71, 98–121; Sally E. Hadden, *Slave Patrols*, 68–152; Jack Kenny Williams, "The Criminal Lawyer in Antebellum South Carolina," 138–50 and "White Lawbreakers in Antebellum South Carolina," 360–73; Laura F. Edwards, "Law, Domestic Violence, and the Limits of Patriarchal Authority in the Antebellum South," 733–70. For more on these masculine tensions within the broader Victorian era, see especially Norman Vance, *The Sinews of the Spirit*, 1–28; Pieter C. Spierenburg, *Men and Violence*; J. A. Mangan, *Manliness and Morality*, 1–6, 35–51; Mark C. Carnes, *Secret Ritual and Manhood in Victorian America*, and Carnes and Clyde Griffen, eds., *Meanings for Manhood*, 1–151, 179–212.
48. E. Brooks Holifield, *The Gentlemen Theologians*.

3. Righteous Honor

1. Mason Locke Weems, *The Devil in Petticoats, or God's Revenge against Husband Killing*, 1. This post–Civil War edition was just one in a long line of reprinted Weems works. As was his custom throughout his career as an author, peddler, and religious cleric, Weems himself published multiple editions of this story, the last of which appeared in 1823 under the revised title *The Bad Wife's Looking Glass, or God's Revenge against Cruelty to Husbands*; Mason Locke Weems, *God's Revenge against Murder, or The Drown'd Wife*, 5.
2. For the most relevant historical literature regarding the cultural tensions between southern honor and religion in tandem, see especially Edward R. Crowther, "Holy Honor," 619–36; Eugene Genovese, "The Chivalric Tradition in the Old South," 188–205; Charity R. Carney, *Ministers and Masters*,

5–37, 138–41; A. James Fuller, *Chaplain to the Confederacy*; John Mayfield, *Counterfeit Gentlemen*, xiii–xxviii, 25–47, 83–104; Steven M. Stowe, *Intimacy and Power in the Old South*, ix–xviii, 5–49; Bertram Wyatt-Brown, *Southern Honor*, vii–xix, 14–15, 60–61, 99–114, 129–47, 298–99, 493, and *The Shaping of Southern Culture*, xi–ix, 83–105. Other works to analyze these cultural values in opposition include Edward Ayers, *Vengeance and Justice*, 9–33, 118–25; Dickson D. Bruce Jr., *Violence and Culture in the Antebellum South*, 12–14, 112–13, 233–40; Ted Ownby, *Subduing Satan*, ix–xii, 1–18, 19–99, 101–64. For more on the antecedents to these ideals during the Revolutionary and Early Republic eras in American society and culture, see especially: Amanda Porterfield, *Conceived in Doubt*, 147–208; Craig Bruce Smith, *American Honor*, 1–21, 98–240; Joanne B. Freeman, *Affairs of Honor*.

3. Clement Eaton, *The Growth of Southern Civilization*, 313–24, and *The Mind of the Old South*, 23, 245–312, 504–10; E. Brooks Holifield, *The Gentlemen Theologians*; Lorri Glover, *Southern Sons*, 17–22, and "'Let Us Manufacture Men': Educating Elite Boys in the Early National South," in Craig Thompson Friend and Lorri Glover, eds., *Southern Manhood*, 22–42; Timothy J. Williams, *Intellectual Manhood*; Evelyn D. Causey, "The Character of a Gentleman." Glover's focus on the patriarchal pressures and filial anxieties animating southern sons during the early national period most directly guided this chapter's generational analysis of the first antebellum generation of white southern men and their emotional experience of prevailing conceptions of honor and piety amid the burgeoning sectional crisis. Other pertinent works on the emerging sectional crisis and its impact on white southern identity include Charles S. Sydnor, *The Development of Southern Sectionalism*; Paul Calore, *The Causes of the Civil War*; Drew Gilpin Faust, *Southern Stories*; Randall C. Jimerson, *The Private War*; James Oakes, *Slavery and Freedom* and *The Ruling Race*; Michael O'Brien, *Intellectual Life and the American South*; David M. Potter, *The Impending Crisis*; Patricia Roberts-Miller, *Fanatical Schemes*; Jeffrey R. Young, *Proslavery and Sectional Thought in the Early South*. Masculine tensions between secular mores and sacred morals abounded during the Victorian Era more broadly as illustrated most poignantly in Norman Vance, *The Sinews of the Spirit*, 1–28; Pieter C. Spierenburg, *Men and Violence*; J. A. Mangan, and James Walvin, *Manliness and Morality*, 1–6, 35–51; Mark C. Carnes, *Secret Ritual and Manhood in Victorian America*, and Mark C. Carnes and Clyde Griffen, eds., *Meanings for Manhood*, 1–151, 179–212.

4. William S. Powell, ed., *Dictionary of North Carolina Biography*, 234–35.
5. Iveson L. Brookes to Jonathan Brookes, February 13, 1818 (emphasis added), ILB-UNC.
6. Iveson L. Brookes to Jonathan Brookes, August 29, 1818 (emphasis added); August 17, September, November 9, 1816; May 10, October 19, November 2,

1817; November 17, 1818; March 22, 1819; January 26, 1820; October 25, 1822; ILB-UNC.
7. Basil Manly Sr. to Captain John Basil Manly, May 21, 1819; October 15, 1817; December 21, 1819; October 11, 1820; Basil Manly Sr. to Charles Manly, January 12, 1824, BMSr, Furman; A. James Fuller, *Chaplain to the Confederacy*, 11–20.
8. Fuller, *Chaplain to the Confederacy*, 43–55.
9. Fuller, *Chaplain to the Confederacy*, 43–55.
10. Basil Manly Sr., church journal entry, March 13, 1837, BMSr, Furman, referencing 1 Chron. 4:9–10.
11. Sermon from Rom. 5:20, September 18, 1828; sermon from James 3:13, 1828; sermon from Heb. 4:2, undated, BMSr, Furman.
12. Basil Manly Jr. and Charles Manly, as quoted in Fuller, *Chaplain to the Confederacy*, 26–27.
13. Basil Manly Jr. and Charles Manly, as quoted in Fuller, *Chaplain to the Confederacy*, 26–27.
14. The most relevant works to emphasize this prevailing perspective include Ayers, *Vengeance and Justice*; Bruce, *Violence and Culture in the Antebellum South*; Thomas J. Carmody, "The Anti-Dueling Movement," 341–66; William S. Cossen, "Blood, Honor, Reform, and God," 23–45; Ownby, *Subduing Satan*. More recently, some scholars have begun to complicate this relationship, pointing toward a more ambiguous personal relationship between southern divines and masculine honor culture. The most relevant works to forward this perspective are Crowther, "Holy Honor," 619–36; Carney, *Ministers and Masters*; Robert Elder, *The Sacred Mirror*; Fuller, *Chaplain to the Confederacy*; David T. Moon, "Southern Baptists and Southern Men," 563–606.
15. For more on the southern honor code's emphasis on masculine self-control see especially Stowe, *Intimacy and Power in the Old South*, 6–49. For more on southern ministers dueling with the pen rather than the sword, see Carney, *Ministers and Masters*, 21–28.
16. Basil Manly Sr., church journal entry, June 4, 1827 (emphasis added), BMSr, Furman.
17. William S. Powell, ed., *Dictionary of North Carolina Biography*, 234–35.
18. Iveson L. Brookes to Jonathan Brookes, August 29, 1818, ILB-UNC.
19. Iveson L. Brookes to Jonathan Brookes, November 11, 1818, ILB-UNC.
20. Iveson L. Brookes to Jonathan Brookes, November 11, 1818, ILB-UNC.
21. Iveson L. Brookes to Jonathan Brookes, November 11, 1818, ILB-UNC.
22. William Bullein Johnson, "Reminiscences," as quoted in Hortense C. Woodson, *Giant in the Land*, 1, 5.
23. Johnson, "Reminiscences," as quoted in Woodson, *Giant in the Land*, 1, 5.
24. William B. Johnson, sermon, "God Is Love," November 4, 1822, William Bullein Johnson Papers, Furman.

25. Richard J. Carwardine, *Evangelicals and Politics in Antebellum America*; Anne C. Loveland, *Southern Evangelicals and the Social Order*.
26. William B. Johnson to James C. Furman, January 1847; William B. Johnson to James C. Furman, November 17, 1847; William B. Johnson to James S. Mims, March 25, 1848; William Bullein Johnson Papers, Furman.
27. William B. Johnson to James C. Furman, October 20, November 19, 1847; January 25, March 10, March 27, April 12, April 28, May 5, 1848; M. L. Mendenhall to William B. Johnson, November 27, 1847; William B. Johnson to James S. Mims, April 15, April 29, May 13, September 2, September 25, October 7, 1848; William Bullein Johnson Papers, Furman.
28. The focus on masculine anxieties emphasized here builds most directly upon the following works Stephen Berry, *All That Makes a Man*, 3–44; Peter S. Carmichael, *The Last Generation*, 2–18, 59–88; Carney, *Ministers and Master*; Christine Leigh Heyrman, *Southern Cross*, 30–64, 91–129; Fuller, *Chaplain to the Confederacy*; Janet Moore Lindman, "Acting the Manly Christian," 393–416; Loveland, *Southern Evangelicals and the Social Order*, 30–64, 91–129; Cynthia Lynn Lyerly, *Methodism and the Southern Mind*, 146–86; Donald G. Mathews, *Religion in the Old South*, 20–38, 120–24; John Mayfield, *Counterfeit Gentlemen*, xiii–xxvii, 25–47; Stephanie McCurry, *Masters of Small Worlds*; Stowe, *Intimacy and Power in the Old South*.
29. Hughes family note on religious clergy and war, 1811; sermon by unnamed preacher, June 1840, HFP, UNC.
30. Sermon by unnamed preacher, June, 1840, HFP, UNC.
31. Sermon by unnamed preacher heard near Winnsboro, South Carolina, June 16, 1849, HFP, UNC.
32. John Bones to James Bones (father), July 24, 1828, HFP, UNC.
33. John Bones to James Bones (father), July 24, 1828, HFP, UNC.
34. Samuel Bones to James Bones (father), October 4, 1834, HFP, UNC.
35. Samuel Bones to James Bones (father), October 4, 1834, HFP, UNC.
36. William Bones to James Bones, March 11, 1830, HFP, UNC.
37. W. G. Stavely to James Bones, August 15, 1832, HFP, UNC.
38. Letter of dismissal from Hopewell Long Cane Presbyterian Church, Abbeville, South Carolina, February 5, 1793, MiFP, UNC.
39. John Dickson to Dr. Joseph Milligan, June 10, 1835, MiFP, UNC.
40. H. K. Silliman to Dr. Joseph Milligan, October 5, 1847, MiFP, UNC.
41. Jane Milligan to Dr. Joseph Milligan, September 12, 1835, MiFP, UNC.
42. Jane Milligan to Dr. Joseph Milligan, November 24, 1835, MiFP, UNC.
43. Dr. Joseph Milligan to Octavia Milligan, July 25, 1848, MiFP, UNC. On the medical profession as a masculine "field of honor" during this period, see especially Robert A. Nye, "Medicine and Science as Masculine 'Fields of Honor,'" 60–79.

44. Whitfield Brooks, journal entry, August 31, 1841; September 1, 1841, in *An Edgefield Planter and His World*, ed. James O. Farmer Jr., 35–36. Page numbers following citations to Whitfield Brooks's journal entries all refer to Farmer, ed., *Edgefield Planter*.
45. Whitfield Brooks, journal entry, January 1, 1842, 50.
46. For more on this conception of fraternal relationships, see especially Anya Jabour, "Male Friendship and Masculinity in the Early National South," 83–111. For the complex relationship between evangelical Protestantism and evolving American gender norms in the late eighteenth and early nineteenth century, especially the contested line between asserting feminine moral authority and submitting to the prevailing patriarchal order, see especially Jean E. Friedman, *The Enclosed Garden*, 1–66; Scott Stephan, *Redeeming the Southern Family*.
47. For more on the prominent role played by women in shaping southern masculine ideals and identities, both within and beyond the confines of evangelical Protestant churches through the early antebellum period, see especially Karen Lystra, *Searching the Heart*; Berry, *All That Makes a Man*, 83–160; Carney, *Ministers and Masters*, 65–90; Elizabeth Fox-Genovese, *Within the Plantation Household*; Friedman, *The Enclosed Garden*, 21–53; Heyrman, *Southern Cross*, 117–205; Cynthia A. Kierner, *Beyond the Household*, 139–211; Mathews, *Religion in the Old South*, 97–134; McCurry, *Masters of Small Worlds*, 135–207; Beth Barton Schweiger, *The Gospel Working Up*, 150–63; Williams, *Intellectual Manhood*, 148–68.
48. "Sermon by unnamed preacher heard near Winnsboro, South Carolina, June 16, 1849," HFP, UNC; "Revivals, November 2, 1854," Edgefield *Advertiser*. For more on the tenuous balance of power between southern courts, law enforcement, and social mores, especially prevailing notions of masculine honor, patriarchal prerogative, and paternalistic obligation, see Peter W. Bardaglio, *Reconstructing the Household*, 3–36; Ariela J. Gross, *Double Character*, 47–71, 98–121; Sally E. Hadden, *Slave Patrols*, 68–152; Craig Thompson Friend and Anya Jabour, eds., *Family Values in the Old South*, 1–16, 62–85, 210–32; Jack Kenny Williams, "The Criminal Lawyer in Antebellum South Carolina," 138–50, and "White Lawbreakers in Antebellum South Carolina," 360–73; Laura F. Edwards, "Law, Domestic Violence, and the Limits of Patriarchal Authority in the Antebellum South," 33–770.

4. Moral Failings

1. Iveson Lewis Brookes to Walker Brookes, August 7, 1846; Iveson Lewis Brookes to John M. Carter, January 28, 1859, ILB-USC. This exchange between Iveson and Walker Brookes is also briefly referenced in Timothy J. Williams, *Intellectual Manhood*, 159, 245n41. Williams references the

exchange as a rare example of candid correspondence regarding sexuality before rightly noting that such candidness about sexual urges and activities, when recorded at all, most typically found the pages of personal diaries, which Williams astutely argues played a vital role in young southern men's "self-construction" toward realizing their ideals of manhood.

2. Williams, *Intellectual Manhood*, 150–68. Williams explores similar dynamics between secular and sacred demands for southern manhood operating on the minds and shaping the actions of the collegiate men he examines, emphasizing how both the tensions and compatibility between these moral and ethical ideals shaped young men's concept of what it meant to be a man (read: white man) in the antebellum South's racialized patriarchy.

3. Scott Stephan, *Redeeming the Southern Family*. Stephan analyzes the role of evangelical women in perpetuating cultural values in their "assigned" domestic capacity within the slave South's racial patriarchy. This chapter extends these perspectives to encompass the role played by southern fathers in this process of transferring such lessons in cultural values to their sons. For more on these dynamics, see Bardaglio, *Reconstructing the Household*, 3–36; Gross, *Double Character*, 47–71, 98–121; Hadden, *Slave Patrols*, 68–152; Drew Gilpin Faust, *Southern Stories*, 15–87; Friend and Jabour, eds., *Family Values in the Old South*, 1–16, 62–85, 210–32; Williams, "The Criminal Lawyer in Antebellum South Carolina," 138–50, and "White Lawbreakers in Antebellum South Carolina," 360–73; Edwards, "Law, Domestic Violence, and the Limits of Patriarchal Authority in the Antebellum South," 733–70.

4. Frederick Law Olmsted, *Journeys and Explorations in the Cotton Kingdom*, 229–30. The primacy of self-mastery within southern manhood, as argued here, has been treated most directly in Christine Leigh Heyrman, *Southern Cross*, 246–50; April R. Haynes, *Riotous Flesh*, 1–55. Other works to point out the importance of self-control or self-discipline within the southern honor code and/or southern evangelicalism include Edward L. Ayers, *Vengeance and Justice*, 27–33; Dickson D. Bruce Jr., *Violence and Culture in the Antebellum South*, 8–12, 233–40; Steven M. Stowe, *Intimacy and Power*, x–xviii, 1–49. For more on the intensifying sectional identities and ideologies among these antebellum generations, see especially Randall C. Jimerson, *The Private War*, 1–49; Timothy J. Williams, *Intellectual Manhood*; Evelyn D. Causey, "The Character of a Gentleman."

5. Iveson Lewis Brookes to Walker Brookes, August 7, 1846, ILB-USC.

6. Iveson Lewis Brookes to Walker Brookes, August 7, 1846, ILB-USC. For more on this conception of biblical morality, see especially David A. DeSilva, *Honor, Patronage, Kinship, and Purity*; Evan Shalev, *American Zion*, 50–83, 151–84.

7. Iveson Lewis Brookes to Walker Brookes, August 7, 1846, ILB-USC.

8. Iveson Lewis Brookes to Walker Brookes, August 7, 1846, ILB-USC.

9. Virginia Brookes to Walker Brookes, July 17, 1849; January 28, 1848; ILB-USC.
10. Walker Brookes to Iveson L. Brookes, November 23, 1853; Harriet Brookes to Iveson L. Brookes, April 5, 1853; December 1853; ILB-UNC.
11. Iveson Lewis Brookes to John M. Carter, January 28, 1859, ILB-USC. Many historians have noted the cultural commonalities between North and South in the antebellum era, especially with regard to the reform impulse and associated increase in moral consciousness initiated by the era's economic, social, and political changes: Richard L. Bushman, *The Refinement of America*; Richard J. Carwardine, *Evangelicals and Politics in Antebellum America*, xvii–xix, 1–49; Lorien Foote, *The Gentlemen and the Roughs*; Reid Mitchell, *The Vacant Chair*, 92–93. These trends predominated throughout the English-speaking Atlantic world during the Victorian era, as exhibited in Norman Vance, *The Sinews of the Spirit*, 1–28; Boyd Hilton, *The Age of Atonement*, 1–251. For works that emphasize divergent regional reactions to these national social and economic transformations, see especially Clayton E. Cramer, *Concealed Weapon Laws of the Early Republic*; Kenneth Moore Startup, *The Root of All Evil*.
12. Sylvester Graham, *Lecture to Young Men on Chastity*, 9–10. For more on Graham, see Stephen Nissenbaum, *Sex, Diet, and Debility in Jacksonian America*; Jayme A. Sokolow, *Eros and Modernization*; John Money, *The Destroying Angel*, 17–27. For more on the emerging antebellum reform culture in America of which Sylvester Graham in particular and many clerics in general played a prominent part, see especially Robert H. Abzug, *Cosmos Crumbling*; T. Gregory Garvey, *Creating the Culture of Reform in Antebellum America*, 1–73; Steven Mintz, *Moralists and Modernizers*; Timothy L. Smith, *Revivalism and Social Reform*.
13. Graham, *Lecture to Young Men on Chastity*, 20–22. For the most relevant analysis of the era's evolving ideals of middle-class masculinity and fatherhood from a broader American and transatlantic perspective, see especially Stephen M. Frank, *Life with Father*; Robert L. Griswold, *Fatherhood in America*; Shawn Johansen, *Family Men*.
14. For the most pertinent analysis of this emerging middle-class culture in the antebellum South, see especially James J. Broomall, *Private Confederacies*, 1–31; Frank J. Byrne, *Becoming Bourgeois*; Tom Downey, *Planting a Capitalist South*; Jennifer R. Green, *Military Education and the Emerging Middle Class*; Stephanie McCurry, *Masters of Small Worlds*; Amanda Reese Mushal, "My Word Is My Bond"; Ami Pflugrad-Jackisch, *Brothers of a Vow*; Beth Barton Schweiger, *The Gospel Working Up*; Jonathan Daniel Wells, *The Origins of the Southern Middle Class*; Jonathan Daniel Wells and Jennifer R. Green, eds., *The Southern Middle Class in the Long Nineteenth Century*. For more on these dynamics, see especially Frank, *Life with Father*;

Griswold, *Fatherhood in America*; Johansen, *Family Men*; John Tosh, *A Man's Place*. For more on the connections between Grahamism and Garrisonian abolitionism as outlined here, see especially Abzug, *Cosmos Crumbling*, 117, 163–82; Nissenbaum, *Sex, Diet, and Debility*, 1, 14, 140–54; Sokolow, *Eros and Modernization*; "Letter from Sylvester Graham, Northampton, [Mass.], to William Lloyd Garrison, March 13th, 1849," Correspondence, March 13, 1849, *Digital Commonwealth*, https://ark.digitalcommonwealth.org/ark:/50959/dv143g59w (accessed August 5, 2020).

15. Iveson L. Brookes, *A Defense of the South*, 1–48. For more on the tangible cultural developments provoking such perceptions of immorality and irreligiosity in antebellum America, see especially John Lardas Modern, *Secularism in America*.

16. Brookes, *A Defense of the South*, 12–18. For more on the broad contours of southern proslavery arguments as they evolved during the antebellum period, see especially Charles S. Sydnor, *The Development of Southern Sectionalism*; David M. Potter, *The Impending Crisis*; William W. Freehling, *The Road to Disunion*, vols. 1 and 2; Paul Calore, *The Causes of the Civil War*; Drew Gilpin Faust, ed., *The Ideology of Slavery*; Lacy K. Ford, *Deliver Us from Evil*, 481–534; Larry E. Tise, *Proslavery*; Patricia Roberts-Miller, *Fanatical Schemes*.

17. Iveson L. Brookes to Brother James, April 10, 1854, ILB-USC; Brookes, *A Defense of the South*, 32–33. Iveson Brookes was not alone among southern clerics in this assessment of the North or his proslavery position. For more on proslavery southern clerics, see especially John Patrick Daly, *When Slavery Was Called Freedom*; Charles F. Irons, *The Origins of Proslavery Christianity*, 133–246; James O. Farmer Jr., *The Metaphysical Confederacy*; John R. McKivigan and Mitchell Snay, eds., *Religion and the Antebellum Debate over Slavery*; David F. Ericson, *The Debate over Slavery*; Mitchell Snay, *Gospel of Disunion*.

18. Iveson Lewis Brookes to Brother Creathe, June 13, 1859; Iveson Lewis Brookes to Walker Brookes, May 10, 1848; ILB-USC.

19. Iveson Lewis Brookes to Brother Creathe, June 13, 1859; Iveson Lewis Brookes to Walker Brookes, May 10, 1848; ILB-USC. Here Brookes acknowledged, and lamented, the corruptions he believed attendant upon the burgeoning market revolution that was sweeping the American landscape. For more on the effects of the market revolution in the antebellum South generally, see especially Charles Sellers, *The Market Revolution*; John L. Larson, *The Market Revolution in America*, 1–168; Scott C. Martin, ed., *Cultural Change and the Market Revolution in America*, 1–12, 89–180, 217–46; Melvyn Stokes and Stephen Conway, eds., *The Market Revolution in America*, 1–257. John Mayfield and Todd Hagstette, eds., *The Field of Honor*, frames much of its collective analysis within the context of the market revolution in the

United States, perspectives reflected and extended here in presenting the moralizing impetus in both North and South as emanating from common origins only to emphasize divergent ends, especially with regards to slavery. For more on clerical responses to the market revolution and their effects on prevailing attitudes toward private and public morality, see especially Mark Noll, ed., *God and Mammon*; Stokes and Conway, eds., *The Market Revolution in America*, 259–309; Fuller, *Chaplain to the Confederacy*, 254–67; Schweiger, *The Gospel Working Up*, 4, 11–54; Sellers, *The Market Revolution*, 202–36; Startup, *The Root of All Evil*; Hilton, *The Age of Atonement*, 1–251.

20. Basil Manly Sr., "'Purity in the Young,' Sermon from Psalms 119: 9 (January 4, 1829)" (emphasis his), BMSr, Furman. For the most thorough account of Basil Manly Sr.'s life and career, especially his southern masculine identity and its evolution during the sectional crisis, see Fuller, *Chaplain to the Confederacy*.

21. Basil Manly Sr., "Seek Ye First the Kingdom of God"; "Because Their Heart Was Tender," sermon from Chron. 34: 27–28 (undated); "To Be Carnally Minded Is Death," sermon from Rom. 5:6 (undated), BMSr, Furman.

22. Basil Manly Sr., "Because Their Heart Was Tender," BMSr, Furman.

23. Basil Manly Sr., "Seek Ye First the Kingdom of God"; "Because Their Heart Was Tender"; "To Be Carnally Minded is Death"; BMSr, Furman.

24. Basil Manly Sr., "Seekest Thou Great Things for Thyself?" sermon from Jer. 45:5 (undated); "Who Is a Wise Man . . . ?" sermon from James 3:13 (1828); BMSr, Furman. For more on Manly in this paternal role—within his own family, his faith, and his profession—see Fuller, *Chaplain to the Confederacy*, 154–211, 228–53.

25. Basil Manly Sr., church journal entries, January 28, February 1, 1827; BMSr, Furman.

26. Basil Manly Sr., church journal entry, April 7, 1828, BMSr, Furman.

27. Basil Manly Jr., diary entries, February 2, 1843; August 16, 1840; June 16, 1842; BMJr, Furman.

28. Basil Manly Jr., diary entries, August 20, 1843; November 15, 1844; BMJr, Furman.

29. Basil Manly Jr., diary entries, June 7, July 18, 1841; July 17, 1842; August 5, 1843; May 8, 1842; November 24, 1844; BMJr, Furman. Williams, *Intellectual Manhood*, 159–68. In his study of white southern collegians during the antebellum era, Williams posits a similar argument regarding the function of personal diaries such as Basil Manly Jr.'s here, including the persistent tension between secular and sacred demands in shaping their concept of ideal manhood and their efforts at "self-construction" to build their character according to that manly image.

30. Basil Manly Jr., diary entries, June 7, July 18, 1841; July 17, 1842; August 5, 1843; May 8, 1842; November 24, 1844; BMJr, Furman.

31. Basil Manly Jr., diary entries, June 7, July 18, 1841; July 17, 1842; August 5, 1843; May 8, 1842; November 24, 1844; BMJr, Furman.
32. "Court of Sessions," April 9, 1845, Edgefield *Advertiser*.
33. "Another Fatal Affray," October 24, 1860, Edgefield *Advertiser*.
34. Dr. Joseph Milligan to Joseph Milligan Jr., June 11, 1846; September 8, 1849, MiFP, UNC.
35. Jane Milligan to Dr. Joseph Milligan, January 12, 1841; Henry M. Bruns to Dr. Joseph Milligan, July 29, 1840, MiFP, UNC.
36. Dr. Joseph Milligan to Joseph Milligan Jr., April 25, 1840; March 15, 1841, MiFP, UNC. On the medical profession as a masculine "field of honor" during this period, see especially Robert A. Nye, "Medicine and Science as Masculine 'Fields of Honor,'" 60–79.
37. Whitfield Brooks, journal entries, March 27, 1842; November 17, 1846; quoted in *An Edgefield Planter and His World*, ed. James O. Farmer Jr., 59, 286.
38. Whitfield Brooks, journal entries, September 6, December 6, December 29, 1841; March 7, 1843; 36, 46, 48, 100–101. Page numbers following citations to Whitfield Brooks's journal entries all refer to Farmer, ed. *Edgefield Planter*. For more on the connections between temperance reform, gender ideals, and the antebellum reform impulse more generally, see especially Holley Berkley Fletcher, *Gender and the American Temperance Movement of the Nineteenth Century*; Elaine Frantz Parson, *Manhood Lost*, 1–74.
39. Whitfield Brooks, journal entries, April 15, July 12, 1842; 63, 73.
40. Whitfield Brooks, journal entries, May 11, 184 (emphasis added); 110. For more on the temperance movement and prohibition initiatives in the antebellum South, see especially Douglas W. Carlson, "Drinks He to His Own Undoing," 659–91; Ian Tyrrell, *Sobering Up*, and "Drink and Temperance in the Antebellum South," 485–510; John W. Quist, *Restless Visionaries*; William J. Rorabaugh, "The Sons of Temperance in Antebellum Jasper County," 263–79.
41. Whitfield Brooks, journal entries, May 24, September 4, 1843; May 10, July 4, August 1, 1844; 111–12, 127, 158, 168, 171.
42. Whitfield Brooks, journal entry, November 5–6, 1844; 186.
43. Whitfield Brooks, journal entries, February 9, April 7, 1845; 206, 218. For more on the prominence of alcoholic consumption in the early republic and antebellum era, see especially William J. Rorabaugh, *The Alcoholic Republic*; Mark Edward Lender and James Kirby Martin, *Drinking in America*, 1–86. For more on the emergence of the temperance movement in reaction to this American habit for pronounced alcoholic consumption, see especially Robert H. Abzug, *Cosmos Crumbling*, 81–104.
44. Preston Brooks, diary entry, 1849; December 25, December 28, 1851, PSB.
45. Preston Brooks, diary entry, December 28, 1851, PSB.
46. Preston Brooks, diary entries, December 28, 1851; August 6, 1849; PSB.

47. The following works in emotions history in the United States were most influential in shaping the analysis herein: Michael E. Woods, *Emotional and Sectional Conflict in the Antebellum United States*, 1–239; James J. Broomall, *Private Confederacies*, 1–32; Carol Z. Stearns and Peter N. Stearns, *Anger and Emotion and Social Change*; Peter N. Stearns, *Jealousy*; Peter N. Stearns and Jan Lewis, eds., *An Emotional History of the United States*; William M. Reddy, *The Navigation of Feeling*. Other works on emotions theory pertinent herein include Rom Harre, ed., *The Social Construction of Emotions*; W. Russell Neuman et al., eds., *The Affect Effect*.

5. The Conundrum of Slavery

1. Basil Manly Sr., speech at South Carolina College, "On the Emancipation of Slaves," April 1821, BMSr, Furman; A. James Fuller, *Chaplain to the Confederacy*, 32–36.
2. Historians' emphasis on evangelical Protestant Christians' early antislavery potential but eventual proslavery collusion during the antebellum era is embodied in Christine Leigh Heyrman, *Southern Cross*, 3–76; Rhys Isaac, *The Transformation of Virginia*; Anne C. Loveland, *Southern Evangelicals and the Social Order*, 186–218; Cynthia Lynn Lyerly, *Methodism and the Southern Mind*, 47–72, 119–75; Donald G. Mathews, *Religion in the Old South*, 66–80. Studies tracing deeper chronological roots of antebellum proslavery defenses include Elizabeth Fox-Genovese and Eugene Genovese, *The Mind of the Master Class*; James O. Farmer, *The Metaphysical Confederacy*; John Patrick Daly, *When Slavery Was Called Freedom*. Charles F. Irons, *The Origins of Proslavery Christianity*, argues that both were essential, as interracial interaction within southern religious communities from the late colonial period through the antebellum period, more than outside abolitionist threats, provided the impetus for the proslavery defense that emerged in the antebellum era.
3. For an analysis of Basil Manly's Sr.'s evolving perspectives on southern slavery, see Fuller, *Chaplain to the Confederacy*, 116–24, 212–27. The most comprehensive analysis of the variety and evolution of white southern perspectives on slavery is Lacy K. Ford Jr., *Deliver Us from Evil*.
4. Peter S. Carmichael, *The Last Generation*, 19–58; Eugene D. Genovese, *The Slaveholders' Dilemma*; Beth Barton Schweiger, *The Gospel Working Up*. All of these works explore some aspect of the perspective emphasized here, which engages white southerners' ambiguous, ambivalent, and often contentious conceptions of history, slavery, and "progress." For more on the intensifying sectional identities and ideologies among these antebellum generations, see especially Timothy J. Williams, *Intellectual Manhood*; Evelyn D. Causey, "The Character of a Gentleman."

5. Basil Manly Sr., "On the Emancipation of Slaves"; Fuller, *Chaplain to the Confederacy*, 32–36. For more on the proscribed antislavery sentiments of Thomas Jefferson as emphasized here, see John Chester Miller, *The Wolf by the Ears*.
6. Basil Manly Sr., "On the Emancipation of Slaves"; Fuller, *Chaplain to the Confederacy*, 32–36.
7. Basil Manly Sr., "On the Emancipation of Slaves"; Fuller, *Chaplain to the Confederacy*, 32–36. For more on the emergence of paternalism as a defense of southern slavery, see Ford, *Deliver Us from Evil*, 141–203.
8. Basil Manly Sr., "On the Emancipation of Slaves"; Fuller, *Chaplain to the Confederacy*, 32–36.
9. Basil Manly Sr., "On the Emancipation of Slaves"; Fuller, *Chaplain to the Confederacy*, 32–36. For more on white southern debates over colonization and emancipation, see Ford, *Deliver Us from Evil*, 299–328, 361–89.
10. Iveson L. Brookes to Bro. Creath, June 13, 1859, ILB-USC; Whitfield Brooks, journal entry, June 16, 1844, 165–66.
11. For more on slavery and secession, see Ford, *Deliver Us from Evil*, 447–80, 505–34.
12. Whitfield Brooks, journal entry, October 30, 1842, 85.
13. Whitfield Brooks, journal entry, August 5, 1844, 172.
14. Basil Manly Sr., church journal entry, January 9, 1828, BMSr, Furman.
15. Basil Manly Sr., church journal entry, March 21, 1828, BMSr, Furman; Fuller, *Chaplain to the Confederacy*, 71–72.
16. William P. Hill, diary entry, November 24, 1846, William P. Hill, diary, 1846–1849, UNC.
17. Whitfield Brooks, journal entry, June 16, 1844, 165–66.
18. Whitfield Brooks, journal entry, June 26–27, 1846, 265.
19. Whitfield Brooks, journal entry, May 25, 1847, 317–18.
20. Basil Manly Sr., church journal entry, June 22, 1829, BMSr, Furman; Fuller, *Chaplain to the Confederacy*, 72–74, 240–41.
21. Basil Manly Sr. to J. L. M. Curry, December 2, 1852, BMSr, Furman.
22. Basil Manly Jr., diary entry, October 4, 1844, BMJr, Furman. On the denominational schisms amidst the sectional crisis over slavery see especially C. C. Goen, *Broken Churches, Broken Nation*. For more on the growing white southern fear, and northern hope, that southern slavery if contained would die of its own inherent maladies, see James Oakes, *Freedom National*, 1–83, and especially *The Scorpion's Sting*.
23. Basil Manly Jr., lecture before the Richmond Athenaeum, "The South in the Nation," 1854, BMJr, Furman. For more on the role of oratory in the masculine culture of the antebellum South, see especially W. Stuart Towns, *Oratory and Rhetoric in the Nineteenth-Century South*, 1–10, 53–74.

24. Basil Manly Jr., "The South in the Nation." For more on this generation gap within broader antebellum American society and culture, see Michael Kammen, *Mystic Chords of Memory*, 1–91.
25. Eugene Genovese, *The Slaveholders' Dilemma*. The psychological interpretation ventured here applies a generational perspective to the ideological and identity crisis confronting many leading white southern men during the sectional controversy over slavery. A similar generational perspective applied to northern political leaders of the era can be found in George B. Forgie, *Patricide in the House Divided*.
26. Basil Manly Jr., "The South in the Nation."
27. Basil Manly Jr., "The South in the Nation."
28. For more on the social and political manifestations of this besieged mentality and its increasingly aggressive defensive posture, see especially Lacy K. Ford Jr., *Origins of Southern Radicalism*, 99–144; Lorri Glover, *Southern Sons*, 165–79; Kenneth S. Greenberg, *Masters and Statesmen*, 85–103, 107–46; Manisha Sinha, *The Counterrevolution of Slavery*.
29. Basil Manly Jr., diary entry, November 23, 1844 (emphasis added), BMJr, Furman. For more on this relationship between white southern honor and slavery, see Kenneth S. Greenberg, *Honor and Slavery*, 24–50.
30. Basil Manly Jr., diary entry, December 22, 1844, BMJr, Furman. For more on the tortured logic of white southern paternalism, especially in relation to proslavery Christianity as they evolved during the antebellum era, see especially Carmichael, *The Last Generation*, 59–88; Charity R. Carney, *Ministers and Masters*, 114–35; Richard J. Carwardine, *Evangelicals and Politics in Antebellum America*, 153–59, 255–58, 269–72, 285–92; Eugene Genovese and Elizabeth Fox-Genovese, *Fatal Self-Deception*; Elizabeth Fox-Genovese and Eugene Genovese, *The Mind of the Master Class*; Greenberg, *Masters and Statesmen*, 85–103; John R. McKivigan and Mitchell Snay, eds., *Religion and the Antebellum Debate over Slavery*; David F. Ericson, *The Debate over Slavery*; Mitchell Snay, *Gospel of Disunion*.
31. Basil Manly Jr., unpublished exposition, "The Duty of Giving Religious Instruction to the Colored Population," undated, BMJr, Furman.
32. Basil Manly Jr., diary entry, February 5, 1843, BMJr, Furman. For more on the biracial complexities of southern evangelicalism, especially in relation to the missions to the enslaved that became increasingly prevalent beginning in the 1830s, see especially John B. Boles, ed., *Masters and Slaves in the House of the Lord*, 1–126; Janet D. Cornelius, *Slave Missions and the Black Church in the Antebellum South*; Sylvia Frey, "Shaking the Dry Bones," 23–44; Charles Irons, *The Origins of Proslavery Christianity*, 97–209.
33. Basil Manly Jr. to Reverend Curtis, February 12, 1844, BMJr, Furman.
34. Basil Manly Jr. to Reverend Curtis, February 12, 1844, BMJr, Furman.

35. Basil Manly Jr. to Reverend Curtis, February 12, 1844, BMJr, Furman. For more on slavery and the southern legal system, see especially Paul Finkleman, ed., *Slavery and the Law*; Ariela J. Gross, *Double Character*; Sally E. Hadden, *Slave Patrols*; Timothy S. Huebner, *The Southern Judicial Tradition*; Thomas D. Morris, *Southern Slavery and the Law*. For more on the tenuous balance of power between southern courts, law enforcement, and social mores, especially prevailing notions of masculine honor, patriarchal prerogative, and paternalistic obligation, see Peter W. Bardaglio, *Reconstructing the Household*, 3–36; Jack Kenny Williams, "The Criminal Lawyer in Antebellum South Carolina," 138–50, and "White Lawbreakers in Antebellum South Carolina," 360–73; Laura F. Edwards, "Law, Domestic Violence, and the Limits of Patriarchal Authority in the Antebellum South," 733–70
36. Basil Manly Jr. "The Duty of Giving Religious Instruction," BMJr, Furman.
37. Basil Manly Jr. "The Duty of Giving Religious Instruction," BMJr, Furman.
38. Basil Manly Jr., diary entry, March 7, 1845; Basil Manly Jr. to parents, February 3, 1845; BMJr, Furman. For the best analysis of the antislavery and abolitionist movements in the North, which Manly Jr. so grossly conflated and indiscriminately despised, see especially Manisha Sinha, *The Slave's Cause*; John R. McKivigan and Stanley Harrold, eds., *Antislavery Violence*. Others to contextualize the movement within social and political reform include Robert H. Abzug, *Cosmos Crumbling*, 129–62; Carwardine, *Evangelicals and Politics in Antebellum America*, 133–43, 235–55, 258–69, 279–318; McKivigan and Snay, eds., *Religion and the Antebellum Debate over Slavery*; Ericson, *The Debate over Slavery*; Steven Mintz, *Moralists and Modernizers*, 117–53; Snay, *Gospel of Disunion*; Bertram Wyatt-Brown, *Lewis Tappan and the Evangelical War against Slavery*. More recently, Margaret Abruzzo, *Polemical Pain*, contextualizes the antislavery and abolitionist movements within the broader emergence of humanitarianism.
39. Basil Manly Jr., diary entry, December 15, 1844, BMJr, Furman.
40. Basil Manly Jr., diary entry, March 5, 1845, BMJr, Furman. For more on the tangled logic of secession in relation to white southern ideals and identities in the midst of the sectional crisis, see especially Charles S. Sydnor, *The Development of Southern Sectionalism*; David M. Potter, *The Impending Crisis*; William W. Freehling, *The Road to Disunion*, vol. 1; Paul Calore, *The Causes of the Civil War*; Peter S. Carmichael, *The Last Generation*, 18, 29–30; Lacy K. Ford Jr., *Origins of Southern Radicalism*, 338–73; Greenberg, *Masters and Statesmen*, 104–46; Sinha, *The Counterrevolution of Slavery*, 187–254; Patricia Roberts-Miller, *Fanatical Schemes*.
41. Basil Manly Jr., diary entries, March 4, March 3, 1845; BMJr, Furman.
42. Basil Manly Jr., diary entry, March 7, 8, 1845; BMJr, Furman.
43. The violence that pervaded the South's peculiar institution belied such paternalistic claims as those advanced by proslavery Christians like Manly Jr.

For more on the inherent violence within the slave system, see especially Dickson D. Bruce Jr., *Violence and Culture in the Antebellum South*; Jeff Forret, *Race Relations at the Margins*, 157–222; John Hope Franklin, *The Militant South*, 63–79; Gross, *Double Character*, 98–121; Hadden, *Slave Patrols*, 41–172.

44. Basil Manly Jr. to parents, April 14, 1845, MaFP-SBHL.
45. Basil Manly Jr. to parents, April 14, 1845, MaFP-SBHL.
46. Basil Manly Jr. to parents, April 22, 1845, MaFP-SBHL.
47. Basil Manly Jr. to parents, April 22, 1845, MaFP-SBHL For more on the nullification crisis and southern separatist sentiments, see especially William W. Freehling, *Prelude to Civil War*.

6. 1856

1. The only scholarly biographical treatment of Preston Brooks is Robert Neil Mathis, "Preston Smith Brooks," 296–310.
2. Stephen Berry, ed., *Princes of Cotton*, xii.
3. For more on this conception of biblical morality, see especially David A. DeSilva, *Honor, Patronage, Kinship, and Purity*; Evan Shalev, *American Zion*, 50–83, 151–84.
4. For analysis of other infamous antebellum affairs of honor at South Carolina College, see Maximilian LaBorde, *History of the South Carolina College*; Louis P. Towles, "A Matter of Honor at South Carolina College, 1822," 6–18; William E. Walker, "The South Carolina College Duel of 1833," 140–42. For more on such extreme violent masculinity at antebellum southern colleges, see especially E. Merton Coulter, *College Life in the Old South*, and Robert F. Pace, *Halls of Honor*. More recent scholars complicate this violent and anti-intellectual view, especially Jennifer R. Green, *Military Education and the Emerging Middle Class in the Old South*; Timothy J. Williams, *Intellectual Manhood*; Evelyn D. Causey, "The Character of a Gentleman."
5. Report of a special meeting of the South Carolina College Board of Trustees, January 4, 1838, PSB.
6. Report of Board of Trustees meeting, January 4, 1838, PSB.
7. "Report of the Secretary of the Faculty for the Expulsion of Preston S. Brooks," South Carolina College, November 27, 1839, PSB.
8. "The Code Duello—A Man of Honor talks of a Famous Duel near Augusta," undated, PSB; Whitfield Brooks, journal entries, November 3–4, 11, 1840, quoted in *An Edgefield Planter and His World*, ed. James O. Farmer Jr., 1. Page numbers following citations to Whitfield Brooks's journal entries all refer to Farmer, ed., *Edgefield Planter*. For the most thorough analyses of the entire Brooks-Wigfall affair of honor, see Alvy L. King, *Louis T. Wigfall*, 20–47; Eric H. Walther, *The Fire-Eaters*, 160–94; Edward S. Cooper, *Louis*

Trezevant Wigfall, 9–21. For more on the broader context in which the duel transpired, see especially James Henry Hammond, *The Hammonds of Redcliffe*, ed. Carol Bleser, 3–18, and *Secret and Sacred*, ed. Carol Bleser, 3–23, 31; Drew Gilpin Faust, *James Henry Hammond and the Old South*, 204–23.

9. Whitfield Brooks, journal entry, November 30, 1840, 5–6.
10. Whitfield Brooks, journal entry, November 30, 1840, 5–6.
11. Whitfield Brooks, journal entry, November 11, 1840 (emphasis added), 2–3.
12. Whitfield Brooks, journal entry, November 11, 1841, 43.
13. Whitfield Brooks, journal entry, January 14, 1843, 95.
14. Whitfield Brooks, journal entries, July 22, August 5, 1843; 121.
15. Whitfield Brooks, journal entry, September 2, 1844, 175–76.
16. Whitfield Brooks, journal entry, April 7, 1845, 218.
17. Whitfield Brooks, journal entries, June 27, 1841; January 1, 1842; 30, 50.
18. Whitfield Brooks, journal entries, July 5, 1841; June 30, 1842; 31, 72.
19. Whitfield Brooks, journal entries, July 24, 1843; March 27, 1844; 121, 151–52.
20. Whitfield Brooks, journal entries, October 30, November 1, November 15, 1843; 133–35.
21. Whitfield Brooks, journal entries, March 6, March 11, March 13, March 15, 1844; 149–50.
22. Whitfield Brooks, journal entry, June 13, 1845, 231–32.
23. Arthur Wigfall, *A Sermon upon Duelling*. For more on antidueling sentiment in the antebellum South, see especially Charity R. Carney, *Ministers and Masters*, 12–24; William S. Cossen, "Blood, Honor, Reform, and God," 23–45; Christine Leigh Heyrman, *Southern Cross*, 211, 246–50; Anne C. Loveland, *Southern Evangelicals and the Social Order*, 180–85. For more on antidueling sentiment within the broader antebellum culture of reform, see especially Robert H. Abzug, *Cosmos Crumbling*, 42–44; Thomas J. Carmody, "The Anti-Dueling Movement," 341–66.
24. Whitfield Brooks, journal entry, May 18, 1846, 259; Colonel Pierce Mason Butler to Captain Preston Smith Brooks, South Carolina Volunteers (SCV), December 6, 1846, PSB; Whitfield Brooks, journal entries, June 8, June 29, November 26, July 10, November 30, 1846; 262, 266, 287, 268, 288.
25. Whitfield Brooks, journal entries, November 30, December 7, December 8, 1846; 288–90.
26. Whitfield Brooks journal entries, December 8, December 31, December 5, 1846; January 2, 1847; 289–90, 292.
27. Colonel Pierce Mason Butler to Reverend Whitefoord Smith, December 26, 1846, Whitefoord Smith Papers, David M. Rubenstein Rare Book and Manuscript Library, Duke University.
28. Public statement of James Davis, former surgeon in the Palmetto Regiment, South Carolina Volunteers, regarding Capt. Preston S. Brooks, October 7, 1847; James Davis, surgeon, Surgeon's Certificate for Captain Preston S.

Brooks, Company D, May 2, 1847; Captain Preston S. Brooks to Adjt. General R. Jones, July 2, 1847; Abner P. Blocker to Captain Preston S. Brooks, January 4, 1848, PSB. In the letter to Adjt. Gen. Jones, Brooks asks to be reassigned to his unit, but should he be denied that request, he asks to be reassigned to the upper districts of South Carolina, implying that his reputation among his Edgefield brethren is withering along with his recruiting prospects. In the letter from Abner Blocker, Brooks's cousin, Blocker makes reference to slanderous comments directed at Brooks by Edgefield neighbors, asserting, "I was pained to hear a few days ago ... that Bill Jones had slandered you this summer in his communications to some of your company. I mean his brother. All that I have to say about it is that I will see when I visit Edge [field] and will put a stop to any talk about you as I did last summer in one or two instances."

29. Captain Preston S. Brooks to Dr. Davis, September 25, 1847; Whitfield Brooks to J. A. Black, January 12, 1848; Captain Preston S. Brooks to Adjt. General R. Jones, July 2, 1847; Adjt. General R. Jones to Captain Preston S. Brooks, September 23, 1847, PSB; Whitfield Brooks, journal entry, September 30, 1847, 340.

30. R. G. M. Dunovant, *The Palmetto Regiment, South Carolina Volunteers, 1846–1848*, 13, quoted in Jack Allen Meyer, *South Carolina in the Mexican War*, 89; Whitfield Brooks to James A. Black, December 20, 1847, PSB.

31. Whitfield Brooks to James A. Black, December 20, 1847, and January 12, 1848; Abner P. Blocker to Capt. Preston S. Brooks, January 4, 1848, PSB.

32. Extracts from the diary of Preston S. Brooks, as copied by his wife Martha, April 1849, PSB. For a recent study that emphasizes the prominent influence of the Mexican War on Preston Brooks's life, see Kenneth A. Deitreich, "The Sly Mendacity of Hints," 290–314.

33. Extracts from the diary of Preston S. Brooks, March 1853, PSB.

34. Charles Sumner, *The Crime against Kansas*, 9, 86. For the most complete analysis of Sumner's speech and reactions to it, see especially Michael D. Pierson, "'All Southern Society Is Assailed by the Foulest Charges,'" 531–57; Carol Lasser, "Voyeuristic Abolitionism," 83–114.

35. Sumner, *The Crime against Kansas*, 5; Charles Sumner to Theodore Parker, May 17, 1856, in *Memoirs and Letters of Charles Sumner*, vol. 3, *1845–1860*, ed. Edward L. Pierce, 438–39; Stephen Douglas as quoted in John Lockwood and Charles Lockwood, *The Siege of Washington*, 98. The best single volume on the caning is Williamjames Hull Hoffer, *The Caning of Charles Sumner*. See also Rachel A. Shelden, *Washington Brotherhood*, 120–43; Harlan Gradin, "Losing Control"; Michael D. Pierson, *Free Hearts and Free Homes*; James Corbett David, "The Politics of Emasculation," 324–45; Manisha Sinha, "The Caning of Charles Sumner," 233–62; Stephen Berry and James Hill Welborn III, "The Cane of His Existence," 5–21. For a rich

set of documents relating to the caning, see T. Lloyd Benson, ed., *The Caning of Senator Sumner*. For a broader analysis of violence in antebellum American politics, see Joanne B. Freeman, *The Field of Blood*.
36. Preston Brooks to J. H. Brooks, Esq., May 23, 1856, PSB. For a more detailed treatment of Keitt's role in the caning, see Holt Merchant, *South Carolina Fire-Eater*. For more on Keitt, see Walther, *The Fire-Eaters*, 160–94, and Stephen Berry, *All That Makes a Man*, 47–64, 79–80. For more on the role of alcohol in fortifying their spirits before the assault, see Hoffer, *The Caning of Charles Sumner*, 71, and Berry and xWelborn, "The Cane of His Existence."
37. "Captain Brooks' Castigation of Senator Sumner," May 28, 1856, Edgefield *Advertiser*, reprinted in Benson, *The Caning of Senator Sumner*, 164–65.
38. "The Right View of the Subject," May 30, 1856, Charleston (SC) *Mercury*, reprinted in Benson, *The Caning of Senator Sumner*, 167.
39. "The Washington Difficulty," May 30, 1856, Laurensville (SC) *Herald*, reprinted in Benson, *The Caning of Senator Sumner*, 164.
40. "Liberty of Speech, of the Press, and Freedom of Religion," June 3, 1856, Richmond (VA) *Enquirer*, reprinted in Benson, *The Caning of Senator Sumner*, 172–73.
41. Untitled editorial, May 28, 1856, Louisville (KY) *Journal*, reprinted in Benson, *The Caning of Senator Sumner*, 168–69.
42. Untitled editorial, May 26, 1856, Wilmington (NC) *Herald*, reprinted in Benson, *The Caning of Senator Sumner*, 169–70.
43. Letter from Congressman John McQueen, October 8, 1856, Edgefield (SC) *Advertiser*, reprinted in Benson, *The Caning of Senator Sumner*, 185.
44. Letter from Congressman John McQueen, in Benson, *The Caning of Senator Sumner*, 186.
45. W. F. Holmes to Preston Brooks, May 27, 1856, reprinted in Benson, *The Caning of Senator Sumner*, 194.
46. Seaborn Jones to Preston S. Brooks, June 1, 1856, reprinted in Benson, *The Caning of Senator Sumner*, 192.
47. Letter from "A Friend Indeed" to Charles Sumner, May 22, 1856, reprinted in Benson, *The Caning of Senator Sumner*, 189–90.
48. For more on the tangled logic of secession in relation to white southern ideals and identities at the height of the sectional crisis, see especially David M. Potter, *The Impending Crisis*; William W. Freehling, *The Road to Disunion*, vol. 2; Randall C. Jimerson, *The Private War*, 124–237; Peter Carmichael, *The Last Generation*, 18, 29–30; Lacy Ford, *Origins of Southern Radicalism*, 338–73; Kenneth Greenberg, *Masters and Statesmen*, 104–46; Manisha Sinha, *The Counterrevolution of Slavery*, 187–254; Patricia Roberts-Miller, *Fanatical Schemes*.

7. The Civil War and Reconstruction

1. The latest death toll figures increase the commonly accepted numbers by 20 percent and are compiled and analyzed in J. David Hacker, "Census-Based Count of the Civil War Dead," 307–48. The best single-volume analysis of the American Civil War in its military, political, and social context is still James McPherson, *Battle Cry of Freedom*. For the most comprehensive single-volume military history of the war, see David J. Eicher, *The Longest Night*. On the expansion of federal power during and after the Civil War, see Richard Franklin Bensel, *Yankee Leviathan*. For an analysis of the national psychological reactions to and effects of this unprecedented death and destruction, see especially Drew Gilpin Faust, *This Republic of Suffering*, and Megan Kate Nelson, *Ruin Nation*.
2. The most comprehensive overview of the postwar social and political landscape is Eric Foner, *Reconstruction*. For an overview of the contested legacies of the Civil War and Reconstruction, see especially David W. Blight, *Race and Reunion*. Other important perspectives on contested postwar cultural memory and its legacies include Alice Fahs and Joan Waugh, eds., *The Memory of the Civil War in American Culture*, 1–129, 157–79; John R. Neff, *Honoring the Civil War Dead*; K. Stephen Prince, *Stories of the South*; Caroline Janney, *Remembering the Civil War*; Robert J. Cook, *Civil War Memories*; Gary W. Gallagher, *Causes Won, Lost, and Forgotten*; Bruce E. Baker, *What Reconstruction Meant*. For African American attempts to shape the southern cultural memory of the war and its results see especially Blight, *Race and Reunion*, 64–77, 300–337, and Kathleen Ann Clark, *Defining Moments*.
3. Beth Barton Schweiger, *The Gospel Working Up*, 91–108; James J. Broomall, *Private Confederacies*, 32–130.
4. Gaines M. Foster, *Ghosts of the Confederacy*; Thomas L. Connelly and Barbara L. Bellows, *God and General Longstreet*; Charles Reagan Wilson, *Baptized in Blood*; William C. Davis, *The Cause Lost*; Gary W. Gallagher and Alan T. Nolan, eds., *The Myth of the Lost Cause and Civil War History*; W. Stuart Towns, *Enduring Legacy*; Adam Domby, *The False Cause*. The prominence of white southern women's initiatives in honoring, commemorating, and memorializing the Confederacy and its soldiers to the foundation of the Lost Cause memory in the New South receive particular emphasis in Karen L. Cox, *Dixie's Daughters*; Sarah E. Gardner, *Blood and Irony*; William Alan Blair, *Cities of the Dead*; Caroline E. Janney, *Burying the Dead but Not the Past*; LeeAnn Whites, *The Civil War as a Crisis in Gender*, 132–224, and *Gender Matters*; Schweiger, *The Gospel Working Up*, 171–94.
5. Basil Manly Jr. to parents, October 26, 1860, MaFP-Furman. For more on the profoundly religious worldviews of both northerners and southerners in the Civil War era, see especially: Randall M. Miller, Harry S. Stout, and

Charles Reagan Wilson, eds., *Religion and the American Civil War*, 3–88, 110–30, 208–49, 360–412; Robert J. Miller, *Both Prayed to the Same God*; Mark A. Noll, *The Civil War as a Theological Crisis*; James H. Moorhead, *American Apocalypse*; Kyle N. Osborn, "Masters of Fate"; George C. Rable, *God's Almost Chosen Peoples*; Sean A. Scott, *A Visitation of God*; Harry S. Stout, *Upon the Altar of the Nation*; Daniel W. Stowell, *Rebuilding Zion*; Andrew Preston, *Sword of the Spirit, Shield of Faith*, 161–74. For more on the emergence and evolution of Confederate nationalism, see especially Drew Gilpin Faust, *The Creation of Confederate Nationalism*, and *Southern Stories*, 88–109; Michael T. Bernath, *Confederate Minds*; Emory M. Thomas, *The Confederate Nation*, 37–166, 190–306; Anne Sarah Rubin, *A Shattered Nation*, 1–138; Stephanie McCurry, *Confederate Reckoning*, 1–84, 310–61; George C. Rable, *The Confederate Republic* and *Civil Wars* and *Damn Yankees*; Paul Quigley, *Shifting Grounds*, 128–213; Ian Binnington, *Confederate Visions*, 1–148.

6. Basil Manly Sr. to children, November 4, 1860, MaFP-Furman. Quigley, *Shifting Grounds*, 16–127.
7. Basil Manly Sr. to children, January 13, 1861, MaFP-Furman; Osborn, "Masters of Fate."
8. Basil Manly Sr. to children, January 13, 1861; Basil Manly Sr. to Basil Manly Jr., January 23, 1861; Basil Manly Sr. to Basil Manly Jr., April 3, 1861; MaFP-Furman.
9. Basil Manly Sr. to children, January 23, 1861 (emphasis his); Basil Manly Sr. to Basil Manly Jr., February 16, 1861, MaFP-Furman. For a general overview of Manly's experience of the Civil War, see A. James Fuller, *Chaplain to the Confederacy*, 287–308. For prevailing white southern religious interpretations of the war more generally, see especially Peter S. Carmichael, *The Last Generation*, 179–211; Eugene D. Genovese, *A Consuming Fire*; Stowell, *Rebuilding Zion*, 3–48; Miller, Stout, and Wilson, eds., *Religion and the American Civil War*, 89–109, 131–86, 297–359; Richard E. Beringer et al., *The Elements of Confederate Defeat*, 32–43, 118–33; Beth Barton Schweiger and Donald G. Mathews, eds., *Religion in the American South*, 99–124; Osborn, "Masters of Fate."
10. Basil Manly Sr. to children, June 8, 1861; Charles Manly to mother Sarah M. Manly, July 22, 1861; Basil Manly Sr. to Basil Manly Jr., February 12, 1862, MaFP-Furman; Osborn, "Masters of Fate."
11. Basil Manly Sr. to children, August 31, 1861; Basil Manly Sr. to son Richard Fuller Manly, October 7, 1861; Basil Manly Jr. to parents, February 13, 1862; Charles Manly to parents, February 14, 1862; Charles Manly to parents, August 8, 1862; Basil Manly Sr. to son Richard Fuller Manly, February 14, 1862; MaFP-Furman. Here the Manlys clearly exhibited the embattled state

of mind common to white southern Christians as analyzed by Genovese, *A Consuming Fire*.

12. Basil Manly Sr. to Basil Manly Jr., February 20, 1862, MaFP-Furman. The Manly family mirrored many others in this constant searching for divine approbation or condemnation for their cause, an emotional cycle that pervaded the rank-and-file of the armies themselves, according to Beringer et al., *The Elements of Confederate Defeat*, 118–33, 154–67; Steven E. Woodworth, *While God Is Marching On*; Kent T. Dollar, *Soldiers of the Cross*; John W. Brinsfield et al., eds., *Faith in the Fight*; John W. Brinsfield, ed., *The Spirit Divided*.

13. Charles Manly to mother Sarah M. Manly, July 22, 1861; Charles Manly to parents, February 18, 1862; Charles Manly to parents, February 19, 1862; Charles Manly to brother Basil Manly Jr., February 10, 1862, MaFP-Furman; Basil Manly Jr. to parents, undated; MaFP-SBHL.

14. For more on women's roles in the Confederate South, see especially Rable, *Civil Wars*; Catherine Clinton and Nina Silber, eds., *Divided Houses*, 3–41, 97–212, 230–45; LeeAnn Whites, *The Civil War as a Crisis in Gender*, 41–63; LeeAnn Whites, ed., *Occupied Women*; Drew Gilpin Faust, *Southern Stories*, 113–92, and *Mothers of Invention*; Miller, Stout, and Wilson, eds., *Religion and the American Civil War*, 229–60; Anya Jabour, "Southern Ladies and She-Rebels; or, Femininity in the Foxhole," in *Manners and Southern History*, ed. Ted Ownby, 1–19; McCurry, *Confederate Reckoning*, 85–217.

15. Sarah M. Manly to son Richard Fuller Manly, April 24, 1861, MaFP-Furman. For the Manly family's wartime experience, see Fuller, *Chaplain to the Confederacy*, 287–308.

16. Sarah M. Manly to children, June 5, 1861, MaFP-Furman.

17. Sarah M. Manly to children, August 1, 1861; Sarah M. Manly to son Richard Fuller Manly, October 7, 1861; MaFP-Furman.

18. Sarah M. Manly to daughter Abby Manly Gwaltney, February 17, 1861; Sarah M. Manly to son Charles, February 20, 1861; MaFP-Furman.

19. Sarah M. Manly to son Basil Manly Jr., March 9, 1862; Sarah M. Manly to sons Basil Jr., Charles, Fuller, and James, March 17, 1862; MaFP-Furman. For more on this prevailing sense that Confederate defeat was a form of divine chastisement, see especially Stowell, *Rebuilding Zion*, 33–48; Jason Phillips, *Diehard Rebels*, 9–39; Miller, Stout, and Wilson, eds., *Religion and the American Civil War*, 187–207, 360–84.

20. Sarah M. Manly to husband Basil Manly Sr., May 4, May 11, June 5, 1862; Sarah M. Manly to son Charles, July 31, August 26, 1862; MaFP-Furman.

21. Basil Manly Sr. to children, February 3, 1862; Basil Manly Sr. to Basil Manly Jr., March 3, 1862; Basil Manly Sr. to children, March 23, 1862; Basil Manly Sr. to Basil Manly Jr., March 26, 1862; MaFP-Furman.

22. Basil Manly Jr. to parents, November 4, 1862, MaFP-Furman.

23. Sarah M. Manly to daughter Abby Manly Gwaltney, October 12, 1863, MaFP-Furman.
24. Basil Manly Sr. to Basil Manly Jr., December 20, 1861, MaFP-Furman.
25. Basil Manly Sr. to children, February 2, 1862, MaFP-Furman.
26. Basil Manly Jr. to parents, March 20, 1865, MaFP-Furman. For an overview of the complicated and various evangelical perspectives on race and religion during the war and into the postwar period, see McCurry, *Confederate Reckoning*, 218–361; Paul Harvey, *Redeeming the South*; Edward J. Blum, *Reforging the White Republic*; Edward J. Blum and W. Scott Poole, eds., *Vale of Tears*, 1–72, 112–63; Miller, Stout, and Wilson, eds., *Religion and the American Civil War*, 167–86, 360–84.
27. Basil Manly Jr. to parents, May 24, 1865, MaFP-Furman. For more on the uneven pace of emancipation across the South, see Katharine L. Dvorak, "After Apocalypse, Moses," in John B. Boles, ed., *Masters and Slaves in the House of the Lord*, 173–91.
28. Basil Manly Jr. to Basil Manly Sr., September 7, 1865, MaFP-Furman.
29. Basil Manly Jr. to Basil Manly Sr., September 7, 1865, MaFP-Furman. For more on white southern efforts to rebuild their religious communities and retain their Black membership while maintaining some semblance of moral authority over them, see Schweiger, *The Gospel Working Up*, 109–27; Stowell, *Rebuilding Zion*, 100–113.
30. Basil Manly Jr. to parents, May 1, 1865; May 4–25, 1865; MaFP-Furman.
31. Basil Manly Jr. to parents, May 4–25, 1865, MaFP-Furman.
32. Basil Manly Jr. to parents, May 4–25, 1865, MaFP-Furman. The most comprehensive analyses of the violence attending Reconstruction on the ground in the South are George C. Rable, *But There Was No Peace*, and Douglas R. Egerton, *The Wars of Reconstruction*. For more on the violent nature of Reconstruction in South Carolina specifically, see especially Richard Zuczek, *State of Rebellion*; Stephen Kantrowitz, *Ben Tillman and the Reconstruction of White Supremacy*, 40–79; W. Scott Poole, *Never Surrender*; Francis Butler Simkins, *Pitchfork Ben Tillman*, 47–77.
33. Basil Manly Jr. to parents, August 15, 1865, MaFP-Furman.
34. Basil Manly Sr. to children, January 20, 1868, MaFP-SBHL; Basil Manly Sr. to children, February 5, 1868, MaFP-Furman; Basil Manly Sr. to children, June 10, 1868, MaFP-SBHL.
35. Basil Manly Sr. to children, July 7, 1865, MaFP-Furman; Basil Manly Sr. to children, February 5, 1868, MaFP-SBHL For more on former Confederate exiles and various exodus schemes, see especially Lawrence F. Hill, "The Confederate Exodus to Latin America, I," and "The Confederate Exodus to Latin America, II," 100–134, 161–99; Robert C. Poister, "The Business of Exile"; Andrew Rolle, *The Lost Cause*; Daniel E. Sutherland, "Exiles, Emigrants, and Sojourners," 237–56.

36. Sarah M. Manly to son Basil Manly Jr., September 13, November 13, 1868; MaFP-Furman.
37. Basil Manly Jr., "A Tribute to Robert E. Lee, 1870," BMJr, Furman.
38. Basil Manly Jr., "A Tribute to Robert E. Lee, 1870," BMJr, Furman.
39. David Blight, *Race and Reunion*, 255–99; Connelly and Bellows, *God and General Longstreet*; Foster, *Ghosts of the Confederacy*; Wilson, *Baptized in Blood*; Davis, *The Cause Lost*; Gallagher and Nolan, eds., *The Myth of the Lost Cause and Civil War History*; Towns, *Enduring Legacy* and *Oratory and Rhetoric in the Nineteenth-Century South*, 101–80; Domby, *The False Cause*. Many historians have highlighted the pivotal role played by southern white women in such Confederate commemoration ceremonies and rituals, and later, in broader Confederate memorialization projects: Blair, *Cities of the Dead*; Cox, *Dixie's Daughters*; Janney, *Burying the Dead but Not the Past*; Whites, *The Civil War as a Crisis in Gender*, 132–224.
40. Broomall, *Private Confederacies*, 108–56.
41. "Testimony of Jerry Thornton Moore, Columbia, S.C.," December 16, 1876, in *Testimony as to the Denial of the Elective Franchise in South Carolina at the Elections of 1875 and 1876*, vol. 1 (Washington, D.C.: Government Printing Office, 1877). For more on the social and political climate of Reconstruction in the South, see especially Foner, *Reconstruction*; Michael Perman, *The Road to Redemption*; Laura F. Edwards, *Gendered Strife and Confusion*; George C. Rable, *But There Was No Peace*; Egerton, *The Wars of Reconstruction*; Baker, *What Reconstruction Meant*, 13–20; Heather Cox Richardson, *Death of Reconstruction* and *West from Appomattox*; Mark Wahlgren Summers, *A Dangerous Stir* and *The Ordeal of Reunion*; Carole Emberton, *Beyond Redemption*; David Prior, *Between Freedom and Progress*; Schweiger and Mathews, eds., *Religion in the American South*, 153–94.
42. For more on the contested memories and legacies of the Civil War era in American society and culture generally, see especially Blight, *Race and Reunion*; Prince, *Stories of the South*; Cook, *Civil War Memories*; Fahs and Waugh, eds., *The Memory of the Civil War in American Culture*; Neff, *Honoring the Civil War Dead*; Gary W. Gallagher, *Causes Won, Lost, and Forgotten*; Lawrence A. Kreiser Jr. and Randall Allred, eds., *The Civil War in Popular Culture*; Foster, *Ghosts of the Confederacy*; Connelly and Bellows, *God and General Longstreet*; Wilson, *Baptized in Blood*; Cox, *Dixie's Daughters*; Gardner, *Blood and Irony*; Blair, *Cities of the Dead*; Janney, *Burying the Dead but Not the Past* and *Remembering the Civil War*; Whites, *The Civil War as a Crisis in Gender*, 132–224, and *Gender Matters*; Schweiger, *The Gospel Working Up*, 171–94; Davis, *The Cause Lost*; Kirk Savage, *Standing Soldiers, Kneeling Slaves*; Gallagher and Nolan, eds., *The Myth of the Lost Cause and Civil War History*; Towns, *Enduring Legacy*; Domby, *The False*

Cause; Frank J. Wetta and Martin A. Novelli, eds., *The Long Reconstruction*; John David Smith and J. Vincent Lowry, eds., *The Dunning School*; Carole Emberton and Bruce E. Baker, eds., *Remembering Reconstruction*; Baker, *What Reconstruction Meant*.

Epilogue

1. For an analysis of the tensions between the Lost Cause faith and the New South creed in the white mind of the postwar South, see especially Gaines M. Foster, *Ghosts of the Confederacy*, 79–159; Charles Reagan Wilson, *Baptized in Blood*, 79–99; David Blight, *Race and Reunion*, 255–99; Peter Carmichael, *The Last Generation*, 213–36; Beth Barton Schweiger, *The Gospel Working Up*, 171–94; K. Stephen Prince, *Stories of the South*, 1–250. For more on the end of Reconstruction and rise of the New South and the Jim Crow era, see especially: Paul M. Gaston, *The New South Creed*; John David Smith, *An Old Creed for the New South*; William Gillette, *Retreat from Reconstruction*; W. Stuart Towns, *Oratory and Rhetoric in the Nineteenth-Century South*, 121–204; LeeAnn Whites, *Gender Matters*, 113–92; Bruce E. Baker, *What Reconstruction Meant*, 21–88.
2. Eustace W. Speer to Elijah Alexander Brown, July 27, 1879, containing copy of "True Manliness" speech delivered July 24, 1879, Elijah A. Brown Papers, Hargrett Rare Book and Manuscript Library, University of Georgia. Elijah Alexander Brown's father, Joseph E. Brown—a former Georgia governor (1857–65), chief justice of the Georgia Supreme Court (1865–70), and U.S. senator (1880–91)—had been born in Pickens County, South Carolina, in 1821 before his family migrated to Georgia during his early childhood. In addition to his political career, Joseph E. Brown also served as the chairman of the Board of Trustees for the Southern Baptist Theological Seminary (1880–94) and figured as the institution's most important donor. His connection to the the seminary also connected him and his family with the institution's founders, including Basil Manly Jr. (and unofficially, his father Basil Manly Sr.), as well as James P. Boyce, John A. Broadus, and William Williams, along with other prominent white Southern Baptists. For more on these connections, see *Report on Slavery and Racism in the History of the Southern Baptist Theological Seminary*, 7, 33–38.
3. W. Speer to Elijah Alexander Brown, July 27, 1879 (original edits and emphasis), Elijah A. Brown Papers, Hargrett Rare Book and Manuscript Library, University of Georgia.
4. Smith, *An Old Creed for the New South*; Perman, *The Road to Redemption*; Heather Cox Richardson, *Death of Reconstruction* and *West from Appomattox*; George C. Rable, *But There Was No Peace*; Carole Emberton, *Beyond*

Redemption; C. Vann Woodward, *Origins of the New South*; Edward Ayers, *The Promise of the New South*; Baker, *What Reconstruction Meant*, 21–88; James C. Cobb, *Away down South*.

5. Baker, *What Reconstruction Meant*, 69–170; Adam H. Domby, *The False Cause*, 76–170; Richardson, *How the South Won the Civil War*, 124–205; Nina Silber, *The War Ain't Over*; Kevin M. Levin, *Searching for Black Confederates*, 68–184; Victoria E. Bynum, *The Long Shadow of the Civil War*, 101–48; Ty Seidule, *Robert E. Lee and Me*;

6. Foster, *Ghosts of the Confederacy*, 79–159; Wilson, *Baptized in Blood*, 79–99; Blight, *Race and Reunion*, 255–99; Carmichael, *The Last Generation*, 213–36; Schweiger, *The Gospel Working Up*, 171–94; Prince, *Stories of the South*, 1–250; Daniel W. Stowell, *Rebuilding Zion*, 162–78; Paul Harvey, *Redeeming the South*, 75–260; Baker, *What Reconstruction Meant*, 21–88; John Hammond Moore, *Carnival of Blood*.

7. Basil Manly Jr., "Our Brother in Black," *Seminary Magazine* 2, no. 5 (May 1889), reprinted in Basil Manly Sr. and Basil Manly Jr., *Soldiers of Christ*, 203–4; A. James Fuller, *Chaplain to the Confederacy*, 310–11.

8. Basil Manly Jr., "Our Brother in Black," in *Soldiers of Christ*, 204–206.

9. Emberton, *Beyond Redemption*; Grace Elizabeth Hale, *Making Whiteness*; Kristina DuRocher, *Raising Racists*; Stephanie Cole and Natalie J. Ring, eds., *The Folly of Jim Crow*; Sarah Haley, *No Mercy Here*; Baker, *What Reconstruction Meant*, 1–68; Domby, *The False Cause*, 1–75; Richardson, *How the South Won the Civil War*, xiii–123; Williamjames Hull Hoffer, *Plessy v. Ferguson*; Henry Louis Gates, *Stony the Road*; Glenda E. Gilmore, *Gender and Jim Crow*.

10. On the intersection of Civil War memory and prejudicial gender and racial politics since 1896, see especially Baker, *What Reconstruction Meant*, 69–170; Domby, *The False Cause*, 76–170; Richardson, *How the South Won the Civil War*, 124–205; Silber, *The War Ain't Over*; Kevin M. Levin, *Searching for Black Confederates*, 68–184; Bynum, *The Long Shadow of the Civil War*, 101–48; Seidule, *Robert E. Lee and Me*. On the broader history and contemporary cultural legacies of such prejudicial dynamics within American society, culture, and politics, see especially Mark Kann, *A Republic of Men*, 155–78; Carol Faulkner and Alison M. Parker, eds., *Interconnections*; Manisha Sinha and Penny Von Eschen, eds., *Contested Democracy*; David A. Bateman, Ira Katznelson, and John S. Lapinski, *Southern Nation*. On the religious dimensions and manifestations of this legacy, see especially Elizabeth L. Jemison, *Christian Citizens*; Michael O. Emerson and Christian Smith, *Divided by Faith*; Robert P. Jones, *White Too Long*; Anthea Butler, *White Evangelical Racism*; Jemar Tisby, *The Color of Compromise*; Eric Weed, *The Religion of White Supremacy in the United States*;

Khyati Y. Joshi, *White Christian Privilege*; Damon T. Berry, *Blood and Faith*; J. Russell Hawkins, ed., *The Bible Told Them So*; J. Russell Hawkins and Phillip Luke Sinitiere, eds., *Christians and the Color Line*; Jesse Curtis, *The Myth of Colorblind Christians*; Kevin M. Kruse, *One Nation under God*; Darren E. Grem, *The Blessings of Business*; Kristin Kobes Du Mez, *Jesus and John Wayne*; Daniel K. Williams, *God's Own Party*; Talia Lavin, *Culture Warlords*.

BIBLIOGRAPHY

Archival and Manuscript Records
Edgefield County Archives, Edgefield, South Carolina
Edgefield District Deed Books, 1786–1869
Edgefield District Judge of Probate: Coroner's Book of Inquisitions, 1844–1860
Edgefield District Judge of Probate: Minutes of the General Sessions Court, 1785–1860

David M. Rubenstein Rare Book and Manuscript Library, Duke University, Durham, North Carolina
Whitefoord Smith Papers, 1807–1893

South Carolina Baptist Historical Collection, James Buchanan Duke Library, Furman University, Greenville, South Carolina
Manly Family Papers
Basil Manly Sr. Papers
Basil Manly Jr. Papers
William Bullein Johnson Papers
Antioch Baptist Church Records, 1830–1982
Big Stephen's Creek (Hardy's) Baptist Church Records, 1803–1947
Dry Creek Baptist Church Records, 1825–1858
Sweetwater (Mt. Lebanon) Baptist Church Records, 1832–1966
Philippi Baptist Church Records, 1814–1917
Red Oak Grove Baptist Church Records, 1812–1882
Republican Baptist Church Records, 1844–1847
Rocky Creek Baptist Church Records, 1831–1875

Hargrett Rare Book and Manuscript Library, University of Georgia, Athens, Georgia
Elijah A. Brown Papers

South Carolina Department of Archives and History, Columbia, South Carolina
Edgefield County Court of General Sessions: Criminal Journals, 1802–1860

South Caroliniana Library, University of South Carolina, Columbia, South Carolina

Preston S. Brooks Papers, 1828–1938
Iveson L. Brookes Papers, 1793–1865

Southern Baptist Historical Library and Archives, Nashville, Tennessee

Manly Family Papers

Southern Historical Collection, Louis Round Wilson Special Collections Library, University of North Carolina, Chapel Hill, North Carolina

Iveson Lewis Brookes Papers, 1785–1868
Hughes Family Papers, 1790–1910
Milligan Family Papers, 1771–1885

Tompkins Genealogical Library, Edgefield, South Carolina

Edgefield Baptist Church Records, 1823–1860
Edgefield United Methodist Church Records, 1790–1860
Harmony Methodist Church Records, 1825–1860
Horn's Creek Baptist Church Minutes, 1824–1860
Little Steven's Creek Baptist Church Records, 1833–1860
McKendree Methodist Church Records, 1817–1860

William S. Hoole Special Collections Library, University of Alabama, Tuscaloosa, Alabama

Iveson L. Brookes Papers
Manly Family Papers

Newspapers

Advertiser (Edgefield, SC)
Chronicle (Augusta, GA)
Hive (Edgefield, SC)
Messenger (Pendleton, SC)
South Carolina Republican (Hamburg, SC)

Other Primary Sources

Brooks, Whitfield. *An Edgefield Planter and His World: The 1840s Journals of Whitfield Brooks.* Edited by James O. Farmer Jr. Macon, GA: Mercer University Press, 2019.

Hammond, James Henry. *The Hammonds of Redcliffe*. Edited by Carol Bleser. New York, NY: Oxford University Press, 1981.

———. *Secret and Sacred: The Diaries of James Henry Hammond, a Southern Slaveholder*. Edited by Carol Bleser. New York, NY: Oxford University Press, 1988.

Isham, Edward. *The Confessions of Edward Isham: A Poor White Life of the Old South*. Edited by Charles C. Bolton, and Scott P. Culcasure. Athens: University of Georgia Press, 1998.

Kennedy, John Pendleton. *Swallow Barn, or, A Sojourn in the Old Dominion*. Baton Rouge: Louisiana State University Press, 1986.

Longstreet, Augustus Baldwin. *Georgia Scenes*. Edited by M. E. Bradford. Nashville, TN: J. S. Sanders, 1992.

Manly, Basil, Sr., and Basil Manly Jr. *Soldiers of Christ: Selections from the Writings of Basil Manly Sr. and Basil Manly Jr.* Edited by Michael A. G. Haykin, Rogers D. Duke, and A. James Fuller. Cape Coral, FL: Founders Press, 2009.

Mylne, William. *Travels in the Colonies in 1773–1775: Described in the Letters of William Mylne*. Edited by Ted Ruddock. Athens: University of Georgia Press, 1993.

Olmsted, Frederick Law. *Journeys and Explorations in the Cotton Kingdom: A Traveller's Observations on Cotton and Slavery in the American States*. Vol. 2. London: Sampson Low, 1861.

O'Neall, John Belton. *Biographical Sketches of the Bench and Bar of South Carolina*. Vol. 1. Charleston, SC: S. G. Courtenay, 1859.

Simms, William Gilmore. *Martin Faber: The Story of a Criminal*. Edited by John Caldwell Guilds. Fayetteville: University of Arkansas Press, 2005.

Sumner, Charles. *The Crime against Kansas*. Boston: J. P. Jewett, 1856.

———. *Memoirs and Letters of Charles Sumner*. Vol. 3, *1845–1860*. Edited by Edward L. Pierce. London, England: Sampson Low, Marston, 1893.

Weems, Mason Locke. *The Bad Wife's Looking Glass, or God's Revenge against Cruelty to Husbands, Second Edition Improved*. Charleston, SC: Printed for the Author, 1823. Reprinted as *The Devil in Petticoats, or God's Revenge against Husband Killing, Advertiser Print*. Edgefield, SC: Bacon and Adams, 1878.

———. *God's Revenge against Murder, or The Drown'd Wife: A Tragedy*. Philadelphia, PA: John Adams, 1808.

Wigfall, Arthur. *A Sermon upon Dueling*. Charleston, SC: A. E. Miller, 1856.

Wilson, John Lyde. *The Code of Honor, or Rules for the Government of Principals and Seconds in Duelling*. Kennesaw, GA: Continental Book Company, 1959.

Woodmason, Charles. *The Carolina Backcountry on the Eve of the Revolution*. Edited by Richard J. Hooker. Chapel Hill: University of North Carolina Press, 1953.

Secondary Sources

Abruzzo, Margaret. *Polemical Pain: Slavery, Cruelty, and the Rise of Humanitarianism*. Baltimore, MD: Johns Hopkins University Press, 2011.
Abzug, Robert H. *Cosmos Crumbling: American Reform and the Religious Imagination*. New York: Oxford University Press, 1994.
Ayers, Edward L. *The Promise of the New South: Life After Reconstruction, 15th Anniversary Edition*. New York: Oxford University Press, 2007.
———. *Vengeance and Justice: Crime and Punishment in the 19th-Century American South*. New York: Oxford University Press, 1984.
Baker, Bruce E. *What Reconstruction Meant: Historical Memory in the American South*. Charlottesville: University of Virginia Press, 2007.
Baptist, Edward E. *The Half that Has Never Been Told: Slavery and the Making of American Capitalism*. New York: Basic Books, 2014.
Bardaglio, Peter W. *Reconstructing the Household: Families, Sex, and the Law in the Nineteenth-Century South*. Chapel Hill: University of North Carolina Press, 1995.
Bateman, David A., Ira Katznelson, and John S. Lapinski. *Southern Nation: Congress and White Supremacy after Reconstruction*. Princeton, NJ: Princeton University Press, 2018.
Beckert, Sven. *Empire of Cotton: A Global History*. New York: Alfred A. Knopf, 2014.
Bensel, Richard Franklin. *Yankee Leviathan: The Origins of Central State Authority in America, 1859–1877*. New York: Cambridge University Press, 1990.
Benson, T. Lloyd, ed. *The Caning of Senator Sumner*. Belmont, CA: Thomson-Wadsworth, 2004.
Beringer, Richard E., Herman Hattaway, Archer Jones, and William N. Still Jr. *The Elements of Confederate Defeat: Nationalism, War Aims, and Religion*. Athens: University of Georgia Press, 1988.
Bernath, Michael T. *Confederate Minds: The Struggle for Intellectual Independence in the Civil War South*. Chapel Hill: University of North Carolina Press, 2010.
Berry, Damon T. *Blood and Faith: Christianity in American White Nationalism*. Syracuse, NY: Syracuse University Press, 2017.
Berry, Stephen. *All That Makes a Man: Love and Ambition in the Civil War South*. New York: Oxford University Press, 2003.
———, ed. *Princes of Cotton: Four Diaries of Young Men in the South, 1848–1860*. Athens: University of Georgia Press, 2007.
Berry, Stephen, and James Hill Welborn III. "The Cane of His Existence: Depression, Damage, and the Brooks-Sumner Affair." *Southern Cultures* 20, no. 4 (Winter 2014).
Binnington, Ian. *Confederate Visions: Nationalism, Symbolism, and the Imagined South in the Civil War*. Charlottesville: University of Virginia Press, 2013.

Blair, William A. *Cities of the Dead: Contesting the Memory of the Civil War in the South, 1865–1914*. Chapel Hill: University of North Carolina Press, 2004.

Blight, David W. *Race and Reunion: The Civil War in American Memory*. Cambridge, MA: Belknap Press, 2001.

Blum, Edward J. *Reforging the White Republic: Race, Religion, and American Nationalism, 1865–1898*. Baton Rouge: Louisiana State University Press, 2007.

Blum, Edward J., and W. Scott Poole, eds. *Vale of Tears: New Essays on Religion and Reconstruction*. Macon, GA: Mercer University Press, 2005.

Boles, John B. *The Great Revival: Beginnings of the Bible Belt*. Lexington: University Press of Kentucky, 1996.

———, ed. *Masters and Slaves in the House of the Lord: Race and Religion in the American South, 1740–1870*. Lexington: University Press of Kentucky, 1988.

Bolton, Charles C. *Poor Whites of the Antebellum South: Tenants and Laborers in Central North Carolina and Northeast Mississippi*. Durham, NC: Duke University Press, 1994.

Brekus, Catherine A. *Strangers and Pilgrims: Female Preaching in America, 1740–1845*. Chapel Hill: University of North Carolina Press, 1998.

Brinsfield, John W., William C. Davis, Benedict Maryniak, and James I. Robertson, Jr., eds. *Faith in the Fight: Civil War Chaplains*. Mechanicsburg, PA: Stackpole Books, 2003.

Brinsfield, John W., ed. *The Spirit Divided: Memoirs of Civil War Chaplains—The Confederacy*. Macon, GA: Mercer University Press, 2006.

Broomall, James J. *Private Confederacies: The Emotional Worlds of Southern Men as Citizens and Soldiers*. Chapel Hill: University of North Carolina Press, 2019.

Brooks, Ulysses R. *South Carolina Bench and Bar*. Columbia, SC: State Company, 1908.

Brown, Richard Maxwell. *Strain of Violence: Historical Studies of American Violence and Vigilantism*. New York: Oxford University Press, 1977 ed.

Bruce, Dickson D. *Violence and Culture in the Antebellum South*. Austin: University of Texas Press, 1979.

Bryan, Carol Hardy. "Basil Manly II: Distinguished Baptist Leader Had Important Ties to Edgefield." *Quill, Old Edgefield District Genealogical Society Newsletter*. March–April 2003.

Burton, Orville Vernon. "In My Father's House Are Many Leaders: Can the Extreme Be Typical?" *Proceedings of the South Carolina Historical Association, 1987*. Aiken: South Carolina Historical Association, 1988.

———. *In My Father's House Are Many Mansions: Family and Community in Edgefield, South Carolina*. Chapel Hill: University of North Carolina Press, 1985.

Bushman, Richard L. *The Refinement of America: Persons, Houses, Cities*. New York: Random House, 1993.

Butler, Anthea. *White Evangelical Racism: The Politics of Morality in America.* Chapel Hill: University of North Carolina Press, 2021.

Bynum, Victoria E. *The Long Shadow of the Civil War: Southern Dissent and Its Legacies.* Chapel Hill: University of North Carolina Press, 2010.

Byrne, Frank J. *Becoming Bourgeois: Merchant Culture in the South, 1820–1865.* Lexington: University of Kentucky Press, 2006.

Byron, Matthew. "Crime and Punishment?: The Impotency of Dueling Laws in the Antebellum United States." PhD diss., University of Arkansas, 2008.

Calhoon, Robert M. *Evangelicals and Conservatives in the Early South, 1740–1861.* Columbia: University of South Carolina Press, 1988.

Calore, Paul. *The Causes of the Civil War: The Political, Cultural, Economic, and Territorial Disputes between North and South.* Jefferson, NC: McFarland, 2008.

Carlson, Douglas W. "'Drinks He to His Own Undoing': Temperance Ideology in the Deep South." *Journal of the Early Republic* 18, no. 4 (Winter 1998).

Carlson, John David, and Jonathan H. Ebel, eds. *From Jeremiad to Jihad: Religion, Violence, and America.* Berkeley: University of California Press, 2012.

Carmichael, Peter S. *The Last Generation: Young Virginians in Peace, War, and Reunion.* Chapel Hill: University of North Carolina Press, 2005.

Carmody, Thomas J. "The Anti-Dueling Movement." In *A New History of the Sermon: The Nineteenth Century*, edited by Robert H. Ellison. Boston, MA: Brill, 2010.

Carnes, Mark C. *Secret Ritual and Manhood in Victorian America.* New Haven, CT: Yale University Press, 1989.

Carnes, Mark C., and Clyde Griffen, eds. *Meanings for Manhood: Constructions of Masculinity in Victorian America.* Chicago, IL: University of Chicago Press, 1990.

Carney, Charity R. *Ministers and Masters: Methodism, Manhood, and Honor in the Old South.* Baton Rouge: Louisiana State University Press, 2011.

Carwardine, Richard J. *Evangelicals and Politics in Antebellum America.* Knoxville: University of Tennessee Press, 1997.

Causey, Evelyn D. "The Character of a Gentleman: Deportment, Piety, and Morality in Southern Colleges and Universities, 1820–1860." PhD diss., University of Delaware, 2006.

Chapman, John A. *History of Edgefield County: From the Earliest Settlements to 1897.* Newberry, SC: Elbert H. Aull, 1897.

Clark, Kathleen Ann. *Defining Moments: African American Commemoration and Political Culture in the South, 1863–1913.* Chapel Hill: University of North Carolina Press, 2005.

Clarke, Simon, Paul Hoggett, and Simon Thompson, eds. *Emotion, Politics and Society.* New York: Palgrave Macmillan, 2006.

Clinton, Catherine, ed. *Confederate Statues and Memorialization.* Athens: University of Georgia Press, 2019.

Clinton, Catherine, and Michele Gillespie, eds. *The Devil's Lane: Sex and Race in the Early South*. New York: Oxford University Press, 1997.

Clinton, Catherine, and Nina Silber, eds. *Divided Houses: Gender and the Civil War*. New York: Oxford University Press, 1992.

Cobb, James C. *Away Down South: A History of Southern Identity*. New York: Oxford University Press, 2005.

Cole, Stephanie, and Natalie J. Ring, eds. *The Folly of Jim Crow: Rethinking the Segregated South*. College Station: Texas A&M University Press, 2012.

Conkin, Paul K. *The Uneasy Center: Reformed Christianity in Antebellum America*. Chapel Hill: University of North Carolina Press, 1995.

Connelly, Thomas L., and Barbara L. Bellows. *God and General Longstreet: The Lost Cause and the Southern Mind*. Baton Rouge: Louisiana State University Press, 1995.

Cook, Robert J. *Civil War Memories: Contesting the Past in the United States since 1865*. Baltimore, MD: Johns Hopkins University Press, 2017.

Cooper, Edward S. *Louis Trezevant Wigfall: The Disintegration of the Union and Collapse of the Confederacy*. Lanham, MD: Fairleigh Dickinson University Press, 2012.

Cordle, Charles G. *Henry Shultz and the Founding of Hamburg, South Carolina: Studies in Georgia History and Government*. Athens: University of Georgia Press, 1940.

Cornelius, Janet Duitsman. *Slave Missions and the Black Church in the Antebellum South*. Columbia: University of South Carolina Press, 1999.

Cossen, William S. "Blood, Honor, Reform, and God: Anti-dueling Associations and Moral Reform in the South." *American Nineteenth-Century History* 19, no. 1 (March 2018).

Coulter, E. Merton. *College Life in the Old South: As Seen at the University of Georgia*. Athens: University of Georgia Press, 1983.

Cox, Karen L. *Dixie's Daughters: The United Daughters of the Confederacy*. Gainesville: University Press of Florida, 2003.

———. *No Common Ground: Confederate Monuments and the Ongoing Fight for Racial Justice*. Chapel Hill: University of North Carolina Press, 2021.

Cramer, Clayton E. *Concealed Weapon Laws of the Early Republic: Dueling, Southern Violence, and Moral Reform*. Westport, CT: Greenwood, 1999.

Crowther, Edward R. "Holy Honor: Sacred and Secular in the Old South." *Journal of Southern History* 58, no. 4 (November 1992).

———. *Southern Evangelicals and the Coming of the Civil War*. Lewiston, NY: Mellen, 2000.

Curtis, Jesse. *The Myth of Colorblind Christians: Evangelicals and White Supremacy in the Civil Rights Era*. New York: New York University Press, 2021.

Daly, John Patrick. *When Slavery Was Called Freedom: Evangelicalism, Proslavery, and the Causes of the Civil War*. Lexington: University Press of Kentucky, 2002.

David, James Corbett. "The Politics of Emasculation: The Caning of Charles Sumner and Elite Ideologies of Manhood in the Mid-Nineteenth-Century United States." *Gender and History*, August 2007.

Davis, William C. *The Cause Lost: Myths and Realities of the Confederacy*. Lawrence: University Press of Kansas, 1996.

Deitreich, Kenneth A. "'The Sly Mendacity of Hints': Preston Brooks and the War with Mexico." *South Carolina Historical Magazine* 113, no. 4 (October 2012).

DeSilva, David A. *Honor, Patronage, Kinship, and Purity: Unlocking New Testament Culture*. Downers Grove, IL: InterVarsity Press, 2000.

Dollar, Kent T. *Soldiers of the Cross: Confederate Soldier-Christians and the Impact of War on Their Faith*. Macon, GA: Mercer University Press, 2005.

Domby, Adam H. *The False Cause: Fraud, Fabrication, and White Supremacy in Confederate Memory*. Charlottesville: University of Virginia Press, 2020.

Downey, Tom. *Planting a Capitalist South: Masters, Merchants, and Manufacturers in the Southern Interior, 1790–1860*. Baton Rouge: Louisiana State University Press, 2006.

Du Mez, Kristin Kobes. *Jesus and John Wayne: How White Evangelicals Corrupted a Faith and Fractured a Nation*. New York: Liveright, 2020.

Dunovant, R. G. M. *The Palmetto Regiment: South Carolina Volunteers, 1846–48. The Battles in the Valley of Mexico, 1847*. Part 2. Charleston, SC: Walker, Evans, and Cogswell, 1897.

DuRocher, Kristina. *Raising Racists: The Socialization of White Children in the Jim Crow South*. Lexington: University Press of Kentucky, 2011.

Eaton, Clement. *The Growth of Southern Civilization, 1790–1860*. New York: Harper Torchbooks, Harper and Row, 1961.

———. *A History of the Old South: The Emergence of a Reluctant Nation*. Prospect Heights, IL: Waveland Press, 1975.

———. *The Mind of the Old South*. Baton Rouge: Louisiana State University Press, 1967.

Edgar, Walter. *Partisans and Redcoats: The Southern Conflict That Turned the Tide of the American Revolution*. New York: HarperCollins, 2003.

———. *South Carolina: A History*. Columbia: University of South Carolina Press, 1998.

Edmunds Jr., John B. *Francis W. Pickens and the Politics of Destruction*. Chapel Hill: University of North Carolina Press, 1986.

Edwards, Laura F. *Gendered Strife and Confusion: The Political Culture of Reconstruction*. Urbana and Chicago: University of Illinois Press, 1997.

———. "Law, Domestic Violence, and the Limits of Patriarchal Authority in the Antebellum South." *Journal of Southern History* 65, no. 4 (November 1999).

Egerton, Douglas R. *The Wars of Reconstruction: The Brief, Violent History of America's Most Progressive Era*. New York: Bloomsbury, 2014.

Eicher, David J. *The Longest Night: A Military History of the Civil War.* New York: Touchstone, 2001.

Elder, Robert. *Calhoun: American Heretic.* New York: Basic Books, 2021.

———. *The Sacred Mirror: Evangelicalism, Honor, and Identity in the Deep South, 1790–1860.* Chapel Hill: University of North Carolina Press, 2016.

Emberton, Carole. *Beyond Redemption: Race, Violence, and the American South after the Civil War.* Chicago, IL: University of Chicago Press, 2013.

Emberton, Carole, and Bruce E. Baker, eds. *Remembering Reconstruction: Struggles over the Meaning of America's Most Turbulent Era.* Baton Rouge: Louisiana State University Press, 2017.

Emerson, Michael O., and Christian Smith. *Divided by Faith: Evangelical Religion and the Problem of Race in America.* New York: Oxford University Press, 2000.

Ericson, David F. *The Debate over Slavery: Antislavery and Proslavery Liberalism in Antebellum America.* New York: New York University Press, 2000.

Fahs, Alice, and Joan Waugh, eds. *The Memory of the Civil War in American Culture.* Chapel Hill: University of North Carolina Press, 2004.

Farmer, James O. *The Metaphysical Confederacy: James Henley Thornwell and the Synthesis of Southern Values.* Macon, GA: Mercer University Press, 1986.

Faulkner, Carol, and Alison M. Parker, eds. *Interconnections: Gender and Race in American History.* Rochester, NY: University of Rochester Press, 2012.

Faust, Drew Gilpin. *The Creation of Confederate Nationalism: Ideology and Identity in the Civil War South.* Baton Rouge: Louisiana State University Press, 1990.

———. *The Ideology of Slavery: Proslavery Thought in the Antebellum South, 1830–1860.* Baton Rouge: Louisiana State University Press, 1981.

———. *James Henry Hammond and the Old South: A Design for Mastery.* Baton Rouge: Louisiana State University Press, 1982.

———. *Mothers of Invention: Women of the Slaveholding South in the American Civil War.* Chapel Hill: University of North Carolina Press, 1996.

———. *Southern Stories: Slaveholders in Peace and War.* Columbia: University of Missouri Press, 1992.

———. *This Republic of Suffering: Death and the American Civil War.* New York: Alfred A. Knopf, 2008.

Finkleman, Paul, ed. *Slavery and the Law.* Lanham, MD: Rowman and Littlefield, 2002.

Fletcher, Holly Berkley. *Gender and the American Temperance Movement of the Nineteenth Century.* New York, NY: Routledge, 2011.

Foner, Eric. *Reconstruction: America's Unfinished Revolution, 1863–1877.* New York: HarperCollins, 1988.

Foote, Lorien. *The Gentlemen and the Roughs: Violence, Honor, and Manhood in the Union Army.* New York: New York University Press, 2010.

Ford Jr., Lacy K. *Deliver Us from Evil: The Slavery Question in the Old South*. New York: Oxford University Press, 2009.

———. *Origins of Southern Radicalism: The South Carolina Upcountry, 1800–1860*. New York: Oxford University Press, 1988.

———. "Origins of the Edgefield Tradition: The Late Antebellum Experience and the Roots of Political Insurgency." *South Carolina Historical Magazine* 98, no. 4 (October 1997).

Forgie, George B. *Patricide in the House Divided: A Psychological Interpretation of Lincoln and His Age*. New York: W. W. Norton, 1981.

Forret, Jeff. *Race Relations at the Margins: Slaves and Poor Whites in the Antebellum Southern Countryside*. Baton Rouge: Louisiana State University Press, 2006.

———. *Slave against Slave: Plantation Violence in the Old South*. Baton Rouge: Louisiana State University Press, 2015.

Foster, Gaines M. *Ghosts of the Confederacy: Defeat, the Lost Cause, and the Emergence of the New South, 1865–1913*. New York: Oxford University Press, 1987.

Fox-Genovese, Elizabeth, and Eugene D. Genovese. *The Mind of the Master Class: History and Faith in the Southern Slaveholder's Worldview*. New York: Cambridge University Press, 2005.

Frank, Stephen M. *Life with Father: Parenthood and Masculinity in the Nineteenth-Century American North*. Baltimore, MD: Johns Hopkins University Press, 1998.

Franklin, John Hope. *The Militant South, 1800–1860*. Urbana: University of Illinois Press, 2002 ed.

Freehling, William W. *Prelude to Civil War: The Nullification Controversy in South Carolina, 1816–1836*. New York: Oxford University Press, 1965.

———. *The Road to Disunion*. Vol. 1, *Secessionists at Bay, 1776–1854*. New York: Oxford University Press, 1990.

———. *The Road to Disunion*. Vol. 2, *Secessionists Triumphant, 1854–1861*. New York: Oxford University Press, 2007.

Freeman, Joanne B. *Affairs of Honor: National Politics in the New Republic*. New Haven, CT: Yale University Press, 2001.

———. *The Field of Blood: Violence in Congress and the Road to the Civil War*. New York: Farrar, Straus, and Giroux, 2018.

Frey, Sylvia. "Shaking the Dry Bones: The Dialectic of Conversion." In *Black and White: Cultural Interaction in the Antebellum South*, edited by Ted Ownby. Jackson: University Press of Mississippi, 1993.

Friedman, Jean E. *The Enclosed Garden: Women and Community in the Evangelical South, 1830–1900*. Chapel Hill: University of North Carolina Press, 1985.

Friend, Craig Thompson, ed. *Southern Masculinity: Perspectives on Manhood in the South since Reconstruction*. Athens: University of Georgia Press, 2009.

Friend, Craig Thompson, and Anya Jabour, eds. *Family Values in the Old South*. Gainesville: University Press of Florida, 2010.

Friend, Craig Thompson, and Lorri Glover, eds. *Southern Manhood: Perspectives on Masculinity in the Old South*. Athens: University of Georgia Press, 2004.

Fuller, A. James. *Chaplain to the Confederacy: Basil Manly and Baptist Life in the Old South*. Baton Rouge: Louisiana State University Press, 2000.

Gallagher, Gary W. *Causes Won, Lost, and Forgotten: How Hollywood and Popular Art Shape What We Know about the Civil War*. Chapel Hill: University of North Carolina Press, 2008.

Gallagher, Gary W., and Alan T. Nolan, eds. *The Myth of the Lost Cause and Civil War History*. Bloomington: Indiana University Press, 2000.

Gallay, Alan. *The Formation of a Planter Elite: Jonathan Bryan and the Southern Colonial Frontier*. Athens: University of Georgia Press, 2007.

Gardner, Sarah E. *Blood and Irony: Southern White Women's Narratives of the Civil War, 1861–1937*. Chapel Hill: University of North Carolina Press, 2004.

Garvey, T. Gregory. *Creating a Culture of Reform in Antebellum America*. Athens: University of Georgia Press, 2006.

Gaston, Paul M. *The New South Creed: A Study in Southern Mythmaking*. Montgomery, AL: New South Books, 2002.

Gates Jr., Henry Louis. *Stony the Road: Reconstruction, White Supremacy, and the Rise of Jim Crow*. New York: Penguin Books, 2019.

Genovese, Eugene D. "The Chivalric Tradition in the Old South." *Sewanee Review* 108, no. 2 (Spring 2000).

———. *A Consuming Fire: The Fall of the Confederacy in the Mind of the White Christian South*. Athens: University of Georgia Press, 2009.

———. *The Slaveholders' Dilemma: Freedom and Progress in Southern Conservative Thought, 1820–1860*. Columbia: University of South Carolina Press, 1992.

Genovese, Eugene D., and Elizabeth Fox-Genovese. *Fatal Self-Deception: Slaveholding Paternalism in the Old South*. New York: Cambridge University Press, 2011.

Gillette, William. *Retreat from Reconstruction, 1869–1879*. Baton Rouge: Louisiana State University Press, 1982.

Gilmore, Glenda E. *Gender and Jim Crow: Women and the Politics of White Supremacy in North Carolina, 1896–1920*. Chapel Hill: University of North Carolina Press, 1996.

Glover, Lorri. *Southern Sons: Becoming Men in the New Nation*. Baltimore, MD: Johns Hopkins University Press, 2007.

Goen, C. C. *Broken Churches, Broken Nation: Denominational Schisms and the Coming of the American Civil War*. Macon, GA: Mercer University Press, 1985.

Gorn, Elliott J. "'Gouge and Bite, Pull Hair and Scratch': The Social Significance of Fighting in the Southern Backcountry." *American Historical Review* 90, no. 1 (February 1985).

Gradin, Harlan. "Losing Control: The Caning of Charles Sumner and the Breakdown of Antebellum Political Culture." PhD diss., University of North Carolina, 1991.

Green, Jennifer R. *Military Education and the Emerging Middle Class in the Old South*. Cambridge, MA: Cambridge University Press, 2008.

Greenberg, Amy S. *Manifest Manhood and the Antebellum American Empire*. New York: Cambridge University Press, 2005.

Greenberg, Kenneth S. *Honor and Slavery: Lies, Duels, Noses, Masks, Dressing as a Woman, Gifts, Strangers, Humanitarianism, Death, Slave Rebellions, the Pro-Slavery Argument, Baseball, Hunting, and Gambling in the Old South*. Princeton, NJ: Princeton University Press, 1996.

———. *Masters and Statesmen: The Political Culture of American Slavery*. Baltimore, MD: Johns Hopkins University Press, 1985.

Grem, Darren E. *The Blessings of Business: How Corporations Shaped Conservative Christianity*. New York: Oxford University Press, 2016.

Griswold, Robert L. *Fatherhood in America: A History*. New York: Basic Books, 1993.

Gross, Ariela J. *Double Character: Slavery and Mastery in the Antebellum Southern Courtroom*. Athens: University of Georgia Press, 2000.

Hacker, J. David. "Census-Based Count of the Civil War Dead." *Civil War History* 57, no. 4 (December 2011).

Hackney, Sheldon. "Southern Violence." *American Historical Review* 74, no. 3 (February 1969).

Hadden, Sally E. *Slave Patrols: Law and Violence in Virginia and the Carolinas*. Cambridge, MA: Harvard University Press, 2001.

Hale, Grace Elizabeth. *Making Whiteness: The Culture of Segregation in the South, 1890–1940*. New York: Knopf Doubleday, 2010.

Haley, Sarah. *No Mercy Here: Gender, Punishment, and the Making of Jim Crow Modernity*. Chapel Hill: University of North Carolina Press, 2016.

Harre, Rom, ed. *The Social Construction of Emotions*. New York: Basil Blackwell, 1986.

Harvey, Paul. *Redeeming the South: Religious Cultures and Racial Identities among Southern Baptists, 1865–1925*. Chapel Hill: University of North Carolina Press, 1997.

Hatch, Nathan O. *The Democratization of American Christianity*. New Haven, CT: Yale University Press, 1989.

Hatley, Tom. *The Dividing Paths: Cherokees and South Carolinians through the Revolutionary Era*. New York: Oxford University Press, 1993.

Hawkins, J. Russell. *The Bible Told Them So: How Southern Evangelicals Fought to Preserve White Supremacy.* New York: Oxford University Press, 2021.

Hawkins, J. Russell, and Phillip Luke Sinitiere, eds. *Christians and the Color Line: Race and Religion after "Divided by Faith."* New York: Oxford University Press, 2014.

Haynes, April R. *Riotous Flesh: Women, Physiology, and the Solitary Vice in Nineteenth-Century America.* Chicago, IL: University of Chicago Press, 2015.

Heyrman, Christine Leigh. *Southern Cross: The Beginnings of the Bible Belt.* Chapel Hill: University of North Carolina Press, 1997.

Hill, Lawrence F. "The Confederate Exodus to Latin America, I." *Southwestern Historical Quarterly* 39 (October 1935).

———. "The Confederate Exodus to Latin America, II." *Southwestern Historical Quarterly* 39 (January 1936).

Hill, Samuel S., Charles H. Lippy, and Charles Reagan Wilson, eds. *Encyclopedia of Religion in the South*, 2nd ed. Macon, GA: Mercer University Press, 2005.

Hilton, Boyd. *The Age of Atonement: The Influence of Evangelicalism on Social and Economic Thought, 1785–1865.* New York: Oxford University Press, 1992.

Hoffer, Williamjames Hull. *The Caning of Charles Sumner: Honor, Idealism, and the Origins of the Civil War.* Baltimore, MD: Johns Hopkins University Press, 2010.

———. *Plessy v. Ferguson: Race and Inequality in Jim Crow America.* Lawrence: University Press of Kansas, 2012.

Holifield, E. Brooks. *The Gentlemen Theologians: American Theology in Southern Culture, 1785–1860.* Durham, NC: Duke University Press, 1978.

Huebner, Timothy S. *The Southern Judicial Tradition: State Judges and Sectional Distinctiveness, 1790–1890.* Athens: University of Georgia Press, 1994.

Irons, Charles Frederick. *The Origins of Proslavery Christianity: White and Black Evangelicals in Colonial and Antebellum Virginia.* Chapel Hill: University of North Carolina Press, 2008.

Isaac, Rhys. *The Transformation of Virginia, 1740–1790.* Chapel Hill: University of North Carolina Press, 1999.

Jabour, Anya. "Male Friendship and Masculinity in the Early National South: William Wirt and His Friends." *Journal of the Early Republic* 20, no. 1 (Spring 2000).

Janney, Caroline E. *Burying the Dead but Not the Past: Ladies' Memorial Associations and the Lost Cause.* Chapel Hill: University of North Carolina Press, 2008.

———. *Remembering the Civil War: Reunion and the Limits of Reconciliation.* Chapel Hill: University of North Carolina Press, 2013.

Jemison, Elizabeth L. *Christian Citizens: Reading the Bible in Black and White in the Postemancipation South*. Chapel Hill: University of North Carolina Press, 2020.

Jimerson, Randall C. *The Private War: Popular Thought During the Sectional Conflict*. Baton Rouge: Louisiana State University Press, 1994.

Johansen, Shawn. *Family Men: Middle-Class Fatherhood in Industrializing America*. New York: Routledge, 2001.

Jones, Robert P. *White Too Long: The Legacy of White Supremacy in American Christianity*. New York: Simon and Schuster, 2020.

Joshi, Khyati Y. *White Christian Privilege: The Illusion of Religious Equality in America*. New York: New York University Press, 2020.

Kammen, Michael. *Mystic Chords of Memory: The Transformation of Tradition in American Culture*. New York: Alfred A. Knopf, 1991.

Kann, Mark E. *A Republic of Men: The American Founders, Gendered Language, and Patriarchal Politics*. New York: New York University Press, 1998.

Kantrowitz, Stephen. *Ben Tillman and the Reconstruction of White Supremacy*. Chapel Hill: University of North Carolina Press, 2000.

Karp, Matthew. *This Vast Southern Empire: Slaveholders at the Helm of American Foreign Policy*. Cambridge, MA: Harvard University Press, 2016.

Kierner, Cynthia A. *Beyond the Household: Women's Place in the Early South, 1700–1835*. Ithica, NY: Cornell University Press, 1998.

King, Alvy L. *Louis T. Wigfall: Southern Fire-eater*. Baton Rouge: Louisiana State University Press, 1970.

Klein, Rachel N. *Unification of a Slave State: The Rise of the Planter Class in the South Carolina Backcountry, 1760–1808*. Chapel Hill: University of North Carolina Press, 1990.

Kreiser Jr., Lawrence A., and Randall Allred, eds. *The Civil War in Popular Culture: Memory and Meaning*. Lexington: University Press of Kentucky, 2013.

Kruse, Kevin M. *One Nation under God: How Corporate America Invented Christian America*. New York: Basic Books, 2015.

LaBorde, Maximilian. *History of the South Carolina College: From Its Incorporation December 19, 1801, to November 25, 1857*. Columbia, SC: Peter B. Glass, 1859.

Larson, John L. *The Market Revolution in America: Liberty, Ambition, and the Eclipse of the Common Good*. New York: Cambridge University Press, 2009.

Lasser, Carol. "Voyeuristic Abolitionism: Sex, Gender, and the Transformation of Antislavery Rhetoric." *Journal of the Early Republic* 28.1 (Spring), 2008.

Lavin, Talia. *Culture Warlords: My Journey into the Dark Web of White Supremacy*. New York: Hatchette Books, 2020.

Leary, Lewis. *The Book-Peddling Parson: An Account of the Life and Works of Mason Locke Weems, Patriot, Pitchman, Author, and Purveyor of Morality to the Citizenry of the Early United States of America*. New York: Algonquin Books, 1984.

Lender, Mark E., and James Kriby Martin, *Drinking in America: A History*. Rev. and expanded ed. New York, NY: Free Press, 1987.

Levin, Kevin M. *Searching for Black Confederates: The Civil War's Most Persistent Myth*. Chapel Hill: University of North Carolina Press, 2019.

Lindman, Janet Moore. "Acting the Manly Christian: White Evangelical Masculinity in Revolutionary Virginia." *William and Mary Quarterly*, 3rd ser., 57, no. 2 (April 2000).

———. *Bodies of Belief: Baptist Community in Early America*. Philadelphia: University of Pennsylvania Press, 2008.

Lippy, Charles H. *Do Real Men Pray?: Images of the Christian Man and Male Spirituality in White Protestant America*. Knoxville: University of Tennessee Press, 2005.

Lockwood, John, and Charles Lockwood, *The Siege of Washington: The Untold Story of the Twelve Days That Shook the Union*. New York: Oxford University Press, 2011.

Long, J. Grahame. *Dueling in Charleston: Violence Refined in the Holy City*. Charleston, SC: History Press, 2012.

Long, Kathryn. "The Power of Interpretation: The Revival of 1857–58 and the Historiography of Revivalism in America." *Religion and American Culture* 4, no. 1 (Winter 1994).

Loveland, Anne C. *Southern Evangelicals and the Social Order, 1800–1860*. Baton Rouge: Louisiana State University Press, 1980.

Lyerly, Cynthia Lynn. *Methodism and the Southern Mind, 1770–1810*. New York: Oxford University Press, 1998.

Lystra, Karen. *Searching the Heart: Women, Men, and Romantic Love in Nineteenth-Century America*. New York: Oxford University Press, 1989.

Mangan, J. A., and James Walvin. *Manliness and Morality: Middle-Class Masculinity in Britain and America, 1800–1940*. New York: Manchester University Press, 1991.

Manly, Louise. *The Manly Family, An Account of the Descendants of Captain Basil Manly of the Revolution and Related Families*. Greenville, SC: privately printed, 1930.

Martin, Scott C., ed. *Cultural Change and the Market Revolution in America, 1789–1860*. New York: Rowan and Littlefield, 2005.

Mathews, Donald G. *Religion in the Old South*. Chicago, IL: University of Chicago Press, 1977.

———. "The Second Great Awakening as an Organizing Process, 1780–1830: An Hypothesis." *American Quarterly* 21, no. 1 (Spring 1969).

Mathis, Robert Neil. "Preston Smith Brooks: The Man and His Image." *South Carolina Historical Magazine* 79.4, October 1978.

May, Robert E. *Manifest Destiny's Underworld: Filibustering in Antebellum America*. Chapel Hill: University of North Carolina Press, 2002.

———. *The Southern Dream of a Caribbean Empire, 1854–1861*. Gainesville: University Press of Florida, 2002.
Mayfield, John. *Counterfeit Gentlemen: Manhood and Humor in the Old South*. Gainesville: University of Florida Press, 2009.
———. "'The Soul of a Man!': William Gilmore Simms and the Myths of Southern Manhood." In "Gender in the Early Republic," special issue, *Journal of the Early Republic* 15, no. 3 (Autumn 1995).
Mayfield, John, and Todd Hagstette, eds. *The Field of Honor: Essays on Southern Character and American Identity*. Columbia: University of South Carolina Press, 2017.
McCurry, Stephanie. *Confederate Reckoning: Power and Politics in the Civil War South*. Cambridge, MA: Harvard University Press, 2012.
———. *Masters of Small Worlds: Yeoman Households, Gender Relations, and the Political Culture of the Antebellum South Carolina Low Country*. New York: Oxford University Press, 1995.
McKivigan, John R., and Mitchell Snay, eds. *Religion and the Antebellum Debate over Slavery*. Athens: University of Georgia Press, 1998.
McKivigan, John R., and Stanley Harrold, eds. *Antislavery Violence: Sectional, Racial, and Cultural Conflict in Antebellum America*. Knoxville: University of Tennessee Press, 1999.
McPherson, James. *Battle Cry of Freedom: The Civil War Era*. New York: Oxford University Press, 1988.
Merchant, Holt. *South Carolina Fire Eater: Laurence Massillion Keitt, 1824–1864*. Columbia: University of South Carolina Press, 2014.
Merritt, Keri Leigh. *Masterless Men: Poor Whites and Slavery in the Antebellum South*. New York: Cambridge University Press, 2017.
Meyer, Jack Allen. *South Carolina in the Mexican War: A History of the Palmetto Regiment of Volunteers, 1846–1917*. Columbia: South Carolina Department of Archives and History, 1996.
Miller, John Chester. *The Wolf by the Ears: Thomas Jefferson and Slavery*. Charlottesville: University Press of Virginia, 1991.
Miller, Randall M., Harry S. Stout, and Charles Reagan Wilson, eds. *Religion and the American Civil War*. New York: Oxford University Press, 1998.
Miller, Robert J. *Both Prayed to the Same God: Religion and Faith in the American Civil War*. Lanham, MD: Lexington Books, 2007.
Mintz, Stephen. *Moralists and Modernizers: America's Pre-Civil War Reformers*. Baltimore, MD: Johns Hopkins University Press, 1995.
Mitchell, Reid. *The Vacant Chair: The Northern Soldier Leaves Home*. New York: Oxford University Press, 1995.
Modern, John Lardas. *Secularism in Antebellum America*. Chicago, IL: University of Chicago Press, 2011.

Money, John. *The Destroying Angel: Sex, Fitness, and Food in the Legacy of Degeneracy Theory, Graham Crackers, Kellogg's Corn Flakes, and American Health History*. Amherst, NY: Prometheus Books, 1985.

Moon, David T. "Southern Baptists and Southern Men: Evangelical Perceptions of Manhood in Nineteenth-Century Georgia." *Journal of Southern History* 81, no. 3 (August 2015).

Moore, John Hammond. *Carnival of Blood: Dueling, Lynching, and Murder in South Carolina, 1880–1920*. Columbia: University of South Carolina Press, 2006.

Moorhead, James H. *American Apocalypse: Yankee Protestants and the Civil War, 1860–1869*. New Haven, CT: Yale University Press, 1978.

Morris, Thomas D. *Southern Slavery and the Law: 1619–1860*. Chapel Hill: University of North Carolina Press, 1996.

Mulder, Phillip N. *A Controversial Spirit: Evangelical Awakenings in the South*. New York: Oxford University Press, 2002.

Mushal, Amanda Reece. "'My Word Is My Bond': Honor, Commerce, and Status in the Antebellum South." PhD diss., University of Virginia, 2010.

Najar, Monica. *Evangelizing the South: A Social History of Church and State in Early America*. New York: Oxford University Press, 2008.

Neff, John R. *Honoring the Civil War Dead: Commemoration and the Problem of Reconciliation*. Lawrence: University Press of Kansas, 2005.

Nelson, Megan Kate. *Ruin Nation: Destruction and the American Civil War*. Athens: University of Georgia Press, 2012.

Neuman, W. Russell, George E. Marcus, Ann N. Crigler, and Michael MacKuen, eds. *The Affect Effect: Dynamics of Emotion in Political Thinking and Behavior*. Chicago, IL: University of Chicago Press, 2007.

Nisbett, Richard E., and David Cohen. *Culture of Honor: The Psychology of Violence in the South*. Boulder, CO: Westview Press, 1996.

Nissenbaum, Stephen. *Sex, Diet, and Debility in Jacksonian America: Sylvester Graham and Health Reform*. Westport, CT: Greenwood Press, 1980.

Noll, Mark A. *America's God: From Jonathan Edwards to Abraham Lincoln*. New York: Oxford University Press, 2002.

———. *The Civil War as a Theological Crisis*. Chapel Hill: University of North Carolina Press, 2006.

———, ed. *God and Mammon: Protestants, Money, and the Market, 1790–1860*. New York: Oxford University Press, 2002.

Nye, Robert A. "Medicine and Science as Masculine 'Fields of Honor.'" In "Women, Gender, and Science: New Directions," *Osiris* 12 (1997).

O'Brien, Michael. *Intellectual Life and the American South, 1810–1860: An Abridged Edition of Conjectures of Disorder*. Chapel Hill: University of North Carolina Press, 2010.

Oakes, James. *Freedom National: The Destruction of Slavery in the United States, 1861–1865.* New York: W. W. Norton, 2012.

———. *The Ruling Race: A History of American Slaveholders.* New York: W. W. Norton, 1998.

———. *The Scorpion's Sting: Antislavery and the Coming of the Civil War.* New York: W. W. Norton, 2014.

———. *Slavery and Freedom: An Interpretation of the Old South.* New York: Alfred A. Knopf, 1990.

Osborn, Kyle N. "Masters of Fate: Efficacy and Emotion in the Civil War South." PhD diss., University of Georgia, 2013.

Ownby, Ted, ed. *Black and White: Cultural Interaction in the Antebellum South.* Oxford: University Press of Mississippi, 2007.

———, ed. *Manners and Southern History.* Oxford: University Press of Mississippi, 2007.

———. *Subduing Satan: Religion, Recreation, and Manhood in the Rural South, 1865–1920.* Chapel Hill: University of North Carolina Press, 1990.

Owsley, Frank L. *Plain Folk of the Old South.* Baton Rouge: Louisiana State University Press, 2008 ed.

Pace, Robert F. *Halls of Honor: College Men in the Old South.* Baton Rouge: Louisiana State University Press, 2004.

Pahl, Jon. *Empire of Sacrifice: The Religious Origins of American Violence.* New York: New York University Press, 2010.

Parson, Elaine Frantz. *Manhood Lost: Fallen Drunkards and Redeeming Women in the Nineteenth-Century United States.* Baltimore, MD: Johns Hopkins University Press, 2003.

Perman, Michael. *The Road to Redemption: Southern Politics, 1869–1879.* Chapel Hill: University of North Carolina Press, 1984.

Pflugrad-Jackisch, Ami. *Brothers of a Vow: Secret Fraternal Orders and the Transformation of White Male Culture in Antebellum Virginia.* Athens: University of Georgia Press, 2010.

Pierson, Michael D. "'All Southern Society Is Assailed by the Foulest Charges': Charles Sumner's 'The Crime against Kansas' and the Escalation of Republican Anti-Slavery Rhetoric." *New England Quarterly* 68, no. 4 (December 1995).

———. *Free Hearts and Free Homes: Gender and American Antislavery Politics.* Chapel Hill: University of North Carolina Press, 2003.

Poister, Robert C. "The Business of Exile: The Money and Memory of a 'Confederate' Family in Cuba." M.A. thesis, University of Georgia, 2012.

Poole, W. Scott. *Never Surrender: Confederate Memory and Conservatism in the South Carolina Upcountry.* Athens: University of Georgia Press, 2004.

Porterfield, Amanda. *Conceived in Doubt: Religion and Politics in the New American Nation.* Chicago, IL: University of Chicago Press, 2012.

Potter, David M. *The Impending Crisis, 1848–1861.* New York: Harper Colophon, 1976.
Powell, William S., ed. *Dictionary of North Carolina Biography.* Vol. 1, A–C. Chapel Hill: University of North Carolina Press, 1979.
Preston, Andrew. *Sword of the Spirit, Shield of Faith: Religion in American War and Diplomacy.* New York: Random House, 2012.
Prince, K. Stephen. *Stories of the South: Race and the Reconstruction of Southern Identity, 1865–1915.* Chapel Hill: University of North Carolina Press, 2014.
Prior, David. *Between Freedom and Progress: The Lost World of Reconstruction Politics.* Baton Rouge: Louisiana State University Press, 2019.
Quigley, Paul. *Shifting Grounds: Nationalism and the American South, 1848–1865.* New York: Oxford University Press, 2012.
Quist, John W. *Restless Visionaries: The Social Roots of Antebellum Reform in Alabama and Michigan.* Baton Rouge: Louisiana State University Press, 1998.
Rable, George C. *But There Was No Peace: The Role of Violence in the Politics of Reconstruction.* Athens: University of Georgia Press, 2007.
———. *Civil Wars: Women and the Crisis of Southern Nationalism.* Urbana: University of Illinois Press, 1991.
———. *The Confederate Republic: A Revolution against Politics.* Chapel Hill: University of North Carolina Press, 1994.
———. *Damn Yankees: Demonization and Defiance in the Confederate South.* Baton Rouge: Louisiana State University Press, 2015.
———. *God's Almost Chosen Peoples: A Religious History of the American Civil War.* Chapel Hill: University of North Carolina Press, 2010.
Ray, Thomas. *Daniel and Abraham Marshall: Pioneer Baptist Evangelists to the South.* Springfield, MO: Particular Baptist Press, 2006.
Reddy, William M. *The Navigation of Feeling: A Framework for the History of Emotions.* New York: Cambridge University Press, 2001.
Richardson, Heather Cox. *Death of Reconstruction: Race, Labor, and Politics in the Post-Civil War North, 1865–1901.* Cambridge, MA: Harvard University Press, 2004.
———. *How the South Won the Civil War: Oligarchy, Democracy, and the Continuing Fight for the Soul of America.* New York: Oxford University Press, 2020.
———. *West from Appomattox: The Reconstruction of American after the Civil War.* New Haven, CT: Yale University Press, 2007.
Rigdon, John. *First Families of Edgefield.* Vol. 1. Powder Springs, GA: Eastern Digital Resources, 2011.
Roberts-Miller, Patricia. *Fanatical Schemes: Proslavery Rhetoric and the Tragedy of Consensus.* Tuscaloosa: University of Alabama Press, 2010.
Robins, Roger. "Vernacular American Landscape: Methodists, Camp Meetings, and Social Respectability." *Religion and American Culture* 4, no. 2 (Summer 1994).

Rolle, Andrew. *The Lost Cause: The Confederate Exodus to Mexico.* Norman: University of Oklahoma Press, 1965.
Rood, Daniel B. *The Reinvention of Atlantic Slavery: Technology, Labor, Race, and Capitalism in the Greater Caribbean.* New York: Oxford University Press, 2017.
Rorabaugh, W. J. *The Alcoholic Republic: An American Tradition.* New York: Oxford University Press, 1981.
———. "The Sons of Temperance in Antebellum Jasper County." *Georgia Historical Quarterly* 64, no. 3 (Fall 1980).
Rothman, Joshua D. *Flush Times and Fever Dreams: A Story of Capitalism and Slavery in the Age of Jackson.* Athens: University of Georgia Press, 2012.
Rubin, Anne Sarah. *A Shattered Nation: The Rise and Fall of the Confederacy, 1861–1868.* Chapel Hill: University of North Carolina Press, 2005.
Sammons Jr., Franklin C. "Failure's Frontier: Ambition, Indebtedness, and Insolvency in Antebellum Alabama." M.A. thesis, University of Georgia, 2011.
Savage, Kirk. *Standing Soldiers, Kneeling Slaves: Race, War, and Monument in Nineteenth-Century America.* Princeton, NJ: Princeton University Press, 1999.
Schwartz, Warren F., Keith Baxter, and David Ryan. "The Duel: Can These Gentlemen Be Acting Efficiently?" *Journal of Legal Studies* 13, no. 2 (June 1984).
Schweiger, Beth Barton. *The Gospel Working Up: Progress and the Pulpit in Nineteenth-Century Virginia.* New York: Oxford University Press, 2000.
Schweiger, Beth Barton, and Donald G. Mathews, eds. *Religion in the American South: Protestants and Others in History and Culture.* Chapel Hill: University of North Carolina Press, 2004.
Scott, Edwin J. *Random Recollections of a Long Life, 1806–1876.* Columbia, SC: Charles A. Calvo, 1884.
Scott, Sean A. *A Visitation of God: Northern Civilians Interpret the Civil War.* New York: Oxford University Press, 2010.
Seidule, Ty. *Robert E. Lee and Me: A Southerner's Reckoning with the Myth of the Lost Cause.* New York: St. Martin's Press, 2020.
Sellers, Charles G. *The Market Revolution: Jacksonian America, 1815–1846.* New York: Oxford University Press, 1991.
Shalev, Evan. *American Zion: The Old Testament as a Political Text from the Revolution to the Civil War.* New Haven, CT: Yale University Press, 2013.
Shelden, Rachael A. *Washington Brotherhood: Politics, Social Life, and the Coming of the Civil War.* Chapel Hill: University of North Carolina Press, 2013.
Silber, Nina. *This War Ain't Over: Fighting the Civil War in New Deal America.* Chapel Hill: University of North Carolina Press, 2018.
Simkins, Francis Butler. *Pitchfork Ben Tillman, South Carolinian.* Baton Rouge: Louisiana State University Press, 1944.
Sinha, Manisha. "The Caning of Charles Sumner: Slavery, Race, and Ideology in the Age of the Civil War." *Journal of the Early Republic* 23, no. 2 (Summer 2003).

———. *The Counterrevolution of Slavery: Politics and Ideology in Antebellum South Carolina.* Chapel Hill: University of North Carolina Press, 2000.

———. *The Slave's Cause: A History of Abolition.* New Haven, CT: Yale University Press, 2016.

Sinha, Manisha, and Penny Von Eschen, eds. *Contested Democracy: Freedom, Race, and Power in American History.* New York: Columbia University Press, 2007.

Smith-Rosenberg, Caroll. *This Violent Empire: The Birth of an American National Identity.* Chapel Hill: University of North Carolina Press, 2010.

Smith, Craig Bruce. *American Honor: The Creation of the Nation's Ideals During the Revolutionary Era.* Chapel Hill: University of North Carolina Press, 2018.

Smith, John David. *An Old Creed for the New South: Proslavery Ideology and Historiography, 1865–1918.* Carbondale: Southern Illinois University Press, 2002.

Smith, John David, and J. Vincent Lowry, eds. *The Dunning School: Historians, Race, and the Meaning of Reconstruction.* Lexington: University Press of Kentucky, 2013.

Smith, Mark M. "'All Is Not Quiet in Our Hellish County': Facts, Fiction, Politics, and Race. The Ellenton Riot of 1876." *South Carolina Historical Magazine* 95, no. 2 (April 1994).

Smith, Timothy L. *Revivalism and Social Reform: American Protestantism on the Eve of the Civil War.* Baltimore, MD: Johns Hopkins University Press, 1980 ed.

Snay, Mitchell. *Gospel of Disunion: Religion and Separatism in the Antebellum South.* New York: Cambridge University Press, 1993.

Sokolow, Jayme A. *Eros and Modernization: Sylvester Graham, Health Reform, and the Origins of Victorian Sexuality in America.* Lanham, MD: Fairleigh Dickinson University Press, 1983.

Spierenburg, Pieter C. *Men and Violence: Gender, Honor, and Rituals in Modern Europe and America.* Columbus: Ohio State University Press, 1998.

Startup, Kenneth Moore. *The Root of All Evil: The Protestant Clergy and the Economic Mind of the Old South.* Athens: University of Georgia Press, 1997.

Stearns, Peter N. *American Fear: The Causes and Consequences of High Anxiety.* New York: Routledge, 2006.

———. *Jealousy: The Evolution of an Emotion in American History.* New York: New York University Press, 1990.

Stearns, Peter N., and Carol Z. Stearns. *Anger: The Struggle for Emotional Control in America's History.* Chicago, IL: University of Chicago Press, 1986.

———. *Emotion and Social Change: Toward a New Psychohistory.* Teaneck, NJ: Holmes and Meier, 1988.

Stearns, Peter N., and Jan Lewis. *An Emotional History of the United States.* New York: New York University Press, 1998.

Stephan, Scott. *Redeeming the Southern Family: Evangelical Women and Domestic Devotion in the Antebellum South.* Athens: University of Georgia Press, 2008.

Stokes, Melvyn, and Stephen Conway, eds. *The Market Revolution in America: Social, Political, and Religious Expressions, 1800–1880.* Charlottesville: University of Virginia Press, 1996.

Stout, Harry S. *Upon the Altar of the Nation: A Moral History of the American Civil War.* New York: Viking, Penguin Group, 2006.

Stowe, Steven M. *Intimacy and Power in the Old South: Ritual in the Lives of the Planters.* Baltimore, MD: Johns Hopkins University Press, 1987.

Stowell, Daniel W. *Rebuilding Zion: The Religious Reconstruction of the South, 1863–1877.* New York: Oxford University Press, 1998.

Summers, Mark Wahlgren. *A Dangerous Stir: Fear, Paranoia, and the Making of Reconstruction.* Chapel Hill: University of North Carolina Press, 2009.

———. *The Ordeal of Reunion: A New History of Reconstruction.* Chapel Hill: University of North Carolina Press, 2014.

Swatos, William H. *Mediating Capitalism and Slavery: A New-Weberian Interpretation of Religion and Honor in the Old South.* Tampa: Department of Religious Studies, University of South Florida, 1987.

Sutherland, Daniel E. "Exiles, Emigrants, and Sojourners: The Post-Civil War Confederate Exodus in Perspective." *Civil War History* 31, no. 3 (September 1985).

Sydnor, Charles S. *The Development of Southern Sectionalism, 1819–1848.* Baton Rouge: Louisiana State University Press, 1948.

Thomas, Emory M. *The Confederate Nation, 1861–1865.* New York: HarperCollins, 2011.

Tisby, Jemar. *The Color of Compromise: The Truth about the American Church's Complicity in Racism.* New York: Zondervan, 2020.

Tise, Larry E. *Proslavery: A History of the Defense of Slavery in America, 1701–1840.* Athens: University of Georgia Press, 1990.

Towles, Louis P. "A Matter of Honor at South Carolina College, 1822." *South Carolina Historical Magazine* 94, no. 1 (January 1993).

Towns, W. Stuart. *Enduring Legacy: Rhetoric and Ritual of the Lost Cause.* Tuscaloosa: University of Alabama Press, 2012.

———. *Oratory and Rhetoric in the Nineteenth-Century South: A Rhetoric of Defense.* Westport, CT: Praeger, 1998.

Tyrrell, Ian R. "Drink and Temperance in the Antebellum South: An Overview and Interpretation," *Journal of Southern History* 48, no. 4 (November 1982).

———. *Sobering Up: From Temperance to Prohibition in Antebellum America, 1800–1860.* Westport, CT: Greenwood Press, 1979.

Underwood, James L., and William Lewis Burke, eds. *The Dawn of Religious Freedom in South Carolina.* Columbia: University of South Carolina Press, 2006.

Vance, Norman. *The Sinews of the Spirit: The Ideal of Christian Manliness in Victorian Literature and Religious Thought*. New York: Cambridge University Press, 1985.

Walker, William E. "The South Carolina College Duel of 1833." *South Carolina Historical and Genealogical Magazine* 52, no. 3 (July 1951).

Walther, Eric H. *The Fire-Eaters*. Baton Rouge: Louisiana State University Press, 1992.

Weed, Eric. *The Religion of White Supremacy in the United States*. New York: Lexington Books, 2017.

Weir, Robert M. *Colonial South Carolina: A History*. Columbia: University of South Carolina Press, 1997 ed.

Welch, William L. "Lorenzo Sabine and the Assault on Sumner." *New England Quarterly* 65, no. 2 (June 1992).

Wells, Jonathan Daniel. *The Origins of the Southern Middle Class, 1800–1861*. Chapel Hill: University of North Carolina Press, 2004.

Wells, Jonathan Daniel, and Jennifer R. Green, eds. *The Southern Middle Class in the Long Nineteenth Century*. Baton Rouge: Louisiana State University Press, 2011.

Wetta, Frank J., and Martin A. Novelli, eds. *The Long Reconstruction: The Post-Civil War South in History, Film, and Memory*. New York: Routledge, 2013.

Whites, LeeAnn. *The Civil War as a Crisis in Gender: Augusta, Georgia, 1860–1890*. Athens: University of Georgia Press, 1995.

———. *Gender Matters: Civil War, Reconstruction, and the Making of the New South*. New York: Palgrave Macmillan, 2005.

———, ed. *Occupied Women: Gender, Military Occupation, and the American Civil War*. Baton Rouge: Louisiana State University Press, 2009.

Wigger, John. *American Saint: Francis Asbury and the Methodists*. New York: Oxford University Press, 2009.

Williams, Daniel K. *God's Own Party: The Making of the Christian Right*. New York: Oxford University Press, 2010.

Williams, Jack Kenny. "The Code of Honor in Antebellum South Carolina." *South Carolina Historical Magazine* 54, no. 3 (July 1953).

———. "The Criminal Lawyer in Antebellum South Carolina." *South Carolina Historical Magazine* 56, no. 3 (July 1955).

———. *Dueling in the Old South: Vignettes of Social History*. College Station: Texas A&M University Press, 2000.

———. *Vogues in Villainy: Crime and Retribution in Ante-bellum South Carolina*. Columbia: University of South Carolina Press, 1959.

———. "White Lawbreakers in Antebellum South Carolina." *Journal of Southern History* 21, no. 3 (August 1955).

Williams, Jeffrey. *Religion and Violence in Early American Methodism: Taking the Kingdom by Force*. Bloomington: Indiana University Press, 2010.

Williams, Timothy J. *Intellectual Manhood: University, Self, and Society in the Antebellum South*. Chapel Hill: University of North Carolina Press, 2015.

Wills, Gregory A. *Democratic Religion: Freedom, Authority, and Church Discipline in the Baptist South, 1785–1900*. New York: Oxford University Press, 1997.

Wilson, Charles Reagan. *Baptized in Blood: The Religion of the Lost Cause, 1865–1920*. Athens: University of Georgia Press, 1980.

Woods, Curtis, John Wilsey, Kevin Jones, Jarvis Williams, Matthew J. Hall, and Gregory Wills. *Report on Slavery and Racism in the History of the Southern Baptist Theological Seminary*. Louisville, KY: The Southern Baptist Theological Seminary, 2018. https://sbts-wordpress-uploads.s3.amazonaws.com/sbts/uploads/2018/12/Racism-and-the-Legacy-of-Slavery-Report-v4.pdf.

Woods, Michael. *Emotional and Sectional Conflict in the Antebellum United States*. New York: Cambridge University Press, 2014.

Woodson, Hortense C. *Giant in the Land: The Life of William B. Johnson, First President of the Southern Baptist Convention, 1845–1851*. Springfield, MO: Particular Baptist Press, 2005 ed.

Woodward, C. Vann. *Origins of the New South, 1877–1913*. Baton Rouge: Louisiana State University Press, 1974.

Woodworth, Steven E. *While God Is Marching On: The Religious World of Civil War Soldiers*. Lawrence: University Press of Kansas, 2003.

Wyatt-Brown, Bertram. *Lewis Tappan and the Evangelical War against Slavery*. Cleveland, OH: Press of Case Western Reserve University, 1969.

———. *The Shaping of Southern Culture: Honor, Grace, and War, 1760s–1890s*. Chapel Hill: University of North Carolina Press, 2001.

———. *Southern Honor: Ethics and Behavior in the Old South*. New York: Oxford University Press, 1982.

———. *Yankee Saints and Southern Sinners*. Baton Rouge: Louisiana State University Press, 1985.

Young, Jeffrey R. *Proslavery and Sectional Thought in the Early South, 1740–1829*. Columbia: University of South Carolina Press, 2006.

Zuczek, Richard. *State of Rebellion: Reconstruction in South Carolina*. Columbia: University of South Carolina Press, 1996.

INDEX

abolitionism, 97–98, 119; defensiveness over slavery as response to, 125–38
Abram (enslaved person), 59
alcohol: and enslaved persons, 58; violence, role in, 36–37, 41, 56. *See also under* vices and self-mastery
Alexander (Mr.), 148
American Baptist Association, schism over slavery, 133–34
American Revolution in backcountry, 24–25
Anglicans, 44–45
Antioch Baptist Church, 50, 59
Appling (enslaved person), 39
Asbury, Francis, 42–43, 45, 46
Atkinson, Abner W., 183
Axon, Jacob, 72
Ayer, L., 122

Baptists, 46–47, 53–54, 77; denominational schism over slavery, 133–34
Benton, Thomas Hart, 34
Bethlehem Methodist Church, 52
Bettis, Francis (also known as Br. Bettis), 55, 59–60
Bill (enslaved person), 41
Bird, Thomas, 143, 145
Bledsoe, Lewis, 56
Blocker, Abner, 147, 225n28
Blocker, John, 147
Blocker, William Butler, 154
Bones, James, 78, 80–81
Bones, James, Jr., 78
Bones, John, 78, 80–81
Bones, Robert, 78, 80–81
Bones, Samuel, 78, 80, 81–82
Bones, William, 78, 82
Botsford, Edmund, 75

Boyd (member of the Antioch Baptist Church), 59
Boyd, Alexander, 32
Brookes, Harriet, 96
Brookes, Iveson Lewis: artist's sketch of, 66; biographical information, 15, 65, 72–73; career of, 65–67; and Manly, relationship with, 68–69; and revival movement, 75–76; on secular versus sacred, 68–69, 73–75, 76–77; on slavery, 98–99, 119; on vices, 91, 93–100
Brookes, Jonathan, 65–67
Brookes, Lucina Sarah Walker, 72–73
Brookes, Prudence Echols Irvin Johnson, 73
Brookes, Sarah Julia Oliver Myers, 73
Brookes, Virginia, 95
Brookes, Walker, 73, 99; on vices, 91, 93–96, 99–100
Brooks, Elizabeth Butler, 85
Brooks, James Carroll, 142
Brooks, Mary Parsons Carroll, 85–86, 108
Brooks, Preston Smith: biographical overview, 15–16; on brother's death, 155–56; caning of Sumner, 113, 157; Congress, election to, 16, 156; daughter's death, 155; father, relationship with, 108, 111–12, 143–45, 151, 153–54; father's death, 155; hip injury, 144, 151, 153; illness and death, 163; law career of, 142; legacy of, 11; and Mexican War, 123, 151–56; portrait of, 140; public image of after caning, 1–2, 163–64; reputation, concern for, 153–54; vices and self-mastery, 111–13; violence, history of, 139, 141–42, 149; Wigfall duel and repercussions, 143–44, 145, 147, 151, 153–54
Brooks, Walker, 15

259

Brooks, Whitfield: on Baptists, 86; on contentment, 119–20; death of, 155–56; on enslaved people, 122–24; family lineage of, 85; on honor, 147–48; portrait of, 86; and Preston, assessment of, 108, 111, 112, 143–45; on Preston and Mexican War, 151–55; on secular versus sacred, 87; on slavery, 119; on son's death, 155; on vice and self-mastery, 108–11; on violence, public, 143–44, 145, 147–50; wife and religion, 85–86, 87
Brooks, Whitfield, Jr., 123–24, 154–55, 163
Brooks, Zachariah, 85
Brooks family, 85
Brown, Elijah Alexander, 185–87
Brown, Joseph E., 232n2
Bruns, Henry, 107
Bruns, Jane Milligan, 107
Buckhalter (member of Horn's Creek Baptist Church), 59
Butler, Andrew Pickens, 34, 147; and Sumner's speech, 156–57
Butler, James, 45
Butler, Pierce Mason, 143, 147, 151, 152–53, 154
Butler, Thomas, 24–25
Butler, William, 24–25, 85
Butler's Methodist Episcopal Meeting House, 45

cane, gutta-percha, 139, 151, 157
caning of Sumner, reaction to, 139, 157–62
Carroll, James P., 143, 147
Carter, John M., 91, 93, 96
Chapman (doctor), 93–94
Cherokee Indians, 23–24
Cherokee War, 23
Chesnut, James, 166
Christian, James H., 37
churches: backsliding, concerns over, 54–62; and enslaved persons, punishment of, 58–61; growth of, 48, 50–51. *See also* Protestantism
Churubusco, battle of, 154–55

Cloud, William, 36
code duello, 21, 33, 71. *See also* dueling; honor; violence
Code of Honor (Wilson), 21–23. *See also* dueling
Colclazuer, William, 58
Colvin, Ansley J., 203n32
Confederacy, 169–75
Cotton, John, 28–30
Cotton, Rebecca "Becky," 28–30, 204n40
Cross (Mr.), 149
Cummings, William, 30–31
Cunningham (Mr.), 149–50
Cunningham, John, 33
Cunningham, William, 25

Davis, E. T., 36–37
Deas, Sambo, 120–21
Denson, Jesse, 72
Devil in Petticoats, The, or God's Revenge against Husband-Killing (Weems), 28–30
Dickson, John, 83
Dinkins, Simion, 60
disfranchisement, 182, 190–92
Dobey, John, 60
Doby, William, 56
Douglas, Stephen A., 157
Dry Creek Baptist Church, 50, 52–53
dueling: formal arrangements, 30–31, 33–34; lines blurred with violence, 34–38; opposition to, 22–23, 150–51; private versus public attributes, 145–46; as rare but pervasive, 85; rhetorical duels, 71–72, 77–78; and self-mastery, 21–23. *See also* honor; manhood; vices and self-mastery; violence

Edgefield, SC: establishment of, 11–12; "first families" of, 25; white settlement of, 23
Edgefield Female Academy, 47, 75
Edgefield Village Baptist Church, 47, 48, 49–50, 51, 53, 69, 75, 86
Ellenton Riot, 183

emancipation: and labor contracts, 177–79; prospect of, 175–77
enslaved persons: and alcohol, 58; and emancipation, prospect of, 175–77; self-mastery, exclusion from, 98; violence against, 39–41, 58, 93, 124–25, 149; violence among, 60. *See also* slavery, whites' views on
Episcopalians, 54
Evans (Methodist preacher), 52
eye gouging, 25, 27

Falkner, Philip, 203n32
Faulkner, Marshall, 55
Findley, Mary, 26–28
Findley, Ned, 26–28, 204n40
Fleming (preacher), 83–84
Foote, Henry, 34
Fort Donelson, 170, 172
Fort Henry, 170
Frierson, Lydia, 124
Furman, James, 77
Furman, Richard, 75, 120–21

Gardner, James, 33
Gellis (Becky Cotton's fiance), 29
Gettysburg, battle of, 175
Glover, Eldred, 36, 57
Glover, Joseph W., 35, 146
God's Revenge against Murder, or The Drown'd Wife (Weems), 26–28
Gomillion, Lovett, 35, 146
Goode, Phillip, 36
Graham, Sylvester, 96–97
Griffin, A. B., 35
Griffin, James, 59
Griffin, S. B., 57
gubernatorial campaign (1840), 143

Haiti, 118
Hamburg, SC, 32, 37
Hamburg Massacre, 183
Hammond, James Henry, 143
Hamp (enslaved person), 41
Harden, Elbert, 40

Harden, Miles, 40
Harden, Russell, 39–40
Harlin, John, 56
Harmony Methodist Church, 47
Harrison, Wade, 197n21
Hart, Oliver, 75
Hatcher, Benjamin, 60
Hill, John, 56
Hill, William P., 122
Hodges, Elizabeth Hughes, 78
Hodges, Nicholas Ware, 78
Holmes, W. F., 161
Holstin, Willis, 55
honor: malleability of, 8–9; and nonformalized violence, 34–38; and piety as contradictory, 4–5; punishment for dishonor, 27–30; scholarship on, 6–7, 9, 10; and violence, 4, 30, 32–33. *See also* dueling; manhood; paternalism and patriarchy; Protestantism; vices and self-mastery; violence
Horn's Creek Baptist Church, 44, 46, 49, 51–52, 55, 57–61
Howl, Alexander, 31
Hughes, A. J., 60
Hughes, John, 78
Hughes, John H., 78
Hughes, Martha Bones, 78
Hughes family, 78–80, 88

Irving (member of Horn's Creek Baptist Church), 59

Jack (enslaved person), 59–60
Jack (enslaved person), 60
Jefferson, Thomas, 117
Jenkins, James, 45
Jenny (enslaved person), 59
Jeremiah (enslaved person), 59
Jim (enslaved person, excommunicated from church), 60
Jim (enslaved person, expelled from church), 60
Jim (enslaved person, reprimanded for "disorder"), 60

Jim (enslaved person, reprimanded for fight with overseer and for swearing), 60
Jim (enslaved person, reprimanded for misdemeanor and abandoning wife), 60
Joe (enslaved person), 58–59
Johnson, Joseph, 75
Johnson, Mary Bullein, 75
Johnson, William Bullein, 47, 48–49, 54–55, 57, 75, 76–78, 87
Jones, Benjamin F., 35
Jones, Bill, 225n28
Jones, James W., 33
Jones, Seaborn, 161
Jones, William S., 33
Joseph (enslaved person), 123–24
journals, use of, 101–2, 103–4, 111–12

Kannady, Davy, 28
Kannady, James, 28–30
Kannady, Stephen, 29
Keitt, Laurence M., 157
Knapp, Joseph M., 202n25

Laborde, Maximilian, 147
Landrum, John, 46
Langford (enslaved person), 121
L. B. (member of Horn's Creek Baptist Church), 58
Lecture to Young Men on Chastity (Graham), 96–97
Lee, Robert E., 181–82
Lipscomb (Mr.), 148
Little Stephen's Creek Baptist Church, 46, 49–50, 55–56, 69
Lost Cause, 166, 181–83, 186–87, 190–92

Mackey, Thomas Jefferson, 12
manhood, 3; scholarship on, 7, 10; and sectional crisis, 126–28. *See also* honor; paternalism and patriarchy; Protestantism; vices and self-mastery; violence
Manly, Basil, Jr.: biographical overview, 14; on the church and enslaved people, 130–31; on Confederacy, 169–70, 174–75; on emancipation and freed people, 176–79; father, similarities to, 102–3; on Lee, 181; photograph of, 117; postwar, 181, 190–92; on revivals, 46–47; on secession, 166–67; on sectional crisis, 126, 137; on slavery, 116–17, 126–28, 129–37; on vices and self-mastery, 102–5, 128–29
Manly, Basil, Sr.: biographical information, 14, 69; and Brookes, relationship with, 68–69; on Confederacy, 170, 174; conversion to Baptist, 68; death of, 181; on emancipation, prospect of, 175–76; on enslaved people's religious state, 120–22, 175–76; father, relationship with, 67–68, 70; on freed people, 179; honor, violent defense of, 71; portrait of, 67; on Reconstruction, 179–80; and revival movement, 75; rhetorical duels, 71–72; on secession, 166–69; on secular versus sacred, 69–70, 76–77; on slavery, 115, 117–19, 124–25; son, similarities to, 102–3; on vices and self-mastery, 92, 100–102, 129, 174
Manly, Charles, 15, 71, 166, 169, 170, 173
Manly, Fuller, 169, 172, 173, 174
Manly, James, 169, 173
Manly, John Basil, 67–68, 70
Manly, Sarah Murray Rudolph, 69, 170–74, 175, 180
Marsh, Samuel, 46
Marshall, Daniel, 44
Mathis, William H., 57
Mayfair, H. H., 60
Mays, Edward S., 56
Mays, George C., 37
Mays, John, 37
McCorkadale (Mr.), 150
McDuffie, George, 30–31, 142
McGowan (Mr.), 149–50
McGowan, S., 33
McKendree Methodist Church, 47
McQueen, John, 160–61
Melton, Robert, 24–25
Melton, William, 24–25
Methodists, 45, 46, 47, 53–54
Mexican-American War, 123, 151–55
Miller, John, 56

Milligan, Jane, 84
Milligan, Joseph, A. S., 16, 106–8
Milligan, Joseph, Jr.: biographical information, 16; on dueling, 85; on secular versus sacred, 83–85; sister and religion, 84, 87; on vices and self-mastery, 106–8
Milligan, Joseph, Sr., 83
Milly (enslaved person), 59
Mims, Hansford, 48
Mims, James, 77
Mims, M., 58
Moore, Jerry Thornton, 183
Moore, Joseph, 78
Moore, Lucy T. Butler, 78
Morgan, Peter, 31
Mt. Lebanon Baptist Church, 52–53
Mt. Tabor Baptist Church, 51, 53
Mt. Vernon Campground, 52

Namdon (enslaved person), 60
Native Americans, 23–24, 25
New Light Baptists, 44–45
New South, 166, 186–87, 190
Newton Theological Institute, 126, 133
Ninety-Six District, 24
Nixon, Alexander, 35
Nobles, W. (enslaved person), 59

Olmsted, Frederick Law, 93
"Our Brother in Black" (Manly Jr.), 190–92
Ously, John, 25

Parrott, Charles, 56–57
paternalism and patriarchy: and contentment, 118, 120; and enslaved persons' religious state, 131–32, 175–77; post-emancipation, 178–79; and self-mastery of slaveholders, 129–32; and violence against enslaved persons, 124–25. *See also* honor; Lost Cause; manhood; Protestantism; slavery, whites' views on; vices and self-mastery
Peggy (enslaved person), 59
Peter (enslaved person), 59

Phill (enslaved person), 149
Pickens, Andrew, 110
Pickens, Susan, 151–52
Plessy v. Ferguson, 192
Posey, Martin, 39
Posey, Matilda, 39
Prather, James W., 25
Price, Charles, 35
Primus (enslaved person), 60
Princeton Theological Seminary, 133–34, 136–37
Protestantism: denominations, commingling of, 42–44, 46–49, 53–54; and dueling, opposition to, 22–23; and enslaved persons, 130–31; and fighting, 55–58; God as judge, 94, 96, 140; piety, tenets of, 3; and reform culture, antebellum, 97–98; and revival movements, 13, 42–44, 46–54, 75–76, 83; scholarship on, 6–7, 10; and vice, protection against, 100–103, 106; and women as shaping men's righteous piety, 87–88. *See also* churches; honor; manhood; paternalism and patriarchy; vices and self-mastery; violence

Quattlebaum, John, 55–56

Rainsford, Thomas, 59, 60
Reconstruction, 178–82; and "Redemption," 183, 186–87
Red Bank Baptist Church, 53
reform culture, antebellum, 97–98
Regulator movement, 23–24
revival movements, 13, 42–44, 46–54, 75–76, 83
Reynolds, James, 37–38, 77
Richardson, John P., 143
Richmond (enslaved person), 41
righteous honor, 4; adaptability of, 186–87, 190–92. *See also* honor; manhood; paternalism and patriarchy; Protestantism; vices and self-mastery; violence
Rocky Creek Church, 50
Roe, Absalom, 202n27
Roe, William, 202n27

Rose (enslaved person), 59
Rudolph, Virginia, 172
Ruffin, Edmund, 166
Russ, Asa, 124
Ryan (member of Horn's Creek Baptist Church), 60

Sally (enslaved person), 59
Samuel (enslaved person), 60
Samuel, Joseph, 37–38
Samuel, Musco, 37–38
Samuel, Wade, 37–38
Samuel, Walker B., 36, 37, 57, 58
Santo Domingo, 118
Scott, Winfield, 154
secession: dissolution, calls for, 160; religious interpretation of, 166–69
segregation, 182, 190–92
Selleck, Fred, 85
Shaw, Stephen, 38
Shiloh, battle of, 169
Shultz, Henry, 32–33
Silliman, H. K., 83–84
Simkins, Eldred, 149
Simons, Lewis, 141–42
slave insurrection, white fear of, 117–18
"slave power" conspiracy, 2
slavery, whites' views on: on loyalty of enslaved people, 123–24; as necessary evil, 115–20; as path to Christianity, 120–23; as positive good, 125–38. *See also* enslaved persons
Smith, Whitefoord, 153
South Carolina College, student discipline, 141–42
Spawn (Mr.), 150
Spincer (enslaved person), 59
Stavely, W. G., 82
Stephen's Creek Baptist Church, 44
Stephney (enslaved person), 40
Stiron (member of Horn's Creek Baptist Church), 57
Sumner, Charles: "The Crime against Kansas" speech, 156–57, 163; image of as martyr, 2; letters to following caning, 161–62. *See also* caning of Sumner, reaction to
Swearingen, E. M., 58
Swearingen, Vann, 55

Taylor, Adam, 35
temperance movement, 109–11
Terry, J. P., 35
Tillman, George D., 36–37
Tillman, John, 37
Tomkins, Samuel, 35
Trinity Episcopal Church, 54, 85

vices and self-mastery: alcohol, 36–37, 41, 56, 95, 105–6, 109–11, 174; and family, 95–96, 101, 107; gambling, 95; greed, 99–100, 101, 107; masturbation, 91, 93–96; and religion and repentance, 54–62; and sectional crisis, 96, 101–2, 104–5, 111, 113–14; sexual transgressions, 59–60, 93, 97, 101; temptations, 93; theft, 59; and vanity, 107. *See also* honor; manhood; Protestantism; violence
Vicksburg, battle of, 175
violence: and alcohol, 36–37, 41, 56; against enslaved persons, 93, 124–25, 149; among enslaved persons, 60; outside honor code, 38–41; post-Reconstruction, 182–83; and religion, 55–58; spontaneous, 25–30, 31–33, 71. *See also* dueling; honor; manhood; Protestantism; vices and self-mastery

Walker, William, 37, 58
Watson, Dick, 154
Weems, Mason Locke, 12, 25–30, 63
White (murder victim), 202n25
Whitlock, James, 56
Wigfall, Arthur, 150–51
Wigfall, Louis T., 143–44, 145, 147, 150–51. *See also under* Brooks, Preston Smith
Williams, Jonathan, 201n25
Williams, Joseph, 40–41

Wilson (Mr.), 148
Wilson, John Lyde, 21–23, 71
women's roles: and Civil War and anxiety, 170–74; and religion and piety, 75, 87–88
Woodmason, Charles, 24, 44–45

Yancy (Mr.), 148
Yangers, U. S., 33
Yates, John W., 201n25
York (enslaved person), 59
Youngblood, James, 56–57
Youngblood, Thomas, 56

RECENT BOOKS IN THE SERIES
A Nation Divided: Studies in the Civil War Era

The Civil War Political Tradition: Ten Portraits of Those Who Formed It
Paul D. Escott

The Weaker Sex in War: Gender and Nationalism in Civil War Virginia
Kristen Brill

Young America: The Transformation of Nationalism before the Civil War
Mark Power Smith

Black Suffrage: Lincoln's Last Goal
Paul D. Escott

The Cacophony of Politics: Northern Democrats and the American Civil War
J. Matthew Gallman

My Work among the Freedmen: The Civil War and Reconstruction Letters of Harriet M. Buss
Edited by Jonathan W. White and Lydia J. Davis

Colossal Ambitions: Confederate Planning for a Post–Civil War World
Adrian Brettle

Newest Born of Nations: European Nationalist Movements and the Making of the Confederacy
Ann L. Tucker

The Worst Passions of Human Nature: White Supremacy in the Civil War North
Paul D. Escott

Preserving the White Man's Republic: Jacksonian Democracy, Race, and the Transformation of American Conservatism
Joshua A. Lynn

American Abolitionism: Its Direct Political Impact from Colonial Times into Reconstruction
Stanley Harrold

A Strife of Tongues: The Compromise of 1850 and the Ideological Foundations of the American Civil War
Stephen E. Maizlish

The First Republican Army: The Army of Virginia and the Radicalization of the Civil War
John H. Matsui

War upon Our Border: Two Ohio Valley Communities Navigate the Civil War
Stephen I. Rockenbach

Gold and Freedom: The Political Economy of Reconstruction
Nicolas Barreyre, translated by Arthur Goldhammer

Daydreams and Nightmares: A Virginia Family Faces Secession and War
Brent Tarter

Intimate Reconstructions: Children in Postemancipation Virginia
Catherine A. Jones

Lincoln's Dilemma: Blair, Sumner, and the Republican Struggle over Racism and Equality in the Civil War Era
Paul D. Escott

Slavery and War in the Americas: Race, Citizenship, and State Building in the United States and Brazil, 1861–1870
Vitor Izecksohn

Marching Masters: Slavery, Race, and the Confederate Army during the Civil War
Colin Edward Woodward

Confederate Visions: Nationalism, Symbolism, and the Imagined South in the Civil War
Ian Binnington

Frederick Douglass: A Life in Documents
L. Diane Barnes, editor

Reconstructing the Campus: Higher Education and the American Civil War
Michael David Cohen

Worth a Dozen Men: Women and Nursing in the Civil War South
Libra R. Hilde

Civil War Talks: Further Reminiscences of George S. Bernard and His Fellow Veterans
Hampton Newsome, John Horn, and John G. Selby, editors

The Enemy Within: Fears of Corruption in the Civil War North
Michael Thomas Smith

The Big House after Slavery: Virginia Plantation Families and Their Postbellum Experiment
Amy Feely Morsman

Take Care of the Living: Reconstructing Confederate Veteran Families in Virginia
Jeffrey W. McClurken

www.ingramcontent.com/pod-product-compliance
Lightning Source LLC
Chambersburg PA
CBHW030822230426
43667CB00008B/1327